D1091449

New Nationalisms of the Developed West

New Nationalisms of the Developed West

Toward Explanation

Edited by
Edward A. Tiryakian
Duke University
and
Ronald Rogowski
UCLA

Boston
ALLEN & UNWIN
London   Sydney

© Edward A. Tiryakian and Ronald Rogowski, 1985
This book is copyright under the Berne Convention.
No reproduction without permission. All rights reserved.

Allen & Unwin, Inc.,
Fifty Cross Street, Winchester, Mass. 01890, USA

George Allen & Unwin (Publishers) Ltd,
40 Museum Street, London WC1A 1LU, UK

George Allen & Unwin (Publishers) Ltd,
Park Lane, Hemel Hempstead, Herts HP2 4TE, UK

George Allen & Unwin Australia Pty Ltd,
8 Napier Street, North Sydney, NSW 2060, Australia

First published in 1985

Library of Congress Cataloging in Publication Data

Main entry under title:
  New nationalisms of the developed West.
Includes index.
1. Nationalism.   2. World politics—1975–1985.
I. Tiryakian, Edward A.   II. Rogowski, Ronald.
JC311.N48   1984   320.5'4   84-16771
ISBN 0-04-320167-9 (alk. paper)

British Library Cataloguing in Publication Data

  New nationalisms of the developed West.
1. Nationalism—History—20th century
I. Tiryakian, Edward   II. Rogowski, Ronald
320.5'4'091812   JC311
ISBN 0-04-320167-9

Set in 11 on 12 point Times by Mathematical Composition Setters Ltd.
Ivy Street, Salisbury, UK
and printed in Great Britain by Mackays of Chatham

Contents

Acknowledgements

This volume presents essays on modern nationalist movements that have challenged in recent years the sovereignty of Western nation-states not from without, but from within their frontiers. It represents the collective effort of a group of scholars to make sense of what underlies "nations against states," so to speak.

Such a collective product is a reflection of many contributions besides those manifest in this book. The editors wish to thank, first of all, the Council for European Studies which awarded us with a planning grant to organize a group of scholars having common interest in contemporary nationalist movements; Dr. Marion Kaplan and Dr. Ionnanis Sinanoglou of the Council were supportive of this project from the start and the "seed money" put at our disposal by the Council made possible the holding of group meetings at both Duke University and Washington, D.C., over a three-year period. This was instrumental in our getting to know each other's frames of reference and each other's pertinent writings; although the reader will note implicit if not explicit methodological and theoretical divergences in the volume, we think (s)he will also find greater coherence and cross-references than in most such collaborative efforts in the social sciences.

A number of scholars who attended the initial planning session at Duke University and/or subsequent meetings could not make a final contribution due to various other commitments. None the less, we would like to indicate to Jeffrey Obler, Françoise Morin, Marcel Rioux, Pierre Simon, and Aristide Zolberg that their inputs constitute an important background dimension which has enriched our thinking and comparative awareness.

We have also benefited from human and institutional resources provided us by our respective universities: at UCLA, Amanda Tillotson and Jeannette Money for editing help, and Charles McNeilly and Lila Merritt for typing and word processing; at Duke, the University Research Council and the Trent Foundation for project grants, and Pat Calebaugh and Linda Lazo-Lane for typing/word processing. In addition, the Center for Advanced Study in the Behavioral Sciences, in Palo Alto,

California, extended a Fellowship to Rogowski during part of the final editing and the writing of the Conclusion. He expresses his thanks to that incomparable institution and particularly to its librarians, Margaret Amara and Bruce Harley; and to the National Science Foundation, whose grant BNS 76-22943 provided some of the funding.

Lastly, besides all the above "support systems," we are also delighted to acknowledge the cordial ties that relate us to our publisher in the persons of Michael Holdsworth and John Whitehead. Their genuine interest in the subject matter of the volume and their unfailing assistance are deeply appreciated.

EDWARD A. TIRYAKIAN
RONALD ROGOWSKI

Notes on Contributors

Jack Brand is senior lecturer in politics at the University of Strathclyde (Glasgow). His major research interests are nationalism and the comparative study of political parties. His books include the coauthored *Political Stratification and Democracy, Local Government Reform in England*, and *The National Movement in Scotland*.

Jacques Dofny is Professor of Sociology at the University of Montreal and vice-president for research of the International Sociological Association. He has extensive publications in French and English on the topics of industrial sociology, social stratification, and the labor unions; he is coauthor of *Nationalism and the National Question*.

Michael Hechter is Professor of Sociology at the University of Arizona. His interests are ethnicity, social change and stratification, and his major publications include *Internal Colonialism: The Celtic Fringe in British National Development, 1536–1966, The Microfoundations of Macrosociology*, and *Principles of Group Solidarity* (forthcoming).

Bud B. Khleif is Professor of Sociology at the University of New Hampshire. He has done extensive fieldwork in the United States, Wales, and Friesland, and is doing fieldwork (1984–5) in Japan on ethnicity and occupations. He has written in the areas of the sociology of occupations and professions, ethnicity, and the politics of language; his most recent volume is *Language, Ethnicity and Education in Wales*.

Margaret Levi is Associate Professor of Political Science at the University of Washington (Seattle). She is currently completing *A Theory of Predatory Rule*, applying rational choice and structural theory to account for variation in revenue production policies in various historical settings.

Juan J. Linz is Pelatiah Perit Professor of Political and Social Science at Yale University. He has been active in building international networks of scholars on comparative politics. Among his extensive multilingual publications pertaining to totalitarian and authoritarian regimes, parties and pressure groups, and peripheralism is the volume coedited with A. Stepan, *The Breakdown of Democratic Regimes*.

Neil Nevitte is Associate Professor of Political Science at the University of Calgary. His research focusses on political change and comparative political ideologies. He is coeditor of *The Future of North America: Canada, the United States and Quebec Nationalism*.

Gunnar P. Nielsson is Assistant Professor of International Relations at the University of Southern California. His research deals with comparative politics, and the roles of ethnicity and nationalism in political integration and disintegration. He is coeditor of *The Study and Teaching of International Relations*.

Oriol Pi-Sunyer is Professor of Anthropology at the University of Massachusetts at Amherst. He has done extensive fieldwork in Latin America and in recent years has been working on the socioeconomic, political and cultural transformations of Spain. His works include *Zamora: Change and Continuity in a Mexican Town, Humanity and Culture* (coauthored), and an edited volume, *The Limits of Integration: Ethnicity and Nationalism in Modern Europe.*

Mario Polèse is director of INRS-Urbanization, a center of regional studies affiliated to the University of Quebec in Montreal. An adviser to both federal and provincial governments in Canada, his main interests lie in the areas of regional development, industrial location, and regional economic policy.

Phillip Rawkins is director of the International Development Centre at the Ryerson Polytechnical Institute in Toronto. He has written extensively on the role of culture, ethnicity, and nationalist politics. He is currently working on the impact of high technology on economic nationalism.

Ronald Rogowski is Professor of Political Science at UCLA. A specialist in West European comparative politics, he relates quantitative analysis and rationalist theory to a wide variety of political data. He is the author of *Rational Legitimacy: A Theory of Political Support.* In 1983–4 he was a fellow at the Palo Alto Center for Advanced Study in the Behavioral Sciences.

Jürg Steiner is Professor of Political Science at the University of North Carolina and *professeur associé* at the University of Geneva. He is the author of *Amicable Agreement versus Majority Rule: Conflict Resolution in Switzerland* and coauthor of *A Theory of Political Decision Modes.*

Edward A. Tiryakian is Professor of Sociology at Duke University. His fields of interest include sociological theory, large-scale societal transformations, and the sociology of modernity. He is the author of *Sociologism and Existentialism*, coeditor of *Theoretical Sociology* and editor of *The Global Crisis: Sociological Analyses and Responses.*

Alain Touraine is director of a research center at the Ecole des Hautes Etudes en Sciences Sociales in Paris. He has done research in North and South America as well as in Europe, and is a specialist on the relation of social movements to modernity. Among his numerous writings are *The Post-Industrial Society, The Self-Production of Society, The May 1968 Movement, The Voice and the Eye*, and *Solidarity.*

Glyn Williams is lecturer in the Department of Social Theory and Institutions at the University College of North Wales. His interests cover political economy, ethnicity and nationalism, and the sociology of language. His publications include *The Desert and the Dream: The Welsh Colonization of Chubut 1865–1915*, and the edited volume, *Social and Cultural Change in Contemporary Wales.*

Introduction

EDWARD A. TIRYAKIAN

"The specter of nationalism haunts equally the bourgeois and the Marxist world. It is a ghost of yesterday and of things to come, but also a liberating spirit for oppressed national groups and minorities seeking autonomy from inherited, involuntary political arrangements."

Thus might well begin a manifesto that in terms of its consequences for existing nation-states would be as revolutionary as the one of 1848. Nationalism is a powerful force, laden with emotions and affect, if not opprobrium, that have obfuscated the reality of this pervasive phenomenon of modern society. And like the phoenix, it has periodically reemerged from its own historical ashes, even in the same country, the same region.

Full justice to nationalism would entail the treatment of all its major waves, starting with the first "long wave" that took place roughly over a 100-year period from the latter half of the eighteenth to the latter half of the nineteenth century. That wave was to a large extent motivated by secular republican ideology, extolling the "nation" as the principle of sovereignty and seeking liberation from alien rule or alien influences, whether the "alien" in question was George III, the Spanish monarchy, the Russian tsar, or the Austro-Hungarian emperor. A second "long wave" would be the one associated with the nationalism of what has become called the Third World. Structurally similar to the first in seeking emancipation from alien rule and alien cultural hegemony, the locale of this wave tends to be outside Western societies and has a predominantly non-Western leadership; in fact many of the instances of this wave are directed toward overthrowing either Western colonial rule or dependency on Western dominance. Early parts of this long wave—which we may say began to crystallize in the aftermath of the European holocaust of World War I—took on a "pan" label, as in Pan-Africanism and Pan-Arabism (Tibi, 1981); but there have also been country-specific movements of national autonomy from alien control, as in the cases of China, Mexico, India, and so on. This wave is not completely spent, but for the most part the breakup of colonial empires and the proliferation of independent countries in the early 1960s particularly, which has so affected the constitution and ethos of the United Nations, may have led social scientists to think that nationalism as a factor for social change was dead.

However, nationalism is alive, as a cursory consideration of its manifestations since the mid-1960s will attest. In the Middle East the decline of Pan-Arab nationalism that had been galvanized by Nasser has been offset by the revitalization of two separate religiously inspired nationalisms, that of Begin's Israel and that of Khomeini's Iran. In the Western Hemisphere, going from North to South, three settings illustrate the kindling of nationalist fervor. In North America the period evidences the militant nationalism of a new generation of French-Canadians in Quebec who opt for a new collective identity as *Québécois* in preference to an older designation as *Canadiens*. Their demands for autonomy, ranging from a linguistic policy that recognizes French as the sole official language of Quebec to more radical demands for political dissociation from the rest of the Canadian federation, provide the basis for an intense political struggle, as much within the Francophone population as between the "two nations" of Quebec. At the same time the major *federal* political figure of the period 1968–84, Pierre Elliot Trudeau, while a staunch foe of Quebec nationalism, is an equally staunch proponent of a resurgence of Canadian nationalism (LeDuc and Murray, 1983), much of which is directed against the United States' control of the Canadian economy. Canadian nationalism in this respect in recent years has involved not only some symbolic or relatively cosmetic changes, such as creating Canadian editions of *Time* and the *Reader's Digest* (Peers, 1979), but also major structural changes launched in Trudeau's 1981 legislative endeavor to "Canadianize" the energy sector, three-fourths of which was foreign-controlled (64 percent by the United States alone) in 1980 (*Canada Today/ D'Aujourd'hui*, 1982). In Central America the Sandinista movement in Nicaragua deserves to be viewed as a successful nationalist movement of liberation from the authoritarian and unpopular rule of the Samoza family, which had made that country an export satellite of the world system at the expense of national development. Finally, in 1982 the Falklands/Malvinas war mobilized the nationalist sentiments of all Argentinians (if not of all Latin America), and generated an equally strong British/English nationalism, dramatically evidenced in speeches in the Commons and in crowds at the departure and the return of the fleet.

In Eastern Europe the Solidarity workers' movement rekindled Polish nationalism which has has so many glorious and so many tragic pages from Kosciusko to Lech Walesa. A short while before Solidarity, the election of Pope John Paul II had renewed Polish ethnic pride at home and abroad. Solidarity has—temporarily or permanently—been put down by Polish military authority, in part because of the real threat of a Soviet military intervention. In turn, if the Soviet Union has been willing to put down by force demands for autonomy in neighboring countries (for instance, Hungary and Czechoslovakia), it is not only for obvious considerations of external security. It may also be viewed as a deterrent to claims for real autonomy from Russian hegemony within the Soviet Union by distinct non-Russian regional minorities who have had a revival of national cultures and/or a rising proportion of the total Soviet population in the past twenty-five years: peoples as diverse as the Ukranians, the Lithuanians, and the demographically dynamic Muslim minorities of Central Asia (Rakowska-Harmstone, 1977; Carrère d'Encausse, 1979; Lapidus, 1984).

Rapid and incomplete as this thumbnail sketch has been, it should suggest the reality if not the significance of nationalism on the contemporary scene.

The present volume does not pretend to do justice to the wide array of nationalism and nationalist movements and manifestations in the modern world. It has a restricted geographical focus, namely advanced Western societies. Further, the contributions are oriented to recent nationalist movements not of nation-states, but of nations against states! Our emphasis is not on descriptive case studies, of which there is no lack in the social science literature, but rather in advancing the comparative analysis of nationalism, which we seek to do theoretically, methodologically, and empirically.

About five years ago the editors of the volume, both of whom were at Duke University at the time, found that they and several of their graduate students shared a common interest in the diversity of Western, regionally grounded nationalist movements. Since these movements were taking place within democratic societies, they combined the advantage of being relatively accessible for empirical study with being theoretically intriguing as anomalies. What did such movements of cultural and political autonomy signify in industrial, technological societies growing more interdependent and aggregated (witness the European Economic Community)? Were these movements like "the mouse that roared," a flickering and amusing nuisance, or did they propose serious new alternatives to existing political arrangements and, therefore, constitute real challenges to existing governmental structures? Were they the tail-end of the counterculture movement that had swept the West in the late 1960s (Yinger, 1982; Leventman, 1982), and which like a meteor had swept past us, leaving little besides a momentary impression of vividness? What sorts of person did the new nationalist movements recruit with what ideologies and what motivations? How did the occurrence, incidence, and spread of these movements relate to nationalist movements, and how did they relate to the conceptual and theoretical framework of sociology and political science, for example, concerning "nation-states," "national development," "political socialization," and even "cycles of protest"? Perhaps we can condense the myriad of questions into one core problem: given a shared paradigmatic view of political modernity (that relating modernization as a significant correlate of the rise of the nation-state), what is the significance of an anomalous phenomenon, that nationalist movements seeking radical decentralization or emancipation from state authority arise at an advanced state of modernization?

At about that time the Council for European Studies encouraged the formation of different groups of scholars working on some problems pertaining to contemporary Europe. Rogowski and Tiryakian were awarded by the Council a three-year planning grant; this made it possible to bring together on several occasions a group of scholars who had done research on some component of recent Western nationalist movements. The most recent meeting of the group as a whole took place over a three-day period at Duke University and Washington, D.C., in October 1980. By that time a consensus had emerged that a volume stressing a comparative outlook on recent Western nationalist movements would be an important contribution to the social science literature. Operating with much more modest resources, the present volume has a model in that edited by Charles Tilly (1975), an output of a summer workshop, and various subsequent meetings of a group of scholars interested in reexamining the formative forces behind the emergence of contemporary nation-states. Recall the major problems of inquiry of Tilly's volume (*ibid.*, p. 602):

(1) Under what conditions do national states rather than some sort of political structures become the dominant organizations in an area?
(2) What are the chief forms taken by national states, and what causes one or another of them to appear?
(3) What determines how strong, durable, effective, and responsive to its own population a national state is?

In a sense we are tacitly dealing in the present volume with a complementary set of problem areas:

(1) Under what conditions do nationalist movements of a regional character come to replace political identification with the nation-state in a given territorial area? (Or what are the structural, cultural, and social-psychological conditions which account for the chief forms of regionally grounded nationalist movements?)
(2) What are the chief forms taken by regional nationalist movements, and what set of causes underlies these?
(3) What determines the vitality, viability, and constituency of such nationalist movements in competition with the resources of the national state? (How does the nature of commitment to such a movement and its political structures compare with that to the nation-state?)

It is by tackling both sets of problems, one dealing centrally with the nature and processes of sociopolitical aggregation, the other with the reciprocal problems of disaggregation, that a considerable advance will be made in the social sciences dealing with political modernization and political identity.

The reader will note a twofold categorization of contributions to this volume. The first part pertains to studies that are more theoretical and methodological in orientation, while the second part contains studies that are more comparative and substantive. However, both parts are intended to be complementary and interrelated. Certainly we trust the pieces to be uniformly comparative in their implication, rather than being so country-specific that the materials cannot be used for research and analysis in settings other than the empirical referents of the particular essay.

The study of nationalist movements in advanced societies began to get important scholarly interest among social scientists somewhere at the start of the 1970s. Without wrangling over what works activated social science interest in the "new nationalisms," we might point to two sources that were immensely heuristic. The first was by a political scientist, Walker Connor, who in this and other writings (1972, 1977) drew attention to treating the new wave of nationalism neither as ephemeral nor as dangerous atavism, but as important subject matter for comparative politics. The second was a book-length study by a young political sociologist, Michael Hechter (1975), who took over the concept of "internal colonialism" (used in the 1960s in a rather rhetorical way by different persons, such as Robert Lafont in France and Robert Blauner in America) and made it the key to a sociohistorical analysis of the persistence of regional consciousness or "Celtic nationalism" in one of the oldest nation-states, Great Britain. Hechter's study, although stopping its data analysis in 1966, was to become as controversial as heuristic in leading to a variety of studies on both sides of the Atlantic either challenging it or following in its footsteps. It is appropriate, therefore, that the present volume give the author the opportunity in "Internal colonialism revisited" to reflect on and expand the scope of his earlier work. As will be seen in this piece, as well as a subsequent one in this volume in which he collaborates with Margaret Levi, Hechter directs his attention empirically to the phenomenon of the waning of the fortunes of nationalist parties in the second half of the 1970s, which in turn leads him to raise microsociological theoretical questions about the nature of group solidarity.

Following this "overture"—for the theme of "internal colonialism" is one that is attended to in several pieces in this volume—we turn our attention to very basic steps involved in the process of explanation, namely, the topics of definition, classification, and categorization (or typologizing). This seems as relevant in the study of nationalism as in anything else, perhaps more so, because so much of the social science literature as well as the more general literature has tended to make a very simplistic and unfortunate double identification. First, there is by and large the identification of "nation" with "state," resulting in treating as *sub specie aeternitatis* the concept of "nation-state." Gunnar P. Nielsson in his careful study "States and 'nation-groups': a global taxonomy" rectifies this false perception by showing the immense global variation in the fit between the two terms and their relation to ethnic groups. Nielsson's taxonomy opens up important areas of research, by no means confined to advanced industrial countries. Secondly, there has been an identification of modern nationalism with claims made by the nation-state. The essay by Edward Tiryakian and Neil Nevitte develops a typology of four principal nationalist orientations, linked to the process of modernization and to the differentiation of nation-states into quite distinct components. This differentiation rests upon a voluntaristic frame of reference regarding nation qua societal community, which the authors argue is to be found in the sociological writings of Marcel Mauss, Max Weber, and Talcott Parsons.

Although in a recent work (1982), he has himself partaken of the common fallacy of equating "nation" with "nation-state," there is no question that the writings of Mancur Olson on collective action, particularly his seminal *Logic of Collective Action* (1965), have led to social scientists (for example, Barry and Hardin, 1982) finding rational structures of action in collective behavior which previously had been associated with irrationality. Nationalist movements—and certainly those taking place within advanced nation-states—have suffered the tarnished image of irrational, atavistic behavior, engaged by lunatics and romantics. However, Olson's influence on the new scholarship of social movements (Oberschall, 1973; Zald and McCarthy, 1979) is manifest in several theoretical essays in the present volume. Ronald Rogowski provides a very general theoretical model, going beyond definition and categorization, in "Causes and varieties of nationalism: a rationalist account." He provides concise definitions of basic terms and postulates, and then goes on to ask from his model what sort of persons will be attracted to nationalism and who will not in societies differentiated by their social division of labor ("plural" v. "pillarized" societies). Taking four kinds of social change as independent variables, he proposes in the form of specific hypotheses what their outcomes will be upon actors opting for nationalism in terms of cost–benefit analysis.

Rogowski's account draws upon a familiar set of actors: elites and nonelites. Economist Mario Polèse in his chapter "Economic integration, national policies, and the rationality of regional separatism" draws upon a unit of analysis familiar to development economics, namely, the region. Focusing upon the regional situation of Quebec in Canada, Polèse's rationalistic model critically examines the question of whether political separation would perforce be economically irrational, in the sense of leading to economic disintegration of the separated region and/or the remaining nation-state. Polèse does not deny that any separation entails costs, but he also proposes conditions under which costs can be minimized and benefits maximized.

Margaret Levi and Michael Hechter also provide a rationalistic model in a theoretically oriented essay which addresses itself to the locations, emergence, and decline of what they call ethnoregional parties. Drawing upon some postulates from political economy, the authors argue that changes in the size of an ethnoregional party vote are a function of that party's ability to supply benefits (public goods) its members value. However, what might be termed intervening variables have to be taken into account: changes in central state policy, which may increase or decrease benefits available through the party, and of course the nature of a cultural division of labor which effects ethnic solidarity that can be mobilized by the ethnoregionalist party.

How do existing regimes respond to protest movements— including those demanding territorial autonomy? An important literature has evolved around the question of how group conflict is met in plural societies or "consociational democracies." Jürg Steiner in "Decision modes toward separatist movements" examines four modes of response (or "decision modes") open to an existing polity when political claims for autonomy are made by one of its components. He draws upon the empirical experience of the accommodations made within Switzerland— the world's oldest "consociational democracy"—by a German-speaking canton (Berne) when faced with demands by a nationalist movement having a different cultural constituency. That this resulted in a new canton (Jura) within the Swiss confederacy in 1979 is for Steiner an empirical springboard to discussing a more rigorous theoretical model of the decision-making *process* (and therefore of its sequences) in situations of intergroup conflict.

During the past fifteen years or so—perhaps provoked by the outburst of such phenomena in so many Western countries— there has been growing serious attention given to social movements directed against established institutional frameworks, values, societal organizations, and so on. Major facets of this vast literature on protest social movements, their dynamics, and their impact on social innovation have been recently summarized by Tarrow (1983). It would seem obvious that the development of the comparative, theoretical explanation of nationalist movements will entail relating these to a broader class of social protest movements. It is highly appropriate that this volume contain a contribution by the French sociologist Alain

Touraine, himself one of the foremost contributors to the new literature on social movements, having studied the May 1968 student movement, the ecology movement, the feminist movement, Solidarity and the antinuclear movement. The selection here is a methodological one, since Touraine has pioneered in the study of social movements by drawing from group dynamics and developing a new method, "sociological intervention," which renovates the participant-observation method. How to make sense of a movement, such as the Occitanist nationalist movement in southern France, entails situating the social scientist within the movement, elucidating from and for its actors its contradictions in order to discover its projects. This in turn gives us a broader perspective on the societal context against which the protest is directed.

The first part ends with a second methodological chapter, that of Bud B. Khleif, who demonstrates that much vigorous new wine can be obtained from the tried-and-true cask of participant-observation methodology coupled with symbolic interactionism. Khleif reviews various theories of ethnic nationalism, the latter treated as a reaction to perceived sociocultural threat, in particular to the perception of cultural suppression; in modern societies this suppression pertains more often than not to the native language. Khleif illustrates his approach, which is both theoretical and methodological, with data gathered in the course of fieldwork in Friesland, where a nationalist regional party emerged in the 1970s seeking autonomy from the Netherlands. One should note that for Khleif a nationalist movement stems from interrelated cultural *and* socioeconomic factors.

Part Two, which deals with empirical case studies, begins with a study by Juan Linz, "From primordialism to nationalism." Linz needs no introduction as a foremost scholar of modern Spain; his comparative interests have as their focus the empirical bases of authoritarian and democratic regimes. The plethora of regional nationalist movements within post-Franco Spain provides rich ground for a comparative study of the bases of nationality and group identity; this Linz analyzes with great subtlety by use of opinion survey data. The title indicates one of his major contentions, namely, that ethnic national identity evolves from "primordial" criteria (language, religion, culture) to more objective and generalizable indicators (territoriality, place-of-work). Linz, as readers will see, does not stop with such a facile unlinear trend, for the Basque data he examines at great length also indicate the persistence of primordialism in nationalist aspirations. This in turn raises the problem of whether the perceived authoritarianism of the existent nation-state would or would not be replaced by a more open society if the radical nationalist movement succeeded in establishing a state for its own territory.

Oriol Pi-Sunyer is a social anthropologist and one of the early social scientists to draw attention to the importance of ethnicity and nationalism in contemporary Western societies (Pi-Sunyer, 1971). His sociohistorical study of Catalonia is drawn from a political economy perspective. Like the Basque area analyzed by Linz, Catalonia represents an instance of nationalism qua social movement which is not generated by deprivation, since both regions have been economically more advanced or developed than the rest of Spain. Pi-Sunyer argues that Catalan nationalism is both very modern and also primordial, since Catalan language and culture have served to maintain Catalan identity through a variety of political and social changes. It is rational in so far as Catalan nationalism functions as a mechanism for solving essentially social problems.

The coupling of Catalonia and Scotland is done by political scientist Jack A. Brand, whose "Nationalism and the non-colonial periphery" compares two societies which were early vanguards of European modernization but later were submerged within Great Britain and Spain respectively. Yet Brand uses the two cases to develop a critique of the "internal colonialism" thesis of Hechter; much of his discussion of regional nationalism takes in as an exogenous variable how the region fares as a function of the fortunes of the imperial system to which it is related.

Great Britain also witnessed in the past fifteen years another vigorous nationalist movement, that stemming from the heartland of Wales. Although the movement for Welsh autonomy is far older and far broader than the political party of Plaid Cymru, the latter is an important crystallization of Welsh nationalism. It still has representation in Westminster and its former head and first M.P., Gwynfor Evans, is surely one of the most articulate advocates of the aspirations of peripheral nationalism (Evans, 1973). Phillip Rawkins has been studying on a comparative basis party organizations and party leadership. He brings another dimension in the study of nationalist movements by examining some of the dilemmas faced by a regional nationalist party—not only when it is out of power and has to make coalitions in order to enlarge its electoral base, but also when it is in power, in the sense of having won seats in the legislative assembly of the nation-state. The protest movement party often emerges, in a sense, as a charismatic party; elected to office, however, it has to make compromises if it is to function, and these compromises often tarnish its charisma. Rawkins's analysis of Plaid Cymru and his comparisons with the Parti Québécois and the Italian Communist Party, among others, will be of interest to many scholars of contemporary Western societies, including those following the development of the "Greens" in Germany, who in 1983 for the first time won parliamentary representation. Welsh nationalism is also the subject of sociologist Glyn Williams's essay, "The political economy of contemporary nationalism in Wales." His neo-Marxist analysis rejects the view that Welsh nationalism is a politically unique phenomenon stemming from a distinctive Welsh culture threatened by modernization. He examines the social structure of Welsh civil society and the marginalization of various elements resulting from intrusions of the British state in carrying out a regional development policy. For Williams, this sort of analysis is crucial to a realistic appraisal of nationalism in social rather than cultural terms; culture—for example, the militant defense of the Welsh language—is for Williams a reflection of social conflict. Readers will find a complementarity between the case of Wales analyzed by Williams and that of Friesland discussed by Khleif; although they stress different aspects, they find the same components of modern "peripheral" nationalism.

Another comparative slant on modern nationalist movements is introduced by political scientist Neil Nevitte in his examination of the religious factor in three settings: Quebec, Wales, and Scotland. The general issue he confronts is what may be called the ambiguous "elective affinity" between religion and modern nationalism: some observers have tended to see modern political movements absorb religious inspiration or take on the functions of religion in providing ideology and a sense of community for their members. This would suggest a blurring of the categories of the religious and the political and, ultimately, of church and state. In the first part of his essay Nevitte argues that the church as a recognized institution played a vital role as the bearer of the national culture, and he suggests three general conditions where religion does contribute to nationalism without being identical to it. He then turns his attention to survey data gathered in Quebec during the fateful electoral campaign of November 1976 and examines the bearing of religious identification upon political orientation.

The final chapter in Part Two is by sociologist Jacques Dofny. Its title "Ethnic cleavages, labor aristocracy, and nationalism in Quebec," is suggestive of the analysis undertaken: a historical examination—using Quebec as a case study—of the interrelation of ethnicity, social stratification, and nationalism. Dofny's essay is addressed to two challenging questions: first, to the phenomenon of a "labor aristocracy" (or "bourgeois proletariat"), which Marx and Engels saw as an instance of false consciousness acting as a brake on the workers' movement; secondly, Sombant's question at the turn of the century as to what accounts for the absence of socialism in North America—a question of continuing actuality to social scientists. Dofny's analysis of Quebec and other comparative materials does much to give rigor to analyzing what is sometimes loosely called "the cultural division of labor," and in doing so he opens up an important reconsideration of the link between the theory of labor aristocracy and a class basis of nationalism.

Lastly, Rogowski's "Conclusion" is more than an editorial summary or reconsideration of the contributions of this volume. It is also an update if not codification of additional materials and analyses of new nationalisms. Further, Rogowski outlines what avenues and research methods seem particularly desirable to deepen the comparative explanation of nationalist movements. Ultimately, he suggests provocatively, what is needed is a theory going beyond nationalism, "a general ... theory of political cleavage." It is a general aspect of science that it endeavors to overcome its own achievements in terms of more general, fundamental theories of the domain of reality it seeks to explain. We seek in this volume to advance the explanation of Western nationalisms, seeing these social movements not as trivia but as genuine problems of social change in the First World. Dialectically, the success of this undertaking points to a necessary *Aufhebung* of nationalism as a research topic for social scientists concerned with the complex sociopolitical process of modernity.

References: Introduction

Barry, B., and Hardin, R. (eds.) (1982), *Rational Man and Irrational Society*? (Beverly Hills, Calif., and London: Sage).

Canada today/D'Aujourd'hui (1982), (Washington, D.C.: The Canadian Embassy, January).

Carrère d'Encausse, H. (1979), *Decline of an Empire: The Soviet Socialist Republics in Revolt* (New York: Newsweek Books).

Connor, W. (1972), "Nation-building or nation-destroying?," *World Politics*, vol. 24, no. 3 (April), pp. 319–55.

Connor, W. (1977), "Ethnonationalism in the first world: the present in historical perspective," in M. J., Esman (ed.), *Ethnic Conflict in the Western World* (Ithaca, N. Y., and London: Cornell University Press, pp. 19–45.

Evans, G. (1973), *Wales Can Win* (Llandybie: Christopher Davies).

Hechter, M. (1975), *Internal Colonialism: The Celtic Fringe in British National Development, 1536–1966* (Berkeley and Los Angeles, Calif.: University of California Press).

Lapidus, G. W. (1984), "Ethnonationalism and political stability: the Soviet case," *World Politics*, vol. 36, no. 4 (July), pp. 555–80.

LeDuc, L., and Murray, J. A. (1983), "A resurgence of Canadian nationalism: Attitudes and policy in the 1980's," in A. Kornberg and H. D. Clarke (eds.), *Political Support in Canada: The Crisis Years* (Durham, N.C.: Duke University Press, pp. 270–90.

Leventman,S. (ed.) (1982), *Counterculture and Social Transformation* (Springfield, Ill.: Charles C. Thomas).

Oberschall, A. (1973), *Social Conflict and Social Movements* (Englewood Cliffs, N.J.: Prentice-Hall).

Olson, M. (1965), *The Logic of Collective Action* (Cambridge, Mass.: Harvard University Press).

Olson, M. (1982), *The Rise and Decline of Nations: Economic Growth, Stagflation, and Social Rigidities* (New Haven, Conn., and London: Yale University Press).

Peers, F. W. (1979), "Tensions over communications," in E. J. Feldman and N. Nevitte (eds.), *The Future of North America: Canada, the United States, and Quebec Nationalism*, Harvard Studies in International Affairs No. 42 (Cambridge, Mass.: Harvard Center for Interntional Affairs; Montreal: Institute for Research on Public Policy) pp. 87–100.

Pi-Sunyer, O. (ed.) (1971), *The Limits of Integration: Ethnicity and Nationalism in Modern Europe*, Research Report No. 9 (Amherst, Mass.: Department of Anthropology, University of Massachusetts).

Rakowska-Harmstone, T. (1977), "The study of ethnic politics in the USSR," in G. W. Simmonds (ed.), *Nationalism in the USSR and Eastern Europe in the Era of Brezhnev and Kosygin* (Detroit, Mich.: University of Detroit Press), pp. 272–94.

Tarrow, S. (1983), "Struggling to reform: social movements, resource mobilization and policy change during cycles of protest," Western Societies Program Occasional Paper No. 15, Center for International Studies, Cornell University, Ithaca, N.Y., May.

Tibi, B. (1981), *Arab Nationalism: A Critical Inquiry* (New York: St. Martin's Press).

Tilly, C. (ed.) (1975), *The Formation of National States in Western Europe* (Princeton, N.J.: Princeton University Press).

Yinger, J. M. (1982), *Countercultures: The Promise and Peril of a World Turned Upside Down* (New York: The Free Press).

Zald, M. N., and McCarthy, J. D. (1979), *The Dynamics of Social Movements: Resource Mobilization, Social Control, and Tactics* (Boston, Mass.: Little, Brown).

PART ONE

Theoretical and Methodological Orientations

1

Internal Colonialism Revisited

MICHAEL HECHTER

Although nationalism is the most powerful political force in the modern world, it is a subject that has received surprisingly little attention at the hands of social scientists (Smith, 1971, p. 3). Nationalism unites individuals with different class interests into a solidary group on some kind of cultural basis. Since it apparently demonstrates the greater salience of cultural affinities over material interests as a basis for the development of group solidarity, the occurrence of nationalism has perplexed structural theorists in general, and economic determinists in particular. From their perspective nationalism is intrinsically unstable because the individuals it seeks to mobilize are always at risk of internal conflict over their divergent material interests. For the same reason idealist scholars have regarded nationalism as further evidence of the irrationality of human behavior and, therefore, of the bankruptcy of economic determinism. Because structuralists felt nationalism to be both insignificant and difficult to explain, they usually chose to ignore it, devoting their energies instead to problems that appeared more significant and that their theories seemed better suited to analyze. This left the field clear for idealists—especially for idealist historians.

However, the events surrounding World War II and the decolonization of the Third World challenged structuralists to come to terms with nationalism. Their favored response was a diffusion theory that conceived nationalism to be a traditionalistic reaction to the incursion of markets, industrialization, and modern styles of life in regions that formerly had been immune to such influences (the prototype is Deutsch, 1966). In this widely accepted view the first stages of market penetration threatened a variety of indigenous social groups and provided the rationale for the establishment of a protective coalition among them. Yet, however strong nationalism might appear to be, it was slated to be undermined by the impinging forces of market society that would tear asunder the existing social structure, replacing it with a different, more modern one. The nationalist movement would soon fragment as the outlines of this new social structure emerged, creating a fundamentally new interest cleavage: that between capital and labor. Nationalism, therefore, was expected to be a temporary emanation, arising, like the fire that consumed the phoenix, only during the transition from tradition to modernity.

In the light of the recent outbreaks of nationalism in developed countries this theory seems wrongheaded. However, retrospective evaluations are always dangerous. Nearly all the classical social theorists had subscribed to a version of this diffusion theory, and it was also buttressed by much social research. The theory thus made a good deal of sense, but it turned out to be empirically misleading.

Internal Colonialism (Hechter, 1975) attacked elements of the diffusion theory and provided an alternative explanation of nationalism. Like its diffusionist predecessor, the new theory assumed that solidary groups were formed by individuals sharing common material interests. Unlike the diffusion theory, however, *Internal Colonialism* suggested that under certain conditions nationalism could continue to persist, if not thrive, in the very midst of industrial society. Whereas the diffusion theory had predicted the inevitable triumph of class over nationalist politics in the industrial setting, *Internal Colonialism* held that this relationship was by no means a determinate one.

Although it escaped the notice of many readers, the central theoretical claim of the book was that the survival of nationalism ultimately depended on the existence of a cultural division of labor—a stratification system giving cultural distinctions political salience by systematically linking them to individual life chances. If an individual perceives that his life chances are significantly limited merely on account of his membership in a particular group, he will either attempt to leave that group or come to see that he shares vital interests with its members and thereby adopt a nationalist identity. Further, industrialization in no way precludes the existence of this kind of cultural division of labor, for the members of advantaged groups will have the means to monopolize their position to the detriment of the disadvantaged. This is precisely the kind of stratification system that internal colonialism invariably produces.

Much of the analysis in the book discusses the evolution of such cultural divisions of labor in Ireland, Scotland, and Wales. The prototype for this discussion is southern Ireland—a stunningly clear example of internal colonial development. The origins of the southern Irish cultural division of labor were to be found in the Cromwellian Settlement of 1642, which expropriated all Catholic landowners and distributed their property to Protestant Englishmen. Had enterprising Catholics any ideas of reclaiming their lands, the Dublin government enacted a set of Penal Laws making such Catholic competition with the Protestants illegal; these were not repealed until 1828. Essentially, this strategy was a precursor of apartheid.

The remainder of the book tried to document the existence of nationalist sentiment in these regions from 1885 to 1966 (but note that this is far from the same thing as nationalist *voting*, for reasons presented elsewhere in this volume—see Chapter 6). It was hypothesized that the persistence of nationalist sentiment was due to the cultural division of labor. But no direct measures of the cultural division of labor were available, and the indirect measures of it used in the study are subject to ambiguous interpretation. Thus despite its elaborate statistical apparatus, the book's central hypothesis—namely, that linking nationalism with the cultural division of labor—was not adequately tested. Unfortunately it remains untested at this writing.

Because *Internal Colonialism* was one of the few attempts to offer a positive theory of nationalism, and the first such study to make a sustained use of multivariate statistical analysis, the book was bound to have a mixed reception. Its appearance was greeted by some with studied indifference, while others excoriated it, and still others embraced it warmly. In general, the book tended to be dismissed by historians, especially by the historians of Ireland, Scotland, and Wales. It was attacked by the proponents of diffusionism and their students, by Celtic area-specialists, and by antinationalists. It was welcomed by the partisans of dependency theory and by Celtic nationalists. And it has been the subject of considerable controversy among a number of (primarily American) sociologists eager to apply their formidable quantitative skills to questions of nationalism (see among others Palloni, 1979; Leifer, 1981; Hannan, 1979; Ragin, 1977, 1979; Nielsen, 1980; Page, 1978; Orridge, 1981).

More revealing, however, was the book's reception within the United Kingdom and Ireland. As might be expected, the dominant English reaction was indifference: the *Times Literary Supplement* (TLS) actually refused to review it, and the leading

sociology journal ignored it. However, there was considerable
enthusiasm for the book among Irish and Welsh readers. The
analysis was quickly adopted into the platform of the Welsh
Nationalist Party (Plaid Cymru), and the *New York Times*
reported (22 April 1977, p. 2) that sales of the book were boom-
ing in the Welsh universities—along with Frantz Fanon's *The
Wretched of the Earth*! but the book's reception in Scotland
was far different, and ultimately more instructive. That the
Highlands were treated as an internal colony was one thing, but
many Scots thought the idea of the Lowlands sharing this
situation was laughable. Even a sympathetic commentator like
Tom Nairn (1977) took this as a central weakness.

Although I had noted that the Scottish case corresponded
least well to the internal colonial model (Hechter, 1975, pp.
342–3), I had failed to draw the proper conclusion from this
observation. If anything, lowland Scotland had been an
overdeveloped peripheral region, not an underdeveloped one.
The Scots had long been innovators in the British context—in
education, finance, technology, and the physical and social
sciences. These are hardly the accomplishments of colonies—
whether internal or external. And the image of the Scots as an
energetic and successful people is far from the image of typical
colonial subjects. Lest Scotland be considered unique,
Catalonia could be offered as an example of an economically
advanced peripheral region which none the less had developed
strong nationalist sentiments.

Thus if internal colonialism was one cause of the growth
of nationalism, other causes of it remained to be discovered
as well. My lack of satisfaction with the indirect measures of
the cultural division of labor drawn from aggregate socio-
demographic statistics led me to other kinds of data sources.
Any direct measure of the cultural division of labor must be
based on cross-tabulations of the relevant cultural categories
with detailed occupational classifications, but such data are
rarely published by governments for obvious political reasons.
However, such cross-tabulations could be derived from the
Public Use Sample tapes of the United States Census, and I
began to explore these as a better means to evaluate the merits
of the concept. In the American context the relevant cultural
groups are, of course, ethnic. Although, for the most part,
American ethnic groups have not developed significant nationalist politics, they are characterized by markedly different levels
of solidarity. For example, they differ considerably in their
rates of endogamy. If a large proportion of the variation in

endogamy among American ethnic groups could be explained by the cultural division of labor, this finding would lend support to the theory proposed in *Internal Colonialism*. With this end in view, the project was undertaken (Hechter, 1978; for other studies utilizing the concept of a cultural division of labor, see Allardt, 1979; McRoberts and Posgate, 1980; special issue, *Ethnic and Racial Studies*, July 1979).

It quickly became apparent that two different kinds of American ethnic groups had high solidarity. On the one hand, groups such as blacks and Hispanics, who were clustered in the lowest reaches of the stratification system, had high levels of solidarity. These groups are in structurally analogous positions to the Irish and Welsh. On the other hand, Yiddish-speaking Jews also had high solidarity, but in no sense could they be regarded as materially disadvantaged. On the contrary, the Jews were the most well-off group in the entire sample. What structural feature could account for their high degree of solidarity?

The answer leapt out from the data: in spite of the fact that the Jews were so well off, and on this account were most unlikely to be solidary, they were simultaneously very highly occupationally specialized. More than any other group, the Jews were clustered in specific occupational niches (they were disproportionately represented as managers and administrators, sales representatives and clerks, physicians, and accountants). There was good reason to suspect that this specialization in relatively prestigious occupations was responsible for their high level of solidarity. Occupational specialization could contribute to group solidarity by promoting the interaction of status equals within group boundaries, as well as by increasing the commonality of members' economic interests. The resulting findings lent support to this reasoning. Thus the cultural division of labor had to have at least two separate and independent dimensions: a hierarchical dimension, in which the various groups were vertically distributed in the occupational structure, and a segmental one, in which the groups were occupationally specialized at any level of the structure.

This new conception of the cultural division of labor, therefore, provided a structural basis for understanding nationalism in Scotland, which may not have experienced internal colonialism to any great degree, but instead had a high level of institutional autonomy. (This is because the Act of Union of 1707 between Scotland and England had established distinctively Scottish legal, educational, and ecclesiastical institutions, all of which differ significantly from their English counterparts.)

Once a region has attained a degree of institutional autonomy by whatever means, this creates a potential basis for the development of a segmental cultural division of labor (Hechter and Levi, 1979). For one of the things such institutions do is to establish occupational niches for incumbents who adhere to the distinctive culture. These incumbents often owe their very jobs to the existence of cultural distinctiveness. There is little doubt that Scottish lawyers face considerable professional competition, but they never face competition from *English* lawyers because the two types of law are incommensurable. In this way Scotland's institutional autonomy provides a substantial material incentive for the reproduction of Scottish culture through history. It also serves to anchor the social base of Scottish ethnicity firmly within the bourgeoisie. The existence of these institutions ensures that nearly all strata in the population come into regular contact with the peripheral culture and thus are likely to identify with it.

Of course, institutional autonomy is not the sole cause of the emergence of ethnic specializations in valued occupations. Neither Catalans nor Spanish Basques—nor, for that matter, American Jews—have had the same kind of institutional autonomy with which Scotland has been blessed. Despite this, each group has none the less managed to gain at least partial control over certain bourgeois occupations in its respective territory.

All told, this research helped resolve the anomaly of Scottish nationalism in the Celtic context, but another question that some critics had raised continued to puzzle me: what could explain the changing fortunes of the nationalist parties themselves? The book had presented evidence—evidence I still find compelling—that the basis for a nationalist coalition had remained roughly constant in these regions from 1885 to 1966. Presumably this was due to the existence of common material interests deriving from the cultural division of labor. There was little reason to believe that the cultural division of labor in Wales or Scotland had changed substantially from 1885 to 1966. Yet the actual course of the nationalist movement—as charted by the numbers and votes nationalist parties could muster—had fluctuated wildly during these years. Popular support for nationalism was at a moderately high level from 1885 to 1914; it diminished from 1914 to 1964 and rose again, meteorically this time, from 1965 to 1978. Since then it has begun to decline once more.

It was obvious that this variation in nationalist voting was due to factors other than the cultural division of labor (see Levi and Hechter in this volume). While patterns of intergroup stratification might have created the possibility of nationalism, they were clearly insufficient to account for political mobilization. This had been recognized in *Internal Colonialism*, which offered an *ad hoc* explanation for the rise of nationalist party activity after 1965 (see Hechter, 1975, pp. 298–310). But this explanation evaded a more fundamental theoretical problem: to understand the conditions under which the individuals in *any* social category (whether defined in class, ethnic, religious, linguistic, or sexual terms) came to develop solidarity with others in that category in order to pursue their collective interests.

Now both the diffusion and internal colonial approaches to nationalism are predicated on the heuristic assumption that most people are rational, self-interested actors. Beginning with this assumption, Marx and Weber had developed an influential theory that solidarity emerges as a result of conflict between groups of individuals having common material interests.

But this conflict theory of group solidarity is inadequate, for it leaves unanswered one very critical question. If the individuals who share common material circumstances are rationally motivated, why should they join forces with their comrades to pursue collective interests? What can they gain, as individuals, by participating in the struggle? A truly rational actor will not join a group to pursue collective ends if, by refraining to participate, he can reap the benefit of other people's activity to obtain these ends. Instead he will opt to be a free-rider when offered the slightest opportunity to do so. The paradox is that, to the degree individuals act as free-riders, they are not likely to participate in groups, or to engage in collective action— either on a class or a nationalist basis.

Awareness of this free-rider problem has led consensus theorists (like Durkheim and Parsons) to conclude that no rational choice analysis could account for the maintenance of solidarity in any group. Instead they argued that individuals could not generally act in unrestrained pursuit of their self-interest, for group solidarity requires that individual action be normatively determined. Thus while conflict theorists suggested that the groups most likely to attain solidarity were interest-homogeneous, they ignored the significance of the free-rider. On the other hand, consensus theorists recognized that groups must induce their members to comply with collective norms to discourage free-riding, but they offered little insight into how this situation comes about.

It gradually became clear that a new theory of group solidarity was required to attack the problem (Hechter, 1983). This new theory seeks to explain the conditions under which individuals comply with the obligations of any group to which they already belong. The more compliance a group demands, and can obtain from, its members, the higher will be its solidarity. The theory treats these obligations as a kind of tax that is charged by the group as a condition of membership. Following this assumption, the compliance of any member is determined by his desire to obtain the benefits provided by membership in that group, as well as by the number and extent of alternative sources of these benefits available to him. Together these factors define the member's dependence on the group. The greater his dependence, the more likely he is to comply with group obligations.

But dependence *per se* is an insufficient cause of compliance. Regardless of an individual's dependence on a group, compliance can only be assured when the group's other members or leaders have the capacity to monitor his behavior in order to discover when he is being compliant and when he is not. For only when selective incentives are provided exclusively to reward the compliant and to punish the non compliant can free-riding be precluded. More formally, dependence and the group's capacity to monitor the behavior of its members are both necessary conditions for solidarity, but neither is by itself sufficient. Solidarity can be achieved only by the joint effects of dependence and group monitoring capacity.

Briefly, the theory proposes that the prospects for group solidarity will be maximized in situations where actors face limited (and, to them, inadequate) sources of benefit; where their opportunities for multiple group affiliation are minimized; and where their social isolation is extreme. But even in these most favorable of circumstances solidarity can only occur when groups have the capacity to monitor members' behavior, so that selective incentives can be dispensed to promote compliance. This clarifies the link to the conflict theories of group solidarity that are currently so popular. While this new theory is consistent with the implicit behavioral axioms of the conflict theories, its predictions differ in that this theory gives critical weight to variables that transform free-riders into collective actors. These variables are either neglected or given short shrift in conflict theories. The problem with the conflict theories is that they specify necessary but insufficient causes of group solidarity. For this reason, it is not surprising that they are of so little use in accounting for the timing of collective action, whether on a nationalistic basis or any other.

Elements of the newer theory have been used to explain the rise and decline of nationalist political parties in Scotland, Wales and Brittany (see Levi and Hechter, in this volume). The theory has also been applied, among other things, to the problems of state formation in early modern Western Europe; to the causes of legislative voting solidarity; and to the relationship between class and ethnic solidarity in the United States and Australia (Hechter, forthcoming). While it is too early to judge the theory's success, it is fair to say that the preliminary results have been encouraging.

How does all this affect the current status of *Internal Colonialism*? I am now inclined to believe that the argument of the book is not so much incorrect as it is incomplete. It is incomplete because it fails to recognize the possibility of segmental cultural divisions of labor in addition to hierarchical ones. Hence it takes too narrow a view of the conditions that promote common material interests among culturally distinct populations. But together with most other conflict-theoretic explanations of group solidarity, it is also incomplete because it fails to attend to organizational mechanisms that are necessary to solve the free-rider problem. The mere existence of common material interests is not a sufficient condition for the establishment of group solidarity or collective action, although it is a *necessary* one (Hechter *et al.*, 1982). In the first place, nationalist organizations must gain sufficient resources to make their members more dependent on them than on rival political organizations. In the second place, to be successful such groups must have the means of monitoring their members' compliance to the movement's goals and procedures. Thus if I were writing the book today, it would raise many of the same questions and provide some of the same answers, but it would have more microsociological analysis.

References: Chapter 1

Allardt, Erik (1979), *Implications of the Ethnic Revival in Modern Industrialized Society* (Helsinki: Societas Scientarium Fennica).

Deutsch, Karl (1966), *Nationalism and Social Communication* (Cambridge, Mass.: MIT Press).

Ethnic and Racial Studies (1979), special issue on internal colonialism, vol. 2, no. 3 (July).

Hannan, Michael T. (1979), "The dynamics of ethnic boundaries in modern states," in Michael T. Hannan and John W. Meyer (eds.) *National Development and the World System* (Chicago: University of Chicago Press) pp. 253–75.

Hechter, Michael (1975), *Internal Colonialism: The Celtic Fringe in British National Development, 1536–1966* (London: Routledge & Kegan Paul; Berkeley and Los Angeles, Calif.: University of California Press).

Hechter, Michael (1978), "Group formation and the cultural division of labor," *American Journal of Sociology*, vol. 84, no. 2 (September), pp. 293–318.

Hechter, Michael (1983), "A theory of group solidarity," in M. Hechter (ed.), *The Microfoundations of Macrosociology* (Philadelphia, Pa.: Temple University Press), pp. 16–57.

Hechter, Michael (forthcoming), Principles of Group Solidarity (Berkeley, Calif., and London: University of California Press).

Hechter, Michael, and Levi, Margaret (1979), "The comparative analysis of ethnoregional movements," *Ethnic and Racial Studies*, vol. 2, no. 3 (July), pp. 260–74.

Hechter, Michael, Friedman, Debra, and Appelbaum, Malka (1982), "A theory of ethnic collective action," *International Migration Review*, vol. 16, no. 2, pp. 412–34.

Leifer, Eric M. (1981), "Competing models of political mobilization: the role of ethnic ties," *American Journal of Sociology*, vol. 87, no. 1 (July), pp. 23–47.

McRoberts, Kenneth, and Posgate, Dale (1980), *Quebec: Social Change and Political Crisis*, rev. ed. (Toronto: McClelland & Stewart).

Nairn, Tom (1977), *The Break-Up of Britain* (London: New Left Books).

Nielsen, François (1980), "The Flemish movement in Belgium after World War II," *American Sociological Review*, vol. 45, no. 2 (April), pp. 76–94.

Orridge, A. W. (1981), "Uneven development and nationalism: 2," *Political Studies*, vol. 29, no. 2 (June), pp. 181–90.

Page, Edward (1978), "Michael Hechter's internal colonial thesis: some theoretical and methodological problems," *European Journal of Political Research*, vol. 6, no. 3 (September), pp. 295–317.

Palloni, Alberto (1979), "Internal colonialism or clientelistic politics? The case of southern Italy," *Ethnic and Racial Studies*, vol. 2, no. 3 (July), pp. 360–77.

Ragin, Charles (1977), "Class, status, and 'reactive ethnic cleavages': the social bases of political regionalism," *American Sociological Review*, vol. 42, no. 3 (June), pp. 438–50.

Ragin, Charles (1979), "Ethnic political mobilization: the Welsh case," *American Sociological Review*, vol. 44, no. 4 (August), pp. 619–35.

Ritter, Kathleen V. (1980), "Natives and settlers: the cultural division of labor in Alaska, 1741–1970," Ph.D. dissertation, University of Washington.

Smith, Anthony D. (1971), *Theories of Nationalism* (London: Duckworth).

2

States and "Nation-Groups"
a Global Taxonomy

GUNNAR P. NIELSSON

A Framework for Inquiry

To analyze better the role of nation-groups[1] and nationalism in domestic and international politics, we need to introduce a more logically consistent conceptualization.

That ethnic groups, nation-groups, and states must be treated as different units of analysis is the first basic assumption in our conceptual framework. A second major assumption is that ethnic groups and nation-groups may persist despite pressures for change that flow from state-building and socio-economic modernization. In other words, nation-groups can adapt to changing societal values.[2] Consequently, the persistence and adaptability of nation-groups should be viewed as an independent and continuous variable in studies of socioeconomic and political change. But nation-group identities should not be carried to the opposite extreme of becoming the basis for a mono-causal, deterministic theory; as Clifford Geertz (1963, p. 124n.) has put it, "Simple primordial sentiment is no more defensible a position than economic determinism." The third major assumption is that nation-group values constitute a significant variable in explaining both intrastate and interstate political relationships.

Nobody has been able to provide precise definitions of the three units of analysis to be used in this conceptual framework.[3] We must, therefore, settle for composites of characterization of the ethnic group, the nation-group, and the state. The characteristics connoted by an *ethnic group* include such social category attributes as common racial identity, culture (including language and religion), kinship, social customs, history, and stable geographic contiguity. The emphasis on ethnic group characteristics often requires differentiating them from social class or secondary, associational intergroup characteristics.

A *nation-group* is an ethnic group that has become politically mobilized on the basis of ethnic group values. (We have adopted the term "nation-group" to stress the differentiation between our conception of "the nation" and the prevailing practice, both among scholars and practitioners, of using the term "nation" or "nation-state" as synonymous with the term "state.") Consequently, *every ethnic group is a potential nation-group*. It is an important assumption in our conceptual framework that a variety of ethnic groups, in a prenational stage, may coexist within a state with one or more nation-groups. Furthermore, nation-groups could change back into ethnic groups (remaining latent nation-groups) or they might dissolve or become assimilated into other nation-groups.

Political mobilization of an ethnic group involves the formation of an ideology (hence nationalism can be defined as an ideology based on nationality values) and the establishment of organizational capacities for participation. When the spatial boundaries of a nation-group's membership coincide with the boundaries of a state,[4] it comprises the ideal case of a nation-state. When one nation-group constitutes a majority of the population within a state, then it is here identified as *the state-nation-group*.[5]

Methodological Approaches

In general, the study of nationalism has been dominated by a combination of sweeping, interpretive historical analyses (Seton-Watson, 1977) and descriptive case studies. As an illustration, five compilations of papers, published during the 1970s (Bell and Freeman, 1974; Glazer and Moynihan, 1975; Said and Simmons, 1976; Bertelsen, 1977; and Heisler, 1977), contained forty-two single case studies focussing on various aspects of "ethnicity" in twenty-four states. More than half of the case studies focussed on nationalism in older, industrialized states. In contrast, the more comparatively oriented work of Crawford Young (1976) focussed exclusively on cultural pluralism in Third World states. Furthermore, there has been a considerable distortion in scholarly orientation, with the vast majority of inquiries devoted to manifestations of conflict. There is very little discussion of successful accommodation within multinational states.* In short, the methodological problems with the studies of ethnicity and cultural pluralism are that they lack (1) comparability across cases, (2) balance between conflictual and cooperative experiences, and (3) a general framework for global, systematic, comparative analysis.

In contrast, studies of socioeconomic modernization, changing political attributes, and patterns of events-interaction among states have increasingly drawn upon newly available global data sets. Aggregate analyses based on these data necessarily adopt the state-centric perspective and the concomitant assumption that states represent culturally homogeneous populations, principally because states collect and report the information. Since multinational states do not report according to the ethnic distribution of their populations, there are no global data sets containing socioeconomic and political attributes of ethnic groups. Therefore, it is still not possible to conduct controlled, cross-sectional, or time-series aggregate analyses of the relationships between nation-group behavior, economic modernization, and political integration.

Consequently, for the time being, systematic qualitative comparative analysis of carefully selected, representative cases of states with diverse national attributes is the best solution of the methodological problems. Through this more modest approach, it might be possible to reach a midpoint between disparate single case studies and global aggregate analysis. The selection of a limited number of representative cases will make the creation of new data more manageable. In addition, cases that represent different state and national attributes will facilitate comparison by drawing on the existing state-centric global data sets on a more selective basis.

The rest of this chapter is devoted to describing and explaining the construction of the taxonomies and the implications for future comparative analysis of ranking states according to the classification schemes developed. The state-centric taxonomy, with its five categories of ethnic fragmentation within states, is presented first. Then follows the introduction of the ethnic-centric taxonomy, which also has five categories according to the extent that the nation-group is dispersed into different states. In the subsequent section the two taxonomies are combined into a matrix within which the global state system is analyzed. Finally, the international regional distribution of states in the two-taxonomy matrix is discussed.

*For precisely such an endeavor, see the essay of Jürg Steiner in this volume (Chapter 7).

The State-centric Taxonomy

In 1981, the global state system consisted of 183 political units, including 168 sovereign states and sixteen dependent territories.[6] The state-centric data set used in this analysis consists of 161 states and three dependent territories.[7]

The first taxonomy is based on a measurement of the degree of ethnic fragmentation *within* each state, calculated as the extent of concentration in each state's population of one nation-group's membership. It ranges from the most nationally homogeneous to the most heterogenous states.

We distinguish five categories of nation-group composition:

(1)   *Single nation-group states*: cases where one nation-group accounts for more than 95 percent of a state's population; ranked according to concentration, from 99·9 to 95 percent.

(2)   *One nation-group dominant states*: cases where one nation-group accounts for between 60 and 95 percent of a

Table 2.1   *Classification of the Global State System by Nation-Group Attributes*

Single nation-group states	One nation-group dominant states	One nation-group dominant states with fragmented minorities	Binational states	Multinational states
South Korea	Greece	Benin	Ecuador	Bolivia
North Korea	Hungary	Malawi	Fiji	Surinam
Portugal	Netherlands	Guatemala	Belgium	Malaysia
St. Lucia	Venezuela	Pakistan	United Arab	Sierra Leone
St. Vincent	China	Soviet Union	Emirates	Canada
Haiti	Austria	Upper Volta	Trinidad	Angola
Japan	Solomon	Afghanistan	Guyana	Guinea-Bissau
East Germany	Islands	Nepal	Peru	Zambia
Hong Kong	Western	Sudan	Bhutan	Kenya
Dominica	Samoa	Ghana	Mauritius	Chad
Kiribati	Lebanon	Namibia	Nauru	Liberia
Puerto Rico	Rwanda	Indonesia	Congo	Nigeria
West Germany	Chile	Gambia	Gabon	Ivory Coast
Poland	Paraguay	Iran	Mozambique	Cameroon
Burundi	Luxemburg	Niger	Central	South Africa
Cuba	Tunisia	Philippines	African	Zaire
Dominican	Honduras	Mali	Republic	India
Republic	El Salvador		Thailand	Uganda
Italy	Finland		Belize	Tanzania

Table continued

Table 2.1 *Continued*

Single nation-group states	One nation-group dominant states	One nation-group dominant states with fragmented minorities	Binational states	Multinational states
South Yemen	Nicaragua		Ethiopia	
Cape Verde	Kuwait		Togo	
Norway	Oman		Senegal	
San Marino	Vanuatu		Guinea	
Taiwan	Yemen Arab		Yugoslavia	
Tonga	Republic			
Bangladesh	Uruguay			
Egypt (UAR)	Israel			
Jamaica	Bulgaria			
Ireland	Syria			
Swaziland	Lesotho			
Jordan	Libya			
Denmark	Vietnam			
Iceland	Romania			
Saudi Arabia	France			
Grenada	Turkey			
Colombia	Bahamas			
Madagascar	Panama			
Brazil	Kampuchea			
Costa Rica	Argentina			
Somalia	Mexico			
Tuvalu	Australia			
Malta	Great Britain			
Sweden	Mauritania			
Albania	Bahrain			
Barbados	Cyprus			
Liechtenstein	New Zealand			
	Mongolia			
	Iraq			
	Singapore			
	Papua New			
	Guinea			
	Algeria			
	Spain			
	Burma			
	Qatar			
	United States			
	Sri Lanka			
	Botswana			
	Switzerland			
	Morocco			
	Czechoslovakia			
	Zimbabwe			
	Brunei			
	Laos			
	Andorra			
	Monaco			
Total 45	62	17	21	19	164

state's population; ranked according to concentration, from 94·9 to 60 percent.

(3) *One nation-group dominant states with fragmented minority nation-groups*: cases where the largest nation-group represents between 40 and 60 percent of a state's population and where there are between seven and twenty-five minority nation-groups; ranked according to concentration, from 60 to 40 percent.

(4) *Bination-group states*: cases where the two largest nation-groups, when combined, represent between 65 and 96 percent of the state's population; ranked according to combined concentration, from 96 to 65 percent.

(5) *Multination-group states*: cases with the highest fragmentation of nation-groups; the three largest nation-groups, when combined, represent between 34 and 97 percent of a state's population, with between five and nineteen additional minority nation-groups; ranked according to combined concentration of the three largest groups, from 97 to 34 percent.

The results of ranking the global state system according to this classification scheme are presented in Table 2.1.

If in conventional usage a nation-state is operationally defined as a single nation-group comprising more than 95 percent of the state's population, then forty-five of the 164 states in the global state system qualify.

There is a marked variation of nation-group pluralism within each of the remaining 119 states. In about half (62) a large majority consists of a single nation-group. Hence the nation-groups in the 107 states in the first two categories have a sufficiently high proportion of the state's population to be identified as state-nation-groups.

The remaining fifty-seven states do not fit the conventional concept of the nation-state. In seventeen states one major nation-group coexists with an extensive fragmentation of minority nation-groups; in another twenty-one states two major nation-groups comprise more than two-thirds of the population; and an even higher degree of fragmentation prevails in nineteen states. In nationally pluralistic states it cannot be assumed that the major nation-group is clearly identifiable as "the state-nation-group." An obvious case in point is South Africa, where the Afrikaner nation-group dominates the political system although it is only a small minority.

This state-centric taxonomy demonstrates very clearly that

the conventional concept of the nation-state fits only one-fourth of the members of the global state system. For nearly one-half of the states in the world, "nation-state" is a misnomer. The remaining middle category can be called nation-states only with great caution.

The complexity found at the state-centric level of analysis is only part of the picture, however. We now examine the compositional attributes of the world's peoples from an ethnic-centric perspective.

The Ethnic-centric Taxonomy

The preceding, state-centric analysis provided indicators for the degree of ethnic fragmentation *within* each state. From that perspective there was a total of 1357 ethnic groups *within* the 164 states that constituted our universe of data. However, the number of ethnic groups is exaggerated, because members of the same ethnic group were counted as separate entities when they resided within different states. To confront this conceptual problem, we created an *ethnic-centric* taxonomy. The ethnic groups' entries were disaggregated and resorted according to their membership, even though they were dispersed over several states.[8]

From this new perspective a global total of 589 ethnic groups was identified. They were classified, initially, according to a simple, five-category taxonomy indicating the number of states over which each ethnic group's membership was dispersed, and whether each ethnic group represented a minority or majority in the various states. The results of this classification are presented in Table 2.2.

In only thirteen cases do all the members of an ethnic group reside in one state and comprise a majority in that state. Even then, their predominance within each state varies considerably, as will be shown later. More than half of all ethnic groups (382, or 55·7 percent) are minorities wholly contained within a single state. There is, therefore, considerable justification for treating many of the issues connected with ethnicity as minority problems. However, the broader inquiry should focus on how minority and majority ethnic groups accommodate each other within and across state boundaries.

More than two-thirds of all ethnic groups, or 399 out of 589, are minorities that constitute no more than 10 percent of the population of any state in which they reside. While some of

Table 2.2 *Distribution of Ethnic Groups, by Degree of Concentration of Membership in States*

	in 1 state	in 2 states	in 3 states	in 4 states	in 5 states	in 6–10 states	in 11–20 states	in 21–40 states	Total	Percentage
Single-state minority ethnic groups	328								328	55·7
Single-state majority ethnic groups	13								13	2·2
Multistate, core state dominant ethnic groups		47	18	7	4	5	2	1	84	14·2
Multistate majority ethnic groups		72	27	13	8	18	5	4	147	25·0
Multistate dispersed ethnic groups			5	3	1	4	1	3	17	2·9
Total	341	119	50	23	13	27	8	8	589	
Percentage	58·0	20·0	8·5	3·9	2·2	4·6	1·3	1·3		100·0

these groups are far from tiny—the largest, the Vighurs in China, numbers 40 million—their median size is under half a million, and 42 percent of such groups represent 1 percent or less of any state's population.

The remaining 190 ethnic groups, each of which comprises more than 10 percent of at least one state's population, are assumed to be the most significant, politicized ethnic groups in the global state system and, as such, will be referred to from now on as nation-groups. They constitute a mixture of "state-nation groups" (when they comprise a majority of a state's population) and significant minority nation-groups within various degrees of multinational states. The degree of multi-state dispersal of these nation-groups is presented in Table 2.3.

The fifty-five nation-groups in the "multi-state, core state dominant" categories consist of cases where more than 95 percent of their memberships reside in one state. Thirty-two of these nation-groups also constitute majorities in their core states of residence and, therefore, can be considered "state-nation-groups" according to our definition. The sixty-nine nation-groups in the "multi-state majority" category consist of cases where between 50 and 95 percent of their memberships reside in one state. Thirty-three of these nation-groups represent majorities in fifty states. When combined with the thirteen single-state majority nation-groups, the cases in these two categories lead to the identification of seventy-eight "state-nation-groups" representing majorities in ninety-five sovereign states. The remaining twenty-three nation-groups in the "multistate, core state dominant," and thirty-two nation-groups in the "multistate majority," category, plus the forty-three nation-groups in the "single-state minority" category, can be classified as significant minority nation-groups, residing in states with a variable degree of multi-national fragmentation.

Ten multistate nation-groups do not have a majority of their membership residing in any one state; others are also very widely dispersed. Among the most notable cases of wide dispersal are:

(1) *The Jews*: dispersed over forty states, the largest concentration of nation-group membership is in the United States where 44 percent of all Jews reside. The second highest concentration of membership is in the Soviet Union where 19 percent reside. The Jews comprise a large majority only in Israel where they represent 89 percent of the population; however, Israeli Jews are only 16 percent

Table 2.3 *Distribution of Nation-Groups Representing More than 10 Percent of at Least One State's Population, by Degree of Concentration of Membership in States*

	in 1 state	in 2 states	in 3 states	in 4 states	in 5 states	in 6–10 states	in 11–20 states	in 21–40 states	Total	Percentage
Single-state minority nation-groups	39								39	20·5
Single-state majority nation-groups	13								13	6·8
Multistate, core state dominant nation-groups		22	15	7	3	2	2	1	52	27·5
Multistate majority nation-groups		21	11	10	6	12	5	4	69	36·2
Multistate dispersed nation-groups			5	3	1	1	4	3	17	9·0
Total	52	43	31	20	10	15	11	8	190	100·0
Percentage	27·4	22·6	16·3	10·5	5·3	7·9	5·8	4·2		

of all Jews. In the remaining thirty-seven states Jews represent very small minorities.

(2) *The Arabs*: dispersed over thirty-seven states, the largest concentration of Arabs is found in Egypt (UAR) where 31 percent of the total membership live. However, the Arabs constitute more than 90 percent of the populations in nine states (Egypt, Saudi Arabia, Yemen Arab Republic, Tunisia, Lebanon, Jordan, South Yemen, Oman, and Kuwait), between 75 and 90 percent of the populations in six states (Algeria, Iraq, Syria, Libya, Mauritania, and Bahrain), between 50 and 75 percent of the populations in two states (Morocco and Qatar) and significant minorities in three states (Sudan, Chad, and the United Arab Emirates). In the remaining seventeen states the Arabs are small minorities.

(3) *The Malays*: dispersed over seven states, they represent an interesting case where more than half of the total membership is located in Indonesia, in which they represent a small minority. However, 35 percent of the Malays live in Malaysia where they constitute one of the two minority nation-groups that dominate that multinational state. They are small minorities in the other five states.

(4) *The Irish*: dispersed over six states, the Irish constitute 98 percent of the population of Eire, but that is only 40 percent of the nation-group membership. Of the remaining Irish, 32 percent reside in Britain and 26 percent in the United States where they are small minorities; the rest live principally in the three "White Dominion" states of Canada, Australia, and New Zealand where they also are very small minorities.

(5) *The Kurds*: dispersed over six states, the Kurds are significant minorities in three: Turkey, Iran, and Iraq.

(6) *Overseas South Asians*: this is a "residual" ethnic group consisting of Indian and Pakistani nationals who have settled in twenty-two states (excluding Britain). They now constitute significant minorities in the United Arab Emirates, Trinidad, Fiji, Guyana, and Suriname.

(7) *Overseas black Africans*: dispersed over fifteen states, this is another "residual" category into which we have aggregated social groups whose African ancestors were settled elsewhere as slaves during the seventeenth and eighteenth centuries. The degree to which they have been integrated into new nation-groups is one of the important research questions to be addressed later in this research

project. The vast majority (91 percent) are located in the United States where they constitute 11 percent of the population. However, the remaining members of this group form the overwhelming majority of populations in the Caribbean states of St. Lucia, St. Vincent, Haiti, Dominica, Jamaica, Grenada, Barbados, and the Bahamas, as well as the African island state of Cape Verde. They also constitute half of the population of Belize and very large minorities in Suriname, Trinidad, and the Yemen Arab Republic.

(8) *Overseas whites/Europeans*: dispersed over thirteen states, this is a third "residual" category, comprised of the vestiges of white European settlement in former colonies. They constitute significant minorities in Namibia, Zimbabwe, the Bahamas, and Nauru.

(9) *The Fulbe*: dispersed over fourteen states, the Fulbe (or Fellatahs) are significant minorities in the sub-Saharan African states of Guinea, Senegal, Mali, Niger, Guinea-Bissau, Mauritania, and Gambia.

(10) *The Armenians*: dispersed over eleven states, the Armenian nation-group is included to illustrate another kind of complexity. Recognized as a separate republic within the Soviet Union where 89 percent of Armenians reside, they constitute very small minorities in Syria, Lebanon, Turkey, Egypt, Bulgaria, Iraq, Greece, Cyprus, and Jordan.

(11) *The Chinese*: dispersed over twenty-seven states, 96 percent of the Chinese reside in the People's Republic of China, but they also constitute the vast majorities in Taiwan, Hong Kong, and Singapore, and significant minorities in Malaysia, Thailand, Brunei, and Nauru.

(12) *The Germans*: dispersed over twenty-eight states, 64 percent of all Germans reside in the Federal Republic of Germany and 20 percent in the German Democratic Republic; in both states they represent more than 95 percent of the population. They also comprise over 90 percent of the population of Liechtenstein, and 69 percent of the population of Switzerland. Austria could be considered another case of a German nation-group-dominated state, although we have treated Austrians as a separate nation-group in this study.

(13) *The Italians*: dispersed over twenty-eight states, 85 percent of all Italians reside in Italy where they represent 98 percent of the population. They also constitute over 90

percent of the population of San Marino, and 10 percent of the Swiss and 17 percent of Monaco's population.

(14) *The French*: dispersed over twenty-four states, the French constitute 81 percent of the population of France, and 56 percent of the population of Monaco; and 30 percent of the Canadian and 18 percent of the Swiss populations, and significant minorities in Mauritius, Vanuatu, and Andorra.

These eleven nation-groups and three "residual" category social groups are the most pronounced cases of wide dispersal over several sovereign states. Combined, they represent majority "state-nation-groups" in forty states and significant minorities in thirty-six. The political behavior of multistate nation-groups and their influence on interstate relations are subjects that have not yet been studied systematically as a significant aspect of international relations.

A more refined ethnic-centric taxonomy has been constructed in order to provide an overview of the range of complexity from single-state nation-groups to widely dispersed, multistate nation-groups. It consists of the following five categories:

Category 1: *single-state nation-groups*: cases where between 75 and 100 percent of a nation-group's membership reside in one state, constituting between 90 and 100 percent of that state's population. The remaining proportion of a nation-group's membership constitutes less than 10 percent of any of the state's populations over which it is dispersed. Ranked according to the degree of concentration: that is, from 100 to 75 percent of the nation-group membership.

Category 2: *single-state majority nation-groups*: cases where 50 to 75 percent of a nation-group's membership reside in one state, constituting between 50 and 90 percent of that state's population. The remaining proportion of a nation-group's membership constitutes less than 10 percent of any of the state's populations over which it is dispersed. Ranked according to the degree of concentration; that is, from 75 to 50 percent of the nation-group membership.

Category 3: *single-state and multistate minority nation-groups*: cases where (*a*) all the members of a nation-group reside in one state, but constitute only a minority (10–50 percent) of that state's population. Such states' populations consist of multiple minority nation-groups. Or where (*b*) the nation-group membership is dispersed over several states and constitutes a significant minority (10–50 percent) of the population in at least one state. Ranked from states with only single-state nation-groups as multiple minorities to states with a mixture of single-state and multi-state nation-groups as multiple minorities.

Category 4:   *multistate majority and minority nation-groups*: cases where a state's population is made up of a combination of multistate nation-groups that constitute only minorities of any state's population and multistate nation-groups that constitute majorities in some of the states over which they are dispersed. Ranked according to states with the lowest to highest proportion of their populations accounted for by a multistate nation-group with majorities in at least one state.

Category 5:   *multistate nation-groups*: cases where nation-group membership is dispersed over several states, but represents the majority of the populations in at least two states. Ranked according to the number of states in which the nation-group constitutes a majority; that is, from the smallest to the largest number of states.

This classification of states (see table 2.4) shows a movement from the least to the most dispersed nation-groups. The first and fifth categories show cases with the least nation-group fragmentation within the states. The third and fourth categories consist of cases with high compositional complexity. According to this rank-ordering, thirty-one states have the high degree of cultural homogeneity characteristic of single-state nation-groups. While the thirty-eight states in the fifth category also are characterized by a high degree of cultural homogeneity, they differ from the first category by sharing cultural identity with majority populations in other states. Increasing national pluralism is found within the thirty-two states in the second category.

The compositional complexity of nation-group attributes within the twenty-six states in the third and the thirty-seven

Table 2.4   *The Global State System in an Ethnic-centric Perspective*

Single-state nation-groups	Single-state majority nation-groups	Single- and multistate minority nation-groups	Multistate majority and minority nation-groups	Multistate nation-groups
Kiribati	Panama	Yugoslavia	Zambia	Western
Tonga	Mongolia	Ethiopia	Angola	Samoa
Iceland	Papua New	Pakistan	Togo	Tuvalu
Madagascar	Guinea	Sierra Leone	Uganda	Laos
Venezuela	Argentina	Central	Chad	Rwanda
Brazil	Romania	African	Canada	Upper Volta
Japan	Australia	Republic	Guyana	Greece
Colombia	Burma	Philippines	Fiji	South Korea
Costa Rica	Vietnam	Liberia	Sudan	North Korea
Cuba	Bulgaria	Kenya	Congo	West Germany
Dominican	New Zealand	Tanzania	Belize	East Germany
Republic	Great Britain	Guinea-Bissau	Morocco	Liechtenstein
Honduras	Mexico	Cameroon	Andorra	Solomon
Chile	Kampuchea	Bolivia	Spain	Islands
El Salvador	Botswana	Indonesia	United Arab	Vanuatu
Swaziland	Burundi	Iran	Emirates	Italy
Denmark	Albania	South Africa	Mozambique	San Marino
Nicaragua	Somalia	Namibia	Zaire	France
Finland	Ireland	Ecuador	Surinam	China
Uruguay	Czechoslovakia	Peru	Ghana	Taiwan
Luxemburg	Guatemala	Gabon	Malawi	Hong Kong
Portugal	Zimbabwe	Ivory Coast	Monaco	St. Lucia
Paraguay	Soviet Union	Niger	Benin	St. Vincent
Netherlands	Afghanistan	Senegal	India	Haiti
Bangladesh	Belgium	Guinea	Malaysia	Dominica
Poland	Sri Lanka	Nigeria	Trinidad	Cape Verde
Malta	Bhutan	Mali	Mauritius	Jamaica
Austria	Nepal	Gambia	Brunei	Grenada
Sweden	Lesotho		Switzerland	Barbados
Norway	United States		Singapore	Egypt (UAR)
Puerto Rico	Israel		Cyprus	Algeria
Hungary	Nauru		Yemen Arab	Saudi Arabia
	Thailand		Republic	Syria
			Qatar	Tunisia
			Bahamas	Lebanon
			Iraq	Jordan
			Bahrain	South Yemen
			Mauritania	Libya
			Turkey	Oman
				Kuwait
31	32	26	37	38 164

states in the fourth category can best be described by a few illustrative cases. The Philippines, in the third category, is an extremely fragmented state, where three single-state nation-groups each account for between 10 and 50 percent of the

Table 2.5 Malaysia as an Illustration of Nation-Group, Multistate Compositional Complexity

Percentage Malaysia's population	Name of ethnic group	Single-state ethnic group	Multistate ethnic group	Percentage ethnic group located in which state		Percentage of state population where located	Total population of ethnic group in 1960
38·3	Malays		X	53·9	Indonesia	5·2	
				34·5	Malaysia	38·3	
				8.6	Thailand	12·9	
				1·8	Singapore	10·1	
				0·8	South Africa	0·4	
				0·3	Sri Lanka	0·3	
				0·1	Cambodia	0·2	9,275,000
35·9	Chinese		X	96·0	China	93·9	
				1·6	Taiwan	98·0	
				0·4	Malaysia	35·9	
				rest dispersed over 19 states			694,000,000
7·2	Tamils		X	90·7	India	7·2	
				6·8	Sri Lanka	23·6	
				1·7	Malaysia	7·2	
				0·5	Burma	0·8	
				0·2	Singapore	5·3	
				0·1	Mauritius	2·2	35,300,000

			Distribution			Population
2·9	Javanese	X	Indonesia	99·4	45·4	43,000,000
			Malaysia	0·5	2·9	
			Singapore	0·1	2·2	
1·1	Banjarese	X	Indonesia	94·0	1·6	1,500,000
			Malaysia	6·0	1·1	
0·6	Malayalis	X	India	99·6	3·7	16,500,000
			Malaysia	0·3	0·6	
			Singapore	0·1	1·2	
0·4	Telugus	X	India	99·4	9·1	40,000,000
			Burma	0·4	0·7	
			Malaysia	0·1	0·4	
			Mauritius	0·05	0·7	
			Singapore	0·05	0·1	
2·9	Ibans	X				
2·0	Dusuns	X				
1·9	Kalimantans	X				
0·9	Sea Gypsies	X				
0·7	Klemantans	X				
0·6	Melanans	X				
0·4	Kadayans	X				
96·3	14 ethnic groups	7	11 different states		7	combined 761,000
						840,336,000

population and eleven ethnic groups each represent less than 10 percent of the population. These fourteen groups together constitute 96 percent of the Philippines' population. Kenya and Tanzania are similar.

Malaysia provides a telling illustration of the even greater complexity that multistate nation-groups bring. As shown in Table 2.5, Malaysia must accommodate seven single-state and seven multistate nation-groups. There are possible linkages to nation-groups in eleven different states, involving the cultural identities of 840 million people. Even beyond the massive membership of the Chinese nation-group, it could involve the cultural identities of 146 million people residing in eight different states.[9]

A Matrix Analysis of the State-Centric and Ethnic-Centric Taxonomies

The degree and major characteristics of nation-group compositional complexity are further refined through analyzing the matrix of the two taxonomies presented in Table 2.6. Juxtaposing the two classification schemes reveals three important clusters of states.

In the first place, we return to the notion of a "best fit" operational definition of the conventional concept of nation-state. The upper left cell of the matrix identifies the nineteen states that would best satisfy the expectation of "one nation in one state." We believe the tight definition can be relaxed a little to include the twelve states in the second column of that ethniccentric category. The resulting thirty-one cases of nation-states should be used as *control cases* in future systematic comparative research, since they are representative of the highest degree of national homogeneity. In them political integration is based on a fusion of national and societal values which serves as the source of legitimacy. Political cleavages are based on differences about societal values. Political disintegration would occur if such value differences became extreme and elites resorted to coercion. Extreme political disintegration would be manifested by revolutionary changes of the regime, but it would not affect the state boundaries or basic structure.

The second major cluster of states conforms worst to the conventional connotation of the nation-state. The thirty-six states in these cells, identified as the third and fourth row and the fourth and fifth columns in the matrix, have the highest degree of compositional complexity, with extensive internal ethnic fragmentation, national pluralism, and linkages to minority nation-group counterparts in several states. They comprise the most obvious research sites for the study of political integration within sovereign states. They are important cases for comparative research on the political mobilization that turns ethnic groups into nation-groups.

We assume that, in multinational states, successful domestic political integration and legitimacy are based on a mixture of shared societal values and mutual respect for the values of the diverse, semiautonomous nation-groups. Political cleavages are caused by irreconcilable value differences between nation-groups or at the level of the whole society. Where differences of social class coincide with ones of nation-group, value differences of these two kinds will often reinforce each other; hence such a coincidence increases the probability of conflict and political disintegration. Extreme political disintegration in these cases is manifested by revolutionary changes not only of political regime, but often of the basic state structure, for example, the disintegration of India and subsequently of Pakistan.

The third cluster of states indicated in the matrix comprises the most representative cases of multistate nations. Cultural identities are shared by large majorities in several states among the twenty-two in the lower-left cell of the matrix. Again we propose that the definition be relaxed somewhat to include the fifteen states in the cells identified as "multistate majority and minority nation-groups"/"one nation-group dominant states." These fifty-two states seem particularly suited for comparative research on the impact of shared cultural identities on interstate relations—one of the less developed subject areas in the study of international relations. Are such nation-groups a basis for cooperative relations among states? Where conflict arises among states sharing cultural identities, we would assume that the issues involve differences over societal values and political ideology, for example, the differences between radical and conservative Arab states.

The states outside of the three clusters have less pronounced nation-group attributes and seem less promising for comparative analysis. The main point is that this matrix provides a first cut at establishing a global perspective from which the variations in nation-group attributes can be assessed and according to which the most representative cases can be selected for future theory-guided, comparative research.

Table 2.6 Matrix of State-centric and Ethnic-centric Taxonomies

	Single nation-group states	One nation-group dominant states	One nation-group dominant states with fragmented minorities	Bination-group states	Multination-group states	Total
Single-state nation-groups	Kiribati Tonga Iceland Madagascar Brazil Japan Colombia Costa Rica Cuba Dominican Republic Swaziland Denmark Portugal Bangladesh Poland Malta Sweden Norway Puerto Rico	Venezuela Honduras Chile El Salvador Nicaragua Finland Uruguay Luxemburg Paraguay Netherlands Austria Hungary				

Single-state majority nation-groups	Burundi	Panama	Guatemala	Belgium
	Albania	Mongolia	Soviet Union	Bhutan
	Somalia	Papua New Guinea	Afghanistan	Nauru
	Ireland	Argentina	Nepal	Thailand
		Romania		
		Australia		
		Burma		
		Vietnam		
		Bulgaria		
		New Zealand		
		Great Britain		
		Mexico		
		Kampuchea		
		Botswana		
		Czechoslovakia		
		Zimbabwe		
		Sri Lanka		
		Lesotho		
		United States		
		Israel		

32

Table continued

Table 2.6 *Continued*

	Single nation-group states	One nation-group dominant states	One nation-group dominant states with fragmented minorities	Bination-group states	Multination-group states	Total
Single- and multistate minority nation-groups			Pakistan Philippines Indonesia Iran Namibia Niger Mali Gambia	Yugoslavia Ethiopia Central African Republic Ecuador Peru Gabon Senegal Guinea	Sierra Leone Liberia Kenya Tanzania Guinea-Bissau Cameroon Bolivia South Africa Ivory Coast Nigeria	
						26
Multistate majority and minority nation-groups		Morocco Andorra Spain Monaco Brunei Switzerland Singapore Cyprus Yemen Arab Republic Qatar Bahamas	Sudan Ghana Malawi Benin	Togo Guyana Fiji Congo Belize United Arab Emirates Mozambique Trinidad Mauritius	Zambia Angola Uganda Chad Canada Zaire Surinam India Malaysia	

Multistate
nation-groups

45	62	17
Tuvalu	Western Samoa	Upper Volta
South Korea	Laos	
North Korea	Rwanda	
West Germany	Greece	
East Germany	Solomon Islands	
Liechtenstein	Vanuatu	
Italy	France	
San Marino	China	
Taiwan	Algeria	
Hong Kong	Syria	
St. Lucia	Tunisia	
St. Vincent	Lebanon	
Haiti	Libya	
Dominica	Oman	
Cape Verde	Kuwait	
Jamaica		
Grenada		
Barbados		
Egypt (UAR)		
Saudi Arabia		
Jordan		
South Yemen		

Iraq
Bahrain
Mauritania
Turkey

37

38

Total	45	62	17	21	19	164

Table 2.7 State-Nation-Groups in the Western State System

Name of nation-group	State of residence	Percentage nation-group membership in major state of residence	Percentage state population	Percentage nation-group membership in neighboring states	Percentage population in neighboring states	Percentage nation-group in four settler societies	Number of states dispersed over
Nation states:							
Icelanders	Iceland	100·0	97·2				1
Danes	Denmark	98·4	97·5	1·6	0·8		3
Finns	Finland	97·1	91·3	2·9	1·5		3
Luxemburgers	Luxemburg	96·7	91·8	3·4	0·1		2
Dutch	Netherlands	94·1	94·7	1·2	0·7	4·7	6
Portuguese	Portugal	95·0	99·7	0·2	0·1		9
Maltese	Malta	87·0	95·7			11·0	4
Austrians	Austria	83·9	93·4	3·8	0·5	13·0	6
Swedes	Sweden	82·0	95·7	4·6	8·3	13·4	6
Norwegians	Norway	78·4	98·0	1·1	0·5	20·5	5
Multistate nations:							
Greeks	Greece	90·8	94·7	6·8		0·9	10
	Cyprus	5·2	78·8				

Group	Country						
Turks	Turkey	95·8	85·7	3·5			10
Italians	Cyprus	0·4	17·2	2·7	9·1		27
	Italy	84·5	98·1				
	Switzerland	0·9	9·2				
	San Marino	0·03	98·0				
French	France	75·1	85·8	9·6	12·9		24
	Canada	10·5	30·1				
	Belgium	7·2	41·3				
	Switzerland	2·0	18·3				
	Monaco	0·03	56·0				
Germany	West Germany	64·3	98·7	24·9	5·9	99·1	28
	Switzerland	4·4	69·3				
	Liechtenstein	0·03	95·0				
Irish	Ireland	39·5	97·7	31·5	29·0	2·4	6
Multinational states:							
English	Great Britain	93·3	81·5	0·1	2·8	1·4	26
Spanish	Spain	95·5	72·8	2·0			15
	Andorra	0·01	61·0				
Flemish	Belgium	93·6	52·7	6·4			3

Table 2.8 Minority Ethnic Groups in the Western State System

Name of ethnic group	State of residence	Percentage ethnic group membership in major state of residence	Percentage state population	Percentage ethnic group membership in neighboring states	Percentage population in neighboring states	Number of states dispersed over	Size of ethnic group membership as of the early 1960s
Andorrans	Andorra	100·0	30·0			1	8,700
Monégasques	Monaco	100·0	18·0			1	4,410
Maoris	New Zealand	100·0	6·9			1	168,000
Frisians	Netherlands	100·0	3·4			1	400,000
Alsatians/ Lotharingians	France	100·0	2·7			1	1,250,000
Bretons	France	100·0	2·4			1	1,000,000
Welsh	Great Britain	99·4	1·9			2	1,000,000
Catalans	Spain	93·5	3·7	0·4		5	5,350,000
Scots	Great Britain	92·4	9·6	0·2	0·4	5	5,520,000
Black Americans	United States	90·7	10·5	9·3	90·0	13	21,410,000
Galicians	Spain	82·9	8·2			7	3,015,000
Basques	Spain	77·3	2·3	14·4	0·3	7	905,000
Kurds	Turkey	47·5	10·5	47·5	17·9	6	6,315,000
Jews	United States	44·3	3·0	2·0	1·4	40	12,414,000
Puerto Ricans	United States	25·2	0·4	74·8	98·9	2	3,180,000
Rhaetoromanians	Italy	87·5	0·7	12·5		2	400,000
	Switzerland	12·5	0·9				
Circassians	Turkey	66·5	0·4	33·5	1·2	4	158,000
Saami	Norway	60·6	0·6	39·4		3	33,000
	Sweden	30·3	0·1				
	Finland	9·1	0·1				
Corsicans	France	100·0	0·6			1	270,000
Gaels	Great Britain	100·0	0·2			1	90,000
Athabaskans	Canada	100·0	0·5			1	85,000
Algonquians	Canada	100·0	0·4			1	75,000
Aborigines	Australia	100·0	0·4			1	40,000
Karapadakh	Turkey	100·0	0·1			1	40,000
Laz	Turkey	100·0	0·1			1	30,000
Cook Islanders	New Zealand	100·0	0·2			1	4,000
Samoans	New Zealand	100·0	0·2			1	4,000

A Comparative Regional Perspective

As might be expected, the European and North and Latin American regions have the highest proportion of homogeneous nation-states. In Europe, only one of the thirty-four states, Yugoslavia, has pronounced multinational attributes (cluster two), while twelve are homogeneous nation-states (cluster one). Eight of the thirty-four states in North and Latin America have a significant degree of national pluralism, and four of those are in the Caribbean, which might be considered a special international subsystem. (The non-Caribbean cases are Bolivia, Canada, Ecuador, and Peru.) Thirteen of the thirty-four American states are homogeneous (cluster one).

By contrast, only two of the twenty-five Asian states, two of the forty-one African ones, and none of the twenty in the Middle East, are "cluster one" nation-states. A majority of the African states, twenty-three of forty-one, falls into the fragmented second cluster. In Asia two states, India and Malaysia, do so; in the Middle East only the United Arab Emirates.

Nation-Groups in the Western State System

We will conclude with an overview of nation-group attributes in the advanced industrialized societies of the West that form the focus of this volume. We take this group to consist of the member states of the OECD, except Japan, and the European "ministates" of Cyprus, Malta, Andorra, Monaco, San Marino, and Liechtenstein.

While of the twenty-nine states in this group only Belgium and Canada can be counted as having high levels of national pluralism, there are in all thirty-two ethnic minorities, twenty-seven of which have no "homeland," that is, no state in which they are dominant. The other five, although minorities locally (for example, the Turks in Cyprus), belong to the category that we have called "state-nation-groups." Details are given in Tables 2.7 and 2.8.

Conclusion

The preceding description and analysis should be viewed as a first step toward explanation of the persistence of national diversity and ethnicity in a modernizing world. The framework for inquiry set forth explicit assumptions and identified the methodological problems. We proposed that systematic comparative analysis of representative cases might be the most practical path for future research. Finally, we developed new classification schemes for ethnic groups and for nation-groups. It remains as a final point to repeat the key questions that should constitute the future research agenda. They are:

(1) How do ethnic groups become nation-groups?
(2) What political forms does the mobilization of ethnic groups into nation-groups take?
(3) How do multination states accommodate their political systems to persistent nation-groups?
(4) How are political integrative/cooperative relations manifested among states with multistate nation-groups?
(5) How are political disintegrative/conflictual relations manifested among states with multistate, nation-group attributes?

Notes: Chapter 2

1 For the definition of this term, see p. 28.
2 This argument is central to Enloe, 1973, and to Young, 1976. Nelson and Wolpe, 1970, reach a similar conclusion in the context of a communal conflict study, and Ross, 1977, forcefully locates this finding in a broader theoretical framework.
3 "The stultifying aura of conceptual ambiguity that surrounds the terms 'national,' 'nationality,' and 'nationalism' has been extensively discussed and thoroughly deplored in almost every work that has been concerned to attack the relationship between communal and political loyalties": Geertz, 1963, p. 197; cf. Tilly 1975, p. 6, and the discussion by Tiryakian and Nevitte, in this volume.
4 We are guided here by Tilly's, 1975, p. 70, definition of the modern state.
5 This is a poor translation of the German concept *Staatsvolk*, which connotes that a state's population is dominated by one particular nation-group.
6 The major data source for the two taxonomies is Taylor and Hudson, 1971. That source in turn drew extensively upon the *Atlas Narodov Mira* for data on ethnic attributes. The *Handbook* compilers augmented the ethnic attribute data from the *Worldmark Encyclopedia of Nations*: see Sachs, 1967. These sources were the basis of the data reconstruction for 131 states. We augmented further for the two Koreas, the new united Vietnam, and Bangladesh, with data from the *Worldmark Encyclopedia*, using the mid-1960s edition rather than the later one, Sachs, 1976, to get population statistics comparable to the *Handbook* data. We subsequently updated for an additional thirty-seven states and fifteen dependent territories, using the following sources: *Worldmark Encyclopedia of Nations*, 5th ed.; *Current National Statistical Compendium*, 1979; *The International Population Census Bibliography: Revision and Update, 1945–1977*, 1980; *The World Factbook*, 1981; *Political Handbook of the World, 1981*; and *The State of the World Atlas*: see Kidron and Segal, 1981.

  Data for the newest thirty-seven states reflect more recent population statistics than those for the original 131 states in the *World Handbook II*, and a certain degree of distortion will occur with the integration of data collected twelve years apart. The new data, however, cover states with relatively small populations, most of them under 1 million. Furthermore, the basic indicators used to classify states are based on proportional distributions, and differential population growth rates should result in only slight errors in the percentage distributions. This exploratory version of a new data set will need periodic updating and refinement. We have worked on the assumption that major changes in the proportional distribution of ethnic groups' populations will occur, by and large, over a long period of time. However, we want to stress the limited accuracy of the data and to take full responsibility for any of the inconsistencies between the data and the listings in the original sources cited above.

7 The seven sovereign states excluded are Vatican City and the new states of Comoros, Djibouti, Equatorial Guinea, the Maldives, São Tomé and Principe, and the Seychelles, for which we have not yet been able to obtain relevant data. The only dependent territories included are those with relatively large populations and special political status, namely Puerto Rico, Namibia, and Hong Kong. The excluded dependent territories are Antigua, Bermuda, the British Virgin Islands, the Cayman Islands, the Falkland Islands, French Guyana, Gibraltar, Greenland, Guadeloupe, Martinique, Réunion, and St. Christopher-Nevis-Anguilla. All are under British or French control except Greenland, which of course is Danish. The combined population of the excluded states and territories is 2,665,000.

8 For the advice and assistance I have received in constructing these data sets, I want to express my gratitude to Professor Charles McClelland and to my students: Paula Hurdle, Rong Yoang, Robert Boydston, Lisa Boswell, Joel Farbstein, Robert Nora, and Shobana Kokatay.

9 For a most interesting comparative analysis of approaches to accommodation among multiple nation-groups in Canada and Malaysia, see Nora, 1980.

References: Chapter 2

Banks, Arthur S., and Overstreet, William (1981), *Political Handbook of the World* (New York: McGraw-Hill).

Bell, Wendel, and Freeman, Walter (eds.) (1974), *Ethnicity and Nation-Building: Comparative, International, and Historical Perspectives* (Beverly Hills, Calif.: Sage).

Bertelsen, Judy S. (ed.) (1977), *Nonstate Nations in International Politics* (New York: Praeger).

Enloe, Cynthia (1973), *Ethnic Conflict and Political Development* (Boston, Mass.: Little, Brown).

Geertz, Clifford (1963), "The integrative revolution: primordial sentiments and civil politics in the new states," in C. Geertz (ed.), *Old Societies and New States: The Quest for Modernity in Asia and Africa* (New York: The Free Press), pp. 104–50.

Glazer, Nathan, and Moynihan, Daniel Patrick (eds.) (1975), *Ethnicity: Theory and Experience* (Cambridge, Mass.: Harvard University Press).

Goyer, Doreen S. (ed.) (1980), *International Population Census Bibliography: Revised and Updated, 1954–1977* (New York: Academic Press).

Heisler, Martin O. (ed.) (1977), "Ethnic conflict in the world today" special issue of *Annals of the American Academy of Political and Social Science*, vol. 433 (September), pp. 32–46.

Kidron, Michael, and Segal, Ronald (1981), *The State of the World Atlas* (New York: Simon & Schuster).

Melson, Robert, and Wolpe, Howard (1970), "Modernization and the politics of communalism: a theoretical perspective," *American Political Science Review*, vol. 64, no. 4, pp. 1112–30.

Nora, Robert (1980), "The effects and reflections of ethnicity in the political, economic, and social spheres of Canadian and Malaysian life," unpublished paper, School of International Relations, University of Southern California (January).

Rejai, Mostafa, and Enloe, Cynthia (1969), "Nation-states and state-nations," *International Studies Quarterly*, vol. 13, no. 22, pp. 140–52.

Ross, Jeffrey A. (1977), "Minorities no more: a framework for the comparative analysis of the mobilization of ethnic identity," unpublished paper presented at the ISA Convention of the International Studies Association, St. Louis, Missouri, 19 March.

Sachs, Moshe V. (ed.) (1967), *Worldmark Encyclopedia of Nations* (New York: Worldmark Press).

Sachs, Moshe V. (ed.) (1976), *Worldmark Encyclopedia of Nations*, 5th ed. (New York: Worldmark Press).

Said, Abdul, and Simons, Ruiz R. (eds.) (1976), *Ethnicity in an Institutional Context* (Brunswick, N.J.: Transaction Books).

Schermerhorn, R. A. (1970), *Ethnic Relations: A Framework for Theoretical Analysis* (New York: Random House).

Seton-Watson, Hugh (1977), *Nations and States* (Boulder, Colo.: Westview Press).

Taylor, L., and Hudson, Michael C. (1971), *World Handbook of Political and Social Indicators II* (Ann Arbor, Mich.: Inter-University Consortium for Political Research).

Tilly, Charles (ed.) (1975), *The Formation of National States in Western Europe* (Princeton, N.J.: Princeton University Press).

USSR Academy of Sciences (1964), *The Atlas Narodov Mira* (Moscow: Department of Geodesy and Cartography of the State Geological Committee of the USSR Academy of Sciences).

Young, Crawford (1976), *The Politics of Cultural Pluralism* (Madison, Wis.: University of Wisconsin Press).

3
Nationalism and Modernity

EDWARD A. TIRYAKIAN
AND NEIL NEVITTE

Introduction

The history of nationalism is a confusing one, and when this is
added to the conceptual morass surrounding "modernization,"
the difficulty of relating the two concerns is compounded.
Nationalism is rarely a central issue in analyses of modernity
and vice versa. Cases can be cited to support the contention that
nationalism is a consequence of modernity, but it can also be
argued that nationalism is an antecedent prerequisite of modernity. Simply to transpose these perspectives suggests a contradiction, but the contradiction is superficial rather than real; it
is at least partly due to the fact that nationalism itself tends to
be regarded as an undifferentiated phenomenon. A necesary
prerequisite to an analysis of the relationship between
nationalism and modernity, in our view, is a reconceptualization of nationalism which can provide a more adequate basis
for comparative analysis.

Contemporary views of nationalism (Smith, 1979, 1981;
Symmons-Symonolewicz, 1968, 1970) quite properly have
moved away from the limiting political and historical orientations which either tie nationalism to a particular part of the
ideological spectrum or which focus on its supposed patho-
logical causes and consequences (Kohn, 1956, p. 322; Hayes,
1926, p. 258). Nevertheless, the widespread tendency to treat
the terms "nation," "state," and "society" interchangeably
reflects a serious conceptual problem which still plagues the
conventional literature. For example, political scientists who
nominate the nation as a sphere of concern offer instead an
analysis of the state or interstate behavior (LaPalombara, 1974,
p. 38; Morgenthau, 1958, p. 38). The resultant state-centric bias

is reflected in contemporary studies of the transnational activities of multinational enterprises and the threat posed to state sovereignty (Keohane and Nye, 1971; Vernon, 1977). In short, while the term nation continues to have wide currency, it is left unanalyzed or it is taken for granted as coextensive with the state, as in nation-state.

In fact there are analytical as well as empirical reasons for upholding the distinction between nation and state or, as one author puts it, for maintaining nation and state as separate units of analysis (cf. Nielsson, in this volume). As a unit of analysis, the state unambiguously stands as a juridical concept relating a governing body to a social group within a defined territory (Plano and Olton, 1969, p. 30; Sondermann *et al.*, 1970, p. 12). In contrast, the substance and reach of nation, as a unit of analysis, is elusive. Ernest Renan, in a seminal essay published in 1882, pointed out that "nation" is more than a set of objective characteristics such as geography, race, language, and so on (Renan, 1970). According to Renan, it is the will of individuals acting in concert that is essential to the definition of nation: a nation is "a daily plebiscite, a living soul, a spiritual principle" (ibid., p. 80). In modern terms we might say that nation is a socially constructed and validated reality. Most contemporary scholars, either implicitly or explicitly, accept the significance of the subjective dimension emphasized by Renan (Kohn, 1961, p. 15; Hayes, 1960, p. 10; Plamenatz, 1973, p. 24; Rustow, 1968). The fundamentally different properties of nation and state make the terms analytically discrete and empirically, as Walker Connor (1972, pp. 319–21) points out, the sociological boundaries of the nation are rarely congruent with the political–legal boundaries of the state. Indeed, it has been convincingly demonstrated that a state which consists of a single national identity, as a strict interpretation of nation-state implies, is the exception rather than the rule (see Nielsson, in this volume).

Although there are serious difficulties in attempting to specify further the underlying subjective dimension of nation, difficulties comparable to the anthropological specification of "culture" and the sociological specification of "solidarity," it is precisely because nation is the reference point of nationalism that the first part of this chapter will try to clarify the character and boundaries of nation. Drawing from the classic sociological literature, we will argue that the concept nation has important voluntaristic and dynamic attributes. Further, we will argue that these attributes, frequently ignored in contemporary social science, provide essential grounding for a definition of nationalism which has comparative utility.

The second part of the chapter, using the reconceptualization of nationalism derived in the first part, aims at blocking-out significant dimensions of the dynamic relationship between nationalism and modernity.

In relating nationalism to the question of modernity, a paramount image of the modernization process—common to liberals, traditional Marxists, and their hybrid offsprings—is to view the central parameters of this process in terms of economic forces and their morphological/ecological correlates and derivatives (industrialization, urbanization and so on). Our perspective, on the other hand, rejoins Zolberg's (1981) excellent critique of Wallerstein's *The Modern World System* (1974), which he faults for glossing over the political features of modernization, or what we might call the political structuration of modernity. If we understand by modernity a set of innovative adaptations to the social, cultural, and physical environments which social actors adopt voluntarily (Tiryakian, 1982, 1984), political innovations (including political identities as well as structures) need to be viewed in a new light as integral to the process of modernization, rather than as peripheral. Nationalism, in its various forms, may be taken as much as an active as well as a reactive element that is at the core of succeeding phases of modernization, as Nairn (1977), partly informed by his readings of Antonio Gramsci, sensed in his brilliant analysis of the nationalisms of Britain.

The present chapter will not endeavor to propose a general theory of nationalism, one that should be able to interrelate nationalism, national development, and societal development; however, we will seek to advance important features of the conceptual framework necessary for a rigorous theory essential to comparative analysis of modernity. A central feature of this conceptualization is a typology which focusses on the external and internal relations of nation and state. The differentiation of the typology is oriented to four major phases of nationalism. The remainder of the chapter applies the typology to two concrete cases, that of France and that of Quebec–Canada.

"Nation" as a Sociological Category

The conceptual "underdevelopment" of nation and phenomena pertaining to it, such as nationalism, is ironical if we consider important sociological attention paid to the subject matter before World War II (for example, Wirth, 1936), and especially around the period of World War I and its aftermath. This was a period when various empires (the Ottoman, the Habsburg, and the tsarist) became fragmented and torn asunder, leading to the problematics of national identity and consequently of the meaning of nationhood. Two major figures who grappled with these problems, Marcel Mauss and Max Weber, are better known for other writings, yet their contributions in this context are still analytically superior to contemporary sociological writings on nationalism and hence merit an extensive discussion. Of particular interest is that their respective analyses converge toward what may be viewed as a dynamic, voluntaristic sociological perspective on the nation.

Mauss's discussion is by far the most extensive treatment of "nation" and "national development" by a sociologist.[1] Mauss begins with a historical overview of the development of nation and nationalism, from the early notion of subjects of a prince living abroad forming a "nation" to the nineteenth-century emphasis of hatred and revolt of what is alien as the hallmark of nationalism. Mauss sees this as a reflection of German jurists identifying nation with state, in spite of the distinction between *Staat* and *Gesellschaft*; this leads to a weak idea of "nation" and to nationalism being "the expression of two reactions: one against what is alien, the other against progress which allegedly undermines national tradition" (Mauss, 1969, p. 577).

Mauss then proposes a fourfold classification of political forms of social life to arrive at societies which may merit being called nations. Mauss's typology is essentially evolutionary, from a kin-based polity to ones marked by a central power of imperium and on to what he sees ultimately as having all the necessary characteristics of nationhood: "a society which is physically and morally integrated, with a stable, permanent, central power, with set boundaries, with its inhabitants relatively morally, mentally and culturally united and consciously committed to a State and its laws" (ibid., p. 584). Mauss observes that only a handful of societies can match his definition; colonies are not nations, and neither are many Latin American countries and East European ones. In fact Western Europe is the major area of nations which have evolved from Germanic and Roman elements (ibid., p. 586).

Mauss views nations *dynamically*: they come into being, continue, and disappear in the world historical process. Nations are also characterized by various levels of *integration*. One level is a geopolitical integration marked by the political autonomy of the nation throughout its frontier and the disappearance of segmentation on the basis of clans, cities, tribes, feudal domains. "In the most achieved of nations," Mauss comments, "the integration between nation and citizen is such that there no longer exist any intermediaries" (ibid., p. 588). Economic integration is equally an important aspect of implementation of the idea of nationhood.[2]

The process of nation-building has more than political (military, administrative, legal) and economic dimensions, however. It has an ideological element, in the sense of a general will (or what might be rephrased a collective aspiration) to create and transmit national unity; and in a related manner it has a major cultural dimension. A nation worthy of the name, observes Mauss, has and believes in *its* civilization (which Mauss understands esthetically, morally, and materially), *its* language, *its* mental life, *its* morality, *its* sense of collective purpose, *its* form of progress. Mauss notes that the process of nation-building entails an important sociological phenomenon of individuation. At the macrolevel the growth of nations in recent times has not led to a uniformity of civilization, but to a greater individuation of nations and nationalities, while at the microlevel a modern nation renders more homogeneous its citizenry (ibid., p. 593).

Instrumental to national individuation or differentiation are various means by which a national group establishes its boundaries. It may do so by the "nationalization of thought and arts," which takes different forms, ranging from copyright laws to classified industrial and scientific secrets. It also establishes boundaries by using ascriptive but socially constructed categories. Two in particular noted by Mauss are race and language; Mauss considers the latter the more important. Since the nineteenth century language policy has emerged as a conscious national activity, whether it is to maintain bilingualism in the case of Basques, Flemish, and so on, or to revive long-forgotten languages (for instance, Gaelic), or to devise a written language where none previously existed. Mauss observes acutely: "If nationalities thus create languages, it is that in modern times, language creates if not the nation, at least the nationality" (ibid., p. 598).

Mauss concludes the essay by viewing a "complete nation" as being a society sufficiently integrated, having to some extent a central democratic power, having a notion of national sovereignty, and having a national character which demarcates it from other such collectivities in terms of race, civilization, language, and a normative system (ibid., p. 604). Some elements may be lacking (for example, linguistic unity in Belgium and Switzerland, political democracy elsewhere), but that is why "complete nations" are more the exception than the rule.

In another fragment written at about the same time ("Nation and Internationalism") Mauss differentiated "society" and "nation." All nations constitute societies, but not all societies are nations. A society may be regulated by an extrinsic super-imposed power (as in the case of a colonial society, or one violently annexed), or it may be regulated by an unstable democratic power. Neither of these fits the criteria of "nation" which Mauss entertains, namely, a stable, permanent central power with a legislative and administrative system, *and* where the notion of rights and duties of citizenship and the rights and duties of the homeland are complementary (ibid., p. 626). Mauss took "complete nations" (in the sense of fulfilling the criteria earlier noted) to be the most advanced forms of social life (ibid., p. 627): "They are the most elevated or superior of societies economically, juridically, morally, and politically, and assure better than preceding forms the rights, life, and happiness of its members."

Still, Mauss's underlying evolutionary and liberal perspective made him view even the most advanced "nations" as capable of further progress in public life, and beyond that, which is not germane for our analysis. Mauss could look into the future and see that the process of national unification might well be extended into an international integration of existing nations in more inclusive economic and moral interdependence (ibid., pp. 626–39).

Obviously much of Mauss's analysis of "nation" appears an important elaboration on Renan, and Mauss does not always maintain the distinction between "nation" and "nation-state," yet his discussion provides a sociological grounding which is lacking in the contemporary literature.

A complementary discussion of "nation" is found in fragmentary form in Max Weber's writings, written at about the same time and independently of Mauss (Weber, 1978, pp. 385–98, 921–6). Like Renan and Mauss, Weber stresses the intersubjective aspect of nationhood; at the same time his discussion emphasizes the political or power aspect of nation: nation implies a political community.

Weber points out that objective characteristics of community do not identify a nation, for the concept "belongs in the sphere of values" (ibid., p. 922), and here Weber means the cultural values of the masses. Political membership in a state does not constitute a nation, nor does membership in a linguistic community define nation. Weber provides illustrations of "national solidarity" among those speaking the same language but there are also contrary examples. National solidarity (his expression) may be connected with differing social structure and mores, "hence with 'ethnic' elements" (ibid., p. 923), or it may be linked "to memories of a common political destiny with other nations" (ibid.). He points out that common descent is not always essential to nationalist consciousness, since "radical 'nationalists' are often of foreign descent" (ibid.). Still, common descent and an imagined common phenotype are frequently ingredients of nationality, and in this respect the sentiment of national solidarity draws close to that of ethnic communities, though Weber quickly adds that "the sentiment of ethnic solidarity does not by itself make a 'nation' " (ibid.).

Weber also noted that the sentiment of nationhood is differentially distributed in the social structure. So, for example, Marxist spokesmen of the proletariat profess indifference and disinvolvement from adherence to a single nation, and within a group formally or objectively recognized as a nation there is a continuum of varied and changeable attitudes toward the idea of "nation" (ibid., p. 924). In brief, Weber points to the multiple meanings of "nationhood" and suggests in passing a conceptual program worth quoting at length:

> In any case, the differences in national sentiment are both significant and fluid and, as is the case in all other fields, fundamentally different answers are given to the question: What conclusions are a group of people willing to draw from the "national sentiment" found among them? No matter how emphatic and subjectively sincere a pathos may be formed among them, what sort of specific actions are they ready to develop? In the face of this value concept of the "idea of the nation," which empirically is entirely ambiguous, a sociological typology would have to analyze all the individual kinds of sentiments of group membership and solidarity in their generic conditions and in their consequences for the social action of the participants. (ibid., p. 925).

Although we do not claim to carry out this very pregnant project of Weber's, the typology of nationalism found later in this chapter will hopefully be seen as a step in a rediscovery of the Weberian patrimony.

Weber also makes the acute observation that the idea of nation is frequently found in intimate association with a cultural myth of a "providential mission," and that such a mission is somehow to be realized through "the peculiarity of the group set off as a nation" (ibid.). This important myth or legend of mission relates the nation in question to cultural values, in the sense that its cultural values are superior, distinctive gifts to mankind; it allows that the welfare of the group which nurtures these values, its survival and enhancement, is necessary for the survival of the precious "culture goods" that are part of the providential mission. Hence the propagation of the "national idea" (ibid., p. 926) is an important cultural dimension of nationalism.[3] Significantly, Weber also grounds his perspective on nation with a discussion of political power and action. A nation essentially strives for achieving or redeeming political autonomy; a nation is fundamentally a political community, and thus the concept of nation is intrinsically linked to that of political power:

> Hence, the concept seems to refer—if it refers at all to a uniform phenomenon—to a specific kind of pathos which is linked to the idea of a powerful political community of people who share a common language, or religion, or common customs, or political memories; such a state may already exist, or it may be desired. The more power is emphasized, the closer appears to be the link between nation and state. (ibid., p. 398)

Weber's emphasis on the linkage of nation to the realm of culture values is apposite—the more so since all nationalist movements entail to some degree claims on behalf of the "national culture"—but we need here to make clear what we understand by "culture." Singer (1968) provides a useful survey of the history and various perspectives associated with this widely used and rather ambiguous concept. Noting an important convergence between the pattern theory and the structural–functional theory of culture, Singer points to recent trends taking culture in the sense of abstract structures underlying observed social relations. These structures "are the systems of meanings, ideologies, conventionalized understandings, and cognitive and unconscious structures, which may be recognized in a given society with varying degrees of consciousness and explicit verbal formulation" (ibid., p. 54).

An understated presupposition of social anthropology and sociology is that for any given complex, organized society, there is an overall coherent set of structures which characterize a culture. This may not preclude the absence of competing and alternative structures—or "subcultures"—but each empirical society has *a* culture, with correspondence and congruence between the set of social structures and institutions on the one hand, and the set of cultural structures on the other.

To carry further the analytical discussion, it is fruitful to examine parts of the conceptual framework advanced by Talcott Parsons, designated as the *theory of action*. The key concept of action is derived from Max Weber, designating that human action has a subjective and voluntary component to it which distinguishes it from mere overt behavioral responses (Bourricaud, 1981).

Amplifying earlier remarks, Parsons proposed that culture be seen analytically as a set of symbolic meaning systems; in so far as this is of relevance to social science analysis culture should be treated as a system of action. He argued:

> A "cultural system" in this sense would then be a system of action (a subsystem, analytically defined as a total system of action) organized about the exigencies of creating and maintaining symbol-meaning systems. (Parsons, 1959, p. 249)

This is crucial because tying culture to action systems not only renders the concept dynamic (that is, treats culture as expressive symbolic structures of social interaction), but also makes it possible to see the nexus of culture and nationalism. It is the nation which, for its survival or enhancement, seeks to create and maintain symbol-meaning systems. The creation and maintenance of culture, its production and reproduction, are vital activities of the nation and of the claims made on its behalf.

Nation as "Societal Community"

From the previous discussion it is a fundamental aspect of the analytical perspective put forth in this chapter that "nation" be recognized as a sociological concept. A nation is a social phenomenon of collective life, marked by a level of inter-subjective consciousness reducible neither to "objective conditions" such as territory, kinship, class (economically understood), and language, nor to other levels of intersubjective consciousness such as class ("for itself"), generation, and so forth. In this respect we follow the fruitful lead of Renan—whose formulation has knowingly or not been followed by a wide array of persons who have subsequently sought an adequate conceptualization, from Mauss and Weber to Rustow (1968). If "nationhood" has, therefore, a phenomenological status, it is also the case that it is grounded in a set of objective structures, no matter how ambiguous or relatively amorphous might be the boundaries of some of these structures: territory, polity, economy, culture (for example, language), and finally, history.

Treated thus, we are now in a better position to understand why there is justification to the implicit substitutability in ordinary language of "society" for "nation." In ordinary usage "American society" is used in the sense of American nation; Americans are nationals of American society—that is, their sociopolitical membership qua Americans is their belonging-ness, rights, and obligations, and adherence to the American nation. Used in this sense, "society" is really constituted in terms of its being a polity, *a political society*. Following Parsons, a feature which differentiates societies relative to other social systems is the key factor of *self-sufficiency*, by which he means "the capacity of the system, gained through both its internal organization and resources and its access to inputs from its environments, to function *autonomously* in implementing its normative culture, particularly its values but also its norms and collective goals" (Parsons, 1968, p. 461; emphasis added). We would argue that the striving to operationalize this capacity, this seeking to function autonomously, is at the core of the major forms or types of nationalism treated in this chapter as salient for the analysis of modernity.

Parsons offers a further conceptual tool in differentiating "society" and drawing attention to its core structure which he terms "societal community"; his formulation bears noting:

> More specifically, at different levels of evolution, it is called tribe or "the people" or, for classical Greece, *polis*, or for the modern world, *nation*. It is the collective structure in which members are united, or, in some sense, associated. Its most important property is the kind and level of solidarity which characterizes the relations between its members. (ibid.)

It would seem appropriate following this to view the solidarity of all members, a diffuse solidarity of adherence to the same historically constituted and evolved societal community, as *national solidarity*. Such solidarity cannot be taken for granted; it is not in this sense an ascriptive solidarity. It has to be fashioned out of competition with other structural bases of solidarity, some of which may involve adherence to a social system of lesser magnitude than the societal community (for instance, the village, the extended family) or, conversely, to one of *greater* territorial and/or temporal magnitude, that is, to a more global social system (for instance, the universal church, the international working class, and so on).

To summarize, then, "nation" is conceptualized as the core structure of society, as its societal community. Further, we treat it within a dynamic and voluntaristic perspective, in the sense that a nation is a historically evolving reality (each nation has its historicity) and that membership in the national collectivity involves an element of subjective choice and commitment. Different actors inhabiting the same territory may evolve different interpretations of what is the identity of their societal community, from which they will have different commitments of political loyalty. From this, different forms of claims on behalf of the nation will ensue, either at the same historical period or in succeeding ones. A further implication of the perspective here entertained is that the boundaries of nation-hood are not frozen—they can expand and contract as criteria of inclusion may change over time (see also Alexander, 1980).

Reconceptualizing Nationalism

The preceding review points to the need of rethinking an adequate conceptualization of the social phenomenon of nationalism. We shall seek to do so in the remainder of this chapter by, first, providing an alternative working definition of nationalism; secondly, by outlining a typology that links nationalism with modernity; and lastly, by illustrating the relevance of the typology to two empirical cases.

Given the general comparative emphasis of this volume as a whole, we propose that nationalism be analytically understood as *the making of claims in the name, or on behalf, of the nation*. This formulation has several advantages. First, by leaving out objective indicators the definition lays emphasis on intersubjective identification with the nation as a requisite of nationalism. It is consonant with the voluntaristic and dynamic character of nation contained in the approach explicated earlier, which allows for the fact that people can and do take on different national identities.

Secondly, national*ism* extends the concept of nation in an important way. The suffix "-ism" points to the active political dimension of the phenomenon. It is not sufficient to regard nationalism as merely an attitudinal "state of mind" or nominal loyalty to the nation. Passive or latent identification with the nation does not necessarily give rise to the making of claims. As Weber noted, nationalism is tied to the issue of political power and therefore, like political power, it is a *relational* concept. By focussing on the act of making national claims (for example, claims which aim to protect or extend the self-sufficiency of the national culture), we intend to stress explicitly the political dimension.

Thirdly, the definition does not pose any limits with respect to the unit of analysis. Individuals as well as groups may make nationalist claims; intellectuals and other cultural elites may make national claims with or without group support. In addition, individuals or groups may be nationalists under one set of circumstances but not another, at different times, or on one issue but not another. The theoretical challenge, of course, is to generalize about the times, the circumstances, and the issues.

Similarly, we make no assumption that the national claims are necessarily advanced through formal institutions and organizations. While there may be a *prima facie* case for historically linking nationalism with the presence of nationalist political parties, the struggle to augment the autonomous capacity of the nation has not been an activity unique to nationalist parties; it may be and has been served as well by voluntary associations such as religious or linguistic ones. Actually the rise of nationalist political parties may even in part be seen as a result of the failure of individuals or groups to achieve their nationalist goals by other means.

The definition advanced here, then, allows for a considerable measure of flexibility. It does not specify that the avenues for making national claims have to be formalized, nor limited to a certain political expression, for example, mass-based participatory liberal democratic parties. Elites prior to or without representative roles can be designated "nationalist," as can open competitive political parties or cultural organizations. In the case of Eastern Europe following World War II, for example, the crucial fact was not so much that East Europeans objectively held rights to make national claims, but rather that they thought they had such rights. National claims were, and are, being made, notwithstanding the fact that the formal mechanisms for claim-making are stifled. In brief, the definition we advance is intended as a general one for comparative analysis and is not restricted or limited to a specific historical panorama.

It will also be noted that the definition avoids the identification of nation with state, since it is the former which is the proper referent of nationalism, though this distinction is frequently obliterated by others. Thus definitions of nationalism such as that of Silvert (1963, p. 19), who treats it as "the acceptance of the state as the impersonal arbiter of human affairs," or that of Kohn (1961, p. 9), focussing on the "nation-state," are equivocal. In making this point we are not saying that nations and states have no overlap, but rather that they are not identical. A national culture, for example, will probably involve a sense of homeland or some territorial anchor which is not necessarily congruent with the state. It may either be enveloped by a state or straddle state boundaries, as is the case with Basque national culture, and there is no guarantee that a national cultural group will enjoy the effective support and protection of the state which may reflect the hegemony of a different group.

Indeed, in multinational states the national culture of the dominant ethnic group may project its culture, for benign or invidious reasons, as the culture of the whole state, thereby relegating other cultures and their groups to dependent and inferior status. This identification may appear spontaneous, albeit it reflects a historical process of one national culture emerging as the "center" and others relegated to the "periphery." For example, some years ago T. S. Eliot wrote about British national culture as including "Derby Day, the Henley regatta, Cowes, the twelfth of August, a cup final, the dog races, the pin table, Wensleydale cheese, etc." (Eliot, 1949, p, 30), unwittingly extrapolating the culture of England to that of the whole of Britain, as if there were no authentic and historically evolving national cultures of Scotland and Wales. Similar identifications of the part for the whole can be shown for other instances (Canada, France, Spain, and so on). The point of differentiating nation from state, and national culture from the official or semiofficial culture of the state, is not to ignore the significance of these ecological social factors but, on the contrary, to increase our awareness of the impact of such factors on the formation of nationalism.

Viewing nationalism as a claim-making activity seeking greater national autonomy from other social environmental impingements is not a perspective restricted only to cases where nations are physically encapsulated by states; it also applies to cases where nations may be constrained by distant imperial states. Thus nationalism as formulated here applies to the demands of African and Asian colonies within the historical context of British, French, and other European imperial systems; to Arab nationalism within the Ottoman Empire; and to Estonian, Polish or Ukrainian nationalism within the tsarist and Soviet political framework. At the same time the capacity of a state to be felt as intruding on the autonomy of a societal community is not limited to the circumstances of formal political domination, since the life situation of a people can be undermined or perceived as being undermined by the economic, political, and cultural tentacles of an "informal" empire. Much of French nationalism under the leadership of Charles de Gaulle drew its stimulus as restoring French autonomy in economic, cultural, and foreign affairs from American intrusion, and similar sentiments are manifest in much of Canadian nationalism under the leadership of Pierre Trudeau.

Nationalism and Modernity: A Typology

The process of modernization necessarily involves a complex set of societal transformations, at the level of ecology (for instance, urbanization) of social structures (for instance, industrialization, bureaucratization, institutional differentiation), and of social-psychological or intersubjective bases of identity, cognitive orientation, and the like. Although much of the literature on modernization takes the economic aspects of social change (for example, class formation, technological development, industrialization) to be the dramatic focus of modernization, we prefer to view the process as a dynamic "total social phenomenon," in the expression of Mauss. This permits us to view nationalism as a fundamental feature of modernization, namely, as not only a political *response* on behalf of the nation made by a group of actors, but also as a political instrument of modernization, in the sense of claim-making on behalf of the nation which seeks to advance modernity through collective action.

The typology that we propose as an heuristic categorization of the interrelationship of nationalism and modernity is one that is based on a double set of relationships: *externally*, on the relation of a given nation-state, having a recognized center of political and economic power, to other nation-states or other external polities; *internally*, on the relation of populations inhabiting recognized territorial ("regions," "provinces," and so on) and cultural demarcations (language, customs, bases of social organization) to the center of the nation-state.

Since the formation of nation-states and their interrelations have been central in discussions of the modernization process, it may be convenient to treat the nationalism of nation-states as an initial type, specified as follows:

Type 1   Claims Made by Elites on Behalf of the Nation-State against either External or Internal Collectivities Whose Territory and Culture Differ from those of the "Nation" Taken as the Societal Community of the Nation-State

The claims may be of a political or economic nature or a combination. Claims may be made that the physical and social space of the societal community (of the nation-state) has to be expanded beyond historical frontiers or that historical frontiers and territories must be "restored." Whatever their nature, the realization of the claims is oriented to increasing the autonomy and sphere of action of the national center in relation to either other nation-states (or external collectivities) or to internal political communities.

It might be remarked that this type of nationalism, historically speaking, is manifest not only as an activity of an established nation-state, but also has been instrumental in the establishment and consolidation of modern nation-states. In the last century, and substantially part of this one, dominant themes of modernity have been those of "progress" and "freedom." These have been effectively used by the first type of nationalism in legitimating its claim-making on behalf of the nation-state. For instance, the justification for the aggrandizement of the nation-state and its spheres of direct influence has frequently been that peripheral peoples (peripheral to the societal community of the nation-state, either within or without its borders) are incompetent and unable to utilize their natural resources, which have to be made more productive and efficient "in the name of freedom." Alternatively, "progress" demands doing away with traditional boundaries, markets, communal political associations, and so on.

However framed, the consequence of this type of nationalism, if the claim-making is successful, is the enhancement or centralization of the powers of the elites acting on behalf of the nation-state. The activity is instrumental in generating or regenerating regime support (particularly when success is in relation to external polities) not only among strata that have provided the electoral base of support for the regime, but also by bringing into the net of "national solidarity" other economic and ethnic strata (who may or may not be territorially differentiated from those providing the core support of the regime).

In terms of the perceived mainstream of the modernization process it is this type of nationalism which has been a dominant force in the aggregation of various parts constituting today's nation-states. To reiterate, this has been accomplished by a double process of making claims against external polities and by making claims against internal autonomous or distinct polities so as to merge them into the larger political unit of the nation-state.[4]

We now turn to responses from the "periphery" to the nationalism of the nation-state. As the core center of the nation-state develops and expands (economically, politically, culturally) there are three important responses that elites of the societal community constituting a peripheral area can undertake (each having historical referents).

Type 2   Nationalism of the Periphery: Identification with the Nation-State

In this instance elites of the periphery, however culturally, territorially, and "ethnically" differentiated from those of the center, find it advantageous to view the interest of the nation as best served by being linked with the nation-state. The nation of origin (or the people of the periphery, or the region) is seen as making contributions in the development of a broader societal community, that of the nation-state in its entirety. In a given period of modernity, when the nation-state is perceived to be in a dynamic growth phase providing greater economic, cultural, and political vistas than the home base of the "periphery," elites of the latter may actively make claims that their contributions (or their community's contribution) will enhance and be enhanced by identification and aggregation with the central regime and its developing "national institutions."

As described, the phenomenon of peripheral nationalism qua identification with the nation-state is of the same sort of ethnic and class "assimilation" by upwardly mobile individuals who leave behind their strata of origin. But in the present context the referents are elites who see themselves acting on behalf of the welfare of their societal community, which they view as linked with integration in the larger polity and economy. These elites in their political activity will be active as leaders in voluntary associations that cross-cut the nation-state (for instance, political parties, unions, and so on).

Although a current image of this identification is that it is a form of co-optation by the "establishment," peripheral nationalism of this sort is one avenue for a peripheral group to gain entry and access to the resources of modernity made possible by the nation-state's economy and polity of size. Given unequal size and resources of the population, it is a rational choice for some peripheral elites to seek to increase the self-sufficiency of their nation by integrating it with a larger unit. As the folk saying goes, "if you can't beat them, join them."

Type 3 Nationalism of the Periphery: Withdrawal (Retreat) from Modernity.

In the face of an expansive, dynamic nation-state making economic, cultural, and political claims against the periphery, a different kind of response may be made in the form of seeking to protect the beleaguered nation or societal community by accentuating its cultural heritage and distinctiveness from that of the nation-state. The nationalism will lay claim to the superiority of the traditional community's way of life, including its system of economic relationships. In so far as the ideology of this form of nationalism stresses a communitarian value against modernist tendencies to dissolve the traditional bonds of community it will tend to have an anticapitalist orientation and to stress the values of an artisanal, agrarian-based economy.

This type of nationalism is one commonly associated with nineteenth-century reactions to centralization and the incursion of capitalist modes of production into formerly peasant and artisanal economies. It might be obvious to label it as "reactionary" or "antimodern" nationalism. Yet in its historical manifestations this type of nationalism covers a whole gamut of movements, past and present, ranging from the French *Félibrige* of Mistral, to Maurras's Action Française, to the Adfer movement in Wales and the *ujamma* nationalism of Nyerere in Tanzania.

Type 4 Nationalism of the Periphery: Overtaking Modernity

The last type of nationalist orientation is one which also emerges in reaction to the existing nation-state and its dominant culture and institutional structures. However, it defines these as "behind the times," as constituting a hindrance to the full accession to modernity of the societal community. The "center" is viewed as socially stagnant and exploitative of "peripheral" peoples, not as a dynamic agent of modernization. The modernity of the "center" is the modernity of yesterday. What is required is the full autonomy of the nation to develop modern institutions and values consonant with the emergent world of tomorrow. This type of nationalism is one that combines acceptance of the cultural development of the nation (including a renaissance of the national language which may have been eclipsed or dominated by the language of the nation-state) with a strong emphasis on extensive social reforms and economic and technological development geared to giving prime benefit to the nation. A social value that is stressed is the participation of the citizenry, or rather of the *demos*, in decision-making processes, and a complementary value is the accountability of officials and leaders to their constituents. There is a stress that the communality of the nation is in contrast to the bureaucratic and hierarchical structures of the nation-state.

The types of nationalist orientation formulated here obviously do not exhaust all empirical instances of nationalism. None the less, we advance this typology as heuristic for the comparative analysis of nationalist movements where a basic relation is that of conflicting claims between "center" and "periphery" within a given nation-state, and between centers of two nation-states. We have sought to emphasize that different actors originating in the same peripheral area or "region" may entertain different understandings and meanings as to the boundaries, purpose, and optimal strategy for the societal community comprising the "nation." Though not part of our consideration, the differences between actors from the same national group as to what and who constitutes the "nation" and what ought to be its relation to the surrounding nation-state may reflect differences in the class location of persons or differences in generational historical experiences or other ties of attachment and detachment to the institutions and elites of the "center." In brief, we have argued that a multiplicity of nationalisms may be found side-by-side within the same territorially based population sharing in common major objective characteristics.[5]

Illustration of the Typology: France and Quebec–Canada

It might be useful to illustrate the applicability of the typology to two different settings which in the course of the modernization process (and reflecting different historical moments and conceptions of that process) have experienced the types of nationalism just discussed.

France

Claims on Behalf of the Nation-State It matters not if we trace the nationalism of the French nation-state to the Hundred Years War or to more recent historical eras, such as the French Revolution, much of French nationalism has been expressed in either expansionary moves against the outside or in defense postures toward external threats. As instances of the latter might be mentioned the great victory of the citizens' army at Valmy during the French Revolution, the national solidarity generated by German invasion in World War I which cemented an otherwise divided country into a coalition Union Sacrée, and in a more recent period the French nationalism of de Gaulle and the nationalist political movement organized around him. General de Gaulle saw the need of a strong French nation-state to maintain the autonomy of the country from the military threat of the Soviet Union and the economic and cultural threat of the United States, hence his championing not only the *force de frappe*, but also the EEC and a strong renovation of French culture led by his Cultural Minister André Malraux, charged with warding off the danger of "anglicization" of the French language. Moreover, as a riposte to the growing postwar influence of the United States and the global Americanization of culture, de Gaulle encouraged a cultural regrouping of the French-speaking world under the loose-knit concept of "francophonie," whose strongest proponent outside of France has been Leopold Senghor of Senegal.

We need not dwell on another aspect of external claim-making, that associated with French imperialism. It may be said to begin with a great modernizer, Napoleon Bonaparte, who legitimated his political invasions by calling on other European peoples to follow the examples of the French Revolution and liberate themselves from traditional and feudal authority structures. In the second half of the nineteenth century French nationalism—imperialism made similar sorts of claims against "backward territories" deemed to require the tutelage of the modern nation-state in order to bring them out of their torpor. The military officer who bravely fought campaigns of colonial warfare under harsh overseas conditions and who did it to bring peace and the benefits of modern civilization to native races is a key nationalist symbolic figure of the Third Republic—whether Faidherbe, Galieni, or Lyautey. Paul Bert, the scientist turned colonial administrator as Governor of Indo-China, was surely displaying the nationalism of the republican nation-state in the symbolic gesture of tacking up the Principles of 1789 when he arrived in Saigon. An important latent function of the claims made by France overseas during the Third Republic in its dynamic phase was to attempt to mobilize support at home for the republican regime which led a rather precarious existence until the turn of the century.

Claims on behalf of the "center" in its external dealings have been matched by claims against internal peripheral polities. From Richelieu and Louis XIV to the Jacobin revolutionaries such as Danton and Robespierre, there is an essential continuity in a vigorous French nationalism seeking a centralization of power at the expense of regional groupings. Local assemblies and regional *parlements* were dissolved or stripped of their fiscal powers, and administrative units traditionally homogeneous were broken into artificial *départements*, whose heads were not locally elected but rather were appointed from Paris. National standardization was achieved in terms of currency and measurements with a new decimal system. This standardization/rationalization was done on behalf of modernity, with a consequence that the autonomy of municipalities and regions was greatly curtailed. The nationalism of the center reached its zenith in the Third Republic in the implementation of a uniform educational system throughout the country and the development of free, public, and mandatory "education laïque." Related to educational policy, French was the only language taught in the public schools, with all other "regional" languages (Breton, Catalan, Provençal, and so on) denigrated as backward dialects.

Claims on behalf of the Periphery   In the 1970s, in the wake of the May 1968 movement, an upsurge of critiques of the central French government and a clamor for regional autonomy became manifest, with a particularly vocal expression in the writings of Robert Lafont at the University of Montpellier, one of the early pre-Hechter users of the concept of "internal colonialism" (1967). Study groups and autonomist movements of different degrees of crystallization were made on behalf of national groupings such as those of Brittany, Alsace, Corsica, and Occitania (Person, 1973: Stephens, 1976; Beer, 1980).

Some of the claims are for the restoration as a medium of instruction of languages which had been suppressed from the school in the previous century, for example, Breton and Provençal. Other claims are for a radical decentralization of administative and economic power. In any case it is the autonomy of the region, its self-determination along the lines of democratic socialism, which is demanded by these movements today.[6]

In the post-World War I setting of France the political orientation of claim-making against the center has been typically from a Marxist socialist perspective, viewing the periphery as being exploited and underdeveloped as a result of capitalist development and Parisian hegemony. Prior to World War I, claim-making of the periphery was much more oriented to maintenance, safeguarding, or protecting the traditional culture and the traditional way of life of the periphery. In the south Mistral and Aubanel were organizers of a movement known as the *Félibrige* which sought to rescue the language of the south, the language of *oc*, from oblivion and disdain; this important cultural movement, limited in its popular appeal, grew in the Romantic era which among other things emphasized throughout Europe the values of self-expression to be found in folk language and folk culture.

Quebec–Canada

Claims on Behalf of the Nation-State Canada experienced first French and then British colonial rule, before achieving in 1867 a measure of independence normally associated with a sovereign nation-state. The British North America Act of 1867 represented Canada's accession to modernity, endowing the country with a constitution that shifted the national political center from Westminster to Ottawa under a confederal arrangement that provided strategic provincial rights. The French Canadian population of Quebec saw the Act as a pact between two nations, but the Anglo-Canadian population saw it more as a pact of different provinces uniting for common economic benefits.

The centralization of power with the federal government has taken many forms but with gathering impetus since World War II, particularly under Liberal federal rule. That English was and is the dominant language of business encourages cultural integration of the majority of recent immigrant groups, both inside and outside Quebec. In 1949 the Supreme Court of Canada was legislated as the final court of appeal in all cases in the nation-state notwithstanding the particular legal tradition of Quebec. Culturally in 1951 the Royal Commission on National Development in the Arts, Letters and Sciences urged that the education of the individual was not exclusively a provincial matter and that indeed the federal government had an obligation to participate in the "general education of Canadian citizens" (Smiley, 1967, p. 44).

The call for the acceptance of the national center as the arbiter of the national economy and of national resources has been led by both British and French Canadians alike, such as Prime Ministers Macdonald, Laurier and St. Laurent. The most striking political personality of recent times in Canada, Prime Minister Trudeau, was equally determined to generate a consensus around the nation-state, which he viewed as requiring a strong central government capable of upholding claims against the particularism and economic selfishness of the periphery. One can say that he was doubly successful in this, first, by his active role in defeating the Quebec government-sponsored referendum of 1980 (which if passed would have given the Parti Québécois government a mandate to renegotiate with Ottawa its political status as a province). Secondly, Trudeau won important concessions from Western oil-producing provinces claiming autonomy in the amount of oil produced and in the markets in which it could be sold.

The primary thrust of Canadian nationalism has been predominantly a British-Canadian affair. Yet it would be missing an important component of Pan-Canadian nationalism if one were to omit the inputs and orientation of Quebec personalities who committed themselves to a greater Canada. This identification with the nation-state is particularly striking in the figures of Prime Ministers Laurier and Trudeau, more than half a century apart. Some of the motivation stems from a desire that the periphery should close ranks with the center in the nature of the "national interest" to maintain Canada autonomous from its larger and more powerful neighbor to the south, the United States. The United States is one target of Canadian nationalism, because the "American presence" is seen as threatening to engulf and absorb Canada both economically and politically. This perception is not only to be found today, but was also held at the turn of the century by two leading Quebec intellectuals, Henri Bourassa (founder of the prestigious *Le Devoir*) and Olivar Asselin, who argued that the economic integration of Canada into the North American economic integration of Canada into the North American state (Levitt, 1972; Asselin, 1909). For some, especially French Canadians, Britain has been another focus of Canadian nationalism. It was only when Bourassa and Asselin realized that Canada for the English-speaking population was not autonomous of its ties to the British Empire (in the Boer War and in World War I) that they turned their nationalist orientation to that of Quebec.

Claims on Behalf of the Periphery The increased economic integration of Quebec within the rest of Canada after 1867 also meant a penetration of the traditional economy by both British and American capital. Industrialization and urbanization brought major transformations in the social structure of Quebec, including massive emigration of a surplus labor force. In the period after World War I, the Liberal Party of Quebec (PLQ) became an important vehicle for modernization and economic development. The defense of traditional Quebec values—particularly those of language and religion—used to differentiate Quebec from its surrounding Anglo-Protestant environment, was actively carried on by Action Française, under the inspiration of l'Abbé Lionel Groulx. His history of Quebec, *Histoire du Canada français* (1950–2), is an important manifestation of the ideology of "survivance," a defensive posture. In the mid-1930s a new political party came together as a result of the crisis of the depression—the Union Nationale, which represented the articulation of a defensive nationalism; its leader was Maurice Duplessis who was to mark Quebec for three decades. For Duplessis, Quebec should retain its cultural heritage and seal itself off from alien subversive forces, particularly those of communism; Duplessis was unsympathetic to the labor movement, even though labor in Quebec was predominantly French-speaking and capital and management predominantly English-speaking. The Union Nationale embodied predominantly an agrarian, small-town support, one ill-equipped to deal with postwar changes in the United States and Canada that had consequences for Quebec.

With the death in office of Duplessis in September 1959 and that of his designated successor in early 1960, leaving the UN in disarray, the stage was cleared for a renaissance of the Liberal Party in the 1960s as a party standing for the economic and cultural modernization and revitalization of Quebec. The Liberal Party under the leadership of Jean Lesage was instrumental in carrying out important stages of what became called the "Quiet Revolution," focussing upon the modernization of education, government planning of industrial development, and the voluntary secularization of society.

The 1960s was a decade of intense change in all sectors of Quebec society, including a sharp rise in national consciousness as Quebec catapulted from a society where traditional elites ran the country pretty much like American city bosses to a politically modernized society where the younger generations sought democratization of decision-making processes. Various manifestations of political nationalism surfaced in that decade in demands of independence or autonomy from Ottawa. These ranged from a right-wing, Maurras-inspired Alliance Laurentienne of Raymond Barbeau to left-wing formations such as the Rassemblement pour l'Indépendance Nationale and the terrorist Front de Libération du Quebéc (FLQ). But these political formations were unable to form an electoral base or to generate popular support outside of limited audiences. They might have met the same fate as the myriad of political formations in France which advocate regional autonomy. However, in 1968 a new party came into being under the leadership of René Lévesque, a former minister in the Liberal regime of Lesage, who felt that the Liberal program shunted aside the question of the political status of Quebec. We need not detail here the dramatic success of the PQ in becoming a broadly supported nationalist party that evolved into a province-wide political machine attracting both progressive and conservative elements.

Contemporary Quebec has a multiplicity of nationalisms. The Parti Québécois represents claims for autonomy leading by electoral means to the independence of Quebec from Canada, while maintaining its economic association. The Liberal Party of Quebec, the opposite party since 1976, had a change of leadership with the eclipse of Robert Bourassa,* representing the industrial and financial elites, and the rebuilding of the party by Claude Ryan, a conservative intellectual, formerly the editor of the widely respected *Le Devoir*. Ryan's nationalism is that of a strong, culturally distinct Quebec within a federal system. There are factions in the Liberal Party of Quebec who are stronger federalists than Ryan, for example, those who are strong supporters of the new Canadian Constitution which does away with Quebec's traditional right to veto constitutional changes. We might also mention the Pan-Canadian nationalism

*Bourassa returned as head of the party in 1983.

of the "French Mafia" in Ottawa, such as Prime Minister Trudeau, Marc Lalonde, Jean Chrétien, and others, who see the future of Quebec as being part of an integrated, bilingual nation-state. Finally, there is a left-wing socialist republican nationalism which has not yet crystallized into a political party, but which has the commitment of a number of intellectuals and labor union leaders.

In brief, the major political choices which are today's options for Quebec reflect different perspectives on the Quebec nation and its horizon.

Conclusion

The conceptual framework advanced in this chapter has led to a typology of nationalism of and within nation-states; the typology centers upon orientations toward modernity concerning actors' conception of the nation understood as a dynamic societal community. What is the prospective for nationalism and modernity in terms of this approach?

A tacit supposition of the modernization theory perspective is that the underlying rationalization trend of the historical process (Moore, 1979) implies at the political level the aggregation of nation-states into larger, more economically and politically integrated units, albeit the process of modernization also necessitates structural differentiation or a complex division of labor. However implicit in modernization theory, a "natural" outcome of the process is that it leads in effect to "one world":

> Those taking a longer view should see international integration in some form as an extension of the process of modernization beyond national frontiers. Those concerned with a future world order should seek to anticipate the problems that lie ahead by learning as much as possible from the experience of societies in their earlier stages of modernization. (Black, 1976, p. 351)

In effect, then, Cyril Black is here proposing an emergent type of nationalism, one which in terms of our basic frame of reference may be formulated as the *making of claims against (the sovereignty of) the nation-state on behalf of the international societal community as the new legitimate source of political authority*. Reasons for making such claims could be several: survival of a common humanity, protection of the global environment, redistribution of strategic mineral resources, and so on. This last stage of nationalism has one appropriate designation, *internationalism*.

Perhaps the present global crisis and the disruptions that have afflicted Western nation-states in the past fifteen years or so present a timely stimulus for a critical appraisal of the presuppositions which have structured our image of modernization and modernity. Beggerstaff has made the telling point that "modern" is "not necessarily a fixed condition or a point in time" (Beggerstaff, 1976, p. 147). In the present context we take this to mean that the trend for increasing political aggregation, seen as the expression or actualization of political "modernity," may be part of a long phase of the historical process but not necessarily of the whole process itself.

There may well have been during the recent "modern period" a surplus of benefits accruing to the aggregation of local and regional parts within a nation-state center. Certainly many of the most ardent nationalists speaking on behalf of a stronger central government and a more unified Canada, Britain, or France came from peripheral regions which in recent years have manifested nationalist movements seeking to wrestle autonomy from the same government. The political and economic advantages of a powerful central government are becoming increasingly questionable and decentralization if not disaggregation may be viewed as modern a tendency as aggregation was a few generations ago, one necessary to revitalize the grassroots productive energies of social actors. Further, increase or development of the nation-state comes at the expense of other things which matter in an existential way of group identity, in "cultural" matters, or in the ability of communal groups to organize and control their own situation. In brief, the identification of the nation with nation-state, an identification which typified the modernization process not that long ago, may be seen today as one that needs questioning: certainly what is good for the state by no means assures what is good for the nation(s), nor for that matter, for the greatest number of persons.

If we wish a truly broad view of the world historical process, one that would permit a more comprehensive and comparative analysis of nationhood and changes in the aggregation and disaggregation of polities, it might be fruitful to contemplate either larger time units or different ones than the 200- or even 500-year period that has marked the recent period, marked in the West by a "civilization of progress" (Tiryakian, 1978). The Roman Empire, which as such lasted as long as our civilization of progress, is an apt referent for comparative purposes. Renewed interest in recent years in cycles and periodicity, including facing up to declines being as much a part of societal change as growth and development, has renewed interest in accounting for the decline of empires, including that of the Roman Empire. Quite suggestive in this vein is the recent essay of Galtung and associates (1980), who see the ultimate ground of the rise and fall of Rome to be expansionism. Galtung extrapolates this to recent Western expansionism, whose days are seen as numbered, and beyond which lies "a successor society to Western imperialism, a society based on smaller, self-sufficient units with more centripetal cosmologies," ones in which the elites will feel more human because less burdened with carrying the world on their shoulders (ibid., p. 146). Galtung might have added to his comparative analysis that modern Western imperialism was vital to the legitimation of the nation-state and to providing a basis of integration of persons from remote peripheral regions, some of which provided fodder for industrial centers while others provided cannon-fodder for imperialistic wars (Enloe, 1980). The breakup of the Roman Empire, of nineteenth-century European and Ottoman empires, and of overseas empires in our own period entail as much a progressive process of disaggregation as a regressive one; for comparative purpose in terms of the typology proposed in this chapter, the underlying nationalism is that of claims for autonomy of the periphery against the (metropolitan) center.

Rejoining the analysis—and vision—of Leopold Kohr (1957), who cogently analyzed the Western situation a quarter of a century ago, the disaggregation of the nation-state into more flexible, autonomous yet interdependent units, each forming a societal community grounded in territory, culture, and history, may be more of a progressive step in human affairs than further aggregation.

Notes: Chapter 3

1 Paradoxically, this is in the nature of an incomplete fragmentary work. Parts of a draft, written around 1920, were published posthumously in 1953–4 as "The nation."
2 Mauss remarks that it is not by chance that the process of German integration in the last century began with a *Zollverein* and doing away with internal customs—an observation equally applicable to the historical beginnings of the United States.

3 Weber's analysis here is suggestive concerning the role of intellectuals in relation to the idea of nation, for on the one hand it is often intellectuals who have been the most adamantly opposed or resistant to nationalism (which Weber noted in mentioning intellectuals who act as spokesmen of the proletariat), and it is also intellectuals (both lay and clergy) who have also been the most articulate proponents of nationalism.

4 We need only mention the emergence of France, Germany, Italy, and Yugoslavia as instances at hand. It might be pointed out in passing that what is "external" and what is "internal" may lack a clearcut distinction, since very often a nationalist movement is directed against an internal power or group which is treated as "alien," that is, really external to the core societal community.

5 There is an important convergence between our analysis and that of Phillip Rawkins in his reporting of four "nationalist types" or "focal representations" in the case of contemporary Welsh nationalism. See also Rogowski's "Conclusion", below.

6 The new Mitterrand Socialist government of France has committed itself to a policy of decentralization, giving regions greater shares of governmental responsibility. If this is implemented, it might mute some of the vocal opposition to Paris-centered rule. It might also be noted that unlike Spain, Britain, and Canada, peripheral nationalism in France has had little success in developing political parties, and even the most successful one in Brittany, the Union Démocratique Bretonne (UDB), has had in absolute terms very little voter appeal, receiving under 5 percent of the popular vote in general or presidential elections.

References: Chapter 3

Alexander, Jeffrey (1980), "Core solidarity, ethnic outgroup, and social differentiation: a multidimensional model of inclusion in modern societies," in J. Dofny and A. Akowowo (eds.), *National and Ethnic Movements* (Beverly Hills, Calif., and London: Sage), pp. 5–28.

Asselin, Olivar (1909), *A Quebec View of Canadian Nationalism* (Montreal: Guertin).

Beer, William, R. (1980), *The Unexpected Rebellion: Ethnic Activism in Contemporary France* (New York and London: New York University Press).

Beggerstaff, Knight (1976), "Modernization—and early modern China," in C. Black (ed.), *Comparative Modernization* (New York: The Free Press), pp. 146–60.

Black, Cyril, (1976), "International integration," in C. Black (ed.), *Comparative Modernization* (New York: The Free Press), pp. 349–51.

Bourricaud, François (1981), *The Sociology of Talcott Parsons* (Chicago: University of Chicago Press).

Connor, Walker (1972), "Nation-building or nation-destroying?" *World Politics*, vol. 24, no. 3 (April), pp. 319–55.

Connor, Walker (1973), "The politics of ethnonationalism," *Journal of International Affairs*, vol. 27, no. 1, pp. 1–21.

Eliot, T. S. (1949), *Notes towards the Definition of Culture* (New York: Harcourt, Brace).

Enloe, Cynthia (1980), *Ethnic Soldiers: State Security in Divided Societies* (Athens Ga.: University of Georgia Press).

Galtung, Johan, Heiestad, Tore, and Rudeng, Erik (1980), "On the decline and fall of empires: the Roman Empire and Western imperialism compared," *Review*, vol. 4, no. 1 (Summer) p. 153.

Hayes, Carlton (1926), *Essays on Nationalism* (New York: The Macmillan Co.).

Hayes, Carlton (1960), *Nationalism: A Religion* (New York: The Macmillan Co.). *A Study of the Psychology and Sociology of National Sentiment and Character* (1944) (London: Routledge & Kegan Paul).

Keohane, Robert O., and Nye, Joseph S. Jr. (eds.) (1971), *Transnational Relations and World Politics* (Cambridge, Mass.: Harvard University Press).

Kohn, Hans (1955), *Nationalism: Its Meaning and History* (New York: Van Nostrand).

Kohn, Hans (1956), "A look at nationalism," *Virginia Quarterly Review*, vol. 32, no. 3 (Summer), pp. 321–32.

Kohn, Hans (1961), *The Idea of Nationalism* (New York: The Macmillan Co.).

Kohr, Leopold (1957), *The Breakdown of Nations* (New York: Rinehart).

Lafont, Robert (1967), *La Révolution Régionaliste* (Paris: Gallimard).

LaPalombara, Joseph (1974), *Politics within Nations* (Englewood Cliffs, N.J.: Prentice-Hall).

Levitt, Joseph (1972), *Henri Bourassa and the Golden Calf* (Ottawa: Les Editions de l'Université d'Ottawa).

Light, Donald, Jr., and Keller, Suzanne (1979), *Sociology*, 2nd ed. (New York: Knopf).

Mauss, Marcel (1969), "La nation" and "La nation et l'internationalisme," in *Oeuvres*, ed. Victor Karady (Paris: Editions de Minuit), vol. 3, pp. 573–639.

Moore, Wilbert E. (1979), *World Modernization. The Limits of Convergence* (New York: Elsevier).

Morgenthau, Hans J. (1958), *Politics among Nations*, 2nd ed. (New York: Knopf).

Nairn, Tom (1977), *The Break-Up of Britain. Crisis and Neo-Nationalism* (London: New Left Books).

Parsons, Talcott (1959), "A rejoinder to Ogles and Levy," *American Sociological Review*, vol. 24, no. 2 (April), pp. 248–50

Parsons, Talcott (1968), "Social systems", *International Encyclopedia of the Social Sciences*, ed. D. L. Sills (New York: The Macmillan Co.), Vol. 15, pp. 458–72.

Person, Yves (ed.) (1973), "Minorités nationales en France," special issue of *Les Temps Modernes*, vol. 29 (August–September).

Plamenatz, J. P. (1973), "Two types of nationalism," in E. Kamenka (ed.), *Nationalism: The Nature and Evolution of an Idea* (London: Edward Arnold), pp. 23–36.

Plano, J., and Olton, R. (1969), *The International Relations Dictionary* (New York: Wiley).

Portes, Alejandro (1976), "On the sociology of national development: theories and issues," *American Journal of Sociology*, vol. 82, no. 1 (July), pp. 55–85.

Rawkins, Phillip (1979), "An approach to the political sociology of the Welsh nationalist movement," *Political Studies*, vol. 27, no. 3 (September), pp. 440–57.

Renan, Ernest (1970), "What is a nation?" in E. Renan, *Poetry of the Celtic Races and Other Studies*, trans. and ed. William G. Hutchison (London: Kennikat Press), pp. 61–83.

Rustow, Dankwart A. (1968), "Nation" in *International Encyclopedia of the Social Sciences* (New York: The Macmillan Co.), Vol. 11, pp. 7–14.

Silvert, Kalman H. (1963), "The strategy of the study of nationalism," in K. H. Silvert (ed.), *The Expectant Peoples: Nationalism and Development* (New York: Random House), pp. 3–38.

Singer, Milton (1968), "The concept of culture," *International Encyclopedia of the Social Sciences*, ed. D. L. Sills (New York: The Macmillan Co,), Vol. 3, pp. 527–43.

Smelser, Neil J. (1981), *Sociology* (Englewood Cliffs, N.J.: Prentice-Hall).

Smiley, Donald V. (1967), *The Canadian Political Nationality* (Toronto and London: Methuen).

Smith, Anthony D. (1979), *Nationalism in the Twentieth Century* (New York: New York University Press).

Smith, Anthony D. (1981), *The Ethnic Revival* (New York: Cambridge Univesity Press).

Snyder, Louis L. (1954), *The Meaning of Nationalism* (New Brunswick, N.J.: Rutgers University Press).

Sondermann, F. A., Olson, W. C., and McLelland, D. S. (eds.) (1970), *Theory and Practice of International Relations*, 3rd ed. (Englewood Cliffs, N.J.: Prentice-Hall).

Spencer, Metta (1982), *Foundations of Modern Sociology*, 3rd ed. (Englewood Cliffs, N.J.: Prentice-Hall).

Stephens, Meic (1976), *Linguistic Minorities in Western Europe* (Llandysul: Gomer Press).

Symmons-Symonolewicz, Konstantin (1968), *Modern Nationalism: Towards a Consensus in Theory* (New York: Polish Institute of Arts and Sciences in America).

Symmons-Symonolewicz, Konstantin (1970), *Nationalist Movements: A Comparative View* (Meadville, Pa.: Maplewood Press).

Tiryakian, Edward A. (1978), "The time perspectives of modernity," *Loisir et Société*, n.s. 1 (April), pp. 125–53.

Tiryakian, Edward, A. (1982), "Modernity: a preliminary conceptualization," paper presented at Fifth Regional Symposium, United Nations University, Milan, November.

Tiryakian, Edward A. (1984), "The changing centers of modernity," in E. Cohen, M. Lissak and U. Almagor (eds.), *Comparative Social Dynamics: Essays in Honor of Shmuel N. Eisenstadt* (Boulder, Colo.: Westview Press).

Vernon, Raymond (1977), *Storm over the Multinationals: The Real Issues* (Cambridge, Mass.: Harvard University Press).

Wallerstein, Immanuel M. (1974), *The Modern World System: Capitalist Agriculture and the Origins of the European World-Economy* (New York: Academic Press), Vol. 1.

Weber, Max (1978), *Economy and Society*, 2 vols., ed. Guenther Roth and Claus Wittich (Berkeley, Calif., and London: University of California Press).

Wirth, Louis (1936), "Types of nationalism," *American Journal of Sociology*, vol. 41, no. 6 (May), pp. 723–37.

Zolberg, Aristide R. (1981), "Origins of the modern world system: a missing link," *World Politics*, vol. 33, no. 2 (January), pp. 253–81.

4

Causes and Varieties of Nationalism
a Rationalist Account

RONALD ROGOWSKI

To sociologists and to many political scientists and historians nationalism is profoundly irrational, a "primordial sentiment" of ethnicity and aggression (for example, Geertz, 1963, pp. 105–57; Connor, 1972, pp. 336–7). To Marxists nationalism has usually seemed all too rational, whether as an expression of early bourgeois desires for more than local markets or as the ideology by which mature capitalism papered over domestic divisions and deluded workers into support of imperialist wars. In contrast to both approaches, I shall advance here a rudimentary "strict rationalist" theory, according to which nationalism is: (1) the product of value-maximizing (but not merely greedy) behavior; (2) based almost always on an accurate appraisal of self-interest and social reality (that is, rarely a consequence of hysteria or delusion); and (3) intimately and specifically connected to the social division of labor and to changes in that division, albeit not in the unadorned way claimed by classical Marxist theory.

Definition

Following Weber (1958, p. 176, and 1964, p. 316), I shall take "nation" to mean a culturally distinct group that could survive as an independent, united, and self-sufficient political entity. "Nationalism," consequently, will mean (as I submit it does in everyday discourse) the striving by members of such a group for territorial autonomy, unity, or independence (cf. Birch, 1978, p. 332). Thus we routinely, and properly, speak of Welsh,

Quebecois, and Arab nationalisms (seeking respectively autonomy, independence, and unity), but not of western Canadian "nationalism" (the efforts for autonomy are based on economic rather than cultural distinctiveness) or, even in the late nineteenth century, of Dutch Catholic "nationalism" (autonomy was sought on a purely cultural and not a territorial basis).

I similarly follow convention in defining the other key term of the argument: by "rational" behavior I shall mean the consistent endeavor, by individual actors, to maximize net benefit, that is, the difference between benefit and cost, where both benefit and cost are evaluated idiosyncratically but consistently (Weber, 1964, p. 18; Riker and Ordeshook, 1973, ch. 2; van den Doel, 1979, s. 2.1).

Premisses

(1) Rationality

Our fundamental assumption, to be tested of course by the empirical accuracy of its deductive implications, is that nationalism is always rational in the sense just given, that is, embraced by the given individual because, and to the extent that, it offers him a greater net benefit (or *mutatis mutandis* a lesser net loss) than do other possible investments of effort. As others have in part already argued, such an assumption must carry far broader implications, for example, that cost−benefit calculations also explain:

(a) individual choices about behavior toward a dominant nation, including assimilation, isolation, apathy, resistance, or minority nationalism (Banton, 1980);
(b) individual choices among contending cultural identifications, including the (actually rather frequent) choice to recover or even invent a cultural identity (Bates, 1974);
(c) individual choices between nationalism and support of rival causes (for example, ones of class or religion) (Rogowski, 1980).

Very generally we are assuming that, among all the courses of action that she or he considers, a given actor chooses that one which maximizes the sum

$$\Delta p \cdot B - C$$

where B is the benefit to be obtained if the course of action is successful, C is the anticipated cost of that course of action, and Δp is the change in the probability of receiving the benefit that the actor can bring about by undertaking the course of action. A Breton youth in the 1880s, for example, might have considered the relative net benefits of assimilation, Breton nationalism, and passivity. Assimilation would have entailed high costs—not only the mastering of French, but a distancing of himself from family and friends—but, if successful, would have opened the door to grander careers than would ever have been available in Finistère or Côtes-du-Nord. But would assimilation, if attempted, have been successful? Would he have gained the requisite facility in the dominant culture's ways, and would he have been fully accepted if he had?

Nationalism, on the other hand, carried heavy costs in the Third Republic. The benefits of autonomy might have been great, but his own contributions could have affected the likelihood of success only slightly. Even if the Breton cause had looked more promising than it did, the temptation to "ride free" (Olson, 1968) would have been great.

Apathy and self-isolation, finally, carried low cost, but—given the backwardness of the area (Berger, 1972, ch. 1)—low benefits. The probability that he could achieve these benefits by his own action, however, was surely greatest here. The choice among the three alternatives was, in Hirschman's sense, a classical one among exit, voice, and loyalty (Hirschman, 1970; cf. Rokkan, 1974).

Even in this simple-minded form, the premiss of rational conduct yields some testable hypotheses. Whatever decreases estimates of cost—typically a successful demonstration that people can "get away" with some defiant action—makes nationalist activity more likely, as does anything that increases the impact of one's own contribution (Δp), for instance, survey results that suggest a nationalist party has a real chance of winning in my constituency. On the other side of the balance collective activity, whether nationalist or proletarian, is made less likely by anything that makes assimilation or emigration less costly; and historians have indeed suggested that the waning of both kinds of revolutionary activism in Europe after 1848 was linked to the rapidly sinking costs and the rapidly rising volume of emigration (Hosbawm, 1975, ch. 11). As Levi and Hechter contend elsewhere in this volume, movements that seem likely to control selective incentives, and thus to offer adherents more control over the benefits they receive (a larger Δp), will logically be likelier to gain support.

But to say all this is still to say less than one would like. We are left guessing, or inferring tautologically from the actions they are supposed to explain, the crucial individual estimates of the benefits to be achieved by the attainment of national autonomy, or by the success of any rival cause.

(2) Calculation of Individual Benefit

Our second premiss, which takes us some way toward resolving the dilemma, is just this: that individuals' preferences for possible future states of society are a joint function of their anticipated positions in those future states and of the "workability" of that future state. More precisely, we postulate that a person's evaluation depends on: (*a*) her estimate of the supply of, and the demand for, her own skill(s) in the future state; and (*b*) her estimate of supply–demand ratios for all other socially important skills in that future state.

I hasten to point out that these provocative hypotheses are not new. Albert Breton (1964) argued that professionals often supported nationalism because they hoped that independence would restrict the supply of candidates for their occupations (cf. Gilpin, 1974). Bates (1974, p. 463) has observed that educationally backward regions and ethnic groups in Africa, unable to supply enough skilled persons to fill all the "occupations of control" in their areas, have often opposed independence, apparently fearing that either chaos or tutelage would follow. More broadly, we may observe that where a group would be unable to meet the demand for a specific skill (or to supply the goods that holders of that skill could produce), it must estimate the ways in which that lack could be met by trade (Banton, 1980, pp. 487–8) and what the terms of that trade would be.

One important implication of this line of argument is that nationalism will be embraced only by cultural groups whose members believe that they can supply all essential skills, or that they can readily compensate by trade for any skills they lack. (This may, of course, provide a partial explanation for the frequent rise of nationalism in areas that suddenly acquire some readily exportable and easily defended resource like oil; but see p. 98.) Absent a highly favourable trading position, however, subjugated cultures in societies characterized by what Hechter (1975) has called a "cultural division of labor" (CDL) are actually *unlikely* candidates for nationalism, at least so long as the CDL is sustained by real inequalities of skill. Further, any previously quiescent or assimilationist group that suddenly espouses nationalism must logically have recently revised upward its estimates of: (*a*) the demand–supply ratio, in a future autonomous nation, for its members' particular skills; (*b*) the likelihood that such a nation would be able to achieve self-sufficiency; or (*c*) both factors.

(3) Realism

Now conceivably these and other crucial estimates could be based on delusion. Louis XIV's expulsion of the Huguenots, like Idi Amin's expulsion of Uganda's Indian population, may have rested on a grave misapprehension of his society's ability to function without that skilled group—or may equally have indicated a willingness to pay the price. Error, however, is expensive, and the costs of avoiding it are usually low. Our axiom of rationality also requires us, therefore, to postulate that people will ordinarily base their estimates of costs, benefits, and probabilities on experience and observation, and will rapidly correct estimates that experience contradicts (cf. Rogowski, 1974, p. 57).

Model

In this preliminary essay we examine the logical implications of the previous postulates for a drastically simplified model of society, in which only two categories of positions exist—call them elite and nonelite—and only two distinct cultural groups. Under our postulate of realism the requisite skills for the two categories of positions are defined by the necessities of the prevailing mode of production.

Two broad kinds of social division of labor are of interest in such a model:

(1) the classical CDL, or "plural" society (Furnivall, 1939; Kuper and Smith, 1969), in which one culture monopolizes the elite positions and skills;
(2) the "pillarized" society (Daalder, 1966, pp. 214–16), in which both cultures have ample numbers of persons with both elite and nonelite skills.[1]

Situations and Hypotheses

I propose now to consider, without any apology except their evident importance, the effects on nationalism, in these two basic kinds of society, of four kinds of social change: (1) social mobility; (2) changes in the mode of production; (3) cultural assimilation or integration; and (4) changes in the terms of trade between cultures.

(1)   Social Mobility in CDLs

Even where one culture monopolizes elite skills, whether by virtue of conquest or of the slow accretions of caste, some movement between elite and nonelite will occur. The least talented or least lucky of the children of the elite will slip downward; and through at least some constricted channels (for example, the church in the Middle Ages) some nonelite off-spring will rise.

The *upwardly mobile* ordinarily face strong inducements to assimilate. Molière's bourgeois felt obliged to learn gentle ways, and generations of Welsh and Irish had to abandon accent or religion, or both, to gain access to elite skills and occupations. Where these barriers hold, mobility is invisible because the camouflage succeeds; and even in the minds of the mobile, the mythic bond between culture and skill remains firm (cf. Bernstein, 1971–5, esp. vol. 1, chs. 2 and 8).

The upwardly mobile will rationally assimilate, however, only so long as the promised rewards can be attained by, and only by, assimilation. If one's best efforts bring only failure or rejection, or if skill and position can suddenly be acquired without assimilation (for instance, in consequence of educational reforms or increased market demand), assimilation will be rejected; and, dangerously for the old elite, one will have visible evidence that the link between skill and culture is delusive: "we" (the nonelite culture) can run things as well as "they."

As soon as enough such unassimilated upward mobiles are at hand the formerly inferior culture becomes a nation, that is, a potentially self-sufficient society; and the upwardly mobile themselves, according to our premises, become the most resolute nationalists, for it is precisely their skills that would be in short supply in an independent state. So great are the potential benefits of autonomy to this group that they may rationally invest in the re-creation or invention of a "nation" from what in present reality is only a welter of tribes or dialects:

Hypothesis 1   In a CDL any failure fully to assimilate to elite culture and position any substantial number of

those of the nonelite who acquire elite skills will
be highly likely to inspire nationalism among
the nonelite; and the unassimilated or un-
accepted upwardly mobile will be the most
fervent nationalists.

The evidence in favor of this proposition seems to me overwhelming. The nationalisms of Southern and Eastern Europe
in the early and middle nineteenth century (Hobsbawm, 1962,
pp. 166–8), those of Norway (Rokkan, 1966, pp. 77–8) and of
Ireland (Inglis, 1973, pt. 2, ch. 2; Lee, 1979, pp. 115–16) in the
later nineteenth century, and in the twentieth century those of
India (Brecher, 1959, pp. 35–8), Quebec (Hamilton and
Pinard, 1976, pp. 9–19), Scotland (Brand, 1978, pp. 146–50),
and Africa (Bates, 1974, pp. 467–8), to name only a few, have
been convincingly linked, in timing and in personnel, to upward
social mobility unaccompanied by assimilation and acceptance.

As one would expect of a strong causal relationship, even
analogous cases present supporting evidence. Merkl (1975, ch.
2 and pp. 105–7) has shown that among the extreme nationalists of the Nazi movement, there is a startling incidence not only
of frustrated upward mobility but of failed emigration: movement to another country, but rapid return with feelings of rejection or discrimination. Gandhi too became a nationalist after
discovering that emigration to South Africa offered no escape
from racial subjugation (Wolfenstein, 1971, pp. 145–52). Even
class-based movements, it seems, whether of the bourgeoisie
or of the proletariat, are more frequently associated with
unassimilated upward mobility than with deprivation or
downward mobility (Brinton, 1930; Lipset and Bendix, 1959,
pp. 66–9).[2]

Downward mobility in a CDL has ordinarily nothing like the
same effects. Where the CDL is a product of conquest or capture, many nonelite positions will already be held by members
of the elite culture (white settlers in Kenya and Rhodesia; Protestant workers in Ulster; poor whites in the American South),
even if under far more favorable conditions. At any rate no
radical innovation is involved if children of the elite move down
to join them. Two partial exceptions should, however, be
noted.

Where members of the elite culture have not previously held
nonelite positions, and where those who move down into such
positions are effectively expelled from the elite culture—treated
often as "tainted," with no chance of return—the thus

derogated group, believing frequently enough that they possess the same capabilities as their former fellows, are in much the same position as the upwardly mobile in the preceding discussion. They will have a strong motive to create and lead a nationalist movement of the nonelite, particularly since any displacement of the old elite (for instance, through independence) would leave the downwardly mobile a near-monopoly of elite skills. Children of mixed marriages in racist societies may be a familiar example; and the analogy from class politics is the role often played by displaced artisans in the leadership of the early working-class movement (Hobsbawm, 1962, p. 253; Thompson, 1963, pp. 240–1; Hobsbawm, 1975, pp. 247–50).

The other chief exception has actually to do with resistance to upward mobility. When members of the nonelite culture begin to acquire elite skills and positions, members of the elite culture who hold nonelite positions will often perceive the change as moving them downward, if only because the change means a widening of the pool of eligibles for elite positions. Any ensuing nationalism of the nonelite will seem an even greater threat. Hence a familiar "red-neck" nationalism, as among the Afrikaner, the Protestant workers in Northern Ireland, or nonelite whites in Rhodesia or the American South, is likely to arise. The demand here is for a "pure" nation of the elite culture, in which the subjugated culture will continue to play at most the role of the *Gastarbeiter*:

Hypothesis 2 In any CDL in which some nonelite positions are held by members of the elite culture, upward movement by members of the nonelite is likely to inspire a "reactive" nationalism among the less privileged members of the elite culture, who will demand restoration of the status quo ante.

Hypothesis 3 Actual downward movement in a CDL is unlikely to engender nationalism unless the downwardly mobile are expelled from the elite culture; and then the nationalism will be one of the nonelite culture, led typically by the downwardly mobile.

(2) Changes in the Mode of Production in CDLs

As both Marx and Mosca demonstrated, changes in a society's mode of production and, therefore, in the skills and habits that are valuable for production, can change almost all else: property, status, belief. With regard to such changes in CDLs three cases will chiefly concern us: (*a*) changes that depreciate or render useless what had been the essential skills of the elite; (*b*) changes that similarly diminish or destroy the value of nonelite skills; and (*c*) changes that alter the optimal scale of production.

Where the *elite*'s crucial skills are devalued, nationalism of the nonelite culture at once becomes possible, for the whole ideological basis of the CDL is impugned. Thus Skocpol (1979) is right to see in the sudden failure of bureaucratic–military elites to defend their societies a crucial—but, I contend, not a sufficient—precondition for mass nationalist revolutions like those of France, Russia, and China. More generally, as Hobsbawm (1962, pp. 164–6) and others have noted, the eighteenth- and nineteenth-century nationalisms of Western Europe were closely connected with the supersession of the cosmopolitan absolutist aristocracies, still based on landholding and office, by more localized manufacturing and mercantile elites. (By contrast, as we have already seen, the contemporaneous nationalisms of Southern and Eastern Europe were largely professional rather than mercantile, and grounded in upward mobility rather than change in the mode of production.)

Yet nationalism need not follow such a change. Where the military skills of the old elite fail, it may simply be displaced by an invading one, as indeed seems to have happened in India and many other colonial conquests (Hobsbawm, 1975, p. 133). Or, as Mosca observed, a fraction of the old elite may well acquire the necessary new skills and use them to eclipse their former fellows, without in any way disturbing the CDL: some at least of what Barrington Moore (1966, p. 438 ff.) has called the "conservative modernizers" fit this category, for instance those German Protestant landholders in Silesia who took up capitalist mining, leaving untouched the subordinate position of their Polish Catholic tenants and workers (Henderson, 1975, p. 56):

Hypothesis 4   In a CDL changes in the mode of production that visibly render obsolete the principal skills of the elite will likely, but not certainly, give rise to nationalism among the nonelite.

Changes in the mode of production that supersede the skills of the *nonelite*, on the other hand, will never by themselves inspire nationalism. In one of Marx's most frequently invoked examples the introduction of British-manufactured cotton cloth into India rapidly destroyed a flourishing textile craft and precipitated mass misery. Yet the catastrophe evoked almost no political response, and certainly no nationalism. It did provide a potent symbol for later generations of nationalists in Gandhi's spinning wheel, universally understood to represent economic independence; but it could do so only after social mobility had created the Indian elite that made independence an achievable dream. So long as the nonelite culture still lacks the skills required for elite positions, and so long as those positions are generally believed to be essential, no deprivation of the nonelite, no matter how horrible, will give rise to nationalism, precisely because a separate existence of the subjugated nation seems unthinkable:

Hypothesis 5   In a CDL changes in the mode of production that render inessential the chief skills of the nonelite will, unless preceded or accompanied by other kinds of change (for instance, unassimilated upward mobility), not give rise to nationalism, even where severe deprivation of the nonelite ensues.

Finally, and as Marxist scholars have long emphasized, changes in the mode of production can indeed stipulate a new optimally efficient scale of production or of markets. While the mercantile capitalisms of the Renaissance flourished best in the city-state—and Venice, to take but one example, developed a patriotism that successors might envy (Plumb, 1961, pp. 97–9)—the manufacturing and early industrial capitalism of the eighteenth and nineteenth centuries required wider access and more secure markets. Hence we often think it "natural" that French, German, and Italian capitalists of the latter period were nationalists, seeking to unite all the territory that could be said to share their respective languages or cultures.

In fact, however, these consequences are natural in a CDL only to the extent that the change in the mode of production not only alters the optimum economic scale, but also displaces the old elite and throws up a new one of something like the optimum geographic dispersal. Where old elites of larger or smaller scale successfully adapt, nationalism can be checked or channeled in ways that defy purely economic optimality. Thus Latin America, with its weak and "deformed" bourgeoisie (see, for example, Cardoso and Faletto, 1979, p. 129, *passim*), has retained a crazy-quilt of boundaries that distort and impede development; and even Germany, under the Empire, remained more decentralized and small than her nonaristocratic capitalists, such as those of the Rhineland, would have wished:

Hypothesis 6   In a CDL changes in the mode of production that alter the optimum scale of production or markets will inspire nationalism only to the extent that they simultaneously displace old elites.

(3) Cultural Integration in CDLs

Frequently the elite in a CDL endeavors to assimilate the nonelite to the "civilized" culture (see, for example, Weber, 1976, esp. pp. 1–8). These efforts, pursued with greater or less brutality, may well succeed: France did develop a unitary culture, and the Cornish and Scottish languages were extirpated. Less frequently elite and nonelite cultures integrate into a hybrid, as seems to have occurred between the Anglo-Saxons and their Norman conquerors.

According to the logic of the present model, neither event will give rise to nationalism so long as the CDL is maintained, that is, so long as the elite skills continue to be monopolized by the elite culture. Indeed, pressure for assimilation usually weakens the nonelite by inducing self-contempt and intense intergenerational and intrapersonal conflict (Loewenberg, 1980; Banton, 1980, pp. 490–1). Only when the elite has been penetrated by unassimilated members of the nonelite, or when elite skills have been visibly superseded, can assimilationist pressure evoke nonelite nationalism:

Hypothesis 7   So long as a CDL remains intact, pressures on the nonelite to assimilate to the culture of the elite will not engender nonelite nationalism.

(4) Changes in the Terms of Trade between Cultures in a CDL.

Even where neither social mobility nor assimilation occurs, and where the fundamental mode of production does not change, events can drastically alter the terms of trade—the extent and the mutuality of dependence—between elite and nonelite. In the twentieth century as in ancient Rome, war has often made elites need nonelites more, and thus has allowed the latter to make substantial gains (Scullard, 1961, p. 52 ff.). World War I made Belgium and Britain, and World War II many colonial governments, vulnerable to demands from long-subjugated cultures (Lorwin, 1966, pp. 158, 161; Rose, 1971, p. 88; Burns, 1970, pp. 379–80). Under other conditions war can equally increase the dependence of nonelites on elites, as it appears to have done in the Middle Ages (White, 1966, ch. 1; Bloch, 1961, pp. 245–8). Such essentially random events as plagues and pioneering, which by respectively decimating the nonelite or expanding its opportunities increase the price that its members can demand for their services, have also radically altered the terms of trade in CDLs. That nonelite demands escalated radically after the opening of new lands in the twelfth century and after the Black Death of the fourteenth century is well known (Bloch, 1961, pp. 276–9; Hilton, 1973, pp. 152–4); and Popkin (1979, pp. 73–82) has argued that similar effects followed the expansion of peasant opportunity in Japan, Latin America, and Vietnam. The discovery or sudden appreciation of a resource that the nonelite can control, I have argued above, will have similar effects. Conversely, a sudden decline in the land–labor ratio (for example, Blum, 1961, pp. 277–81, 422–41) or the loss of some vital resource can greatly weaken the position of the nonelite.

In a CDL, as in other caste or class societies, changes like these will alter the degree of subjection. The nonelite will gain or lose some rights, economic differences will diminish or grow. Only where they benefit the nonelite extremely, however, can changes in the terms of trade by themselves provide a basis for nationalism. So long as the subjugated culture lacks some crucial elite skill, even wealth will leave it in the unsure position of those Renaissance republics that kept mercenary armies (Machiavelli, 1513, ch. 12). The advantage from altered terms of trade is also often too transitory to serve as a reliable base of national existence. Interestingly even among the Islamic states, not oil wealth but the emergence of indigenous technical and professional elites has been the surest predictor of the strength of nationalism:

Hypothesis 8   Except where they (*a*) extremely improve the position of the nonelite and (*b*) appear to be of relatively long duration, changes in the terms of trade between elite and nonelite cultures in a

CDL are unlikely by themselves to give rise to nationalism.

Social Mobility in Pillarized Societies

In pillarized societies, by definition, each culture possesses adequate numbers of persons to carry out both elite and nonelite functions. Hence political autonomy is usually possible, yet often it is not pursued. We must try to see what calculations affect that choice.

In our simplified model we suppose two such cultures coexisting within a single state. Each has its own elite, each its separate avenues of recruitment and mobility. By a kind of Gresham's law, wider opportunity for the nonelite in one pillar, possibly including substantially higher rates of upward mobility, will encourage rational members of the other pillar to assimilate, the more so the greater the difference in opportunity. Thus many Welsh adopted English culture in the nineteenth century, and many Castilians today not only migrate into the industries of Catalonia, but adopt Catalan language and culture.

In such movements there is often as much "push" as "pull," for example, when modernizing landlords in nineteenth-century eastern Germany forced their tenants to migrate into the industries of the Ruhr. But the loss of substantial numbers of a pillar's nonelite can in other circumstances threaten to turn the intracultural terms of trade sharply against the affected pillar's elite. Obviously where nonelite numbers diminish but demand holds constant, the position of the nonelite is strengthened.

In this situation, as Meadwell (1982) has argued persuasively from the examples of nineteenth-century Brittany and Quebec, an *elite-led* nationalism of the less flourishing culture is likely. By achieving autonomy or statehood, these elites reason, they will gain means to stem the outflow. Even short of that, a movement of "national consciousness" can invoke social controls against emigration, by equating it with desertion and treason. "Manipulative" nationalism of this kind is wholly distinct from, and often in conflict with, the "radical" form (the labels are quite unsatisfying) led by rising new elites[3]: in Quebec the Union Nationale v. the Parti Québécois (see pp. 103–4).

Alternatively, when the less promising culture already dominates the state, it will simply impose policies that check movement and assimilation; and then the elites of the more flourishing pillar may seek control or autonomy to preserve the flow of new labor into their domain. Surely the recent revivals of Catalan and Croatian nationalism owe something to this latter phenomenon. Reaching further back, one suspects that American Republicans' emphasis in the 1850s on "free soil" and the repeal of the Fugitive Slave Laws had a similar motivation:

Hypothesis 9   When rates of social mobility or opportunity are appreciably higher in one culture than in another in a pillarized society, elite-led nationalism is likely to result, typically within the culture with fewer opportunities, but sometimes also (particularly when the less flourishing culture dominates the existing state) among the culture of greater opportunity.

Changes in the Mode of Production in Pillarized Societies

A fundamental change in a pillarized society's mode of production can have two chief effects. (1) The elite skills of the new order may be mastered only, or very disproportionately, by members of one of the cultures (Lijphart, 1977b, pp. 57–8). As Weber noted at the outset of *The Protestant Ethic and the Spirit of Capitalism*, business in Germany tended by the end of the nineteenth century to be dominated overwhelmingly by Protestants. In our simple two-class model such a change must eventually transform the pillarized society into a CDL, with one of the formerly equal cultures now subordinate. Such a development can inspire nationalism among either culture: in the threatened group something akin to what Barrington Moore has called a "Catonist" reaction, which rejects the new ways as alien and vulgar; or on the part of the now more advanced culture, self-assertion as the *Staatsvolk*, and impatient dismissal of the other group as backward and benighted. The Belgian Catholics of the mid-nineteenth century may be taken as representative of the first tendency (Lorwin, 1966, pp. 154–5), the German Protestants and seculars in the *Kulturkampf* as typical of the second.

(2)   Change in the mode of production can so change crucial transaction costs in a pillarized society as to make previous patterns of coexistence impossible. As Katzenstein (1977, p. 295) and Zolberg (1979) have observed, linguistic differences, and *a fortiori* most other cultural differences, are tolerable in

the basic productive activities of the primary and secondary sectors, but may impose high costs in the "high tertiary" sectors that produce and distribute mainly information. Put more simply, pidgin and rough translation suffice in the factory and on the farm, but not in the office. Hence with economic modernization, assimilation or segregation (that is, monoglot enterprises) may become an economic necessity, and a struggle for domination of these leading economic sectors may well ensue. Similarly, dietary and commensal taboos that were easily adhered to under familial and guild production may become unbearably costly in large-scale enterprises:

Hypothesis 10   Change in the mode of production in a pillarized society is highly likely to give rise to nationalism and, particularly when the new mode attaches high economic costs to the maintenance of traditional patterns of coexistence, to national conflict.

Assimilation and Integration in Pillarized Societies

Where modes of production and rates of economic growth are roughly the same in both cultures of a pillarized society, both elites will have many reasons to oppose assimilation or integration between the nonelites. A unified nonelite would be more powerful (for the full argument, see Rogowski, 1974, ch. 5) and would constitute a larger pool of candidates for elite positions in either pillar. Yet the elites are more powerful if they *are* integrated with each other, and they have more opportunities to become so (multilingual education, social contacts, travel). Hence in pillarized societies the elites are often significantly, if rather secretly, integrated; but any prospect of a similar merger of nonelites will likely call forth in both pillars an *elite-led* cultural, and rather hypocritical "nationalism," whose main purpose is to keep the nonelites divided. (For a generally favourable view of the phenomenon, see Lijphart, 1977a, pp. 87–103; far more critical is Kieve, 1981, pp. 318–19.)

Any effort at forcible assimilation in a still-intact pillarized society, on the other hand, will lead at once to demands for autonomy or independence throughout the attacked culture. Only if—as some totalitarian regimes have understood only too well—the elite of such a culture is first absorbed, exiled, or liquidated, can defensive nationalism of this kind be avoided. The continuing active presence of an indigenous elite, I suspect, goes far to explain why Alsatians and Poles reacted differently to assimilationist pressure than did the Welsh or Cornish:

Hypothesis 11   In a pillarized society whose cultures are at roughly the same level of economic development the elites will usually cooperate to prevent integration or assimilation between their respective nonelites; and as part of their effort, will often support conservative nationalisms of their respective cultures.

Hypothesis 12   Any effort at forcible assimilation of one culture in an intact pillarized society will arouse intense nationalism among both the elite and the nonelite of the attacked culture.

Changes in the Terms of Trade in Pillarized Societies

Despite their relative self-sufficiency, the cultures of a pillarized society must ordinarily engage in some exchange and must develop some mutual dependency. They also evolve political relations and expectations about the costs and benefits of state action. (For what I see as examples from Italian and Swiss history, see respectively Allum, 1973, pp. 3–4; Lijphart, 1977a, pp. 31, 89–97). These relations and expectations define the terms of intercultural trade in a broad sense.

When these terms of trade so change as to violate the original anticipations of either side, a reassessment of the benefits of continued political unity can be expected. A classic case, as Pi-Sunyer argues elsewhere in this volume, is Catalonia. In the latter half of the eighteenth century, having benefited both from natural endowments and from Spanish royal policies of tariff protection and imperial preference, Barcelona developed an astonishingly vigorous textile industry, and Catalonia became the peninsula's economically most advanced province (LaForce, 1965, ch. 1 and pp. 144, 151–61; 179). Seemingly able to influence governmental policy to suit their interests, Catalan business elites raised few objections to Castilian dominance of politics and administration (LaForce, 1965, pp. 14–15, 17, 167). When, after the loss of most of the Spanish Empire during and after the Napoleonic Wars, the Catalan elites' demands for increased protection were rejected by the rural-dominated central government, the illusion of influence was shattered; and the manufacturing bourgeoisie began its embrace of Catalan nationalism.

In the antebellum United States too, as Beard and Beard (1930, p. 678) long ago observed, "in [the] clash of sectional interests, the outstanding issue of (the 1820s and 1830s) was the tariff." Southern agricultural elites, who had anticipated that federal tariffs would be imposed only for revenue, were shocked by the protective duties of 1824; and the further increases of 1828 moved some to consider nullification and secession. Changes that negate previous power-sharing arrangements, as in Cyprus and Lebanon, are similarly likely to stimulate nationalism:

Hypothesis 13   In a pillarized society any substantial decline in the net benefit that either culture anticipates from continued unity will greatly increase the likelihood of nationalism among that culture.

It should perhaps be emphasized that this connection is *not* hypothesized to hold for CDLs (see hypothesis 8).

Varieties of Nationalism

We can perhaps usefully recapitulate by noting the conditions that the preceding hypotheses have associated with specific kinds of nationalism.

What can be called *radical nationalism*, accompanied by social revolution, led by new elites and often ready to employ violence at an early stage of the struggle, appears to be produced: (1) *only* in what had been CDLs, and (2) only as a consequence of unassimilated upward mobility, or of changes in the mode of production that supersede the old elite.

Hegemonist nationalism, which pursues with missionary zeal the assimilation of "inferior" cultures, has equally specific origins: (1) above all, in a previously pillarized society in which one culture has come to monopolize the elite skills of a new mode of production, but also (2) in an economically expanding CDL in which aspects of the subjugated culture (often language) constrict entry into the workforce.

Defensive nationalism, led usually by traditional elites and concerned chiefly with the preservation of traditional culture, occurs: (1) only in recently or still pillarized societies, and (2) only against efforts at compulsory assimilation. Depending on the situation, it can resist passively (for example, the minority nationalities in the German Empire) or violently (the Bretons in the French Revolution).

Table 4.1   Varieties of nationalism and their hypothesized incidence in specific types and conditions of societies

	Condition: stability, or type of social change				
Type of society	*Stability*	*Unassimilated upward mobility*	*Change in mode of production*	*Cultural assimilation*	*Change in terms of trade*
Cultural division of labor	no nationalism	radical nationalism	possibility of radical nationalism	no nationalism	possibility of conservative nationalism
Pillarized society	manipulative nationalism	manipulative nationalism	hegemonial and/or defensive nationalism	defensive nationalism	conservative nationalism

Conservative nationalism, again socially un- or even anti-revolutionary but concerned with achievement of a broader autonomy, can proceed according to this analysis from only one source, namely, changes in the terms of trade in either CDLs or pillarized societies. The latter are the far more likely source.

Manipulative nationalism, finally, is led by traditional elites but not really embraced by them; they use it only to keep nonelites divided or to keep emigration from bidding up the effective wages of "their" nonelites. This cynical "nationalism" appears rather ordinarily in steady-state pillarized societies, and even more predictably and powerfully in pillarized societies affected by uneven rates of opportunity and social mobility.

I attempt to summarize these hypothesized linkages in Table 4.1. Obviously I consider that a preliminary examination of the evidence supports them. Whether they withstand more rigorous testing will tell us something about the merits of rationalism as an explanation of nationalism.

Notes: Chapter 4

For their criticisms of earlier drafts of this chapter, I am grateful to (in alphabetical order) Michael Hechter, David Laitin, Hudson Meadwell, Phillip Rawkins, Edward A. Tiryakian, and Ekkart Zimmermann, and all of the participants in the September 1980 meetings of the Research Planning Group. I owe special thanks to James Coleman, to Laitin, and to Zimmermann, for having pointed me to pertinent literature that I did not know. All remaining errors and omissions I modestly claim for myself.

1   Obviously there is a third logical possibility, in which neither culture has a monopoly of elite skills but one does monopolize nonelite positions and skills. I shall try to

show presently that such a situation is inherently explosive and ephemeral (see pp. 92–3).

2 Indeed, for many of the unassimilated upwardly mobile, the choice between class-based and nationalist politics is often unclear, as was for example the choice between Socialism and Zionism for many East European Jews before World War II, or between Socialism and nationalism for the young Nehru: see Brecher, 1959, p. 33.

3 Gourevitch's otherwise valuable contribution seems to me to neglect the "manipulative" nationalisms touched on here: see Gourevitch, 1979.

References: Chapter 4

Allum, P. A. (1973), *Italy—Republic without Government?* (New York: Norton).

Banton, Michael (1980), "Ethnic groups and the theory of rational choice," in UNESCO, *Sociological Theories: Race and Colonialism* (Paris: UNESCO), pp. 475–99.

Bates, Robert H. (1974), "Ethnic competition and modernization in contemporary Africa," *Comparative Political Studies*, vol. 6, no. 4, pp. 457–84.

Beard, Charles A., and Beard, Mary R. (1930), *The Rise of American Civilization* (New York: The Macmillan Co.).

Berger, Suzanne (1972), *Peasants against Politics: Rural Organization in Brittany, 1911–1967* (Cambridge, Mass.: Harvard University Press).

Bernstein, Basil B. (1971–5), *Class, Codes and Control*, 3 vols. (London: Routledge & Kegan Paul).

Birch, Anthony H. (1978), "Minority nationalist movements and theories of political integration," *World Politics*, vol. 30, no. 3, pp. 325–44.

Bloch, Marc (1961), *Feudal Society*, trans. L. A. Manyon (London: Routledge & Kegan Paul).

Blum, Jerome (1961), *Lord and Peasant in Russia: From the Ninth to the Nineteenth Century* (Princeton, N. J.: Princeton University Press).

Brand, Jack (1978), *The National Movement in Scotland* (London: Routledge & Kegan Paul).

Brecher, Michael (1959), *Nehru: A Political Biography*, abridged ed. (Boston, Mass.: Beacon Press).

Breton, Albert (1964), "Economics of nationalism," *Journal of Political Economy*, vol. 72, no. 4, pp. 376–86.

Brinton, Clarence Crane (1930), *The Jacobins: An Essay in the New History* (New York: The Macmillan Co.).

Burns, James MacGregor (1970), *Roosevelt: The Soldier of Freedom* (New York: Harcourt Brace Jovanovitch).

Cardoso, Fernando Henrique, and Faletto, Enzo (1979), *Dependency and Development in Latin America*, trans. Marjory Mattingly Urquidi (Berkeley, Calif.: University of California Press).

Connor, Walker (1972), "Nation-building or nation-destroying?" *World Politics*, vol. 24, no. 3 (April), pp. 319–55.

Daalder, Hans (1966), "The Netherlands: opposition in a segmented society," in Robert A. Dahl (ed.), *Political Oppositions in Western Democracies* (New Haven, Conn., and London: Yale University Press).

van den Doel, Hans (1979), *Democracy and Welfare Economics*, trans. Brigid Biggins (Cambridge: Cambridge University Press).

Furnivall, J. S. (1939), *Netherlands India: A Study in Plural Economy* (Cambridge: Cambridge University Press).

Geertz, Clifford (1963), "The integrative revolution: primordial sentiments and civil politics in the new states," in C. Geertz (ed.), *Old Societies and New States: The Quest for Modernity in Asia and Africa* (New York: The Free Press), pp. 105–57.

Gilpin, Robert (1974), "Integration and disintegration on the North American continent," *International Organization*, vol. 28, no. 4, pp. 851–74.

Gourevitch, Peter Alexis (1979), "The re-emergence of 'peripheral nationalisms': some comparative speculations on the spatial distribution of political leadership and economic growth," *Comparative Studies in Society and History*, vol. 21, no. 3, pp. 303–22.

Hamilton, Richard, and Pinard, Maurice (1976), "The bases of Parti Québécois support in recent Quebec elections," *Canadian Journal of Political Science*, vol. 9, no. 1, pp. 3–26.

Hechter, Michael (1975), *Internal Colonialism: The Celtic Fringe in British National Development* (London: Routledge & Kegan Paul; Berkeley and Los Angeles; Calif.: University of California Press).

Henderson, W. O. (1975), *The Rise of German Industrial Power, 1834–1914* (Berkeley and Los Angeles, Calif.; University of California Press).

Hilton, Rodney (1973), *Bond Men Made Free: Medieval Peasant Movements and the English Rising of 1381* (New York: Viking Press).

Hirschmann, Albert O. (1970), *Exit, Voice, and Loyalty: Responses to Decline in Firms, Organizations, and States* (Cambridge, Mass., and London: Harvard University Press).

Hobsbawm, Eric J. (1962), *The Age of Revolution: 1789–1848* (New York: New American Library).

Hobsbawm, Eric J. (1975) *The Age of Capital: 1848–1875* (New York: Charles Scribner's Sons).

Inglis, Brian (1973), *Roger Casement* (New York: Harcourt Brace Jovanovitch).

Katzenstein, Peter J. (1977), "Ethnic political conflict in South Tyrol," in M. J. Esman (ed.) *Ethnic Conflict in the Western World* (Ithaca, N. Y., and London: Cornell University Press), pp. 287–323.

Kieve, Ronald A. (1981), "Pillars of sand: a Marxist critique of consociational democracy in the Netherlands," *Comparative Politics*, vol. 13, no. 3, pp. 313–37.

Kuper, Leo, and Smith, M. G. (eds.) (1969), *Pluralism in Africa* (Berkeley and Los Angeles, Calif.: University of California Press).

LaForce, James Clayburn, Jr. (1965), *The Development of the Spanish Textile Industry, 1750–1800* (Berkeley and Los Angeles, Calif.: University of California Press).

Lee, J. J. (1979), "Sub-national regionalism or sub-state nationalism: the Irish case," in W. Link and W. Feld (eds.), *The New Nationalism: Implications for Transatlantic Relations* (New York: Pergamon), pp. 114–18.

Lijphart, Arend (1977a), *Democracy in Plural Societies: A Comparative Exploration* (New Haven, Conn. and London: Yale University Press).

Lijphart, Arend (1977b), "Political theories and the explanation of ethnic conflict in the Western world: falsified predictions and plausible postdictions," in M. J. Esman (ed.), *Ethnic Conflict in the Western World* (Ithaca, N. Y., and London: Cornell University Press), pp. 46–64.

Lipset, Seymour Martin, and Bendix, Reinhard (1959), *Social Mobility in Industrial Society* (Berkeley and Los Angeles, Calif.: University of California Press).

Loewenberg, Peter (1980), *Walther Rathenau and Henry Kissinger: The Jew as a Modern Statesman in Two Political Cultures*, Leo Baeck Memorial Lecture No. 24 (New York: Leo Baeck Institute).

Lorwin, Val R. (1966), "Belgium: religion, class, and language in national politics," in R. A. Dahl (ed.), *Political Oppositions in Western Democracies* (New Haven, Conn., and London: Yale university Press), pp. 147–87.

Machiavelli, Niccolo (1513), *The Prince*.

Meadwell, Hudson (1982), "The political economy of cultural mobilization; Quebec and Brittany, 1870–1918," paper presented at Third Conference of Europeanists, Washington, D. C., 29 April–1 May.

Merkl, Peter H. (1975), *Political Violence under the Swastika: 581 Early Nazis* (Princeton, N.J.: Princeton University Press).

Moore, Barrington, Jr. (1966), *Social Origins of Dictatorship and Democracy: Lord and Peasant in the Making of the Modern World* (Boston, Mass.: Beacon Press).

Olson, Mancur, Jr. (1968), *The Logic of Collective Action* (New York: Schocken Books).

Plumb, J. H. (1961), *The Italian Renaissance: A Concise Survey of its History and Culture* (New York and Evanston, Ill.: Harper Torchbooks).

Popkin, Samuel (1979), *The Rational Peasant: The Political Economy of Rural Society in Vietnam* (Berkeley, Calif.: University of California Press).

Riker, William H., and Ordeshook, Peter C. (1973), *An Introduction to Positive Political Theory* (Englewood Cliffs, N.J.: Prentice-Hall).

Rogowski, Ronald (1974), *Rational Legitimacy: A Theory of Political Support* (Princeton, N.J.: Princeton University Press).

Rogowski, Ronald (1980), "Understanding nationalism: the possible contributions of a general theory of political cleavage," paper presented at annual meeting of the International Studies Association, Los Angeles, 19–22 March.

Rokkan, Stein (1966), "Norway: numerical democracy and corporate pluralism," in R. A. Dahl (ed.), *Political Oppositions in Western Democracies* (New Haven, Conn., and London: Yale University Press), pp. 70–115.

Rokkan, Stein (1974), "Entries, voices, exits; toward a possible generalization of the Hirschman model," *Social Sciences Information*, vol. 13, no. 1, pp. 39–53.

Rose, Richard (1971), *Governing without Consensus: An Irish Perspective* (London: Faber).

Scullard, Howard H. (1961), *A History of the Roman World from 753 to 146 BC*, 3rd ed. (New York: Barnes & Noble).

Skocpol, Theda (1979), *States and Social Revolutions: A Comparative Analysis of France, Russia, and China* (Cambridge: Cambridge University Press).

Thompson, E. P. (1963), *The Making of the English Working Class* (New York: Vintage Books).

Weber, Eugen (1976), *Peasants into Frenchmen: The Modernization of Rural France 1870–1914* (Stanford, Calif.: Stanford University Press).

Weber, Max (1958), *From Max Weber: Essays in Sociology*, trans. and ed. Hans Gerth and C. Wright Mills (New York: Oxford University Press/Galaxy Books).

Weber, Max (1964), *Wirtschaft und Gesellschaft: Grundriss der verstehenden*

Soziologie, ed. Johannes Winckelmann (Cologne and Berlin: Kiepenheuer & Witsch).

White, Lynn, Jr. (1966), *Medieval Technology and Social Change* (New York: Oxford University Press/Galaxy Books).

Wolfenstein, E. Victor (1971), *The Revolutionary Personality: Lenin, Trotsky, Gandhi*, paperback ed. (Princeton, N.J.: Princeton University Press).

Zolberg, Aristide (1979), round-table remarks, session of Council of European Studies Research Planning Group, Duke University, 30 August −3 September.

5

Economic Integration, National Policies, and the Rationality of Regional Separatism

Mario Polèse

Introduction

In this chapter we propose a conceptual framework for analyzing regional separatism. The costs and benefits (to the region) from separation will vary under different conditions; they will also vary according to the degree of separation desired. Following from our definition of separation, we propose to break down the economic aspects of separation into three composite dimensions, where each dimension both represents an exogenous variable describing existing economic links (affecting the potential costs and benefits of separation) and an endogenous variable which may be integrated into the separatist option, thus modifying it and the associated costs and benefits.

Our analysis basically is concerned with the Western industrialized world. We exclude the possibility of outright "colonialist" exploitation and refer, by definition, to regions within existing states. Much of our reasoning is derived from a broader study (Bonin and Polèse, 1980) on the costs and benefits of varying forms of economic association between the Province of Quebec and the rest of Canada under conditions of political sovereignty for the former. The basic thrust of our analysis nevertheless goes beyond the particular conditions of the Quebec situation.

The region is treated as if it were a distinct and homogeneous decision-making unit (which of course it is not), whose objective it is to maximize its welfare, defined either in terms of total or per capita gross regional product.

Defining Separation

We may consider a region as separate when it ceases to be a region: when it assumes the status of a state.

In strictly legal terms this means the assertion of sovereignty and, at least in principle, the recognition of that sovereignty by other members of the international community. Interregional links are replaced by international links. Despite occasional practical difficulties—for example, the case of Taiwan today, or Rhodesia between 1965 and 1980, or indeed Canada before 1931—this strictly legal definition of separation is both clearcut and simple; a state is either recognized as sovereign or it is not. We shall call this political separation or, equivalently, "sovereignty," "independence," or "full political autonomy."

The economic notion of separation is much less clearcut. If we look at increasing levels of separation as a continuum, we may locate the region along three distinct but related dimensions according to the region's position on each:

(1) the level of economic integration (or disintegration), defined here as the absence (or inversely the importance) of institutional barriers to trade and to factor movements between the regions of the system;[1]
(2) the importance (or absence) of systemwide economic policies and institutions to which the region is subject, including and in addition to those needed to ensure economic integration;
(3) the level of interregional transfer payments.[2]

The higher a region's score on each dimension, the further it is from full economic separation. Each dimension may thus equally be understood as an attempt to distinguish between the economic concept of region, as opposed to the concept of state.

A high score on the first dimension means that a region has no real borders in economic terms; its economy is necessarily open; and barriers to trade do not exist.[3] Goods and factors flow freely between regions of the same state. No such freedom of movement need exist between states, although it may prevail there also, as in the case of a common market. The absence of barriers to trade and factor movements is thus not necessarily incompatible with political separation. But while various levels of economic integration are compatible with the concept of state, a high level of economic integration is basic to the concept of region.

A second feature distinguishes the region from the state in terms of economics. Basic economic policy decisions are, in general, determined at the level of the state, not the region. Regional governments may exist and possess broad powers, as in the case of a federal system; but such tools as trade policy, monetary policy, and at least in part fiscal policy traditionally remain in the hands of the "national" government. A state is, in principle, an autonomous unit in terms of all economic policy matters. It may choose to share its prerogatives with other governments or to coordinate its actions, especially if this is needed to maintain economic integration; and this may entail institutions which carry out systemwide policies similar to those of a sovereign government. But a state, in contrast to a region, is free to choose.

A third factor increasingly distinguishes regions from states, especially among modern industrial societies: regions may derive a significant portion of their income (or, inversely, incur losses) from interregional transfer payments channeled through the larger state.[4] Certain states may equally give or receive transfer payments (to or from other states), as in the case of foreign aid, but such payments are generally small compared to interregional payments and far more volatile.

In sum, full *economic* separation would mean: the erection of significant trade barriers (or, in the extreme case, the cessation of all trade); the discontinuance of all common systemwide economic policies, agreements, or institutions; and the suspension of all transfer payments. At the other end of the spectrum full economic union would entail free trade, common economic policies and institutions, and possibly interregional transfer payments. Similarly, in the extreme case approaching political union, common policies and institutions (including a common currency) would cover a very wide range of activities. Under conditions of *political* union (nonsovereign regions) the functions and objectives implied in the three dimensions are usually assumed by the "national" government, for they express the classical policy objectives of the modern state: integration of the "national" market (efficiency maximization under free market conditions), economic growth and stabilization, and redistribution of wealth.

Although political and economic autonomy are traditionally related, they do not necessarily follow from each other. A nonsovereign entity may possess all or most of the economic characteristics of a state (for instance, Hong Kong), while certain sovereign states may satisfy all or most of the economic conditions of a region (for instance, Luxemburg and certainly ministates like Liechtenstein or Monaco).

The Limits of Economic Analysis

The rationale underlying demands for regional political separatism or autonomy need not be economic. This is in part linked to the very nature of regional autonomist movements and in part to the incapacity of economic analysis to come to terms with long-range macroproblems.

As Hansen (1978) points out, it is difficult to explain regional separatism in terms of regional disparities. Among regions where independence movements exist, we find some whose per capita income is below that of the existing state average (for example, Quebec, Brittany, and Scotland) and some whose per capita income is above that level (for example, Croatia, Catalonia, and the Basque country).

Economic grievances may well be among the factors that impel a region to seek full political autonomy, but they will rarely suffice to explain why independence is entertained at all as a possible option. In the Canadian case Quebec is neither the poorest nor the richest province. The Atlantic provinces, all poorer than Quebec, may with some justice feel themselves to be "exploited" (to use Hansen's term); yet sovereignty is not entertained as a feasible solution. At the other end of the scale independence has not been seriously considered by richer provinces such as Ontario or Alberta[5] which may, with equal justice, see themselves as "subsidizing" the rest of Canada (specifically via transfer payments).

If the Canadian experience can be generalized (and it probably can), the drive for full regional autonomy will have its roots elsewhere, in a deep-seated sense of regional identity, which in turn may be traced back to any number of factors including economics: language, culture, ethnicity, religion, geography, and so on. In short, for independence to be considered at all, the inhabitants of a region (or a significant proportion thereof) must see themselves as forming a distinct *nation*.[6] The origins of a sense of nationhood fall beyond the scope (or competence) of this chapter. Suffice it to say that, in all cases where significant regional independence movements exist, the advocates of that option call themselves "nationalists". One thus speaks of Scottish, Basque, or Quebecois nationalists. By the same token the proponents of independence

always speak of national independence (or even national liberation), while their opponents generally prefer to use the word
"separation," thus stressing the sense of loyalty to the larger
state.

Political separation is a long-term commitment based on the
wager that a society will, over the long run, be better off if it
forms a sovereign state. Economics really has very little to say
about this. It is, for example, impossible to say if Belgium
would today be better or worse off if it had remained part of
the Netherlands (or of France for that matter), or if Ireland
would be better or worse off if it had remained part of the
United Kingdom. As Kuznets (1966) has consistently pointed
out, economic growth defined as a long-term rise in per capita
income is largely a matter of culture, organization, and institutions. Nor is per capita national income always correlated
positively with national size. Equally, in models of the Denison
(1974) type, the "residual" (which is largely a measure of our
ignorance) continues to explain the larger portion of per capita
economic growth. On the other hand, culture, organization,
and institutions may in part be a function of the region's
political status and, therefore, pertinent to the debate over
sovereignty.

Economics basically remains a static science emphasizing
efficiency maximization (resource allocation) under given conditions. Economics thus tends, by nature, to be antiseparatist (or
antinationalist if one prefers) in as much as nationalism is traditionally equated with protectionism;[7] see for example Migué
(1979) in the Canadian case. This largely limits the effects of
separation to the erection of trade barriers. The long-term
effects on the region of a redefinition of statewide policies are
admittedly far more difficult to analyze, although the "static"
allocation and redistribution effects of national policies (including transfer payments) lend themselves more easily to economic
analysis.

Yet for most regions, the rationale for separation will in part
be based on the postulate that the positive effects of a redefinition (or regionalization) of statewide policies will, over the long
run, outweigh the negative effects of diminishing economic
integration. By the same token the greater visibility of immediate "static" costs (associated with trade barriers and/or the
cessation of transfer payments) v. the uncertainty of future
gains probably goes a long way to explaining the difficulties of
many separatist movements. For example, the popular perception of the immediacy of short-term "static" costs v. the uncer-

tainty of future gains undoubtedly played a role in the May 1980 defeat of the Quebec government's proposal for sovereignty-association.

This does not mean that the economic implications of separation cannot be put to scrutiny, but only that the analyst must remain aware of the limits of the tools at his disposal. In this sense the analysis that follows is necessarily partial, dealing only with those economic aspects that can be captured by our conceptual framework.

The Costs and Benefits of Separation

Given our three-dimensional framework, let us then consider the possible costs and benefits of political separation, depending on the existing (and desired) level of economic separation. Changes in position on each dimension will imply costs. We assume that the region seeks the most economically profitable solution compatible with political separation. A region may wish (of course) to maximize its political and economic autonomy, even at the cost of diminishing economic welfare (at least in the short run); but we shall not consider this alternative, since we are only considering *economic* costs and benefits. Rationally the region will consider its performance, as a region, on each dimension in order to evaluate the potential costs and benefits of varying changes in position and, in turn, formulate its separatist option so as to minimize cost and maximize benefits. (See Table 5.1.)

Economic Integration: Trade Flows

Given free trade at the outset, economic disintegration should represent a cost for the region. Those costs, at least in "static" terms, are fairly easy to estimate (see, for example, Hazeldine, 1978, and Courville, 1979, in the Canadian case). The potential costs are basically a function of two variables:

(1) the importance of trade between the regions;
(2) the importance of the protection (*vis-à-vis* third-party states) which that trade enjoys.

In the case of very little trade, as might be the case between very distant regions, the costs would be minimal and the region should thus be fairly indifferent as to the maintenance (or cessation) of economic integration. Equally, in the case where

Table 5.1 *The Economic Dimensions of Regionalism/Nationalism*

Description	Dimension 1 Economic integration	Dimension 2 Systemwide economic policies	Dimension 3 Interregional transfer payments
Definition	Absence of institutional barriers to interregional trade and factor flows	Systemwide (common) policies and institutions: may include various elements: fiscal policies (subsidies, incentives, investments, etc.): monetary policy and regulatory measures	Net regional redistribution of public expenditures (and revenues), channeled through the systemwide government
Systemwide objective	Integration of "national" (system) market: efficiency maximization	Economic growth and stability of the system	Equity: redistribution of income
Government intervention	Essentially a supervisory or regulatory function	In part a fiscal function, but also a regulatory function dealing chiefly with trade, transportation, and financial institutions	Wholly a fiscal function
Compatibility with the political separation (sovereignty) of composite regions	Compatible	Partial compatibility; largely compatible for regulatory functions; less so for many fiscal measures	Incompatible, at least not at the level usually understood for political unions
Costs or benefits of separation	Depends on the importance of interregional trade (and other flows) and on the level of outside protection	Depends on the importance of systemwide policies and on their regional impact	Depends on the net interregional balance (and relative importance) of central government expenditures and revenues
Quantification of impact	Direct static effects fairly easy to measure	Very complex; almost impossible to measure dynamic effects	Direct effects very clear, less so for indirect dynamic effects

intense trade relationships do exist but in the absence of protectionist policies towards other states, the costs of separation should be minimal, since we may assume that such trade will remain competitive and also that the (politically) separate region will continue to be integrated into the rest of the world economy.

The second variable, the level of protectionism, is a measure of the degree of integration of the state (from which the region is separating itself) with other multistate systems or states. The greater the level of integration, or of international economic collaboration if one prefers, the less should be the costs of separation. Thus in the case of a region separating from the Netherlands, for example, the costs would be reduced to the extent that the Netherlands already functions in a broader competitive context (Benelux and the European Economic Communities, EEC) and the region would also continue to function in that context. By the same token, in the Canadian case, the reduction of Canadian–United States trade barriers should over the long run reduce the potential costs to Quebec of separation, again assuming that Quebec would continue to function within the same context.

In the extreme case of total world economic integration there would in principle be no costs to separation in terms of trade, since political independence would no longer be related to trade barriers.[8] It is thus not entirely surprising that many regional separatist movements tend to be antiprotectionist (or more precisely, "continentalist"), contrary to the traditional antinationalist wisdom. European regionalist movements often look to European integration as their solution.

In the case where the system is very protectionist toward third parties, and where significant interregional trade is at stake, the costs of economic separation may be important.[9] This fairly well represents the Canadian case, where internal trade enjoys a relatively high level of protection (Dauphin, 1978; Martens and Corbo, 1978). Quebec's desire specifically to maintain economic integration with the rest of Canada (Quebec, 1979) is thus rational, logically following Canada's past and present protectionist policies.

Economic Integration: Factor Flows

The costs and benefits of interrupting factor flows depend on the importance of those flows that affect the region. Interregional capital flows are extremely difficult to measure, and so too is their impact on the region. Labor flows are fairly easy to determine, but a disagreement exists as to their ultimate regional impact; the neoclassical model holds that labor migration has a dampening effect on regional disparities, but this may not necessarily be true under all conditions (Polèse, 1978).

Concerning labor flows, the costs of economic separation may be significant for labor-exporting regions, where the rest of the larger state constitutes an important destination, for example, Puerto Rico *vis-à-vis* the United States or Corsica relative to mainland France. As in the case of trade, the relative openness of other states would serve to reduce costs, both for the region and for individuals, in that they would provide alternative destinations for labor emigration. We would thus expect labor surplus regions to favor economic integration at this level, both within the existing state and with other states. This may be less clear for labor-importing regions, since alternative sources of labor exist in most cases; also states generally seek to control immigration and not emigration (at least among Western democracies).

In part because the regional economic effects of migration are difficult to estimate, the rationale for maintaining (or disrupting) free labor flows may equally depend on other factors, especially if migration is linked to factors like ethnicity, culture, and language, which may in part be at the core of the region's quest for political autonomy. But precisely because the region will often possess a very different culture from that of the rest of the system, interregional labor mobility may already be very low (this is certainly the case between French Quebec and English Canada), and separation as such is likely to have little regional economic (or cultural) impact.[10] The political costs of establishing new barriers to migration may, on the other hand, be very high, especially if there is a long tradition of free interaction between regions:[11] people do not in general appreciate border controls or limits to their freedom of movement. It is interesting to note in this respect that almost total freedom of movement continues to exist between the Republic of Ireland and the United Kingdom, but this is also rational in regional economic terms (certainly for Ireland), since the Republic is a net labor-exporting region.

Capital-exporting regions could benefit from increased autonomy in so far as barriers to capital movements would permit them to stem such outflows or, more precisely, increase the net rate of regional capital formation. But unlike labor flows, capital flows are extremely difficult to control; many economists would maintain that controls are ineffective at best and counterproductive in more cases than not (in fact repelling or discouraging outside investment). To the extent that the state already functions within a relatively open world economy (in terms of money flows) and that the region would also continue to do so, it is unlikely that the region would gain much from separation in terms of controlling capital flows. Thus it is unlikely, for example, that a separate Scotland, within a European framework, would significantly increase its capacity to reduce capital outflows. By the same token and to the extent that an orderly economic multistate framework already exists, and that the region is accepted into it, the costs of separation will also be minimized.

In sum, on the first dimension, in a world of total freedom of movement for all goods and factors (total economic integration) both the potential costs and benefits from separation would be minimized. At this point political separation is, in economic terms, analogous to simple political autonomy. Correspondingly, pure autonomist movements (no political separation) would not be based on a desire to modify significantly this dimension.

Statewide Economic Policies

While political separation (and *a fortiori* simple autonomy) need not necessarily entail economic disintegration, it *must* mean a change in the political process underlying statewide economic policies, and logically a change in the regional impact of those policies. Regions should thus expect to reap benefits on this dimension by altering their political status. It is unlikely that a change in position on the first dimension (economic disintegration) would *as such* bring gains to the region without its being linked to possible benefits on the second dimension.

The costs or benefits from political separation on the second dimension are basically a function of two variables:

(1)　the importance of economic policies determined at the statewide level, or at any other level where the state is the basic decision-making unit;
(2)　the impact of those policies on the region.

The Importance of Central Economic Policies

If few or no economic policies are determined at the state (or international) level, little economic rationale would seem to exist for separation. Correspondingly, as the economic powers of the region grew (in a very loose federation, for example), so the economic rationale for separation would decrease; up to the point where the region would in fact acquire the powers of a state. Depending on one's point of view, devolution (as in the Scottish case) may thus be seen as either a way to forestall sovereignty or as a halfway house to political separation. Thus one might argue that the powers of the Province of Quebec, which have increased since the nationalist upsurge of the 1960s, make the need for full autonomy less urgent. If this is true, then Quebec "indépendentistes" are partly victims of their own success of the reforms which they have called forth.

In the extreme case of decentralization, that is to say, a totally free market economy without state intervention, the economic rationale for separation would cease to exist, since the state would no longer be an economic agent. That would also mean that there would be no costs to separation on this dimension. Thus, as Boisvert (1980) notes, Norway's separation from Sweden in 1905 entailed few visible costs, a fact that he explains in part by the very limited powers of the state at that time, both in terms of regulation and public expenditures. Inversely as the economic power of the state grows, including the associated costs and benefits, so the rationale for political separation, or at least increased autonomy, grows. It is thus not surprising that regional autonomist movements are in part a post-Keynesian phenomenon. As the state is increasingly perceived as the chief architect of the economy, so the powers that the state embodies increasingly become the object of contention. If, on the other hand, the state despite its powers is seen as intrinsically inefficient in economic terms, or if its real impact on the larger statewide economy is considered questionable, then logically the case for separation would also appear less clear.

Following the same line of reasoning, the impetus for political separation should increase as the number and importance of global, continental, or multistate organizations or economic decision centers grows; for the state remains, in principle, the chief participating decision unit in such organizations. Examples such as the General Agreement on Tariffs and Trade (GATT), the International Monetary Fund (IMF), or the European Economic Community (EEC) immediately spring to mind. To the extent that economic relations or policies are internationalized, and dependent on relations between states, the region would appear to have an interest in possessing a distinct international identity.[12] If, after all, Luxemburg and Ireland are present at the negotiating table, why not Brittany or Puerto Rico? Conversely, to the extent that regions participate in processes of international decision, even if only as part of larger state delegations, the rationale for political separation will weaken.[13]

The Regional Impact of Central Government

In most cases we would expect the economic rationale for increased autonomy or political separation to be based on the postulate that existing statewide policies are detrimental to the region, or at least not as beneficial as they could be, or again that the existing state does not sufficiently represent the region's interest on the international plane. It is indeed difficult to imagine a region wishing to separate for economic reasons if existing state economic policies are perceived as acting in its favor. Given the number and the variety of state policies, it is in most cases impossible to measure rigorously their net impact on the region. The regional impact of central government policies thus often becomes a subject of political debate. In the Canadian case the Quebec government tends to stress the detrimental effects of federal policies (Quebec, 1979), while the federal government stresses the positive impacts (Canada, 1979).

Looking at Canada, we in fact found that different central government policies often tend to act at cross-purposes and to cancel out each other's interregional effects, so that the net aggregate impact of government intervention on the regional distribution of economic activity may be far less than expected given the importance of government programs (Bonin and Polèse, 1979). It would indeed be difficult to show that federal intervention has significantly affected Quebec's aggregate relative economic standing within Canada in one direction or the other.[14]

To this extent those favoring sovereignty have some warrant to argue that any federal policies have basically served to confirm existing trends, first, to accentuate the concentration of economic activity in Ontario and, more recently, at least not to retard the Western movement of the Canadian economy.[15] At another level Fortin (1980a) argues that the goods and services provided by the federal government may simply not reflect the consumer preferences of the Quebec population. This in part raises the question of applying "national" homogeneous policy criteria to a system composed of regions with varying cultures, economic structures, and geographical characteristics. But Fortin (1980b) equally suggests that Quebec would stand to gain from a distinct fiscal policy, within the limits allowed by a common currency, given the difference in economic structures and business cycles.

It is reasonable to assume that specific policies, not necessarily linked to economic integration, could often be at least as efficiently carried out at the local level: housing, labor retraining, harbor administration, and so on, not to mention education and health, which are already provincial responsibilities in Canada. Reasoning on a statewide level, the problem largely comes down to determining which is the most efficient (spatial) level for implementing a given policy. In many cases there is no *a priori* reason for believing that it need be the larger state. In such cases political separation or increased autonomy may mean a more efficient framework for policy implementation and formulation.

For other economic policies, however, regionalization may enter into conflict with the desire to maintain the economic integration of the system.[16] The absence of trade barriers necessarily means a common trade policy toward third parties, except in the case of a free trade area, the most elementary case of economic integration. In this sense we may speak of a *tradeoff* between the costs of economic disintegration and the benefits of distinct regional economic policies. This tradeoff will vary from region to region. As already noted, the cost of economic separation on the first dimension could be fairly important in the Canada–Quebec case, given the present level of protectionism. On the other hand, the potential benefits of forming distinct economic policies, especially with respect to trade and capital flows, appear relatively limited in both the Canadian and the Quebecois cases, given the high degree of interdependence with the North American economy. Under present conditions the tradeoffs in this case would appear to favor the maintenance both of economic integration and of protection *vis-à-vis* third parties.

The decision to maintain economic integration and common policies need not mean that the region approaches the existing statewide policies. The absence of internal barriers to trade is one thing and the impact of central policies another: even if economic flows are unimpeded, their intensity and direction may in part be a consequence of certain central policies. In other words, "unbalanced growth" (as expressed by the direction of economic flows) is not necessarily a consequence of economic integration as such, but may also in part be a result of "unbalanced" economic policies, which may or may not accompany economic integration.[17] For an economy where capital is mobile but labor is not, for cultural reasons for example, we should expect compensatory policies to ensure a "balanced" distribution of demand, or to achieve adjustment through other (price) mechanisms: flexible factor prices, regionalized monetary policies, and so on. In short, the separating region that wants to maintain economic integration and associated common policies must necessarily assume that new common policies will better serve its interests than the old, or at least that systemwide policies determined within a new framework compatible with political separation will not worsen its situation. Thus, in the Canadian case, the maintenance of a common trade policy, implying the present level of protectionism, can be interpreted as a short-term, cost minimization decision, which need not necessarily mean that the composite regions (specifically Quebec) agree with the long-run structural effects of the present policy.

Given common policies, the question thus boils down to a choice of political processes. The region implicitly assumes that it will have more political "clout" in determining common policies as a sovereign state than it has within the framework of a political union.[18] From the point of view of the whole system we may equally ask which is the more efficient framework for managing the economy. Exactly the same economic result could, in theory, be produced by one central government, or by several sovereign states joined in an economic association. Whether this is in fact possible often depends more on political judgment than on economics. Much of the debate in the Canadian case centered around the comparative efficiency of sovereignty-association v. federalism for managing the Canadian economy (Maxwell and Pestieau, 1980; Smiley, 1980).

Interregional Transfer Payments

Unlike the previous dimension, the impact of interregional transfer payments, defined as the net interregional distribution of central government expenditures and revenues, is relatively easy to determine, at least in "static" terms. Thus, a region which is "subsidizing" the rest of the system should, in principle, gain from political separation, while the opposite would be true for a region being subsidized. In the Canadian case Quebec has been a net subsidized region since about 1973 (it was a net subsidizer before); the net inflow of federal expenditures into Quebec currently accounts for about 2 percent of gross regional product (Canada, 1978). Logically, a politically sovereign Quebec should have to forgo this income, at least in part, since we have postulated that interregional transfer payments are incompatible with political separation (Table 5.1), at least at the level that generally prevails within a political union.[19] According to our framework, separation on this dimension, unlike the two previous ones, automatically accompanies political separation.

In the cases where central government expenditures do constitute an important source of regional income, and thus a net inflow, separation could indeed appear very costly, at least in static terms. This is certainly true of Atlantic Canada as well as of many traditionally "peripheral" regions in other Western nations. Autonomist groups in such regions are faced with a dilemma; indeed, the popular call may be for more central government spending and thus implicitly for greater dependence on the central government. For such regions heavily dependent on transfer payments, we may speak of a tradeoff between money and power; or in terms of our framework between the regions' relative positions on dimensions 2 and 3.

This raises the question of the long-term, nonstatic effects of transfer payments on productivity, innovation, efficiency, and so on. If we take only the direct impact of transfer payments, it is clear that a net inflow must be beneficial. But for a system whose policies include significant redistributive elements, this leads to the somewhat troublesome conclusion that the poorer a region is, relative to the rest of the system, and thus the greater its net receipts of central government expenditures, the more the region is profiting from political union. Following this line of reasoning, "peripheral" regions such as Corsica, Ulster, or Sicily, which are relatively dependent on central government generosity, would be considered as the chief beneficiaries of political union, a proposition with which many inhabitants of those regions would undoubtedly take issue. Many would probably maintain that these payments are simply a "just" compensation for the regional impact of "unbalanced" systemwide policies whose effects are more profound but also more difficult to measure. Courchene (1978) argues, in the Canadian case, that many transfer schemes only serve to prolong regional disparities, by concealing the need for necessary adjustments. Yet it is difficult totally to deny their utility. The resolution of this debate falls beyond the scope of this chapter.

Finally, for the Quebec example, we may summarize the Lévesque government's 1980 proposal of sovereignty-association as follows within our three-dimensional framework: Quebec was willing to accept costs on the third dimension; it did not expect to incur significant costs or benefits on the first dimension, precisely because it intended to leave it unchanged; and it hoped to reap significant benefits on the second dimension, especially in the long run. As we have seen, the costs are easier to measure than the benefits and this is probably true in most cases.

Conclusion

Given our framework, we hypothesize that the costs of regional separatism would be minimized—or benefits maximized—or both, under the following conditions:

(1) Little trade or other economic relations between regions; or, in the opposite case, the maintenance of interregional economic integration, and/or the existence of economic integration as a general world (or multination) rule; as a corollary, the presence of an orderly world economic system, or of multistate blocs, into which the separated region would be accepted.
(2) A perception that systemwide ("national" or international) policies have either had little significant effect on the underlying spatial trends of the economy, or that their effects have been clearly unfavourable for the region, *and* that separation would increase or at least not diminish the region's capacity to influence those policies.
(3) Evidence that interregional governmental transfer payments either have a marginal effect on the regional economy or translate into a net outflow of money.

This is the ideal case. For many regions, located in Western nations where redistributive policies are important, conditions 2 and 3 are probably in conflict. The first condition is largely limited to a cost minimization objective: to the extent that it is not met, the region must equally consider tradeoffs between possible losses on condition 1 and possible gains on 2 and/or 3.

But given the present state of the art, it is impossible to determine rigorously tradeoffs between dimensions of differing timeframes and levels of quantification. In most cases the debate surrounding separation or regional autonomy will thus remain largely noneconomic, if only because of the political content of some of the economic dimensions themselves.

Notes: Chapter 5

I should like to thank my colleagues at the Institut national de recherche scientifique (INRS), Raymond Bazinet, Yves Bussière and Marc Termote, for their comments, as well as Bernard Bonin at the Ecole nationale d'administration publique, Caroline Pestieau of the C. D. Howe Research Institute (Montreal) and Pierre Fortin of Laval University (Quebec City). Another version of this chapter has previously appeared in the *Canadian Journal of Regional Science*, vol. IV, no. 1, 1981, pp. 1–19, which we would like to thank for its kind cooperation.

1   This is not necessarily equivalent to the importance of trade between regions. Thus there is relatively little trade betwen Quebec and British Columbia (two Canadian provinces); trade between Quebec and New York State is certainly more important despite the existence of legal trade barriers. As for all flows, trade is also a function of mass and distance.

2   This dimension, unlike the two others, is not a primary element of the economic region–state continuum. Interregional transfer payments are, in other words, not a necessary condition of regional (as opposed to state) existence, while economic integration and systemwide policies are.

3   Barriers to trade and to factor movements do in fact exist between certain regions, as in the case of American states or Canadian provinces.

4   The expression "transfer payments" is employed here as a proxy for all central government expenditures, since in regional accounting terms this distinction is of little significance. The question thus becomes; does the central government spend more (or less) in a region than it receives from it, abstracting from the national debt?

5   In more recent years a small independence movement has in fact emerged in western Canada. But if our reasoning is correct, such a movement would stand little chance of success if it is based purely on economic grievances (that is, without the prerequisite existence of a sense of western Canadian nationhood).

6   The word "nation" is used here in the sociological sense. Some would say, in the Quebec case, that the defeat of the Quebec government's proposal for sovereignty-association may thus in part be traced back to an insufficient sense of Quebec nationhood, compared to the feeling of loyalty to the Canadian whole. Implicitly we may surmise that the sense of Canadian identity is still very strong in Quebec.

7   Another way of defining the debate is between economists who see nationalism as a consumption good and those who see it as a production good.

8   Correspondingly, simple regional autonomy (without political independence) involves no significant costs on this dimension, since simple autonomy is not, in principle, related to trade barriers.

9   It would be more accurate to say that the costs to the region are difficult to predict, but the costs to the individual may be more apparent. For labor mobility, we may thus talk of a possible conflict between the perceived regional weal and the individual weal.

10   Conversely, in cases where mobility is important, we may easily imagine a region wishing to control immigration in order to "protect" its ethnic makeup. The desire to control interregional immigration may thus be a powerful impetus to autonomy

or separation. In the Quebecois and Belgian cases this control is in part indirectly achieved through regionalized language legislation.

11 Perceived costs to individuals may in part be considered as a proxy for political costs.

12 On the other hand, one might say that the region is trading one minority status (on the intranational level) for another (on the international level).

13 Admittedly, at this point, the political distinction between state and region starts to become fuzzy.

14 Abstracting for the moment from regional transfer payments, our third dimension.

15 Inhabitants of the region need not feel that central government policies are intentionally detrimental. To the extent that the underlying spatial trends of the economy seem to be going against the region, they may simply feel that state policies are doing little to arrest those trends.

16 This conflict of objectives will be minimized if there is little trade between the regions or, in another context, if economic integration is the general world (or continental) rule.

17 "Unbalanced" growth may equally be attributed to other factors such as differential resource endowment or changing international demand. Since the 1973 energy crisis this factor has become increasingly important and, in the Canadian case, largely explains Alberta's recent prosperity and the increasing tensions between energy-producing provinces and the central government.

18 Although this question falls within the realm of political science, we as economists may postulate that political separation will more likely increase the region's bargaining power the less its power already is. Thus a region that dominates a state will feel little impetus to separate. Some would say that this is the case for Flanders today, in Belgium, for Ontario in Canada, and certainly for England in the United Kingdom. Conversely, minority regions will feel more political pressure to separate. This is certainly one of the most compelling arguments for Quebecois sovereignty, since Quebec accounts for 27 percent of the Canadian population, with demographic trends predicting a further decline. On the other hand, Slovenia, one of Yugoslavia's smallest republics, remains very loyal to the Yugoslav federation, in part because it offers a sense of security against larger, neighbouring Italian and German cultures. Some might wish to draw a parallel with Canada–Quebec and its large American neighbor.

19 Perhaps the most notable exception to this rule is the Common Agricultural Policy (CAP) which does involve fairly important interstate transfer payments. On the other hand, the recent tensions within the EEC are largely attributable to the CAP. We may equally refer to less costly EEC programs such as the European Investment Fund or Regional Development Fund.

References: Chapter 5

Boisvert, Michel (1980), *Les Implications économique de la souveraineté-association: le Canada face à l'expérience des pays nordiques* (Montreal: Les Presses de l'Université de Montréal).

Bonin, Bernard, and Polèse, Mario (1979), "The regional impact of national policies: lessons from the Canadian experience," paper presented at the 1979 Meeting of the Regional Science Association, Los Angeles, November.

Bonin, Bernard, and Polèse, Mario (1980), *A Propos de l'association économique Canada Québec* (Quebec City: Ecole Nationale d'Administration Publique).

Canada (1978), *Provincial Economic Accounts, Experimental Data*, catalogue 3-1100-505 (Ottawa: Statistics Canada).

Canada (1979), *Understanding Canada*, series of studies prepared under the auspices of the Canadian Unity Office (Ottawa: Government of Canada).

Courchene, Thomas (1978), "Avenues of adjustment: the transfer system and regional disparities," in Michael Walker (ed.), *Canadian Confederation at the Crossroads* (Vancouver: Fraser Institute).

Courville, Leon, Dagenais, M., Nappi, C., and Van Peeterson, A. (1979), *La Sensibilité des industries au commerce interrégional: le cas du Québec, de l'Ontario et du reste du Canada* (Quebec City: Ministère des Affaires Intergouvernementales).

Dauphin, Roma (1978), *The Impact of Free Trade in Canada*, No. 22–56 (Ottawa: Economic Council of Canada).

Denison, E. F. (1974), *Accounting for United States Economic Growth 1926–69* (Washington, D. C.: Brookings Institute).

Doder, Dosko (1979), *The Yugoslavs* (New York: Vintage Books).

Fortin, Pierre (1980a), "La souveraineté-association est-elle un projet économiquement viable?," *Critère*, no. 28, pp. 153–76.

Fortin, Pierre (1980b), *Unemployment, Inflation and Economic Stabilization in Quebec* (Montreal: C. D. Howe Research Institute), pp. 143–52.

Hansen, Niles (1978), "Economic aspects of regional separatism," *Papers of the Regional Science Association*, vol. 41, pp. 143–52.

Hazeldine, Tim (1978), *The Costs and Benefits of the Canadian Customs Union* (Ottawa: Economic Council of Canada).

Kuznets, Simon (1966), *Toward a Theory of Economic Growth* (New York: Norton).

Martens, A. and Corbo, V. (1978), *Le Tarif extérieur canadien et la protection de l'activité manufacturière québécoise, 1966–74*, cahier 18 (Montreal: Centre de Recherche en Développement Economique, University of Montreal).

Maxwell, Judith, and Pestieau, Caroline (1980), *Economic Realities of Contemporary Confederation* (Montreal: C.D. Howe Research Institute).

Migué, Jean-Luc (1979), *Nationalist Policies in Canada: An Economic Approach* (Montreal: C. D. Howe Research Institute).

Polèse, Mario (1978), "The impact of international migration on the regional labor market: a Quebec case study," *Papers of the Regional Science Association*, vol. 41, pp. 153–65.

Quebec (1979), *Quebec–Canada: A New Deal—the Quebec Government Proposal for a New Partnership between Equals: Sovereignty-Association* (Quebec City: Government of Quebec).

Smiley, Donald (1980), "The association dimension of sovereignty-association: a response to the Quebec White Paper," Discussion Paper No. 8, Queen's University Institute of Intergovernmental Affairs, Kingston, Ontario.

Termote, Marc (1980), *Migration and Settlement: Canada* (Laxenberg, Austria: International Institute for Applied Systems Analysis).

6

A Rational Choice Approach to the Rise and Decline of Ethnoregional Political Parties

MARGARET LEVI AND MICHAEL HECHTER

Since the mid-1960s ethnoregionalism, or nationalism based on ethnic distinctiveness and territorial claims within established states, has emerged as a significant source of political organization within the Western democracies. This is not the ethnoregionalism of tribal societies only recently incorporated with other tribes into a single political entity. Nor is it the ethnoregionalism of territories whose unique languages and cultures are still strong and well. Rather these are movements by people whose traditional ways have nearly disappeared (or are disappearing rapidly) and whose political incorporation is not a matter of decades but of centuries.

The reemergence of ethnoregionalism in the advanced industrial democracies presented a paradox to scholars. Diffusion theories of national development anticipated that the spread of markets, industrialization, urbanization, and national systems of education, politics, administration, and conscription would diminish regional political, economic, and cultural distinctiveness. Even Marxists, who might have been sympathetic to the implied issue of national liberation, subscribed to a version of the diffusion model. After all, it is the Marxist prediction that capitalist societies will divide along class, not ethnic or territorial, lines. Despite this, ethnoregionalism did arise and with it an increasingly extensive academic literature attempting to analyze its reemergence. However, the synthetic work within this literature, while often provocative, tends to be based on impressionistic data (see, for example, Anderson, 1978; Connor, 1977; Esman, 1977; Mayo, 1974; Orridge, 1981; Ronen, 1979; Smith, 1977; 1981). Most empirical research tends to focus on case studies in a single country (see, for example, Hechter, 1975; Nielsen, 1980; Olzak, 1978) or one region (see, for example, Aull, 1978; Brand, 1978; Dulong, 1975). No one has yet undertaken a serious comparative analysis of ethnoregionalism in developed societies (for two partial exceptions, see Allardt, 1979; and Gras and Gras, 1982). We still lack a model that enables us to compare ethnoregionalism in different regions and states. There is no theory to indicate the critical variables and to permit us to organize in a systematic way the wealth of material already or potentially available. This chapter represents the cautious beginning of such a project.

To this end, it poses three separate questions. One question concerns *the geographical distribution* of ethnoregionalism. Why does it occur in Wales and not East Anglia, in Brittany and not the Dordogne? By definition, of course, ethnoregionalism can occur only where existing cultural markers (Barth, 1969) can be used to support a claim to ethnic distinctiveness. However, cultural distinctiveness is not sufficient to account for the variation among movements. Scottish nationalists are more successful electorally than the Welsh; Spanish Basques engage in more terrorist action than do the Catalans. This suggests that a theory linking social, economic, and political factors with ethnic distinctiveness is needed in order to explain the variations in the form and size of ethnoregionalist movements.

Another major question confronting scholars is *the timing* of ethnoregionalism. Despite controversies about measurement and cause, considerable evidence indicates that regional sentiments and political orientations exist even when they are not being expressed as demands for autonomy, home rule, or devolution (Budge and Urwin, 1966; Hechter, 1975; Ragin, 1977; Shaber, 1973). What catalyzes their expression in political terms? In particular, under what conditions do ethnoregional political parties gain strength? The Scottish National Party (SNP) was founded in 1934 and Plaid Cymru in 1925, but each only began to attract significant percentages of the vote in the late 1960s. The Flemish Volksunie (or VU) attracted increasing electoral support after 1958. The Quebecois produced a strong ethnoregionalist party in the 1970s that still (mid-1984) controls the provincial government, and Catalan nationalists were very successful in their 1980 elections. There are many other examples of political activity that suddenly emerged in the ethnoregions in the 1960s and 1970s. Yet an adequate explanation of their timing has yet to be developed.

Finally, what is *the future* of the ethnoregional movements? There is reason to believe that ethnoregionalism, at least in its autonomist form, is a cyclical phenomenon. It has risen and fallen several times over the past centuries in the same regions. In all likelihood it will decline once again. However, the conditions under which such a decline is likely to take place must be specified.

The purpose of this chapter is to develop a set of testable hypotheses that account for variations in the location, size, and timing of ethnoregional movements. The focus is on ethnoregional political parties in democratic countries where such parties are legal. The possible causes of these parties' existence are investigated, and the fluctuations in their membership and shifts in the percentage of the votes these parties attract in national, regional, and local elections. This is not to deny that ethnoregionalism may take other forms, such as cultural revival or terrorism. However, party organizations, members, and votes are quantifiable indicators of the probable success of a major strategy used by ethnoregionalists in advanced industrial democracies.

The Geographical Distribution of Ethnoregional Parties

By definition, the first precondition for the development of an ethnoregional party is the persistence of a separate and distinct ethnic identity linked to a particular territory. The maintenance of minority languages, religions, or cultural traditions may be indicators of such an identity. However, ethnoregional parties have also gained members in regions such as Scotland where the language, religion, and culture are clearly not the central issues or bases of membership, as well as in regions where they are being re-created rather than merely maintained, as is the case in Brittany and Wales.

The theory of internal colonialism (Hechter, 1975) offers another source of ethnic identity. It posits that ethnoregional movements are most likely to occur in economically dependent territories with ethnically distinctive populations that are characterized by hierarchical cultural divisions of labor (CDL). The result is reactive ethnicity. Although the model seems to fit certain cases fairly well, it came under attack for its failure to make adequate distinctions among the ethnoregions. It is plausible to argue that Wales or Brittany are dependent, but a case can be made that Scotland and Catalonia have experienced "relative overdevelopment" (Nairn, 1977, pp. 181–95,

199–215). Moreover, the theory fails to consider substantial differences in the ability of the ethnoregion's bourgeoisie to resist internal colonialism (Palloni, 1979, esp. p. 363). Finally, it does not take into adequate account differences among the states that practice internal colonialism (Verdery, 1979, pp. 379–80). Such observations lead Gourevitch (1979) to argue that strong "peripheral nationalism," which unfortunately he does not define, is most likely to occur where there is non-congruence between a state's economic and political cores and where the ethnoregion dominates in one of these dimensions, usually the economic. While this hypothesized correlation about the relative strength of the ethnoregional movement and the position of the ethnoregion in the state may be correct (although it is as yet untested), it begs important questions. Most important, it provides no clues as to why ethnoregional-ism is stronger in these areas, why ethnoregionalism also takes place in totally peripheral regions, or why there are variations in the movements even among the "stronger" peripheries.

In his 1978 reformulation of the cultural division of labor Hechter (also see Allardt, 1979, pp. 37–42, 49–51) extends his previous conception to distinguish two analytically distinct forms of the CDL: (1) a hierarchical form, in which the various ethnic groups in a territory are vertically distributed in the occupational structure; and (2) a segmental form, in which the ethnic groups are occupationally specialized at any level of the structure. In both kinds of situations cultural markets have political and economic consequences, for they strongly affect the individual's life chances. Although empirical data are still scanty regarding the configurations of CDLs in various countries and the relative degree of group solidarity produced by the forms of the CDL, there are indications that both hierarchy and segmentation are sources of ethnic identification (Armstrong, 1980; Hechter, 1978; Ritter, 1979). However, the two different kinds of CDL are likely to produce different goals among those individuals affected. Persons in a hierarchical CDL will seek to expand their occupational horizons, while those who occupy privileged positions in segmental CDLs may seek to maintain their station. As we shall see, this difference has implications for which state policies are most likely to catalyze the political salience of their ethnic identity.

Stratification is an important precondition of collective action. However, as numerous theorists since Marx have pointed out (see, for example, Stinchcombe, 1965), stratifica-tion cannot lead to collective action unless it also promotes informal organization among the stratified population. Peasants who live on their separate plots of land and only come together to exchange in a distant market place are unlikely to develop collective solidarity. On the other hand, workers who interact with each other regularly in the factory or Jews who are forced to live together in a ghetto possess communication networks and bases of trust that are essential for the development of a political organization. There are probably very few cases where the CDL does not imply regular patterns of interaction among the ethnic population. None the less, it is possible to conceive of such an instance, for example, where an ethnic group monopolizes the occupation of itinerant peddler. This suggests that the major factor promoting interaction, other than the CDL itself, is the existence of sites in which members of the ethnic group regularly meet.

Since the two kinds of CDLs we have identified rest on different patterns of stratification, they also tend to have distinctive sites of ethnic interaction. A hierarchical CDL has particularly strong effects on residential and social interaction. Members of each ethnic group tend to live together, to play together, and often to pray together. But to the degree they are dispersed throughout many occupations they do not work together. In this case they are also likely to be dispersed among various unions, if they are unionized at all.

Individuals subject to a segmental CDL, on the other hand, are concentrated in discrete occupations, in some cases relatively prestigious ones, rather than whole strata. This not only affects life chances, making ethnic background a requirement— or at least an advantage—for certain jobs, it also affects interaction since it ensures that members of the ethnic group come into regular and sustained contact with one another at work. Moreover, such occupational specialization usually leads to organization through craft unions and professional associations. Thus, although both kinds of CDL are likely to produce patterns of regular interaction, the intensity of intraethnic interactions is stronger in the case of the segmental CDL.

However, not all bases of interaction are work-related. Shared religions, languages, and cultures, each of which can provide the cultural markers of a CDL, are bases of voluntary associations in which regular interaction also occurs. Churches, language societies, and festivals such as the Welsh *eisteddfodau* or the Breton *pardons* also promote an organizational infrastructure within the ethnoregion. Given that such an infrastructure is an important source of recruitment and contributions for explicitly political organizations (Stinchcombe, 1965, p. 144 ff.), the extent of these voluntary associations probably has important consequences for the growth of ethnoregional parties. Moreover, the skilled leadership produced by such groups can often mobilize resources not readily available otherwise (Frohlich *et al.*, 1971).

Thus the impetus for the establishment of ethnoregional political parties emanates from any given region's CDL. The more hierarchical and/or segmental this CDL is, the greater the potential for the politicization of ethnic distinctions. The more sites of interaction the CDL creates, the easier it will be to mobilize potential followers. One extremely important implication that can be drawn from this is that territories without significant CDLs will not develop ethnoregional parties. Moreover, since the CDL may not be as significant in some areas of the ethnoregion as in others, the strongholds of the party should vary accordingly. In other words, the existence of a CDL alone should explain most of the variation in the geographical distribution of these parties.

The Determinants of Ethnoregional Political Activity

Our next task is to explain individual participation in and votes for ethnoregional political parties. Why do people belong to such parties? Why do people choose to vote for these parties? Why does a larger percentage of the population support the parties in one ethnoregion than in another? Why do individuals give and withdraw their support when they do? Our answer to these questions starts with the assumption that individuals are rational actors; decisions to engage in ethnoregional collective action are based on the individual's calculation that benefits outweigh costs. These calculations vary with time and place. Thus at issue are the factors that alter these calculations.

There are really two separate decisions that must be explained with regard to ethnoregional political parties: (1) the decision to join such a party, and (2) the decision to vote for it. Obviously a complex of factors influences a decision to support, by membership or vote, an ethnoregional party, and somewhat different factors influence each of these decisions. We argue that all of these factors can be reduced to two major sets of variables, the demand for benefits available from the party and the supply of these benefits that exists elsewhere. A discussion, first, of ethnoregional party membership, and then of ethnoregional party votes will indicate more precisely how these variables affect indidvidual choices.

The Determinants of Ethnoregional Party Membership

The theory of group solidarity (Hechter, 1983) predicts that individuals will most likely be attracted to and comply with an organization when it offers benefits that are both valued and not readily available elsewhere, Moreover, these benefits generally take the form of selective incentives, that is, inducements or sanctions contingent on membership (Olson, 1965). An ethnoregional party offers its members a social network, a compatible ideology promising the preservation of a culture or the achievement of statehood as well as, potentially, positions of prestige, power, and income that other parties presumably provide. In other words, any political party's membership, or at least its leadership, is composed largely of individuals who either have limited access to social networks or benefits available through other organizations, or perceive the party as an easier path to the benefits they seek. Regional variations in the demand for and supply of benefits should largely account for the relative size of different ethnoregional parties at any given time. Shifts in the demand for and supply of benefits within a region should largely account for fluctuations in any given party's membership over time.

We, therefore, predict that ethnoregional party membership will increase: (1) as more individuals find that membership in the party is their only or main avenue of advancement; and (2) as there is an increase in the benefits, especially the selective incentives, offered by the party.

Discrimination on the basis of cultural markers is one possible cause of a demand for ethnoregional party membership as a means of advancement. Certainly there is a reason to believe that talented individuals are attracted to religious and political organizations where other avenues of mobility are blocked (Oberschall, 1973, pp. 160–1). However, for the most part discrimination in such public organizations as political parties has decreased in the industrial democracies during the past several decades. This suggests that the more likely cause of an increased demand for the benefits of an ethnoregional party lies with a rise in education and skills among the ethnically distinct population that encourages some of its members to seek opportunities not traditionally sought by individuals in that ethnic group. It is fairly well documented that voluntary associations, including political parties, depend largely on individuals with sufficient resources in time and money to allow participation in an organization (Lipsky and Levi, 1972; Wilson, 1973, p. 156 ff.). To the extent that leadership positions are relatively closed to new members of traditional parties, and to the extent that they are relatively open in the ethnoregional party, the demand for ethnoregional party membership should increase, given an increase in individuals who would seek such positions.[1]

Neither the socioeconomic characteristics of its constituents nor the lack of mobility through other parties and organizations is sufficient to explain the variations and fluctuations in membership. The ethnoregional party itself must be able to supply benefits potential members value, or else nonparticipation would be the more rational choice. Although the CDL may account for why people perceive it in their interest to engage in collective action around questions of ethnicity, one of the most important findings of the recent literature on social movements is that interest is not sufficient to sustain political organization. In addition, the organization must be able to mobilize the resources necessary to pay staff, attract party workers, and mount campaigns (see, for example, Lipsky and Levi, 1972; McCarthy and Zald, 1977; Oberschall, 1973; Olson, 1965; Stinchcombe, 1965; Tilly, 1978; Wilson, 1973).

One major fount of organizational resources is the discretionary wealth of the ethnoregion. Regions vary in their natural resources, geography, dominant industries, and general level of development. Although it seems likely that an ethnoregion whose ethnic groups are distributed in a hierarchical cultural division of labor is likely to be poorer than an ethnoregion with a segmental CDL, this does not necessarily follow. The standard of living could be generally high throughout the ethnoregion even if its constituent ethnic groups are stratified hierarchically. What is crucial is the extent to which the wealth of the area is sufficient to produce leisure time, discretionary funds, and skills among the inhabitants that can be used to build and support political parties.

Resources such as those we have just described are very important in accounting for variations in the relative size of membership *once the party is able to mobilize them*. Regions with more of these resources should produce larger ethnoregional parties, *ceteris paribus*.[2] However, parties cannot always transform the resources of the ethnoregion into selective incentives that actually attract and maintain membership. To sustain members even rich parties must eventually hold out the possibility of office and influence.

The most important factors affecting the transformation of resources into selective incentives are: (1) the extent to which the laws and rules of the central state encourage the development of such parties; and (2) the extent to which state structure and policies enable the party to provide patronage to its militants.

Not only do the laws of the central state have to permit the existence of an ethnoregional party, they also can be more or less encouraging of the voluntary associations and/or cultural institutions on which such a party may depend (Rose, 1954; Hechter and Levi, 1979). Moreover, the electoral system itself is a major determinant of the size of the party. As Duverger contended, proportional representation, constituency elections, and other mechanisms developed to encourage multipartism do in fact produce third parties (Lipset, 1960, pp. xiii–xiv; and Rokkan, 1970, p. 168). In other words, ethnoregional parties are likely to be relatively larger where the electoral arrangements present minimal obstacles to the success of such parties in winning offices, an important benefit of party activism. Since ethnoregions vary with regard to such electoral arrangements, they should also vary on this account with respect to their ability to attract members.

The electoral system not only makes it easier to form a party, it also can increase (or reduce) the amount of patronage available through the party. However, an even more important determinant of patronage is the institutional autonomy of the ethnoregion. Federal systems and devolution of administration to the local or regional level mean that jobs in the administrative, educational, and legal systems are capable of coming under the control of an ethnoregional party. Quebec under the Parti Québécois is a notable case in point. But the importance of institutional variables for the development of ethnoregional parties is nowhere more clearly illustrated than in contemporary Spain. The new Spanish constitution actually specifies two different routes by which the inhabitants of its regions may gain self-government—and thereby assume control over a host of resources that were formerly under the exclusive control of the central state. Among the powers granted to autonomous regions in Spain are control over regional governmental institutions, local government structures, public works and transportation systems, agriculture, livestock grazing, the use of wilderness areas, environmental protection, irrigation systems, fishing rights, economic development policy, cultural patrimony, and the promotion and regulation of tourism. It is easy to see that the powers granted to the autonomous regions are considerable. As a result of this constitution, traditionally ethnoregionalist parties in Catalonia and the Basque country have been strengthened, and wholly new parties have developed in regions such as Andalusia, which had no prior experience with ethnoregional political parties (see Greenwood, 1980).

By this reasoning, the size of ethnoregional party membership will increase when the party is able to provide more patronage to its members. Since the possibility of patronage is largely determined by the region's institutional autonomy, this variable should act to set limits on the size of each party's membership and should also explain a large part of the variation in the relative size of ethnoregional parties in different regions.

Even parties in institutionally autonomous ethnoregions fluctuate in size, however and this can only be accounted for by changes in the amount of patronage flowing to the region. It is our argument that the major catalyst to such fluctuations is changes in central state policy that have the effect of directly increasing the benefits available through the party.[3] Affirmative action and regional economic development programs are two examples. As an organized voice of the ethnoregion's inhabitants and as an organization that can exert electoral pressure on the major parties, ethnoregional parties can use these programs as a means of obtaining additional resources and patronage to support membership. Such programs inevitably produce new bureaucracies that must be funded and staffed. Moreover, regional economic development plans almost always involve grants to particular localities and industries, and the decisions about who gets such grants become an impetus to increased demand for the party and to an increased supply of its benefits.

Another kind of state policy that can have major consequences on the ability of the ethnoregional party to provide selective incentives is government reform of representative, electoral, or administrative arrangements. When these have the effect of increasing patronage opportunities, party membership should grow. When they have the effect of reducing patronage through the party, membership should decline.

To recapitulate our argument so far, the size of an ethnoregional party is largely determined by the extent to which it is able to supply benefits its members value. This depends, first, on the demand for such benefits. Only where there is a

CDL can such a demand exist, but it will increase as the skills and educational levels of the ethnic population rise without a corresponding rise in opportunities for advancement through other organizations. The second and more important determinant of membership size is the availability through the party of patronage and other selective incentives. This depends in part on the resources of the ethnoregion, but leadership will be able to mobilize potential organizational resources to support an ethnoregional party only to the extent the electoral arrangements of the state and the institutional autonomy of the ethnoregion permit the translation of those resources into patronage opportunities. These factors should account for variations in the relative membership size of ethnoregional parties. Fluctuations in membership, however, are accounted for by changes in state policy that alter the electoral system, that affect the degree of institutional autonomy an ethnoregion possesses, or that modify the size of the patronage "pie." Changes that increase patronage will result in larger ethnoregional parties; changes that decrease patronage will have the opposite effect. Moreover, over the long run the state can undermine demand for the party altogether by eliminating the cultural division of labor.

The Determinants of Ethnoregional Party Votes

Party voters are measured by the number of people who vote for ethnoregional party candidates in national, regional, or local elections. Party members and activists can be expected to vote for the party. More interesting are those actors who have not made such a public commitment to the party. Indeed, what differentiates the member and the voter is the kind of commitment each expresses. The member pays dues and contributes time and energy. On the other hand, the voter need only engage in a single and secret act. The member is an identifiable object of rewards and punishments, while the voter is not. In other words, the voter is probably not subject to selective incentives *per se*, and his/her calculus may be quite dissimilar from that of the member. The literature suggests that economic strains and the incentives of the party system are two major determinants of the rise of third parties (see especially Pinard, 1971, pp. 247–50). However, these are rather general political and economic factors; they do not explain the calculations of individual voters.

We assume that individuals who vote for ethnoregional parties have already made the decision to vote. Thus we are not addressing the problem of the free-rider, since it is the non-voters who are the free riders (Downs, 1957; Olson, 1965) and here we are concerned only with the voters. It seems that those who do vote believe—for whatever reason—that by this act they are exerting political pressure on the major political parties, the government, or both.[4] This is not to suggest that all of the voters for the ethnoregional party must be in sympathy with its platform. Obviously the party will try to mobilize those with a potential for ethnic identity, as we have already described it. However, the evidence from Scotland, at least, is clear that the SNP attracted voters who sought neither devolution nor autonomy (Miller *et al.*, 1977, p. 100). Some of the votes for ethnoregional parties, then, come from voters who calculate that the vote for the party is simply a means of exerting pressure for desired changes or of protesting the policies of the major parties.

We expect that voters, somewhat like members, are subject to shifts in the demand for and supply of benefits by the ethnoregional party. However, since the benefits cannot be transformed into selective incentives for voters, the benefits here are the public goods the party provides, not its individual inducements. The major public good is the promise of change, whether through improvements in the economic and social condition of the constituents or through modifications of the platforms of the traditional parties to reflect voter concerns more closely. The extent to which the party can pressure the government into making such improvements or the major parties into altering their programs depends, ultimately, on the skills of the ethnoregional party leaders and on their ability to mount successful electoral campaigns. Our next step is to investigate the factors that account, first, for the demand for change, and secondly, for the ability of the party to deliver what it promises.

One catalyst to demands for change is dissatisfaction with government. This can take the form of generalized loss of confidence in political institutions and leaders, a phenomenon that appears to be growing throughout the Western world (Inglehart, 1977). Economic decline may be one precipitant of its expression in political form. Experience with a party in power that had broken promises of change may be another. However, such dissatisfaction is likely to take the form of a vote for an ethnoregional party only when the voter either wants to protest the policies of a traditional party without totally defecting to the major opposition or when the voter has an actual preference for the ethnoregional party platform. In the first case, it should be noted, the voter need not even be a member of the latent ethnic group. This is probably necessary only in the second case.

Another factor affecting the extent to which voters perceive the ethnoregional party as an important pressure group is the extent to which ethnic identity is politically salient. In such a case the ethnoregional party is the logical vehicle for expressing the demands of the ethnic populace, since its platform usually directly reflects their concerns.

It appears that one major impetus to ethnic mobilization is intensification of competition for jobs or niches between the members of different ethnic groups (see especially Hannan, 1979; Nielsen, 1980; Ragin, 1979; Tilly, 1978, pp. 144–5; and Olzak, 1978). Competition can be precipitated by industrialization, modernization, or state intervention (on this point, see Fox *et al.*, 1982) that creates new resources or threatens old resources over which the ethnic group has a claim. As a result, the party is sought as a vehicle for preserving past privileges or achieving new ones. However, in either case the precondition of ethnic mobilization is a CDL producing a latent group whose ethnic identity is made more salient by the existence of competition.[5]

We argue that the major catalyst to an increased demand for an ethnoregional party is a change in state policy that markedly affects intergroup competition. Industrialization, urbanization, modernization, migration, and state penetration have been going on for a long time without significant effects on the membership of ethnoregional parties. Affirmative action rules, cultural preservation programs, and regional economic development plans, on the other hand, are more recent and may cause individuals to see themselves as residents of an ethnically distinct territory, with a right to claim central state resources on that basis.

Still, even a strong ethnoregional party sympathizer is not likely to choose to vote for the party unless there is reason to believe it can be effective as a pressure group. The party must be credible. Credibility is determined by the size of the membership and by the relative success of the party in elections. Even a single victory can promote confidence in the party. The resources on which the ethnoregional party draws become very important here. The money to finance candidates, the allies attracted to the cause, and the skills of leaders in manipulating media and organizing campaign workers all are important determinants of electoral success. Where voters have a demand for an ethnoregional party, the factors that explain the relative size of membership go a long way toward explaining the relative number of voters. Even so, a large membership that is inefficiently utilized may achieve far less than a smaller party that uses its resources fully.

Actual changes in party platforms or new government actions in response to the existence of the party also legitimate the ethnoregional party as a pressure group. Parties that are competing with the ethnoregional party for the votes of a particular constituency are most likely to make such concessions, especially if a national election is scheduled in the near future. However, there is a paradox here. The very concessions that promote ethnoregional party support in the short run may undermine the demand for that party in the long run, as stronger, more viable parties take over components of the program previously monopolized by the ethnoregional party.

According to this analysis, many votes for an ethnoregional party are votes for a pressure group. Thus its ability to attract votes depends not only on the extent of dissatisfaction with current parties and policies, on a resurgence of ethnic identity, or on the ability of the party to mount campaigns and win elections. It also depends on the extent to which other issues mobilize potential voters and other parties' platforms meet those demands. A voter is more likely to support an ethnoregional party in a national election when it is relatively costless to throw the vote away. This is most likely to occur when one major-party candidate is a "shoo-in" and, therefore, a third party vote is symbolic. It can also be the case if the major parties seem to the region's electorate to be nearly identical. Once again a third party vote has meaning without being costly. On the other hand, in tight elections between parties with vastly different programs, the rational individual will vote for the party that most closely represents his or her preferences. This is obviously true of the voter who supports the ethnoregional party only as a means to pressure the major parties. However, it is also likely to be true of the ethnoregionalist if the national-level issues seem more important than the regional ones. This might, for instance, explain some of the fluctuation in the SNP and Plaid Cymru votes. The choice between Conservatives and Labour in 1974 was a choice between Tweedledum and Tweedledee. But with the advent of

Mrs. Thatcher as the head of the Conservatives at a time when the economic problems of Britain had become rather severe, the 1979 election took on quite another cast.

Our analysis suggests that a vote for an ethnoregional party is not the norm. Voters will, we expect, return to their traditional parties if the voters' goal is not autonomy, a benefit promised uniquely by ethnoregional parties, but is either more limited recognition of ethnoregional concerns or protest against the platforms of the other parties. Alternatively, voters can become disillusioned with the ethnoregional party as a strategic mechanism if it experiences no electoral success or wins no concessions. This will lead to votes for other parties, to nonvoting, or, given a strong enough demand for ethnoregional change, to the development of other forms of organization.

To recapitulate, voters are most likely to be attracted to an ethnoregional party when they are seeking changes that a vote for the party might help to effect. The demand for change is predicated on dissatisfaction with the current government and on the political salience of ethnic and ethnoregional identity. These factors are most likely to be transformed into a vote for an ethnoregional party when state policies exist that can be targets of approval or attack. The likelihood that an ethnoregional party can help effect change is determined by its strength as a party; that is, by its ability to mobilize resources, members, and victories, and by evidence that it is able to wrest concessions from the established parties and from the government. Votes for the ethnoregional party will decline to the extent the government increases the satisfaction of the ethnoregional electorate with its policies, and to the extent the ethnoregional party is co-opted or fails to influence government decisions. They will also decline if the voter perceives another party as better able to effect the changes that are sought.

These hypotheses deserve further investigation.[6] The problem of ethnoregional party voting is as complex as any in political sociology, and it is likely that progress in understanding it will remain slow until larger-scale historical and comparative studies are carried out. This chapter has presented a rather simple framework for the collection of data that can, at least in principle, serve as an adequate evidentiary basis for the comparative study of ethnoregional politics. But the really hard work remains to be done.

We make no claim that the preceding model provides an exhaustive account of variations in ethnoregional politics.

Indeed, the model derives from the simple and overly restrictive behavioral postulates of political economy. It is likely that a more adequate model—even one based on these same restrictive behavioral assumptions—would specify additional relevant determinants of ethnoregional voting and would, therefore, be even more complex. But the present model seems to us complicated enough. It locates the most important determinants of ethnoregional voting at the level of the state's constitutional arrangements and policies. If ethnoregional parties are illegal, or if they are legal but because of peculiar electoral arrangements have little chance to win votes, or if they cannot provide patronage or offer selective inventives, then ethnoregional voting will not be a problem for either central rulers or social scientists.

One final point is worth special emphasis. It has long been traditional to see ethnoregionalism as a phenomenon that is intimately related to processes of industrialization and to the expansion of national markets. Diffusion theorists predicted that as industrialization and the extension of markets proceeded, ethnoregionalism would diminish apace. More recently others (see Hannan, 1979) have predicted somewhat different outcomes. But if the argument presented here is correct, then it is clear that the relationship between industrialization, or economic development, and ethnoregionalism is far from determinate.

There is no necessary link between industrialization and the CDL—as the South African case makes crystal clear. Nor is there any necessary link between industrialization and a region's institutional autonomy, or the regional policies adopted by central states, or the constitutional arrangements of these states themselves. The determinants of these key causal variables are largely unexplored in our model. But it is safe to guess that future research will reveal that their antecedents are at least as complicated as the causes of ethnoregional voting— and probably a good deal more so. Thus neither industrialization nor market expansion by itself can provide much help in accounting for different patterns of ethnoregional political activity.

Notes: Chapter 6

Several people offered helpful comments on an earlier draft of this chapter. In particular, we wish to thank Malka Applebaum-Maizel, Mary Brinton, William Brustein, Debra Freidman, and John Keeler.

1   By understanding rising educational and skill levels as a factor that changes the demand for the benefits of ethnoregional party membership, the observations of several scholars concerning the leadership role played by teachers and other members of the "new middle class" begin to make theoretical sense: see, for example, Khleif, 1978, and Beer, 1977.

2   Allardt's recent study of the resources possessed by forty-six linguistic minorities in fourteen West European nation-states adds further weight to this argument: see Allardt, 1979, pp. 52–65. However, he does not adequately specify the relationships between the kinds of resource and the kinds of movement they will produce. Nor does he discuss the mechanisms by which these resources can be utilized. Thus it is difficult to interpret his findings.

3   This argument is inspired by research on black militants during the 1960s. For example, see Levi, 1974.

4   For a relatively sophisticated discussion of the decision to vote for ethnoregional parties, see Green, 1982. Unfortunately we have not had the time to take this interesting, but very recent, article into account.

5   This formulation should make it clear that the reactive ethnicity model and the competitive ethnicity model are not alternatives as some have argued: see Hannan, 1979; Nielsen, 1980; Ragin, 1977. Since the basis of the cultural division of labor is occupational niches, competition for those niches should precipitate ethnic mobilization on the basis of an ethnic identity the CDL preserves.

6   A preliminary investigation using evidence from Scotland, Wales, and Brittany has been carried out by the authors and is available from them in a larger, unpublished version of this chapter. Paul, 1980, has also found this model useful in explaining a different but related problem, the rise of Slovak nationalism in Hungary at the turn of the century.

References: Chapter 6

Allardt, Erik (1979), *Implications of the Ethnic Revival in Modern Industrialized Society* (Helsinki: Societas Scientarium Fennica).

Anderson, Malcolm (1978), "The renaissance of territorial minorities in Western Europe," *Western European Politics*, vol. 1, no. 2, pp. 123–43.

Armstrong, Tim (1980), "Intergroup relations and differential fertility: the case of 1900 Utah," paper presented at the Pacific Sociological Association, San Francisco.

Aull, Charlotte (1978), "The British bureaucracy, Welsh culture, and Welsh political nationalism," unpublished paper, Department of Anthropology, Duke University, Durham, N. C.

Barth, Fredrik (1969), *Ethnic Groups and Boundaries* (Boston, Mass.: Little, Brown).

Beer, William R. (1977), "The social class of ethnic activists in contemporary France," in M. J. Esman (ed.), *Ethnic Conflict in the Western World* (Ithaca, N.Y., and London: Cornell University Press), pp. 143–58.

Brand, Jack (1978), *The National Movement in Scotland* (London: Routledge & Kegan Paul).

Budge, Ian, and Urwin, D. W. (1966), *Scottish Political Behavior* (New York: Barnes & Noble).

Connor, Walker (1977), "Ethnonationalism in the first world: the present in historical perspective," in M. J. Esman (ed.), *Ethnic Conflict in the Western World* (Ithaca, N.Y., and London: Cornell University Press), pp. 19–45.

Downs, Anthony (1957), *An Economic Theory of Democracy* (New York: Harper & Row).

Dulong, Renaud (1975), *La Question bretonne* (Paris: Armand Colin).

Esman, Milton J. (1977), "Perspectives on ethnic conflict in industrialized society," in M. J. Esman (ed.), *Ethnic Conflict in the Western World* (Ithaca, N.Y., and London: Cornell University Press), pp. 251–86.

Fox, Richard G., Aull, Charlotte, and Ciminio, Louis (1981), "The developmental phases of ethnic nationalism," in Charles Keyes (ed.), *Ethnic Change* (Seattle, Wash.: University of Washington Press), pp. 198–245.

Frohlich, Norman, Oppenheimer, Joe A., and Young, Oran R. (1971), *Political Leadership and Collective Goods* (Princeton, N.J.: Princeton University Press).

Gourevitch, Peter Alexis (1979), "The reemergence of 'peripheral nationalisms': some comparative speculations on the spatial distribution of political leadership and economic growth," *Comparative Studies in Society and History*, vol. 21, no. 3, pp. 303–22.

Gras, Solange, and Gras, Christian (1982), *La Révolte des régions* (Paris: PUF).

Green, Leslie (1982), "Rational nationalists," *Political Studies*, vol. 30, no. 2, pp. 236–46.

Greenwood, Davydd J. (1980), "Castilians, Basques, and Andalusians" paper presented at the Department of Anthropology Colloquium, University of Massachusetts, Amherst, Mass., October.

Hannan, Michael T. (1979), "The dynamics of ethnic boundaries in modern states," in M. T. Hannan and J. Meyer (eds.), *National Development and the World System* (Chicago: University of Chicago Press), pp. 253–75.

Hechter, Michael (1975), *Internal Colonialism: The Celtic Fringe in British National Development, 1536–1966* (London: Routledge & Kegan Paul; Berkeley and Los Angeles, Calif.: University of California Press).

Hechter, Michael (1978), "Group formation and the cultural division of labor," *American Journal of Sociology*, vol. 82, no. 2 (September), pp. 293–318.

Hechter, Michael (1983), "A theory of group solidarity," in M. Hechter (ed.), *The Microfoundations of Macrosociology* (Philadelphia, Pa.: Temple University Press), pp. 16–57.

Hechter, Michael, and Levi, Margaret (1979), "The comparative analysis of ethnoregional movements," *Ethnic and Racial Studies*, vol. 2, no. 3 (July), pp. 260–74.

Inglehart, Ronald (1977), *The Silent Revolution* (Princeton, N. J.: Princeton University Press).

Khleif, Bud B. (1978), "Ethnic awakening in the first world: the case of Wales," in Glyn Williams (ed.), *Social and Cultural Change in Contemporary Wales* (London and Boston: Routledge & Kegan Paul), pp. 102–19.

Levi, Margaret (1974), "Poor people against the state," *Review of Radical Political Economy*, vol. 6, no. 1, pp. 76–98.

Lipset, Seymour Martin (1960), "Party systems and the representation of social groups," *Archives Européenes de Sociologie*, vol. 1, no. 1, pp. 50–85.

Lipsky, Michael, and Levi, Margaret (1972), "Community organization as a political resource," in Harlan Hahn (ed.), *People and Politics in Urban Society* (Beverly Hills, Calif.: Sage), pp. 175–99.

McCarthy, John D., and Zald, Mayer N. (1977), "Resource mobilization and social movements: a partial theory," *American Journal of Sociology*, vol. 82, no. 6, pp. 1212–41.

Mayo, Patricia Elton (1974), *The Roots of Identity* (London: Allen Lane).

Miller, W. C., with Sarlvik, Bo, Crewe, Ivor, and Alt, Jim (1977), "The connection between SNP voting and the demand for Scottish self-government," European Journal of Political Science, vol. 5, no. 1, pp. 83–102.

Nairn, Tom (1977), *The Break-Up of Britain* (London: New Left Books).

Nielsen, Francois (1980), "The Flemish movement in Belgium after World War II," *American Sociological Review*, vol. 45, no. 2 (April), pp. 76–94.

Oberschall, Anthony (1973), *Social Conflict and Social Movements* (Englewood Cliffs, N.J.: Prentice-Hall).

Olson, Mancur (1965), *The Logic of Collective Action* (Cambridge, Mass.: Harvard University Press).

Olzak, Susan (1978) "An ecological-competitive model of the emergence of ethnicity: the French-Canadian example," paper presented at the American Sociological Association, San Francisco, Calif., 6 September.

Orridge, A. W. (1981), "Uneven development and nationalism," *Political Studies*, vol. 29, no. 1, pp. 1–15; and vol. 29, no. 2, pp. 181–90.

Palloni, Alberto (1979), "Internal colonialism or clientelistic politics? The case of southern Italy," *Ethnic and Racial Studies*, vol. 2, no. 3, pp. 360–77.

Paul, David (1980), "Slovak nationalism and the Hungarian state, 1870–1910," paper presented at the CSEN Seminar, University of Washington, Seattle, April.

Pinard, Maurice (1971), *The Rise of a Third Party* (Englewood Cliffs, N.J.: Prentice-Hall).

Ragin, Charles (1977), "Class, status, and 'reactive ethnic cleavages': the social bases of political regionalism," *American Sociological Review*, vol. 42, no. 3, pp. 438–50.

Ragin, Charles (1979), "Ethnic political mobilization: the Welsh case," *American Sociological Review*, vol. 44, no. 4, pp. 619–35.

Ritter, Kathleen V. (1979), "Internal colonialism and industrial development in Alaska," *Ethnic and Racial Studies*, vol. 2, no. 3, pp. 319–40.

Rokkan, Stein (1970), *Citizens, Elections, Parties* (New York: McKay).

Ronen, Dov (1979), *The Quest for Self Determination* (New Haven, Conn.: Yale University Press).

Rose, Arnold (1954), "Voluntary associations in France," in A. Rose (ed.), *Theory and Method in the Social Sciences* (Minneapolis, Minn.: University of Minnesota Press), pp. 72–115.

Shaber, Sandra (1973), "The political consequences of regional imbalances in socio-economic development: electoral alignments and socio-economic regionalism in modern France." Ph.D dissertation, University of Pennsylvania.

Smith, Anthony D. (ed.) (1977), *Nationalistic Movements* (New York: St Martin's Press).

Smith, Anthony D. (1981), *The Ethnic Revival* (Cambridge and New York: Cambridge University Press).

Stinchcombe, Arthur (1965), "Social structure and social organizations," in *Handbook of Organizations*, ed. James March (Chicago: Rand McNally), pp. 149–93.

Tilly, Charles (1978), *From Mobilization to Revolution* (Reading, Mass.: Addison-Wesley).

Verdery, Katherine (1979), "Internal colonialism in Austria-Hungary," *Ethnic and Racial Studies*, vol. 2, no. 2, pp. 378–99.

Wilson, James Q. (1973), *Political Organizations* (New York: Basic Books).

7

Decision Modes Toward Separatist Movements
some Conceptual and Theoretical Considerations

JÜRG STEINER

In many countries around the world the political authorities are confronted with the question of what decision modes they should use in dealing with separatist movements. For example, should the demand of these movements be put to a popular vote, or is it preferable to seek an accommodation with the separatist leaders? In this chapter I wish to present a conceptual framework which allows one to classify the decision modes available to political authorities. Moreover, I will discuss possible explanations of variation in these decision modes. As an illustration, I will use the Swiss case of the Jura to show how the abstract ideas may work in a concrete empirical situation.

This particular research focus may be justified in terms of its relevance for daily political life. There is already a large literature that explains the rise of separatist movements from a structural approach. Although such structural explanations are useful on scholarly grounds, they are often of little help for the day-to-day operations of the political authorities. The Jura case may serve to illustrate this point: the separatist movement developed in the three most northern districts of the canton Berne, and the demand was not for separation from Switzerland but merely from the canton Berne. These three districts were in two important ways in a minority position in the canton Berne. Together with three other districts in the Jura region they formed a French-speaking minority in the predominantly German-speaking canton. Secondly, and in contrast to the southern part of the Jura, the three northern districts were also religiously in a minority, being Catholic in a predominantly

Protestant canton. This structural position of a double minority has often been used to explain why the separatist movement had its strength in the northern part of the Jura (see, for example, Mayer, 1969). I have offered this explanation myself, and I still think that it contributes importantly to an understanding of the Jura problem.

The weak point of such a structural explanation is, however, that it tells the political authorities very little about how to deal with a separatist movement. Structural features such as the linguistic and religious composition of a population are usually "givens" which cannot easily be changed by the political authorities. What the authorities need to know is which decision modes they should use in order to find a solution for a separatist problem. Thus if we wish to be useful advisers, we should have something to say about these decision modes. Even if we are not interested in giving advice but only in explanations, an analysis of decision modes should be most fruitful because it helps us to get a handle on short-term changes that cannot be explained from a structural approach.

For the Jura problem, we can register many dramatic changes since World War II, the most dramatic being the foundation of the canton Jura at the beginning of 1979. A structural approach is useful for an understanding of the movement as a whole, but it cannot explain the particular events that have led to the foundation of the new canton. Here we need additional approaches, and one of these is to look at changes in the decision modes of the political authorities. Our research indeed shows many strong changes in the decision modes of the Bernese authorities towards the Jura separatist movement. What we need, first, is a clear conceptualization of these decision modes.

Conceptualization of Decision Modes

The consociational literature has made an important effort to conceptualize decision modes in the context of separatist movements (see, for example, the useful overview in McRae, 1974). I take this literature as a starting-point, but I shall try to refine its typology of decision modes. The key concept of this literature is consociational decision-making, a concept which was developed in contrast to competitive decision-making. Before the rise of the consociational literature, the term competitive decision-making was often used more or less as a synonym of democratic decision-making. To many authors it appeared as the only democratic way to apply the principle of "one man one vote" and to resolve conflicts in a competitive way through a voting procedure. In Northern Ireland, for example, the Protestant leaders argued time and again that a separation from Britain could only take place by a majority vote. The authors of the consociational literature were struck by the rareness of the competitive decision mode in some countries which were otherwise considered as fully democratic. It was noted, for example, that in Switzerland the majority principle is relatively rarely used to resolve conflicts between the German-speaking majority and the three linguistic minorities. It was for this noncompetitive decision pattern that the term consociational decision-making was coined. The theoretical argument was then put forward that a predominance of consociational decision-making made it less likely that a separatist movement would gain strength. In Switzerland there was a dangerous "trench" between German and French-speakers during World War I; that this "trench" did not lead to any strong separatist movement was explained by the predominance of consociational decision-making.

I have argued elsewhere that the concept of consociational decision-making is not clearly enough defined, with the result that confusion has developed about its exact meaning (Steiner, 1981). From its intellectual history, consociational decision-making means primarily the absence of competition. But such an absence may have different reasons, and accordingly I suggest that the concept of consociational decision-making should be broken down in more specific terms. These terms are, in principle, applicable to any societal conflict. In the present context, I will try to illustrate what the terms mean when they are applied to the decision modes of political authorities toward separatist movements.

A first noncompetitive strategy of political authorities toward separatist movements may be a strategy of *amicable agreement*. By this I mean that the authorities try to negotiate with the separatist leaders a solution that is acceptable to both sides. It is important for this decision mode that the negotiations take place between roughly equal partners, so that the decision develops from a free bargaining process.

A lack of competition in the decision process may also be due to the tendency of the authorities to *repress* the demand of a separatist movement. The criticism has often been raised that consociationalism is a repressive form of decision-making. I agree that decisions by repression are sometimes subsumed under the broad umbrella of consociational decision-making. It should contribute to conceptual clarity if we distinguish whether, in the decision process, the conflicting groups have roughly the same status or whether one group is clearly superordinate to another. This distinction has already been made in an excellent article by Ian Lustick (1979), who differentiates "cooperative efforts of rival sub-unit elites" from a control model with "effective exertion of the superior power of one sub-unit." Decisions by repression are not only similar to the control model of Lustick, but also to the concept of nondecisions as used by Peter Bachrach and Morton S. Baratz (1975). These two authors claim "that political consensus is commonly shaped by status-quo defenders, exercising their power resources, and operates to prevent challenges to their values and interests" (ibid., p. 901). Thus, according to Bachrach and Baratz, the defenders of the status quo are a superordinate group which is usually able to repress demands of the challengers to the status quo. If these challengers are separatist movements, there are many ways in which their demands can be kept off the political agenda, for instance, by shrewd parliamentary maneuvers.

A third noncompetitive option for the authorities is to refer the problem of separatism to a third party, such as an expert committee of "wise men." This third party is asked to listen to both sides and to interpret a decision from the sense of the discussion. As Dorff and I have shown elsewhere, it happens frequently in all kinds of political situations that a third party interprets a decision from the sense of a debate (Steiner and Dorff, 1980). For such *decisions by interpretation* to be successful, it is usually sufficient that none of the conflicting groups openly object; to go along with the decision in a tacit way is behavior often practiced in such situations.

We have now described four decision modes which the authorities of a country can use when they are confronted with a separatist movement. They can put the demands of the separatists to a majority vote, they can seek an amicable agreement, they can try to repress the demands, or they can hope for a decision by interpretation by a third party. If we analyze events in a temporal sequence, we should be able at each decision point to determine which strategy the authorities pursue. The fascinating aspect is that this strategy may change from decision point to decision point, so that we will get a whole sequence of decision modes. If we compare the various separatist movements around the world, we may see that there

1: repression → interpretation → majority vote → amicable agreement

2: amicable agreement → majority rule → interpretation → repression

Figure 7.1 *Hypothetical cases 1 and 2*

is great variation in the sequence of decision modes used by the political authorities. In the two hypothetical cases in Figure 7.1 the decision modes follow each other in reversed order. In the first example the authorities begin with repression and then ask a third party for an interpretation; afterwards they try to work with the majority principle and, finally, seek an accommodation. In the second example the authorities attempt, first, amicable agreement, then turn to majority rule, then refer the matter to a third party and end up with repression. Having described for many cases such sequences of decision modes, we find the theoretically interesting question to be how variation in these sequences influences the development of the separatist problem. Which sequence has the highest probability that the outcome will be separation and which other sequence will most likely lead to a reintegration of the separatist movement in the current political system? It would also be interesting to see how the sequence in the decision modes influences the degree of violence resulting from a separatist problem. On the other side of the causal chain it would be exciting to explain why the political authorities went for a particular sequence in their decision modes. Before we engage further in such theoretical discussions, we have first to determine whether our conceptualization of sequences of decision modes is operational if we are confronted with empirical data. As an illustration, I shall use in the next section the case of Jura separatism.

The Example of Jura Separatism

Before the French Revolution, the Jura belonged to the bishopric of Basel, a feudal clerical principality of the Holy Roman Empire of the German nation. Originally the bishop resided in the city of Basel, but when it adopted the Reformation in 1529, the episcopal court moved to Porrentruy in the northern part of the Jura. The southern districts of the Jura significantly pursued a special historical development by entering a series of defensive alliances with the Swiss Confederation and especially with the city of Berne. Following the lead of Berne, these southern districts converted to Protestantism but still remained under the sovereignty of the bishop. At the Congress of Vienna the Jura was considered a masterless territory and was given to Berne as compensation for other territories that Berne had lost. Berne was not enthusiastic about the arrangement, and in the Jura itself there was some strong opposition to the annexation by Berne. Even in the nineteenth century, then, the relation between the Jura and the other parts of the Berne canton was quite stormy, and separatism was an issue almost from the beginning.

In order not to get lost in too many historical details we pick up the story of the Jura question only after World War II. According to my reading of this most recent period, the decision strategies of the Bernese authorities can be classified in roughly the following manner (Steiner, 1974) (see Figure 7.2).

During and immediately after World War II, it was relatively easy for the Bernese authorities to keep the demands of the Jura separatists off the political agenda, because the agenda was already overloaded with huge problems related to the war situation. In 1947, however, an incident in the Bernese Parliament brought great publicity to the Jura question once again. Because of his language, a Jurassian member of the cantonal Cabinet was denied the important Department of Public Works. There was an uproar in the Jura, and a long list of grievances was put forward to the Bernese authorities. At this point the authorities changed their decision strategy and attempted to come to an amicable agreement with the Jura leaders. The authorities tried to negotiate a package of reforms, accepting some of the Jura leaders' demands while rejecting others. The authorities, for example, recognized the Jurassian flag as the official flag of the Jura and guaranteed two Jurassian seats in the cantonal Cabinet. Other demands were rejected, such as the establishment of a second chamber in the cantonal Parliament in which the Jurassians would have held half of the seats. The militant separatist leaders rejected all negotiations that aimed at a solution within the Berne canton. In 1947 they founded the Rassemblement Jurassien, which drew its main support from the Catholic north.

A new turning-point was reached in 1959, when a referendum

Repression → amicable agreement → repression → interpretation → repression → majority vote

Figure 7.2 *Decision modes of the Bernese authorities toward the Jura separatists since World War II.*

was held based on a popular initiative by the Rassemblement Jurassien. The goal of this initiative was to allow a special referendum among the Jura population on the question of separation. But this initiative was rejected in a popular vote in the canton as a whole. In the Jura itself a strong difference was revealed between the north and the south, with the former accepting and the latter rejecting the initiative. The total result within the Jura showed a narrow defeat of the initiative. Based on these overall results the Bernese authorities considered the Jura question as settled: not only the German-speaking majority of the canton, but even the Jura itself did not want a special referendum on the question of separation. Thus in the early 1960s the Bernese authorities believed that the issue of Jura separatism could be removed from the political agenda. As before 1947, a period of repression began.

The Rassemblement Jurassien reacted to this repression of their demands with a tighter organization, founding, for example, a very agressive youth group. There now occurred several incidents of violence, including the blowing up of a military barrack and a railway line. Although the separatist leaders disapproved of terrorism, they were widely blamed as those morally responsible. The reaction of the Bernese authorities to these new developments was a change in decision strategy. Around 1966 the authorities recognized that the Jura question could not be swept from the political agenda. The new strategy was to refer the problem to a third party, which was to listen to both sides and interpret a decision from all the arguments. The authorities appointed a committee of four "wise men", who all had a high reputation in Swiss political life. They came from the four largest parties in Switzerland; two were French-speaking, two German-speaking. Two of the committee members were former members of the federal government, the two others current members of the federal Parliament. The committee tried to contact all groups involved in the Jura question, but here again the separatist leaders rejected all negotiations with the argument that the principle of separation was not negotiable. Thus any solution of the committee which would take account of both separatist and antiseparatist arguments would be unacceptable.

Seeing that the committee of "wise men" would be unable to interpret a decision acceptable to all sides, the Bernese authorities around 1969 again changed their decision strategy. They turned now to the majority principle, an idea which had already been launched by the separatists with their popular initiative in 1959. What was unacceptable to the Bernese authorities in the 1950s now became their own strategy in the 1970s. But there was also an important new element in how the authorities tried to apply the majority principle. Rather than having a single referendum on the Jura question, a whole series of referendums was organized.

At first the populace of the entire canton accepted a constitutional amendment which allowed the question of separation to be put to a popular vote among the Jurassians. In a second step the Jura decided by a narrow margin for separation. In a third referendum the southern districts of the Jura decided not to participate in separation, but to remain with the Berne canton. Fourthly, individual communities along the new frontier between the canton Berne and the canton Jura could decide whether they wished to change their district and consequently also their canton. Finally, it was decided in a nationwide referendum to accept the Jura as a new canton in the Swiss Confederation. The new canton began to function on 1 January 1979.

This series of referendums was not yet the end of the Jura question. The Rassemblement Jurassien continues to claim the southern districts too as part of the new canton. The rationale for this claim is that the electorate that decided on the separation was not correctly defined. The immigrants from the German-speaking part of the canton should not have been allowed to vote, while the Jurassians who had emigrated elsewhere should have been permitted to participate. In contrast to the Rassemblement Jurassien, the Bernese authorities now consider the Jura question as definitively settled. Demands in the southen districts to separate from the Berne canton and to join the Jura canton are to a large extent repressed.

Theoretical Considerations

One may argue with details of the above description. But I hope that it demonstrates that the proposed conceptualization of decision modes can be applied to a concrete empirical example. Having described the decision modes used by the Bernese authorities in the Jura problem, a further task would now be to explain these decision modes. I limit myself to a few considerations about the direction in which such a theory could be developed.

My main interest is to relate various decision-making elements and thus to develop a broadly based decision-making theory. Applied to our empirical case this means that I try to explain the decision modes of the Bernese authorities through other decision-making elements. I see these elements in particular in three directions. First, it seems plausible that the decision modes of the Bernese authorities were influenced by the decision modes chosen by the Jura separatists. Secondly, I expect that the decision mode chosen by the Bernese authorities at a particular time depended on their decision modes at earlier time points. Thirdly, the decision modes which the Bernese authorities used for their internal decision-making may have had an impact on the decision modes that they used toward the separatists. Trying to explain a particular decision mode in such a way, through other decision-making elements, has the advantage that causal interactions in an entire decision-making system can be revealed. This gives us a handle on short-range changes. If the overall structural situation remains the same, a particular decision pattern can probably best be explained by referring to other decision patterns.

That the Bernese authorities since World War II changed their decision mode so many times in the Jura question can hardly be explained through structural features of the problem, which remained fairly unchanged during the entire time period. It is more reasonable to assume that the Bernese authorities reacted to changes in the decision modes of the separatists, to their previous experiences with particular decision modes, and to changes in their own internal decision-making. Having said all this, we have of course also to explain how the whole decision system develops over time; and here, finally, structural features of the decision situation have to enter the theory. Applied to our empirical case I do not deny at all that it is important to consider, for example, the linguistic and religious dimensions of the Jura problem. These structural features can help us to explain why the entire decision system has developed in a particular direction.

In a theory-building effort one would have to compare, for example, the structural features in Canada and the canton Berne in order to explain how the decision systems have developed in the two cases. My overall approach is not to play structural and decision-making explanations against each other, but to integrate both in a broader theory. The question is not what matters more, structure or politics. Both matter, of course, but in different links of the causal chain.

References: Chapter 7

Bachrach, Peter, and Baratz, Morton S. (1975), "Power and its two faces revisited: a reply to Geoffrey Debnam," *American Political Science Review*, vol. 69, no. 3 (September), pp. 900–4.

Lustick, Ian (1979), "Stability in deeply divided societies: consociationalism versus control," *World Politics*, vol. 31, no. 3 (April), pp. 325–44.

McRae, Kenneth (ed.) (1974), *Consociational Democracy: Political Accommodation in Segmented Societies*, Carleton Library No. 79 (Toronto: McClelland & Stewart).

Mayer, Kurt B. (1969), "Einige soziologische Aspekte des Jura Problems," *Schweizerische Zeitschrift für Volkswirtschaft und Statistik*, vol. 105, no. 2 (June), pp. 230–6.

Steiner, Jürg (1974), *Amicable Agreement versus Majority Rule: Conflict Resolution in Switzerland* (Chapel Hill, N.C.: University of North Carolina Press).

Steiner, Jürg (1981), "The consociational theory and beyond," *Comparative Politics*, vol. 13, no. 3 (April), pp. 339–54.

Steiner, Jürg, and Dorff, Robert H. (1980), *A Theory of Political Decision Modes: Intra-Party Decision Making in Switzerland* (Chapel Hill, N.C.: University of North Carolina Press).

8

Sociological Intervention and the Internal Dynamics of the Occitanist Movement

ALAIN TOURAINE

A Divided Movement

What is the nature of the Occitanist movement? What is its direction? How important is it? These are all trap-questions which we must be wary of. Those who identify a social movement with an ideology, with an appropriate speech, may say that such and such is the actor's intention, such and such the meaning of his message, for they conceive of a social movement as a person speaking, reflecting, resolving. Our research, however, has enabled us to dismiss this incorrect representation, which wrongly assumes that the Occitanist movement has a single or central direction. This movement in fact belongs to the great family of Third World nationalisms; it is also a defense action by a preindustrial, merchant economy and society endangered by the rapid evolution of a single, advanced, industrial society. And what is there in common between a national liberation movement and protest movements which might be those of a regional pressure group? Indeed, the liberation movement may even be both produced by a will and determined by realities that are foreign to the actors' awareness; the crisis of industrial values gives renewed importance to roots, to traditions, and to the troubled search for an identity. The crisis of the national state—and more particularly the crisis of the French republican state of the Third and Fourth Republics— has driven the traditional cadres, especially the teachers, to defend their threatened influence and to react to the loss of their influence by countering the French state with an Occitanist state, which although resembling the French state would still be opposed to it. None of these hypotheses can be fully accepted, for they all make the same mistake of saying this is the essence, this is the true nature of the Occitanist movement.

Our first and perhaps most important conclusion is that the Occitanist movement does not have one sole direction and that it is pointless to seek for its nature, for it has no principle of unity. We searched constantly for this nature yet never succeeded in causing it to emerge. Was this a failure of the method? By no means, for this negative result led us in the right direction. Instead of painting a full-length portrait of the Occitanist movement, we must analyze Occitanist action as work aimed at integrating mutually opposed components. This action is not the outward manifestation of an Occitanist movement, but rather an effort toward creating this movement. Every social movement is the combination of a definition by the actor of himself, of his opponent, and of the stakes of their struggle. If these three definitions are congruent, the movement becomes formed, as happens for instance when workers come out in opposition against the industrialists for the social and political control of industrialization. If, however, these definitions do not belong to the same mode of analyzing society, the action remains disintegrated: it may be violent or, instead, weak and heteronomous, but in no instance will it succeed in forming a social movement. In order for this movement to be produced work must be undertaken on transforming the main directions of the action.

Occitanist action is an endeavor to construct an Occitanist movement out of three divergent forces. This action defines the Occitanist actor in cultural terms; if there were no Occitan language to be defended, there would be no Occitanist struggle—since the struggle has taken its name from the *langue d'oc*. The opponent is defined here in national terms, with frequent reference to conquest and invasion, even when there is no mention of obtaining independence. And, finally, the stakes in this struggle are often declared in economic terms, relating to the defense or revival of the regional economy. The visitor to Occitania will observe numerous manifestations of cultural defense: language schools, Occitan singers, regionalist gatherings and folklore meetings; expressions of revolutionary nationalism fired by Cuban, Algerian, Vietnamese, or Basque examples; and protests, which may be made by the winegrowers or the miners, or else—in a different spirit—by the self-managing modernizers of the Confédération Française et Démocratique du Travail (CFDT). But there is nothing that would necessarily lead to these three types of action becoming united: they are more readily opposed to one another than complemented by one another. The nationalists are equally critical of the new *Félibres** and the folklorists as they are of the regionalists; those who defend this culture are more often attached to a confined area or to a region—Gascony, Auvergne, Provence—than to Occitania as a whole; the modernizers are mistrustful of cultural or political integralism. Instead of choosing imperiously from among the various possible directions of Occitanian action, one must instead more humbly ask oneself in what respect cultural defense, nationalist ideology, and economic demands are interdependent. This is so difficult a question, and one to which the answer has so often evaded the groups which sought it, that one might put forward the idea that this interdependence has never really existed and that its absence has been concealed by the submission of Occitan action to a great ideological principle of political unity deriving from outside: the leftism in which was steeped first the *Lutte Occitane* and later the *Union de la gauche* from 1971 to 1977. One is obliged to conclude, then, that the breakdown of the French left after 1977 led to the weakening and even the disintegration of the Occitanist movement. (It doesn't seem to have been stimulated by the sweeping victory of the Socialist Party in 1981. The new government took important measures in favor of regional decentralization and of the teaching of regional languages, but without being pushed forward by demonstrations.)

The teachers are defending a gravely threatened language, the trade unionists are defending employment or income, and the militants are devising a nationalist program progressing from autonomy to independence—but there is nothing to bring them together. For several years the Occitanists and the wine-growers seemed to be united, but this may have been in appearance only. Since the Occitanist movement is incapable of creating a party or an organized movement, and since it is torn apart by the political and unionist conflicts spreading throughout the French left, and is still as much divided between "political" and "cultural" adherents as it was twenty years ago—and far more than it was ten years ago—can it be said that the movement really exists?

---

*The original *Félibres* were members of a cultural association, the *Félibrige*, founded in 1854 by the poet Mistral. This movement sought the renewal and safeguard of the distinct languages and culture of southern France.

Right from the start, our research dismissed the most customary reply to this question. Nationalists everywhere constantly answer by saying that the unity of the national movement is provided by the national reality itself; the language, culture, and history common to all the inhabitants of the same territory, or at least to the great majority of them. Czech or Polish nationalists have appealed to their language and to their national history, occasionally to their religion, as is being done today by the Basques, the Catalans, and even the Corsicans. This nationalism also exists in Occitania, but it is weak because the Occitan language has been enfeebled and because the national Occitan history is unreal.

What might unite the different forms of Occitanian action is something quite different. It is, first of all, an awareness of impending downfall and collective depth; not the idea of what is commonly owned but the sense of the threats hanging over everyone, threats of population exodus, impoverishment, aging and growing dependence. In a Western Europe led on by belief in growth Occitania is, first of all, the France of decline, losing its governing class, its capital, and its young, and becoming the "solarium" of Europe. The southerners, as soon as they have revolted against the disdain of the northerners (industrialists and centralizers), become Occitanist and enter, strongly or weakly, into the Occitanist movement. This is what contrasts the Occitanist movement with many of the branches of the Breton movement which—particularly between the two World wars—has called upon Celtic culture and even the Celtic race in the fight against domination by the Latins. This ethnism, present in the National Occitan Party or in the Poble d'Oc, has never succeeded in exerting a large influence upon the Occitanist movement, which—perhaps because it has been linked to the middle classes and to small independent farmers, radical or socialist—has been as far removed as possible from integralism and fundamentalism. It has constantly been more critical and protesting than communitarian; it speaks far more of the future than of the past and leaves little room for mysticism. This awareness of decline and downfall might have allowed for *passéist* (or "past-oriented") reactions; but the Occitanist movement is directed far more toward the future.

What is happening is that the downfall of Occitania is being experienced at the same time as the decline of republican France. These two significations should not be separated. Occitanism has two directions: one for Occitania, which it wishes to save, and one for French society, not for the

managers and administrators, but for a nation from which the
state is moving away to become increasingly identified with the
large companies and modern sectors from which it accepts that
a large portion of the population should be excluded. The
Occitanist movement is neither entirely regionalist nor entirely
nationalist, for it is fighting against the French state but in the
name of a country which is both Occitanian land and a land
with a republican population. Those who speak of a national
Occitan state and those who devise regional development plans
are equally isolated, while the Occitanist movement becomes
reinforced each time it draws closer to the basic communities,
at the elementary level where the French left and Occitanian
culture merge in order to oppose the centralizing, capitalist, and
bureaucratic state.

The Search for Unity

This, then, explains both the constant, insurmountable division
of the Occitanist movement into two opposing tendencies, and
the no less constant efforts to unite them. National affirmation
and the struggle against regional and economic underdevelopment are two deeply opposed forces, but they are also substantially linked to each other by their common opposition to the
French national state which, after having been an often brutal
but effective integrating agent, is increasingly becoming an
agent of the domination and dualization of society while at the
same time losing its political sovereignty, economic autonomy,
and cultural particularity.

The division and opposition of the various components of
Occitanist action may be easily perceived; by contrast, the work
of the movement, its endeavor to discover or reconstruct its
unity, does not emerge so easily. Those who believed that the
convergence of cultural, economic, and political struggles
occurred both naturally and of necessity were mistaken. In the
early 1970s this convergence was strengthened; today the trend
is the reverse. Events do not generate a direction which might
be divulged to the observers directly from the mouths of the
protagonists and their spokesmen. Most of the studies on social
movements are satisfied with limelighting the actors and
transcribing their ideology. This idle approach, the risks of
which may be reduced only by historical distance, leads to the
worst of errors whenever present history is involved. It would
be all too easy to relate, at some years' remove, the errors of

judgment and the astonishing reversals of opinion by certain highly committed authors.

We must, then, return to the method we have used, that of sociological intervention, revised specifically to enable social movements to be studied (Touraine, 1981). The researchers progressively led the militants to analyze their movement as being the search for a synthesis between nationalism and "developmentalism," between faithfulness to a past and the construction of a future. The groups passed through three main stages. First, the *populist* stage, that is, the feeling that it is by safeguarding the past that one can invent a future through battling against decadence, dependence, and invasion. But this first synthesis is far from being firm; one swiftly realizes that there is even greater opposition than there is complementarity between the restoration of the past and modernization. The researchers then had to press the groups beyond this stage which they had reached on their own throughout their self-analysis. It was necessary to present a more highly developed analysis, stressing the opposition between the chief components of the group's actions and the need, but also the difficulty, of finding a synthesis for them.

The key stage of the intervention led to two results. The groups' behavior revealed the validity of the researchers' predictions, but at the same time the militants attested to their failure, for they did not succeed in developing the synthesis which they recognized as being necessary and which they accepted in the manner defined by the researchers. Some months later the group from Limoges reached the same stalemate position as had been encountered by the groups from Carcassonne and Montpellier; the group from Paris broke down before a problem which it was even less able to resolve. The groups' inability to develop a synthesis between nationalism and developmentalism, and the failure—in this respect—of their conversion was for us a revelation of the absence of any intrinsic principle of unity in Occitanian action: this is an important result and one which must be measured with accuracy. It does not indicate that Occitanian action is vain or unimportant; it means rather that this action cannot be effective unless it recognizes its own inherent duality and defines itself as an effort to unite two components which can never be united. But the groups' ability to follow up the researchers' theories— which may be described as the success of the conversion— reveals with equal strength that the Occitan movement has not been destroyed, split in two, by the existence within it of conflicting tendencies which it wishes to preserve, and also that there is intercommunication between these two battlefronts, particularly in their general opposition to the French state.

This double result, which represented the main contribution of the intervention, led us somewhat later to develop a new theory. Before discussing it, let us stress once again the usefulness of our method. We created groups into which we introduced certain hypotheses, and we observed whether they produced intelligible effects; whether the militants, once they had themselves taken these hypotheses in hand, led the discussion and analysis along clear, coherent, and stable lines; and whether they were capable of conducting the analysis of their past, present, and future. An irrelevant analysis can only create disorder and confusion, for the sway which the researchers may hold over a group can last for only a certain time and can never be sufficiently strong to lead each member of the group to behave over a long period in conformity with the hypotheses whose predictions as to his own behavior are unknown to him. We noticed not only in the case of the Occitanists, but also in that of the antinuclear militants and even of the students, that the researchers' hypotheses were relevant and that they gave rise to meaningful discussion in the groups. What was new here was that this group self-analysis, guided and stimulated by the researchers' intervention, resulted in a practical deadlock or rather in a series of repeated failures. The groups were perfectly well aware of this, recognized their failure and analyzed it with remarkable perspicacity, sincerity, and courage.

By the end of the central phase of work, carried out not only in Montpellier and Carcassonne but also in Limoges and Paris, we were able to state that Occitan protest action in its entirety is functioning as a search for an absent movement and that this action has not succeeded in finding the unity desired.

The Unity and Duality of Occitan Action

This failure was serious; it forced us to recognize that a unified and integrated Occitanist movement cannot exist, which accounts for the constant and serious weakness of all Occitanist movements. It also led us to introduce a new, weaker, hypothesis. If the Occitanist movement had not succeeded in unifying its various components, was it at least able to control the tensions and direct the movement toward weakly integrated but effective action? If Occitania was subject to an internal colonialism, it was because it was both dependent and integrated: it should, therefore, be possible to generate collective action which would take into account these two aspects of the Occitanian situation and thereby appeal to a historic nationalism, while at the same time acting within the framework of French society. Was not this what the Volem vivre al païs (VVAP) had been seeking from 1974–78: to be an Occitanist movement allied to the French left? Was not this the direction taken by the wine-growers in their action of defending a country and yet bringing pressure to bear upon the French government, sometimes through the intermediary of high-ranking figures, and at other times through direct action, even violence? This double situation—with one foot in and one foot out—did not allow for the production of a strong ideology or powerful movement; nevertheless, it was able to generate an effective strategy. Is trade unionism in a much different situation when it speaks in the name of the class struggle, while still seeking to develop collective negotiations?

The difference between this and the preceding phase of intervention must be properly understood. In the former stage the purpose was to integrate two of the senses of Occitanist action for its own sake: the struggle for the defense of a cultural identity and the demand for economic development; the purpose now is to combine two senses, one for Occitania and one for French society, and hence to accept that the Occitanist movement is simultaneously both an Occitanist action and a reaction to the crisis of the French national state.

It was this that engendered our hypothesis concerning the increasing dualization of French society which was being developed at the same moment both by the government spokesmen and by the industrialists. International competition, they claimed, made it necessary to strengthen an effective and dynamic "battleforce" while keeping the remainder of the country as a "territorial army," slower in its movements and weaker in its productivity and earnings. This we would express with different connotations by saying that France has renounced its social, economic, and cultural integration and has accepted this dualization against which the Latin-American progressivists have fought so hard. The Midi, or south of France, is becoming a "mezzogiorno," a controlled drift toward underdevelopment, occasionally disguised behind deceptive labels such as the opening-up of tourism, the sweet life, or even defense of the patrimony.

All of this has deeply altered the direction of Occitanist

action. It had been opposed to an all-powerful, centralizing state, defending the Federalists against the Jacobins. Now we have shown the movement that its opponent has renounced the unity of the republic and accepted the controlled and dependent autonomy of the sectors and regions destined to underdevelopment. In these conditions Occitanist protest becomes an element of the struggle against the dualization of French society: hostility toward central power becomes tranformed—through a reversal that is often not yet perceived—into defense of the diversity and autonomy of French society, which are the conditions of its real integration and opposed to the disintegration caused by the increasingly brutal domination of the center over the periphery.

The Occitanist movement can thus become the ally of the French forces of the left, if they abandon their Jacobinism. In this respect the development of the Communist Party is important and has made possible a real convergence beween its action and that of the Occitanists. Conversely, the recession of socialist influence in the Languedoc may be explained by the attachment of most of these high-ranking regional and departmental officials to their role as favored interlocutors of the central power. According to this hypothesis, the Occitanist movement cannot in itself be a social movement, thought it may constitute half of such a movement if it succeeds in becoming the partner of a French left fighting the breach between state and nation enforced by the great alliance between the state and the industrial battleforce.

The impact of this fresh hypothesis on the Occitanist groups, particularly that of Montpellier, was considerable. Many of the militants saw in it the unhoped-for solution to their difficulties. Our conclusions, however, were more cautious. The introduction of this hypothesis into the groups had only limited effect, simply because it was our interpretation of a logical change rather than the observation of a real reversal in the French left, which more often remains *étatiste* and centralistic. The strengthening of the Occitanist movement depends on a possible transformation of the French left, and until this occurs the movement will inevitably be torn apart. On the one hand, it is reduced to cultural protest taken in hand by the parties and trade unions of the French left; on the other hand, it is attracted by an independentist program and fascinated by the example of the Corsicans and the Basques. Between this revolutionary nationalism and a close association with the Communist or Socialist parties the distance is so great that the unity of the

Occitanist movement, which is already weak, cannot help being shattered.

Such was the situation at the time when this research study was concluded. The very unity of the Institute for Occitanist Studies was being called into question: struggles between different tendencies were tearing apart the VVAP movement; relations between the wine-growers and the Occitanists had almost entirely disappeared; the Communist Party was expanding its influence; the cultural militants were falling back on defense of the language; and certain activists had thoughts of using violent methods of action. The Union of the Peoples of Occitania (UPO), which had just been created at the instigation of *Aici e Ara*, will inevitably be defined more by its resistance to communist influence and by its nationalism then by its intention to gather together all the Occitanist militants.

This negative conclusion—far removed from our expectations, difficult to utter, and even more difficult to hear—does not exclude even in the short term the protest actions or "blows" such as those of which the militants of the Perigord and the Limousin dream. But it does lead to the greatest importance being given to the organizational difficulties of Occitanist action and to the struggles by which the movement is split and which one would be mistaken to reduce to personal confrontations.

Does this conclusion mean that the Occitanist movement is without importance and without effect? Our research in no way permits such an interpretation. This impossible movement is at the same time a necessary one. The student movement which we analyzed in 1976 (Touraine *et al.*, 1978) was in a state of disintegration, decadent, declining and blind, an apparently effective activism which was none the less void of direction. The Occitan movement, although divided, is overflowing with direction. Nothing permits us to gloss over the duality of our conclusions: the Occitan movement tends constantly to become divided, and at the time of our research it was receding and threatened by a breach between nationalism and social and economic defense. But it continued to work against this inner disruption and to seek ways of refocussing itself by shifting closer toward its base and to its permanent *raison d'être*—the defense of the country. A simpler, more enthusiastic, or on the contrary, more dramatic conclusion might perhaps be more alluring; however, it could not but deceive the Occitans and strengthen the tendencies toward the disruption of their movement. Our own conclusion, the outcome of a series of investigations and demonstrations, should at least enable one to achieve as close as possible a rapprochement between the analyses of social movements and the militants concerned with gaining an understanding of the conditions and the nature of their action.

Nationalism or an Antistate Struggle?

On both sides people are wondering in particular if the Occitanist movement can follow the way opened up by the movement of the nationalities in the nineteenth century and further enlarged by the national liberation movements of the twentieth century. Our research would seem to lead us in a direction contrary to this hypothesis, showing that the Occitanist struggles have exemplary importance of quite a different nature. Up till now nationalism has almost always been linked to the creation of a national state and has, therefore, been what we would call a historical movement rather than a social movement. Nationalism tends to be an antielitist movement rather than a class movement, aimed at controlling change and at creating a specific mode of development rather than at fighting against a ruling class, battling against an outside enemy rather than a social opponent.

In his speech of 1882 on "What is a nation?," Renan defended the right of peoples to decide on their own national affiliation, and challenged the "ethnoregional" theories which caused the nation to be based on race, language, and religion; but after stating that what constitutes a nation is not speaking the same language nor belonging to the same ethnographical group, he added it is "to have common glories in the past, a common will in the present; to have done great things together, to will to do the like again" (Renan, 1970, p. 81), thus closely associating nation and state, for how could a nation without a state accomplish "great acts"? An analysis very close to his is that of Otto Bauer, who defined the nation as a "community of fate" and as a "desire for communal existence," by contrasting nation with class, which is a "community of character" (Bauer, 1924). This voluntarism, common both to the inheritor of the French Revolution and to the Austro-Marxist, is different from historical nationalism which goes back not to a common will or desire, but to a common origin. This is a concept which was developed in particular by the Germans in the late eighteenth and early nineteenth centuries, by the nationalities of Central Europe who had been deprived of their national existence, and also by the Jews who, either in the Bunds or in the Zionist organizations, appealed to the rights of a historicocultural group. The Catalans were susceptible to German romantic thought, as is shown by the "Oda a la Patria" by B. C. Aribau, a work which marked the beginning of the *Renaixença*. In all these instances the nation wished to be identified with a national state, and the national protest was political and historical rather than social. Renan did not oppose the nation to the state, but national states to empires.

It is once nationalism develops in colonized countries that its nature changes and the political struggle becomes associated with a social struggle. Anti-imperialism calls both upon national liberation and on the class struggle: it creates a movement which is simultaneously historical and social. This model, rather than that of the nationalities of Central or Eastern Europe in the nineteenth century, is the one which dominates the mind today. Frantz Fanon and Jean-Paul Sartre, during the Algerian War—and Sartre once again during the trial of the Basque nationalists at Burgos—provided the best-known expressions of this model. And the more brutal the foreign domination it is combating, the stronger it becomes. It took hold in Ireland, first, during the times of James Connolly and the national revolutionary uprising of 1916, and then in our own times even in the two IRAs. And even more strongly in Euskadi, where the repression exercised by the Franco regime was even more brutal. Algerian and particularly Maoist influences led the Basque ETA, beyond its own divisions, to appeal both to Marxist ideology and to a national liberation movement in which the national petite bourgeoisie could find its place. Here we are far from the thinking of the first Marxists, of Marx, Engels, and even Rosa Luxemburg, who were mistrustful of nationalism, which was above all bourgeois in their eyes, and opposed to it the class struggle and proletarian internationalism. This opposition was followed, particularly in Asia and Latin America, by the union of class struggles and national struggles against imperialism and its allies, the oligarchy and the corrupt "comprador" bourgeoisie. This union was ideologically strong but politically weak, and it led to the creation of absolute states.

This antiimperialist and proletarian nationalism is very much present in the Occitanist movement, but it is still minoritarian and intermingled with very different themes. How is one to speak of historical nationalism in a region which has never had a national history? Some intellectuals may compare Occitania with one part or another of Africa, or else compare the Occitans to the Indians. These comparisons are indeed accepted because they help toward an arousal of national consciousness, but they are so clearly metaphorical that they do not involve any political consequences. Occitanist action belongs to a different ensemble, that of resistance struggles waged by a society and a culture against the incursion of the forms of organization and life which are dominant and imposed by a state.

If the word "nationalitarian" (*nationalitaire*) is so often used, it is not because it clearly defines the aim of such a movement—for we have seen how confused it was—but because it separates in a new way the defense of a nation and the creation of a state. It is difficult to understand what is meant by a nation without a national state, but it is easy to grasp the nature of a struggle carried out in the name of a sociocultural body against an increasingly total state.

Regionalism is a limited and most often conservative form of this defense. It breaks with the progressivism inherited from the Enlightenment, which contrasted innovation to tradition, the general or universal to the particular. Regionalism, like all other forms of particularism, instead opposes diversity to uniformity, rootedness to proletarization, initiative to dependence. The ethnographical analyses of D. Fabre and J. Lacroix (1975) are nourished by a nonconservative version of this regionalism.

Far more violent is the reaction of communitarian fundamentalism of the Iranian type which takes the form of a rejection of dependent modernization and an appeal to the absolute values which lead to theocracy. The contrast between this fundamentalism and the national revolutions of the preceding period is all the more striking. While the national revolutions—the most recent of which overthrew the negus in Ethiopia—struggled against tradition and oligarchy in the name of a national revolutionary will which was to open by force the way to progress, the Khomeinist movement is both nonnational and antirevolutionary. It has fought against a state, and its success has led to the disintegration of this state. And even in the West, does not the success of John Paul II derive from the fact that he has opposed religion, as a popular and communitarian force, to the domination of states? What a reversal this is in relation to the era of national construction directed either by the bourgeois parties, by enlightened despots, or by revolutionary, political, and military forces! And is not the uprising of the Polish workers in 1980, which is a class struggle, even more a nationalitarian struggle—the defense of a society against an almost foreign state by which it is dominated?

The Occitanist reaction is located between these two opposing forms of resistance to the modernizing state. It is a struggle both against technocracy and against the force of big capitalism concentrated in the name of a cultural specificity. Its struggle, which is more directly social, is nourished by its national consciousness. All these forms of antistate behavior are more social movements than historical movements. They make scarcely any appeal to a new mode of development, of historical change; they speak in the name of a people rather than that of a destiny; they are battling against rituals and apparatuses, which in France brings the struggle of the Occitanists closer to other struggles, that of the ecologists in particular. In all the Occitanist groups there emerges a strong sensitivity toward the antinuclear movement, and often also an opening up toward the woman's liberation struggles. But this resistance to technocratic domination and to the dualization it entails may also take on forms other than that of a social movement. This is also true of the antinuclear and ecologist movement. All may reject modernity and desire restoration rather than progress, they may also fall into the mold of a dominant model: the appeal to local life, to handicrafts, and to rural activities seems at times to anticipate the wishes of the technocrats, who are glad to see part of the population accepting of its own accord to live with limited aspirations and resources. Conversely, they can also go to the point of a complete break, at the risk of being drawn into escalating violence, which occasionally mobilizes the people but may also isolate the activists.

On what condition do these forms of resistance produce social movements? They must, first, be backed up by a principle of resistance sufficiently strong to avoid the traps and the limitations of regional development. This principle can be only a powerful awareness of cultural identity, and hence of national difference. Secondly, and conversely, it is necessary that the defence of a country or of a region should also cause a general social struggle to emerge and, consequently, to be associated with social forces located within the dominant system. All research shows that these two conditions are necessary and complementary, that the Occitanist or Breton movement cannot be built up by choosing only between either national specificity or, instead, participation in the social struggles of the "hexagon" (France). The movement can be created only by associating these two forces of its action.

This conclusion enables us to understand the work of the militants, of organizations and ideologists, for their work is organized around this central point which remains empty. We believe that this work may produce a movement, but we have also observed that the principle of the integration of struggles constantly tends to become weakened, which in the case of the Occitanist movement has led to the action being split between an antiimperialist tendency and an anticapitalist tendency.

All national movements which are not backed up by a national ruling class, as in Catalonia—either because this class does not exist, as in Corsica, Occitania, or Britanny, or because it is hand-in-glove with the dominant state, as in the Basque country—are drawn both toward a movement of national liberation and toward an economic defense more or less powerfully marked by class struggles. If repression is weak, this bipolarization results in confusion and instability; if it is powerful, as in Ireland and particularly in Euskadi, a breach occurs between the two forms of struggle, one of which gives priority to armed action in the service of nationalist objectives, while the other sees itself more as a politicomilitary struggle, which means that it is more Marxist and tends to give priority to the class struggle rather than to nationalism. In Euskadi national action prevails completely over class action owing to the strength of the national consciousness itself and to the existence of a powerful nationalist party concentrated around the middle classes. In Occitania, on the other hand, independent nationalism is little expressed, remaining confined to small groups such as the one which publishes *Aice e Ara*, and it is not openly demanded by any of the chief leaders of the movement, even if Y. Rouquette and P. Maclouf are quite close to such a standpoint. By contrast, however, the necessary link with the French left and the priority given to the defense of workers, farmers, and wine-growers have frequently been proclaimed; and they have been defended by Robert Lafont, who is highly critical of extreme nationalism, the substantiality of which he has called into doubt.

Our conclusion is that although it may become enriched by its nationalist anti-imperialist components and by its economic claims, the Occitanist movement—like the Breton movement under other forms—can develop only by following the nationalitarian path, by defining itself as an antistate movement, which is the only way for such movements to integrate national consciousness and social struggles. In writing these lines we are not thinking of going beyond the results of our research. It is certainly not up to us to indicate to the militant Occitanists what their policy or strategy should be, but we would not be meeting their expectations if we were not to tell them clearly what conclusions our intervention had led to and what the historical nature of their action is, that is, on what condition it can develop and make its mark on history.

The militant Occitanists have agreed not only to carry out their self-analysis with us, but also to participate in our work, which means enabling us today to present publicly our analyses and conclusions. We in turn would like our published study to be useful to them. Its purpose is not to interest the spectators of history or the lovers of exoticism; rather its aim is to help the Occitanists to mark their collective existence more powerfully tomorrow than they have today, by showing them that the Occitanist movement is possible provided it is built up both around a position which is at once national and Occitanist, and around resistance to the dualization of French society. The aim of all sociological intervention is to define the maximum of possible action, and hence of knowledge, and to help the actors to become even more fully actors.

The Occitanist movement has need of such reflexion, for it is weak and frail. When it is not involved in a great revolt by the wine-growers, it attracts gatherings far less numerous than those which occur at folklore festivals; and its language schools themselves attract far more militants than its political organizations. It is possible that little by little it may dissolve as the regional crisis worsens, and that it may be replaced both by violent revolts and by an increasing dependence on the central powers. This would be a great misfortune for Occitania and for French society, because the Occitanist militants are agents of change in a none-too-dynamic society and because they are fighting against the dualization and disarticulation of French society. It is our hope that we have revealed the importance of their action far more than its weakness.

In wishing to render useful service to the militant Occitanists, our research has by no means distanced itself from its own objectives of knowledge. On the contrary, it has shown that the Occitanist struggle belongs partially, weakly, but truly to the body of struggles by which the vital social movement of our times and of the coming period is borne: the resistance of the "territories" and the "publics"—to use our customary words— to the sway of a technocracy which is increasingly dominating the state. We do not separate our defense of sociological intervention as a method for studying social behavior from our effort to bring out the historical nature of the social movements of today and from our assistance to the development of the Occitanist struggles. We believe that knowledge must be an instrument of liberation.

Our last word must be to define the contribution of this research to knowledge. Our research has studied the Occitanist movement, which sees itself both as class action—or at least left-oriented action—and national action. Has our research discovered in this movement a specific manner of combining these two great actors in social struggles—class and nation?

Not only is our answer negative, but our intervention has been so active and our attempts to help the groups construct a synthesis of the two orders of struggle have been so numerous and prolonged that we feel justified in going beyond the Occitan case to state that these two orders of struggle—class struggle and national struggle—are of different natures. They may be intermingled, may even join, but they cannot be unified. Class struggles are directed against social domination in a type of society and in a pattern of production; national struggles fight against a state—national or foreign—which appears as an obstacle, as the principal opponent of development. Class struggles are the subject of synchronic analysis, national struggles of diachronic analysis, of a study of change.

One objection, however, immediately rises: is not the weakness of the link between the two struggles more the weakness of the Occitanist movement itself? And in colonial situations, does not one have by contrast a powerful unity between social struggles and national struggles? This reasoning is weak. The stronger the external constraints are, the more the two orders of struggle become intermingled, which results particularly in the production of ideologies proclaiming their fundamental unity, even their identity. As soon as these constraints weaken, especially after decolonization, one finds instead that a separation occurs between nationalism and the workers' or peasants' movement, which generally leads to the triumph of the nationalists over the revolutionaries, and of the military over the unionists. The thinking of F. Fanon has cast light upon the national liberation struggle of Algeria; but it has none the less been contradicted by the Algerian reality and by the subsequent split between the comrades-at-arms of the day before.

Our intervention penetrates far more deeply into the functioning of social struggles than does a description of the events. And the very weakness of the Occitanist movement makes clearer the impossibility of transferring directly from one style of struggle to another, or even of combining them. This is not to say that there cannot exist struggles which are both social and national, but it must be recognized that there can be no unity in such struggles, that they are constantly threatened by a breach between the two sides of their action and that, consequently, they can have strength and importance only in periods of crisis.

Such then, is the situation of the Occitanist movement: it becomes weakened and disappears if it is not both national and social at the same time, but it can never integrate these two components into its thought or action. It is only ideologically that it unifies them, but the ideas proclaimed in such profusion between 1970 and 1976 have not stood up to the test of fact, nor have they made it possible to construct the national and popular action for which they believed they had provided the formula. The failure of this movement is but a weak and distant echo of the far more important failure of Third Worldism reinforced by an anticapitalism derived from the West and at the same time the inheritor of the movements of national liberation.

The Occitanist movement can survive and act only if it recognizes that it must combine the orientations of two different forms of action instead of establishing their unity. This perhaps is impossible and could lead toward a break which would set up a complete and violent opposition between the activists of an independently oriented movement and those who would subordinate their economic and cultural demands to the objectives of a French political party. But if we recognize the importance of the Occitanist movement, it is because it constantly and stubbornly endeavors to bring together the two struggles which spontaneously move apart from each other, and to combine them; it is capable both of recognizing and of living with its double nature. The life of the Occitanist movement is made up of centripetal efforts alternating with the centrifugal attractions which tend to separate social and national action.

It is hardly likely that these efforts will succeed in constructing a movement of sufficient strength to effect a rapid and deep-reaching change in the situation of the Occitans, but they are nevertheless important. They have already achieved a striking transformation in the consciousness of the Occitanian periphery and they are breaching the pride of the centralist powers. In particular, the Occitanist movement has directed the defense of a cultural specificity toward the future rather than toward the past, and toward modernization and not regionalist restoration, and this protects it from reactionary and authoritarian temptations. It takes part in the defense of society against the state, which in France is also the defense of the weak against the strong. Though incapable of overthrowing domination, it has the strength necessary to challenge it and weaken it; and though too weak to stir up large-scale organized action, it is strong enough to extend its influence over public opinion. It will not spark off a revolution, but it is an important agent of the social struggles which are now developing.

Note: Chapter 8

This is a version of materials appearing in Alain Touraine and François Dubet, with Zsuzsa Hegedus and Michel Wieviorka, *Le Pays contre l'état. Luttes Occitanes*, Paris, Seuil, 1981.

References: Chapter 8

Bauer, Otto (1924), *Die Nationalitätenfrage und die Sozialdemokratie* (Vienna: Wiener Volksbuchhandlung).

Fabre, Daniel, and Lacroix, Jacques (1975), *Communautés du sud. Contribution a l'anthropologie des collectivités rurales Occitanes*, 2 vols. (Paris: Union générale d'éditions).

Renan, Ernest (1970), "What is a nation?" in E. Renan (ed.), *Poetry of the Celtic Races and Other Studies* (Port Washington, N.Y.: Kennikat Press), pp. 61–83; first published in France, 1882.

Touraine, Alain (1981), *The Voice and the Eye: The Analysis of Social Movements* (New York: Cambridge University Press).

Touraine, Alain, Dubert, François, Hegedus, Zsuzsa, and Wieviorka, Michel (1978), *Lutte étudiante* (Paris: Seuil).

9

Issues of Theory and Methodology in the Study of Ethnolinguistic Movements
the Case of Frisian Nationalism in the Netherlands

BUD B. KHLEIF

Introduction

The purpose of this chapter is twofold: (1) to sketch out a theoretical framework for viewing ethnolinguistic movements, particularly those in Western Europe; and (2) to deal substantively with one case study, that of the Frisians in the Netherlands. The framework serves as an ultimate context for the case study, which reciprocally helps to make the particular illuminate the general. At the outset we should say that we prefer to view method merely as an aspect of theory, not vice versa. This way, we shall hope to eschew reductionism and get to see things in larger contexts.

We present our sociocultural framework as a series of explicit assumptions, woven into an overall pattern. We may have to deal with some fundamental questions or concepts—for instance, what is "nationalism"?—giving them working definitions. Our perspective is essentially that of the old Chicago school of sociology: we are guided by formulations advanced by R. E. Park, E. C. Hughes, G. H. Mead, Robert Redfield, Herbert Blumer, and others; we prefer fieldwork as a method; we view symbolic interactionism as a key for unlocking social structure; we are concerned with macro- more than microconsiderations; we often like to go back to Weber and Simmel and attempt to link them with more modern writers. *Issues are always relative to an ethos* (cf. Mills, 1959, pp. 128–31; Ellul, 1964, pp. xiii–xx)!

What is the interrelationship of social structure and nationalism? How do we account for the rise of nationalism in the post-1945 era? What are the stigmata of nationalism (somewhat in the post-crucifixion sense)? How is nationalism nurtured and maintained? How has it fared in Friesland, particularly since the end of World War II? These will be the questions for exploration here.

Nationalism and the Social Structure

Sociologists often use three concentric contexts for understanding social organization among humans: *macro-*, *meso-* or intermediate, and *micro-*. The first is the level of social classes and ethnic groups within the nation-state; the second is the level of institutions; and the third is that of the household. We will work herewith essentially from the *macro-* to the *meso-*, rarely for our current purposes being concerned with the *micro*level. At times we will go beyond the nation-state to link some phenomena with an international configuration, the world-system or world-economy.

(1) In the final analysis, perhaps, when sociologists get to contemplate not only their own society, but also their own sociology as a calling or trade, some may come to the conclusion—as Alain Touraine has done—that there is actually no such thing as "society" as a viable sociological concept, only "social movements" (Touraine, 1980a, 1973, 1981b). This is precisely the notion of an earlier American sociologist, Robert E. Park, who thought of society as a group of competitive groups that are in *temporary* balance—or peace treaty—perpetually modifiable and negotiable by future generations (Park and Burgess, 1921, p. 665; cf. Khleif, 1971, pp. 144–5). This notion—of Park and of Touraine—emphasizes that *change is a constant in human affairs*, not equilibrium; for the *balance* is always *temporary*. This is our initial and fundamental assumption for viewing ethnic and linguistic stratification across generations. We should wonder not so much why there has been an ethnic resurgence in a given sociopolitical era, but more realistically perhaps, why there has *not* been one!

(2)   (*a*) A corollary of the aforementioned notion is that history—including contemporary history—abounds with instances of "shell nationalism" or "hollow-core nationality," that is, one that is almost obsolete or quite dormant, but that can be refilled several generations later. Ethnic relations, then, need not be examined only when they are flaring up, but also when they are dormant or semidormant (Khleif, 1980a, p. 38). (*b*) How ethnicity—that is, ethnic pride or ethnic identity—is transmitted from generation to generation has not received adequate conceptualization in sociology or anthropology. In this regard we would like to single out the helpful works of Mannheim (1952), Bourdieu (1979), and more recently Menes (1982).

(3)   A necessary, if not sufficient, condition for national assertiveness, for the rise of the part against the whole, seems to be a major upheaval or war during which representatives of minorities may at times not only endure sacrifices, but also prove themselves worthy in the eyes of the majority, with nationalist movements thereafter gathering strength. New intellegentsia, new spokesmen and spokeswomen, for example, arose among the Welsh, the Frisians, and the Quebecois subsequent to World War II, part of the acceleration of white collar job opportunities and the opening up of higher education—the gateway to the professions—increasingly to inhabitants of historically neglected regions (Khleif, 1978).

(4)   Manifest or latent, a "theory of the state" is always necessary for explaining nationalism and its corroborative socioeconomic and ethnolinguistic stratificational and institutional arrangements, be it the nationalism of a majority, that is, of a dominant group that has traditionally controlled the nation-state, or of a rising minority. In this regard our working theory of the state is a combination of (*a*) conflict theory—in the sense that the state can basically be regarded as a sort of hegemony of a ruling group over a number of less powerful ones—and (*b*) "contractarian" theory—in the sense that the state provides services to meet social needs and professes sentiments of an ever-increasing equality for various segments of its population (cf. Hechter and Brustein, 1980, pp. 1089–90).

Conflict theory, as a theory of the state, is in line with the notions of Park and Touraine, expressed above. Our combination of conflict and contractarian theory is in line with what Alan Wolfe (1977) has termed the "dual state," the welfare state of Western Europe, particularly after World War II, a state with a seemingly popular politics and economic concessions to rank-and-file citizens, one with a "frontstage," so to speak, where an audience of citizens is entertained with a particular politics, and a "backstage" where the actual power, hidden from the audience, is held. The post-1945 welfare state has extended its "contractarian" avowals, for example, in the form of social services to heretofore neglected ethnic groups in outlying regions, making them more speedily middle class and white collar. The nationalist movements of such groups can be understood, then, as an attempt to get to the backstage of the "dual" state!

(5) (*a*) The world as we know it—that is, the interrelated intrapenetrated world economic system with its overall technological homogenization, monetary and energy crises, and supranational inflation and unemployment— began in the nineteenth century when the whole globe was turned into a single social system serving an industrial culture radiating out of Western Europe and North America. It was Western colonialism that consolidated the world into a single social system serving the needs of Western industrialism (Worsley, 1973, pp. 50–3). The phenomenon of the "world-system" is currently attracting a lot of intellectual interest, particularly in relation to the effect of such system on individual nation-states and with regard to upheavals, tensions, and changes in this overall system (cf. Wallerstein, 1974, 1979, 1980; Bergesen, 1980; cf. Gunder-Frank, 1969). Whereas for all practical purposes the nation-state may be regarded as the foremost macrosociological context for examining ethnolinguistic and nationalist phenomena, it can in turn be regarded merely as a subunit of the world-system, as the internal workings and traditional stratificational arrangements of the state are subjected to somewhat uncontrollable influences from the outside. (*b*) Wallerstein's world-system theory is actually a *world-market* theory, the world market being the central mechanism of international capitalism, the central expression. The world market creates and re-creates capitalist social relations (of "shearers" and "shorn" in Talleyrand's terms—cf. Warren, 1980; Jenkins, 1970) on a world scale, an *international system of*

stratification in which sovereign states are individual units. Two further notions may explain how people in a region of the nation-state—for instance, in a distinct ethno-linguistic territory, such as Wales within Britain and Friesland in the Netherlands—may experience firsthand the vicissitudes of the international market:

(i) We refine the idea of "market" further by bringing in Weber's notion of "market situations," that is, his tripartite typology of people's class situations or "life chances" with reference to—(*a*) the *labor market*—employers v. employees, (*b*) *money market*—creditors v. debtors, and (*c*) *commodity market*—buyers v. sellers; landlords v. tenants (Rothman, 1978, p. 22; Wiley, 1967, p. 531). These three types of markets obtain within nation-states and, more important, *between* them.

(ii) Because headlong expansionism and relentless profit maximization seem to be inexorably built into the world capitalist market, and because the sky seems to be the limit when it comes to production or "supply," while human capacity to consume is limited, the excess of supply over demand periodically creates a socioeconomic crisis. Every fifty years or so the world market seems to go through distinct economic (Kondratieff) cycles, each of which is composed of both a "growth" or expansion phase and a "stagnation" or contraction one (Wallerstein, 1980, pp. 168–9). In other words, national growth rates tend to follow a regular pattern (Rostow, 1980), which influences the priorities of the nation-state; for instance, whether to give continued financial support for bilingualism or for the cultural activities of minorities. Kondratieff cycles, with their duality, are the temporal dimension to the threefold spatiality of core, semiperiphery, and periphery of the world-system.

(6) A fundamental structural change in the nature of industrial society in the West, in the "control mechanism" of the world-system located in Western Europe and North America, has occurred essentially after 1945. The major features of this distinct transformation include extension of industrialization, tourism, and investment into hitherto somewhat isolated but ethnically distinct regions, for example, Flanders in Belgium, Brittany and Corsica within

France, and Quebec in Canada (Khleif, 1979a, p. 2). In other words, nationalist movements in the underdeveloped or traditionally rural regions of the underdeveloped world—"the Third World in the First World" are perhaps a case of decolonization within the nation-state (especially one that had lost its empire), subsequent to decolonization without it: an extension of, and a sequel to, nationalist movements of the Third World (Khleif, 1980a, p. 2). If this formulation is essentially correct, then what is needed is a typology of internal colonization situations and the decolonization efforts connected therewith, including, for example, attempts at devolution in Wales, Scotland, and Corsica (cf. Khleif, 1980a, pp. 317–31; Simon, 1982; Ashworth, 1977, pp. 55–7).

(7) The transformation of the First World into a "post-industrial" society with a "core" of countries devoted to sales and service of products and a "periphery" of countries engaged in actual industrial manufacturing, mining, or specialized one-crop agriculture for the benefit of the core has also been accompanied by what can be termed a postindustrial *Verbindungsnetzschaft* (Richmond, 1969, pp. 278–80): by a global communication network emanating from the First World, by-passing traditional kin-based or market-based primary or secondary groups and information screening and processing associations within which the person is anchored, to go directly to the individual to give him/her the feel of "instant knowledge" of world events and of instant impact. Note that the world's major news agencies are those of the First World: Associated Press and United Press International in the United States, Reuters in Britain, and Agence France-Presse in France. The postindustrial society, based on electronic and cybernetic technologies, is where Marshal McLuhan's "global village" is created, where traditional social bonds are threatened with erosion, where the seemingly all-permeating or never-ending bombardment of consciousness by the core media is especially resented by rising nationalists. In other words, the cultural assertiveness of such places as Brittany, Corsica, Wales or Friesland faces a double jeopardy: the language of the dominant group within the nation-state (the "national" language), and the langue of the core of the world system English, or more accurately perhaps, American English! This sort of double threat, national and international, near

and far, is a major theme in the writings of nationalist spokesmen and spokeswomen in Wales, Brittany, and Quebec (cf. for example the writings of Ned Thomas in Wales, Morvan Lebesque in Brittany, and Françoise Loranger in Quebec).

(8)   In the final analysis, in the activity we tend to call *"social science"* (that is, a suprapersonal knowing), there is perhaps no psychology without a sociology, no sociology without an anthropology, and—to push this concatenation further—no anthropology without a multiplicity of connotations and denotations that extend awareness to larger and larger horizons: no anthropology without poetry or the appreciation of poetry! This means socioculturally that psychological mechanisms for explaining social movements may be logically necessary but insufficient. One has to appreciate *process*; to appreciate the rise of a new group or class and of what triggers its concoction of appropriate nationalist ideology; to appreciate what in the words of George Simmel makes the far near and the near far; and to appreciate Park's definition of "structure"—of the structure of the present, as *"process* in slow motion"! In addition, and contrary to what is experienced by the average person in TV-drenched America (sometimes unjustly accused of having no poetry in his life and of using "crime-drama" for entertainment), poetry continues to have a central importance in European society not only for members of dominant majorities, but especially for members of resurgent ethnolinguistic minorities, for example, the Welsh in Britain and the Frisians in the Netherlands (Khleif, 1980a, pp. xiv, 23–4, *passim*; Khleif, 1982, pp. 5–6).

Methods and Frameworks in the Study of Ethnolinguistic Movements

We would like to comment briefly on two theoretical perspectives in the study of nationalist movements or of social movements in general: the so-called "rationality model of individual actors" and the social activism model. The former, often favored by survey-oriented researchers concerned with voting behavior, tends to assume that human behavior is guided first and foremost by rational criteria; it is an individual-

centered rather than a community-centered approach.*
Moreover, the "rationality model" seems often to communicate
an *ideology of rationality* focussed on the individual in isolation, a calculating creature, motivated chiefly by economic
gain. This model, in our opinion, neglects *network* people in
favor of *atomistic* ones; it cannot account for historically con-
ditioned reactions undetected in the objective situation, for the
historical memory of a group. More important perhaps, the
"rationality model" seems to neglect the constant financial and
emotional sacrifices made by people involved in nationalist
movements—sacrifices that anyone having a first-hand (that is,
fieldwork) knowledge of an ethnic movement readily notices.
All theoretical models make assumptions about the nature of
human nature, for example, about whether individual actions
are premeditated, calculated, logical. The *self-interest* or
"rationality model of individual actors" neglects the group as
a source of rationality. It neglects the historical situation of the
group in relation to other groups. It assumes that individual
actors behave as if they were isolated from one another. Within
the total picture of national, ethnic, or political behavior, the
notion of rationality is of limited scope; the social context for
"rationality" is more important and needs to be specified.

A promising innovation is the social activism model in the
study of social movements—for example, the Occitan nationalist movement and the antinuclear energy movement. This
approach is synonymous with the research activities of Alain
Touraine in France (Touraine, 1980a, 1980b, 1981a, 1981b).
Basically it attempts to make human actors sociologists of their
own situation, treating them as activists and as analysts of their
activities. This approach, also called "sociological intervention," requires not only intellectual skills of the highest order
and incisive logic; more important, superb training in group-
work, in understanding and channeling group processes, in
forging a unity between theory and practice, in having a command of psychoanalysis and of therapeutic work as well as of
sociology. Very few sociologists or anthropologists, either in
Europe or elsewhere, have engaged in such advocacy-cum-
conceptualization.

Often what accounts for ethnolinguistic resurgence can be
summarized into sets of dichotomies, for instance, exogenous
v. endogenous factors, economic v. social-psychological ones,
and so forth. Two perspectives, however, seem to tie together

*See the chapters by Rogowski, and by Levi and Hechter, in this volume.

such dichotomies: (1) the world-system perspective, and (2) the internal colonialism metaphor. The two in turn are inter-connected.

We have earlier dealt with the world-system as an inter-national market one, suggesting that it may be the ultimate context for the study of nationalist movements. We now turn to the second perspective.

The Internal Colonialism Metaphor

A colonial analysis of the inner workings of an advanced industrial society such as Britain or the United States is only of recent vintage among sociologists (Khleif, 1972, pp. 12–13). In American sociology this explanatory orientation is a by-product of the black civil rights movement of the 1960s, although there were scattered echoes of it prior to that (Khleif, 1980b, p. 20). Basically, "internal colonialism" is the classical "external" colonialism of Western European countries applied, in a turning-of-the-tables stance, not overseas to remote places, for example, to pre-1947 India, but to regions within Western states, including the United States (Barrera, 1979; Hechter, 1975, 1980; Moore, 1970).

The dynamics of "internal colonialism" are as follows: the colonized become *possessions* of the conqueror; they are *administered from the outside* by representatives of the domi-nant group who are imported from the metropolis; their culture is systematically destroyed; they are the object of an ideology of racism; they are systematically excluded from the higher rewards of the occupational structure; their dignity is con-stantly assailed (cf. Blauner, 1972).

Obviously one dynamic—for instance, administration from the outside—does not a whole analytic concept make: "internal colonialism" has been criticized on a number of counts (see, for example, the chapters on Wales, Scotland, the Basque country, and Catalonia in Foster, 1980; Rawkins, 1981, pp. 11–18; Isajiw, 1981, pp. 23–4; cf. Murvar, 1982, pp. 14–16). In spite of its lack of precise indicators, and of overall typology of the various forms it takes in different environments (Lustick, 1980, pp. 74–5; cf. Zureik, 1979, pp. 10–30; Smooha, 1978, pp. 11–47, 151–82), we prefer to think of "internal colonialism" as a *metaphor* rather than a concept, useful in some instances in establishing historical analogies. It is, we believe, a *relative-deprivation model* which describes how access to objectively determined high-status occupations is regulated, and, more important, how such access is interpreted in ethnic regions such as Wales or Scotland, where the inhabitants have entered a "postcolonial" phase of rather open avenues to the national metropolitan culture and its central political institutions! Whereas some Welshmen may use "internal colonialism" as an analytic vehicle for explaining English–Welsh relations (Khleif, 1978, pp. 113–14, and 1980a, pp. 30–3), in Friesland one encounters a rather social-psychological variant of it called "dominance" (fieldnotes, September 1980). The heuristic value of "internal colonialism" is that such a metaphor may stimulate cross-cultural analysis of the overall dialectics of oppression, oppression in its ethnolinguistic, male–female, or social-class manifestations (Khleif, 1982, pp. 20–1). Allegorically, "internal colonialism" is a pregnant concept because it points to a range of phenomena of which the Western European variety, when compared with others worldwide, is perhaps the mildest form (Cohen, 1972, for example, treats linguistic restriction or cultural "banning" as a form of subordination and "spiritual murder"; see also Gladwin, 1980). We are not yet ready to abandon this metaphor: it has social-psychological resonance that leads to social structural considerations!

We are now ready to integrate the world-system—that is, world market—and the internal colonialism perspectives. We suggest that they are linked through a number of intermediary processes relevant to the post-1945 era, such as the following.

(1) (*a*) The importance of multinational corporations not only as arenas for social mobility in a given country or locale, but as arenas that often mix together in some industrial or manufacturing enclaves in formerly rural areas, diverse populations with different linguistic or cultural commitments. This means, among other things, that the status of traditional elites is reduced. (*b*) This is in line with Gellner's hypothesis about the rise of nationalism, a hypothesis that incorporates both economic and cultural factors:

> As the wave of industrialisation and modernisation moves outward, it disrupts the previous political units [which are] generally either small and intimate ... or large but loose and ill-centralised. The two prongs of nationalism, he [Gellner] suggests, tend to be a *proletariat* and an *intelligentsia*: the former is first uprooted and then gradually incorporated in a new national community; the latter

provides *new cultural definitions* of group membership which are widely diffused with the development of mass literacy and a national educational system which industrialisation itself makes necessary. (Gellner, 1964, cited and augmented in Bottomore, 1979, p. 102; emphasis added).

We suggest that, in the post-1945 era, the new cultural definitions have been focussed on maintenance of a traditional language, as, for example, in Wales and Friesland where there is still a thriving literature in the native tongue.

(2) Multinational corporations help to create a new middle and upper middle class: a managerial class that benefits from the importation of *Gastarbeiter* in the expansion phase of the Kondratieff cycle; a class that buys up "second homes" and "holiday homes" at an accelerated rate, particularly in rural areas (for instance, Englishmen in Wales, Frenchmen in Brittany and Corsica, and Germans and Dutchmen in Friesland). This encroaches on the local people's sense of territoriality, particularly where the local people are a numerical majority in their historical homeland.

(3) To a great extent, however, the rise of a new middle class in outlying regions of Western European nation-states has been closely linked to the doubling and tripling of college and university enrollments in the post-1945 era. This has produced a middle class with ethnic commitments forged during childhood in working-class households and by the experience, however fleeting, of ethnolinguistic or social subordination. Many of the spokesmen and spokeswomen of resurgent nationalism in the West European peripheries are members of this class.

(4) Hand-in-hand with the creation of a new university-educated middle class has been the expansion of health and welfare services to newly industrializing peripheries. Often, the high-echelon members of welfare bureaucracies in such regions have been representatives of linguistically and politically dominant groups from the metropolitan regions, thus signifying blocked opportunity for qualified local natives. The social-psychological mechanism of "relative deprivation" is the other side of the coin for "rising expectations": a feeling of exclusion from lucrative administrative jobs in one's own region. Here "internal colonialism" may be expressed as "dominance," a feeling of sociocultural siege.

(5) We now come to our central hypothesis, which takes into

account both economic and cultural factors. We believe economic factors are important but prefer to treat them in a Weberian manner, anchoring life chances not merely of individuals, but more important of whole ethnic groups, in market relations and, ultimately, in the occupational structure. We, therefore, define ethnicity as *political mobilization*, a reaction to perceived sociocultural threat. The supreme symbol of unity often becomes a traditionally suppressed native language, which cuts across internal divisions, vested interests, and feelings of inferiority. *We locate the politics of ethnicity in the post-1945 era in the transformation of group relations as a result of change in the systems of labor in the "postindustrial" society.* We shall apply different facets of this hypothesis to Friesland.

Application to Friesland

There are three facets to our central hypothesis, and we present them as subhypotheses: the quest for community; the corollaries of the expansion of the post-1945 welfare state; and the inhabitants' feelings of linguistic inferiority or cultural suppression that are akin to those of a colonial situation (cf. Khleif, 1982, pp. 15–20).

(1) The "Quest for Community" Hypothesis

Rapid industrialization of formerly rural areas and their closer integration with the national economy produce a sense of impending rootlessness and of the loss of the traditional "props" of identity. As Erik Erikson (Kinloch, 1974, p. 74) has pointed out, identity is the basic link between the "core" of the person and the collective or community culture: the person is anchored into a group through identification with it. Ethnicity may be regarded as a search for roots, for identity, for the creation of a *Gemeinschaft* in the midst of *Gesellschaft*, for checking social atomization in a rapidly urbanizing environment. The increasing emphasis on ethnic identity can be interpreted as a self-protective response to the increasing homogeneity of modern life. The emphasis on an ancestral language, for example, as an aspect of uniqueness and authenticity, cannot be bought or mass-produced (Khleif, 1978, pp. 104–5): "something we can call our own," something as the Welsh would say "Y Pethe" ("Ours," "Our very thing").

Consider the following:

(a)   Middle- and upper-middle-class Dutch immigrants to the Frisian countryside usually speed up its linguistic Dutch-ification (Gorter, 1981a, p. 3; cf. Wenger, 1978, p. 124, regarding Anglicization of traditionally Welsh-speaking areas). They buy "country houses" (van der Plank, 1978, p. 82). The proportion of persons who are monoglot Dutch-speakers in Friesland is growing: there are no longer any monolingual Frisians in Friesland (a similar situation exists in Wales in relation to Welsh) and Frisian-speakers are bilingual (Gorter, 1981a, p. 3; cf. Smith, 1977, regarding the bilingualism of the village community of Teherne, Friesland, and the increased use of Dutch).

(b)   In the 1950s and 1960s intensive urbanization took place in Friesland: the urban population jumped from 30 percent of the total to 50 percent. This further marginalized the countryside and its language (ibid., p. 76).

(c)   Rural Frisians, migrating to town and faced with what appeared to them to be the stigma of speaking an inferior language (Frisian), often shifted to speaking Dutch (ibid., p. 76) and raised their children as Dutch-speakers. The urbanized village of Stiens in Friesland, for example, tripled its population in a short time: newcomers to it, strangers in a new environment, began to speak Dutch, "to pretend to have a high status" (fieldnotes, 19 September 1980). This is a well-known phenomenon of migration and immigration, where newcomers tend to shift from a less esteemed to a more esteemed dialect of the same language or, if they have the rudiments of one, to another language altogether.

(2)   The "Welfare State" Hypothesis

Historically the following phenomena have been related to one another and treated as mutually reinforcing: industrialization, migration, urbanization, bureaucratization, cultural homogen-ization, and the establishment of service agencies (Khleif, 1980b, pp. 4–5). The growth of the welfare state after 1945 has had important social, political, and linguistic consequences for Friesland, among which:

(a)   There has been substantial immigration into Friesland of people whose mother tongue is Dutch: "Many of them came as *managers or as higher officials* with industrialization and the growth of the bureaucracy of the welfare state; or they came as owners of second-homes" (Gorter, 1981b, p. 4; emphasis added). What seems to make a difference is not merely the exodus of capable natives, but the influx of non-Frisians into Friesland to occupy *high-echelon positions*: as van der Plank put it, "A large number of non-Frisians occupy the *dominant positions* in the province: most of these positions are in fact occupied by persons who have moved in from elsewhere" (van der Plank, 1979, p. 87; emphasis added).

(*b*) Regionalism in Europe was encouraged by development of the European Economic Community (EEC). This, together with perceived threats to cultural identity and blockage of high-status economic opportunity, may have led in the 1970s to the establishment of a nationalist regional party, the Frysk Nasjonale Partij. That party obtained one-tenth of the vote in the first elections (Stephens, 1978, p. 579; van der Plank, 1979, p. 76).

(3) The "Internal Colonialism" Metaphor: Institutional Control

During fieldwork in the Netherlands, in 1980, I made it a point to ask whether "internal colonialism" was in any way useful in explaining Frisian–Dutch relations, whether any writer in the Netherlands had ever used it. The response I got from both Dutch and Frisian informants indicated that the term itself was unfamiliar to them, though readily understandable. The concept that was current among the people with whom I spoke was invariably "dominance": the dominance of the Dutch language, of the central government, of the central bureaucracy. "Dominance" seemed to signify both control from outside Friesland and encroachment from within it. From the way "dominance" was uttered, one got a mental picture of a double siege, within and without, irritating but not debilitating! Yet if one goes back to the history of the resurgence of the Frisian language, one may find indications to support a colonial analogy, particularly with reference to the *institutional control of consciousness* (for instance, control of cultural identity and language in the context of education and worship: in two out of the three sectors of the home–church–school trinity traditionally concerned with socialization of the new generation, as well as in courts of law):

(*a*) In 1897, for example, S. Bartstra, a Protestant minister and a Frisian who had spent his career in Indonesia, wrote a paper in Dutch entitled "De Ontfriesching van het Friesche Volk" ("Defrisianization of the Frisians," an expressive title), in which he objected to the teaching of Holland's history in the primary schools of Friesland rather than Frisian history—much as Indonesians were taught Dutch history rather than Indonesian history. One suspects that for Bartstra, at the time, the colonial analogy was too close for comfort.

(*b*)   Twenty-five years ago a Frisian school inspector visiting Frisian primary schools would use *Dutch* with teachers despite their poor knowledge of Dutch, and even though he could have communicated with them much more easily and naturally in Frisian (fieldnotes, 15 September 1980). This is reminiscent of accounts about Algerian schools even today, where an Arab inspector would insist on speaking French to teachers whose French was faulty or unmanageable.

(*c*)   In 1951 a Frisian street vendor in one of the towns of Friesland dared write in Frisian on his pushcart, an offense that brought him before a municipal judge in Leeuwarden, the capital of Friesland. The judge ridiculed the faulty Dutch of the street vendor in the process of fining him. This incensed a prominent Frisian journalist, poet, and playwright, Fedde Schurer, who wrote an editorial criticizing the judge's disdain for the Frisian defendant and his native language. The community issue, of course, was: couldn't Frisians use Frisian in Friesland? Fedde Schurer's trial for contempt of court was scheduled before the same judge on Friday 23 November 1951 in Leeuwarden. Friday, being the cattle market day for lots of farmers from the countryside, brought even more of them into town to follow the trial. The local police feared a riot and overreacted by indiscriminately using their billy clubs on the crowd that had assembled in front of the courthouse. The central government feared that things might get out of hand; it transferred the judge (by coincidence named Hollander, that is, pertaining to the traditionally dominant province of the Netherlands, a symbolism not lost on the Frisians) and got the case dismissed. Much more important, the Dutch Parliament passed a law early in 1952 permitting the teaching of Frisian in primary schools, even its use as a medium of instruction in the early grades; also Frisians were allowed to speak Frisian in courts of law, though Frisian documents, unlike those written in Dutch, are not yet legally binding. In Frisian annals Friday 23 November 1951 is a day of cultural self-assertiveness and pride in Frisian identity; the historic day is known in Frisian as *Kneppelfried*, that is, the "Friday of the cudgels." The ethnic and identity connotation is that things began to happen fast after that day! We have dwelt at length on this incident, because it represents internal colonial situations in other West European states where "submerged nations" exist.

(*d*) The traditional language of worship in Friesland has been, since the seventeenth century, Dutch. This is because the Bible was translated into Dutch earlier, and because the first Calvinist missionaries who came to Friesland were Dutch and also used Dutch texts for hymns and common prayer. The Bible was translated into Frisian only during World War II (Fedde Schurer had helped in that); a new Frisian translation of the Bible and *Book of Hymns* appeared only in 1978. Now the new generation is used to reading the Bible or reciting some Psalms or the Lord's Prayer in Frisian, whereas their parents only know them in Dutch (the church sermons continue to be mostly in Dutch, although some church magazines now carry an occasional article in Frisian). An informant put it this way: "The older generation thinks you don't pray to God, or speak to God, in Frisian: he only understands Dutch [laughter]! ... Yes, resistance of the older generation to sermons in Frisian [sermons have to be in the master language]. In church you use Dutch. At home Frisian was spoken, but when the father read the Bible or prayed, it was in Dutch ... It has to do with the higher or lower status of the language. Take my grandfather—as far as he was concerned, 'You couldn't talk about God in Frisian—that was horrible!' [said with distinct emphasis, the facial features lighting up in portrayal of both affection for the 'old codger' and amusement at his sternness]. My grandfather never went to church if he heard that someone was going to preach in Frisian! ... No I don't really think it's *suppression of the Frisian language*; I think it's a matter of *bicultural situation*" (fieldnotes, 17 September 1980).

(*e*) Language is an index of social position, of power, of the capacity to command deference. An inferior languge is an inferior person, at least social-psychologically and in relation to some situations or spheres of daily life. It is no wonder, then, that language has become the chief marker of ethnicity, the synonym for cultural identity and authenticity in movements of national resurgence in West European regions.

With regard to the Province of Friesland in the Netherlands and to the domains of Frisian–Dutch language use, Frisian has been traditionally in a relation of *stable diglossia* to Dutch, that is, the *high* variety of language (Dutch) was kept for formal domains (worship, formal education, courts of law, government departments, and overwhelmingly the mass media), whereas the *lower* variety (Frisian) was kept for informal use in everyday life (the home and the farm). Nationalism in Friesland means *inter alia*, the extension of the public or "official" domains of language use, of Frisian, into a variety of institutions and giving it what could be termed a *market value* (cf. Brazeau, 1964).

It is precisely in this attempt at giving *institutional support* for the language that the extent of its *institutional restriction* is fully and painfully comprehended, the extent of its "colonial" or subordinate status, the extent of its sociopolitical and socioeconomic constraints. A language ideology, among other things, serves to mobilize an ethnic group to break traditional *structural constraints* on the social mobility of its members through the passage of legislation to bilingualize governmental service institutions and business establishments, *bilingualizing* both the public and private sectors. The link between language and nationalism, the socioeconomics of it all, can be precisely formulated: a reaffirmation of linguistic identity, coupled with an ideology of collective rights, not only expands linguistic space and ethnic jurisdiction—an emotionally satisfying accomplishment in its own right—but also expands job opportunities (Khleif, 1979b, p. 72).

The current *Tynged yr Iaith* (Fate of the Language), the Welsh title of a famous British Broadcasting Corporation (BBC) radio lecture by the Welsh poet and playwright Saunders Lewis, a fateful and evocative title for language problems in general, what the Flemish would call *Taalstrijd*, or "language struggle", of the Frisian language can be summarized by a twofold hypothesis. (*a*) Without legislation by the Dutch Parliament, first and foremost, and by-laws by the provincial government and municipalities in Friesland to extend the domains of the Frisian language, to make it "official," there will be increased Dutchification of the informal realms of life in Friesland, a considerable threat to the Frisian language. (*b*) This means, as is currently being noticed, that there will be an increasing shift from a *stable diglossia* of Dutch and Frisian to an unstable one, to what Gorter (1981a, p. 7) calls "transitional bilingualism," with Dutch eventually gaining the upper hand in the home and outside it in Friesland.

A language ideology, of course, has emotional and economic consequences: an emphasis *inter alia* on the traditional cultural slogan of *Frysk en Frij* ("Frisian and free"), on a measure of independence and what Pietersen (1978, p. 380) has called the "right to exist," the freedom to be, an echoing of the efforts of the Frisian nationalist E. B. Folkertsma, head of the Fryslân Frij (Friesland Free), an organization established in the 1930s that called for decentralization and interdependence. Said Folkertsma (cited in Harris, 1956, p. 14; emphasis added): "We accept our political unity with the Netherlands as both desirable and necessary, but if unity of the Netherlands is to continue strong and vital, *the life must not be sqeezed out of its component parts.*" The "life" is the life of the language, of the cultural integrity of the Frisian community, of its socioeconomic fortunes.

Dynamics of Nationalist Movements

We have maintained that the rise of nationalist movements has been a response to the creation of new market situations that have been also accompanied by feelings of social dislocation, by threats to traditional community, and by a "double whammy" of status reduction of traditional elites and rising-expectations-cum-relative-deprivation of a new university-educated middle class. New systems of labor, new market relations, produce new vistas of "life chances" and a new intelligentsia with ideology-creating proclivities that make "ethnicity" or "nationalism" understandable as a *socially constructed phenomenon* (cf. Berger and Luckmann, 1967, pp. 37–46), an intelligentsia that defines sociocultural reality for others since human reality is, after all, a matter of social definition. In Friesland activists follow closely what goes on in Wales; in Wales what goes on in Scotland and Quebec; and so forth. Through cross-contacts nationalist movements seem to acquire—that is, for different parts of Western Europe—a sort of "cumulative directionality" (cf. Schermerhorn, 1964).

What sociologists call "social movements" are all political movements, whether the women's liberation movement or religious movements. In other words, religious movements are political movements using a religious idiom. They are all, of course, socioeconomic movements and seem to share some common characteristics or "quests," which we identify with particular reference to our principal concern: nationalist movements.

(1) People engaged in a nationalist movement, particularly the intelligentsia that engages in turning out an appropriate ideology, usually seek a *respectable genealogy*. They want to build a future from the past and forge a continuity in the life of the group, a continuity broken by negligence or by an oppressor. They look for a glorious past to edit the present. Hence the history of the group, if necessary, begins to be *rewritten*, dusted up and edited in terms of present needs, present concerns, and putative enemies or adversaries. Instances of treachery or betrayal by others are emphasized (cf. what the Welsh call "Brad y Llyfrau Gleision" or "Betrayal of the Blue Books," that is, the 1847 Parliamentary Reports by three English commissioners who maligned them and their language, creating among the Welsh such a sense of outrage that it led to an awakened nationalism—see Khleif, 1980a, pp. 106–13).

Along with the glorious pages of the past the historic memory of the Frisians consists, for example, of (*a*) the praise the Roman historian Tacitus (c. 55–120) has bestowed upon them: "The name of the Frisians is glorified among the Germans" (Tacitus, *Annals*, book IV); (*b*) of the fact that the North Sea used to be known as Mare Frisium, ("Frisian Sea") until about the tenth century; and (*c*) of the Battle of Warns on 26 September 1345, when they defeated the Hollanders (Dutch) (which is to say that historically the Frisians were never *conquered* by the Dutch, but joined them in a federation at a later date); and so forth. Among the nationalist or literary heroes of the Frisians, for example, are Japiks, Kalma, Bartstra, the Halbertsma brothers, and as mentioned earlier Fedde Schurer.

(2) In addition to a respectable genealogy, nationalists cultivate a sort of supernatural or mystical emphasis that asserts the group's unique traits. This is what Weber aptly termed a *providential mission* (Gerth and Mills, 1958,

p. 176); and Malinowski, the *myth charter* of a group, a sort of "justification by precedent" (cf. Malinowski, 1955, pp. 144–6). There is a myth of "chosenness," of "special status" in all nationalist movements.

(3) History provides heroes and a "providential mission," acting as nourishment for identity; sometimes it also provides *slogans* (such as *Frysk en Frij*—"Frisian and Free"). Not all slogans are historical, of course; many are contemporary. Slogans are rallying points, asserters of group uniqueness, defiers of oppression, expressers of pride.

These characteristics or dynamics we have sketched out are intended as matters of *process*, of symbolic interactionism, for comparison and contrast of a number of cases. Here, then, the social-psychological is considered a response to the socioeconomic or social structural.

Conclusion

In their resurgence ethnolinguistic groups seek to control institutions and institutional settings. One of those institutions, perhaps the chief success so far for Frisian (and Welsh) nationalism, is the *school*, the arena for bringing up a new generation, and more important, the pathway to the world of work. Nationalist groups have often attempted a *bilingualization of work settings, of the occupational structure*: governmental departments and service agencies, commercial and business establishments, and the mass media. When it comes to bilingualization of the world of work, the success of nationalist movements in Western Europe has been limited (Khleif, 1980a, pp. 81–99, and 1982, pp. 25–8). There is, obviously, an *interlocking* of the institutions of the nation-state: the dominant group that controls one tends to control the others; the dominant nationalism, the nationalism of the majority, is considered the unifying symbol for all groups. This in part accounts for the difficulty of linguistic and cultural "desegregation" or bilingualization of public institutions, particularly now in the contraction phase of the post-1972 economic cycle. Economic priorities determined by the central government of a nation-state seem now to portray financial support to minority languages as a luxury (for instance, in the United States), as a legitimate check on further political demands by the periphery (for instance, as shown by the results of the 1 March 1979 referendum on Welsh and Scottish devolution in Britain), and as a curb to extending the Frisian language as a subject and medium of instruction upward to secondary schools (bilingualism in Friesland prevails in the primary schools, unlike in Wales, where it continues in some schools through the sixth form, the equivalent of the American twelfth grade). Out stocktaking stops with 1982, the year of seemingly widespread unemployment and recession in the North Atlantic region.

References: Chapter 9

Ashworth, Georgina (ed.) (1977), *World Minorities* (Sunbury: Quartermaine House), Vol. I.

Barrera, Mario (1979), *Race and Class in the Southwest: A Theory of Racial Inequality* (South Bend, Ind.: University of Notre Dame Press).

Berger, Peter L., and Luckmann, Thomas (1967), *The Social Construction of Reality: A Treatise in the Sociology of Knowledge* (Garden City, N.Y. Doubleday/Anchor).

Bergesen, Albert (ed.) (1980), *Studies of the Modern World-System* (New York: Academic Press).

Blauner, Robert (1972), *Racial Oppression in America* (New York: Harper & Row).

Bourdieu, Pierre (1979), *Outline of a Theory of Practice* (New York: Cambridge University Press).

Bottomore, Tom (1979), *Political Sociology* (New York: Harper & Row).

Brazeau, E. J. (1964), "Language differences and occupational experiences," in M. Rioux and Y. Martin (eds.), *French Canadian Society*, Carleton Library No. 18 (Toronto: McClelland & Stewart), pp. 296–307.

Cohen, Jean (1972), "Colonialism and racism in Algeria (*circa* 1955)," in A. H. Richmond (ed.), *Readings in Race and Ethnic Relations* (Oxford: Pergamon).

Ellul, Jacques (1964), *The Technical Society* (New York: Vintage Books/ Random House).

Foster, Charles H. (ed.) (1980), *Nations without a State: Ethnic Minorities in Western Europe* (New York: Praeger).

Gellner, Ernest (1964), *Thought and Change* (London: Weidenfeld & Nicolson).

Gerth, H. H., and Mills, C. Wright (eds.) (1958), *From Max Weber: Essays in Sociology*, GB–13 (New York: Oxford University Press/Galaxy Books).

Giles, Howard, Bourhis, R. Y., and Taylor, D. M. (1977) "Towards a theory of language in ethnic group relations," in H. Giles (ed.), *Language, Ethnicity, and Intergroup Relations* (New York: Academic Press, pp. 307–48.

Gladwin, Thomas (1980), *Slaves of the White Myth: The Psychology of Neocolonialism* (Atlantic Highlands, N.Y.: Humanities Press).

Gorter, Durk (1981a), "The advancement of Frisian by the provincial government," paper presented at Second Colloquium on Language and Integration in Europe, Urbino, Italy, 16–20 September, mimeo.

Gorter, Durk (1981b), "The use of teleboard for language-teaching in Friesland," paper prepared for *International Journal of the Sociology of Language*, mimeo.

Gunder-Frank, André (1969), *Capitalism and Underdevelopment in Latin America* (New York: Monthly Review Press).

Harris, E. Howard (1956), *The Literature of Friesland* (Assen: Van Gorcum).

Hechter, Michael (1975), *Internal Colonialism: The Celtic Fringe in British National Development, 1536–1966* (London: Routledge & Kegan Paul; Berkeley and Los Angeles, Calif.: University of California Press).

Hechter, Michael (1980), "'Internal colonialism' revisited," paper presented at Second Conference of Europeanists, Washington, D.C., 24 October, mimeo.; revised version, in this volume.

Hechter, Michael, and Brustein, William (1980), "Regional modes of production and patterns of state formation in Western Europe," *American Journal of Sociology*, vol. 85, no. 5 (March), pp. 1061–94.

Isajiw, W. W. (1981), "Nationalism and community change in Quebec and Flanders," paper presented at Annual Meeting of the Society for the Study of Social Problems, Toronto, Canada, 22 August, mimeo.

Jenkins, Robin (1970), *Exploitation: The World Power Structure and the Inequality of Nations* (London: MacGibbon & Kee).

Khleif, Bud B. (1971), "The school as a small society," in M. L. Wax, S. Diamond and F. O. Gearing (eds.), *Anthropological Perspectives on Education* (New York: Basic Books, pp. 135–55.

Khleif, Bud B. (1972), "A socio-cultural framework for understanding race and ethnic relations in schools and society," paper presented at the Annual Meeting of the Society for Applied Anthropology, Montreal, Canada, 17 April, mimeo.

Khleif, Bud B. (1978), "Ethnic awakening in the First World: the case of Wales," in Glyn Williams (ed.), *Social and Cultural Change in Contemporary Wales* (London and Boston: Routledge & Kegan Paul), pp. 102–19.

Khleif, Bud B. (1979a), "Ethnicity and language in understanding the new nationalism: the North Atlantic region," paper presented at First Conference of Europeanists, Washington, D. C., 30 March, mimeo.

Khleif, Bud B. (1979b), "Language as an ethnic boundary in Welsh–English relations," *International Journal of the Sociology of Language*, vol. 23, no. 1–2 (Summer), pp. 59–74.

Khleif, Bud B. (1979c), "Language as identity: towards an ethnography of Welsh nationalism," *Ethnicity*, vol. 6, no. 4 (December), pp. 346–57.

Khleif, Bud B. (1980a), *Language, Ethnicity, and Education in Wales*. (The Hague: Mouton).

Khleif, Bud B. (1980b), "The nation-state and the control of consciousness: towards a sociology of schooling, language, and colonialism," paper presented at the Annual BERA Conference on the Sociology of Education, Cardiff, Wales, 3 September, mimeo.

Khleif, Bud B. (1982), "Ethnicity and language with reference to the Frisian case: issues of schooling, work and identity," in K. Zondag (ed.), *Bilingualism in Friesland* (Franeker, Friesland: T. Wever).

Kinloch, Graham C. (1974), *The Dynamics of Race Relations: A Sociological Analysis* (New York: McGraw-Hill).

Lustick, Ian (1980), *Arabs in the Jewish State: Israel's Control of a National Minority* (Austin, Texas: University of Texas).

Malinowski, Bronislaw, (1955), *Magic, Science, and Religion*, A-23 (Garden City, N. Y.: Doubleday/Anchor).

Mannheim, Karl (1952), "The problem of generations," in K. Mannheim, *Essays on the Sociology of Knowledge* (London and Boston: Routledge & Kegan Paul), pp. 276–323.

Menes, Bonnie (1982), "Generational transmission of national identity: the case of Alsace, 1871–1914," paper presented at Third Conference of Europeanists, Washington, D. C., 30 April, mimeo.

Mills, C. Wright (1959), *The Sociological Imagination* (New York: Oxford University Press).

Moore, J. W. (1970), "Colonialism: the case of the Mexican-Americans," *Social Problems*, vol. 17, no. 4 (Spring), pp. 463–72.

Murvar, Vatro (1982) "Submerged nations surfacing in research: review of two books," *Contemporary Sociology*, vol. 11. no. 1 (January), pp. 14–16.

Novak, Michael (1973), *The Rise of the Unmeltable Ethnics: Politics and Culture in the Seventies* (New York: The Macmillan Co.).

Park, R. E., and Burgess, E. W. (1921), *Introduction to the Science of Sociology* (Chicago: University of Chicago Press).

Pietersen, Lieuwe (1978), "Issues and trends in Frisian bilingualism," in J. A. Fishman (ed.), *Advances in the Study of Societal Multilingualism* (The Hague: Mouton), pp. 343–99.

van der Plank, P. H. (1979), "Frisian bilingualism in the Netherlands and Germany," *Plural Societies*, vol. 10, no. 1 (Summer), pp. 71–95.

Rawkins, Phillip M. (1981), "Culture as a dynamic factor in the analyis of nationalist movements," paper presented at Annual Meeting of the Society for the Study of Social Problems, Toronto, Canada, 22 August, mimeo.

Richmond, Anthony A. (1969), "Sociology of migration in industrial and post-industrial societies," in J. A. Jackson (ed.), *Migration*, Sociological Studies No. 2 (Cambridge: Cambridge University Press).

Rostow, W. W. (1980), *Why the Poor Get Richer and the Rich Slow Down* (Austin, Texas: University of Texas).

Rothman, Robert A. (1978), *Inequality and Stratification in the United States* (Englewood Cliffs, N.J.: Prentice-Hall).

Schermerhorn, Richard A. (1964), "Towards a general theory of minority groups," *Phylon*, vol. 25, no. 2, pp. 238–46.

Simon, Jacques-François (1982), "Corsican test-bed for a devolutionary experiment," *Manchester Guardian Weekly* (Le Monde section), vol. 126, no. 2 (10 January), p. 12.

Smith, James Floyd (1977), "Language use and language attitudes in a bilingual community: Terherne, Friesland," Ph.D. dissertation, Department of German Studies, Stanford University.

Smooha, Sammy (1978), *Israel: Pluralism and Conflict* (Berkeley, Calif.: University of California Press).

Stephens, Meic (1978), *Linguistic Minorities in Western Europe* (Llandysul, Dyfed, Wales: Gomer Press).

Touraine, Alain (1973), *Production de la société* (Paris: Seuil).

Touraine, Alain (1980a), "Social movements," paper presented at the Center for European Studies Colloquium, Harvard University, 17 April.

Touraine, Alain (1980b), *Titres et travaux d'Alain Touraine* (Paris: Center for the Study of Social Movements, Sorbonne).

Touraine, Alain (1980c), "The Occitanist movement," paper presented at Second Conference of Europeanists, Washington, D. C., 24 October, mimeo.; published as Chapter 8 in this volume.

Touraine, Alain (1981a), *Le Pays contre l'état. Luttes Occitanes* (Paris: Seuil).

Touraine, Alain (1981b), *The Voice and the Eye: An Analysis of Social Movements* (New York: Cambridge University Press).

Wallerstein, Immanuel (1974), *The Modern World System*, 2 vols. (New York: Academic Press), Vol. I, 1974; Vol. II, 1980.

Wallerstein, Immanuel (1979), *The Capitalist World-Economy* (New York: Cambridge University Press).

Wallerstein, Immanuel (1980), "The future of the world economy," in T. K. Hopkins and I. Wallerstein (eds.), *Processes of the World-System* (Beverly Hills, Calif.: Sage).

Warren, Bill (1980), *Imperialism: Pioneer of Capitalism* (London: Verso).

Wenger, G. Clare (1978), "Ethnicity and social organization in north-east Wales," in G. Williams (ed.), *Social and Cultural Change in Contemporary Wales* (London and Boston: Routledge & Kegan Paul), pp. 120–32.

Wiley, Norbert (1967), "America's unique class politics: the interplay of the labor, credit, and commodity markets," *American Sociological Review*, vol. 32, no. 4 (August), pp. 529–41.

Wolfe, Alan (1977), *The Limits of Legitimacy: Political Contradictions of Contemporary Capitalism* (New York: The Free Press).

Worsley, Peter (1973), *The Third World* (London: Weidenfeld & Nicolson).

Zureik, Elia T. (1979), *The Palestinians in Israel: A Study of Internal Colonialism* (London and Boston: Routledge & Kegan Paul).

PART TWO

Comparative Analyses

10

From Primordialism to Nationalism

JUAN J. LINZ

Introduction

Very often in the social sciences, in the absence of hard data, the conceptualization of social phenomena tends toward reification, the use of relatively simple typologies, a preference for dichotomies, and so on. This is certainly the case with much of the literature using the terms "nation" and "ethnicity" in the study of peripheral or emerging nationalisms or of drives for devolution in old states. The ambiguous results of elections and referendums in which the aspirations of peripheral nationalists were at issue should have led to a more careful and empirical analysis, to a consideration of the multiple and different types of identity and of the very imperfect correspondence between them and the political expressions of nationalism. Data collected in the various peripheries of Spain and in the French Basque country will allow us to explore more systematically some of the complexities involved.

The subject of different cultural and/or political aspirations is generally left undefined by the use of generic expressions like the Basques or the Welsh, or of terms like the Basque nation, people, ethnic group, and so on. Little effort is made to define more precisely who is meant by those terms, what distinguishing characteristics are used to include someone in those categories, and how to verify the degree to which such a collective entity is a reality, experienced as such by its assumed members. It is generally left to the reader of both political statements and academic writings to fill those concepts with empirical referents. However, both in the political tracts and the academic analyses, those concepts have very different content, resulting in much misunderstanding.

Much of the theorizing of nationalist ideologists and

academics focusses on what has been called primordial ties or identities, initially labeled as such in the work of Edward Shils or Clifford Geertz (1963, p. 109). Primordial ties have been defined as relations based on a common language, culture, distinctive religion, or kinship. The writings of the founding fathers of the nationalist movements certainly refer constantly to these primordial elements. However, such ties constitute a weak and uncertain basis for political action and, ultimately, for the creation of an independent nation-state, at least in the context of the old states of Europe.

Karl Deutsch in his classic work *Nationalism and Social Communication* (1966) might have been wrong in assuming that with increased modernization, industrialization, and therefore communication, many minor nationalities would be absorbed and assimilated into the larger nation-state. Yet there can be little question that, in the old states of Europe, the primordial elements have been weakened, in some cases perhaps irremediably, by those processes. Particularly in highly industrialized regions, as is the case in the Basque country and Catalonia in Spain, internal migrations since the late nineteenth century have produced a heterogeneous population in which the descendants of immigrants and immigrants of recent decades constitute a large proportion. The natural processes, as well as the deliberate action of the state, have produced a loss of the traditional languages, a cultural assimilation, and an identification with the larger nation-state. To build in such a context a national consciousness, a hegemonic nationalist movement, and ultimately a nation-state, on the basis of the primordial characteristics, turns out to be plagued with difficulties.

The creation of any even partially self-governing political unit involves the definition of a territory; and in the context we are discussing the primordial elements are not equally distributed over the territory that would constitute a viable basis for a polity. Nationalists quickly turn toward history to define the boundaries, claiming either an area in which sometime in the past those primordial elements were dominant or, more often, historically created administrative boundaries. Only to the extent that the social group aims at the defense of the right to maintain its culture and folkways without the support of legally binding norms, and to the extent that it is willing to recognize the cultural heterogeneity resulting from the displacement by outside influences of the primordial characteristics, will the definition of the ethnic community or the nation be based on the primordial elements.

To the extent that the social group aims at creating a political community with some form of self-government it will have to define membership territorially. In that case, if the defense of the primordial characteristics against alien cultural elements is carried to its extreme, the only options are assimilation or the more ominous policy of discrimination and, potentially, expulsion of those unwilling to accept those primordial values. A third alternative is to abandon the emphasis on those primordial characteristics and to define membership in the new community exclusively in voluntaristic terms; by including those who want to share the national identity, or by simply accepting as members all those who live in the territory, irrespective of their sharing the primordial characteristics or of their desire to identify with the emerging community.

Our hypothesis, therefore, is that ethnic peripheral nationalism will move from an emphasis on primordial elements to a definition based on territoriality. That is, the definition would change from an emphasis on common descent, race, language, distinctive cultural tradition, in some cases religion, to one based on "living and working" in an area, on a willingness to identify with that community, or on both. Contrary to much of the theorizing on the subject, primordialism might be the original source of nationalism, but ultimately nationalism's political implications are incompatible with primordialism. This hypothesis has emerged out of the analysis of data from surveys of the Spanish and French Basque country and, to some extent, is confirmed by data from Catalonia and Galicia.[1] The comparison of these regions, in which nationalist sentiment is of a very different intensity,[2] and the analysis both of ideological texts and of the attitudes of the population about what defines a Basque, a Catalan, or a Galician, has suggested the hypothesis formulated above. It justifies the title of this chapter, "From primordialism to nationalism."

If the basis of a strong nationalist feeling, leading to political nationalism, were a strong primordial sentiment, we would expect that a stronger nationalist sentiment, expressed by a widespread and strong sense of national identity, by a large vote for nationalist parties, and by a strong desire for political independence, would be associated with an emphasis on primordial elements in the definition of national identity. We would, therefore, expect that in the Spanish Basque country, where nationalism as measured by any of those indicators is stronger than in the French Basque country, the emphasis on primordialism would be greater and stronger. Similarly, we would expect that in Catalonia, where nationalism is less violent, where the nationalist parties obtain fewer votes, where the dominant desire is for political autonomy within Spain rather than for independence, the emphasis on primordial elements in defining Catalanicity would be weaker. And similarly, within each of these regions, we would expect those with the strongest nationalist views to be most committed to a primordial identity. Although the data are not as neat as we would wish, the basic patterns point in the opposite direction: the most extreme nationalism in the Basque country seems to be associated with a *territorial*, rather than a *primordial*, conception of the nation.

The analysis is complicated by the fact that a significant proportion of the population in both the Spanish Basque country and Catalonia is either immigrant or descended from recent immigrants. Many of these persons identify themselves fundamentally as Spaniards or "as Spanish as Basque" or "as Spanish as Catalan," and only a minority consider themselves Basque or Catalan.[3] Obviously immigrants' definitions of what allows someone to consider himself Basque or Catalan should be kept distinct from the definition espoused by the native Basque or Catalan population.

The immigrants, and even more the children of immigrants, find themselves cross-pressured in the context of nationalist politics in those regions between two distinct and to some extent contradictory ways of defining who is Basque or Catalan. If the peripheral nationalists were not aspiring to political hegemony, it would be easy for the immigrant, and for those identifying as Spanish among descendants of immigrants, to define as Basque or Catalan those sharing certain primordial characteristics. But in the context we are discussing such a definition would exclude them from the emerging political community and would in a sense deprive them of full "citizenship." Therefore, when forced to choose between a primordial and a territorial definition, they naturally incline toward the latter. This is not the case in regions where primordial cultural movements and identity have not been transformed into political nationalism, for example, in the French Basque country: there a primordial view of who is a Basque seems actually to be stronger among those identifying themselves as Frenchmen.

To avoid misunderstandings we should stress that our analysis is based on contemporary data. Certainly in the past, particularly in the earliest stages of peripheral nationalism, ideologists and followers of the movement undoubtedly based their identity on primordial characteristics, and their public action was based on the defense of those primordial characteristics.[4] We should, therefore, qualify our statement that nationalism is not simply an expression of primordial sentiments by saying that advanced or mature nationalism is not based on them, although in its origin primordialism was the main basis of an incipient nationalism.

In the history of ethnic consciousness and political action, we would discover that in an initial stage there would be considerable correspondence between the self-categorization and the categorization by others, especially by the dominant group at the center. A significant part of the population would reject, or at least underevaluate, the significance of the primordial element used in self-categorization by the more militant segment of the community. The more militant nationalists, who emphasize the primordial elements, will reject as alien all those not sharing these elements and claim the loyalty of all those endowed with them. They will label as traitors those who do not feel proud of the primordial characteristics and consider *déraciné* those who have abandoned them.

At a later stage those not sharing any of the primordial characteristics will use them to define as members of the minority those with the primordial characteristics. As a reaction against the more radical political minority that stresses those primordial characteristics and the demands derived from them, opponents will formulate negative or repressive policies against those sharing the primordial characteristics, irrespective of their pride or identification with them. At an even later stage both the nationalists and their opponents are likely to develop an interest in underevaluating the primordial elements and will emphasize the territorial components with opposite purposes: in the case of the nationalists to create a territorial basis for a future nation-state; in the case of the central state to give a territorial basis to a reorganization of authority patterns by granting autonomy or devolution to territorially elected bodies that reject the emotional and political implications of a primordially based nationalism.

It is probably not inevitable that ethnic groups and linguistic minorities should go through these different phases. It is very likely that some of them, particularly small and geographically dispersed ones in basically rural or traditional settings, might be satisfied with the recognition of their primordial claims, sometimes on the basis of recognition of a personal rather than a territorial categorization. We can imagine that the Lapps in the Northern countries and some small minorities in Central Europe and Italy would be satisfied with what we would call a primordial stage. It could also be argued that larger minorities, whose culture and social identity is quite assured because a large number share and value the primordial characteristics, might strive mainly for recognition and some public support for their autonomy within the old state. In the Spanish case the Catalan culture in the Balearic Islands, the Galician in Galicia, and even to a certain extent the Catalan in Catalonia, could stop short of a territorial definition of the linguistic, cultural, national minority status within Spain. It is not easy to account for why, in some other cases, a territorial definition of membership displaces the emphasis on primordial characteristics, as it seems largely to have done in the case of Basque extreme nationalism. One factor that might account for the transition from one to another stage would be the takeover of the minority's claims by cultural and social organizations or their channeling through the existing party system rather than through a nationalist party. We would go even further to argue that a transition to the third stage might depend not so much on the presence of a nationalist party, but on a competition between different nationalist parties within a self-governing territory within the state.

Who Can Consider Himself a Member of an Ethnic Community?

In the DATA survey in the Spanish and French Basque country and the one carried out by Richard Gunther and associates of the University of Ohio in other regions of Spain, it was asked: "Which of the following conditions are necessary, so that a person could consider himself Basque [or Catalan, Galician, Valencian, in the respective regions]?" The alternatives (asked independently) were, in the DATA study, "to live and work in the region of residence," "to speak the respective language," "to descend from a family of the ethnic group," "to have been born in the region." In the Ohio study the last two alternatives were combined into one.

The answer in the five peripheral regions under consideration show some surprising patterns. (The data from Euskadi, Catalonia, and Galicia are summarized in Table 10.1.) The alternative "living and working" is most often chosen in Valencia by 82 pecent, but in that region 79 percent also chose "to be

Table 10.1 *Proportion Saying that a Certain Condition Is Necessary for Someone to Consider Himself Basque, Catalan, Galician, by Identity Chosen of Residents in Euskadi, Catalonia, or Galicia Respectively*

Identity chosen and region	Condition			
	Live and work in	Speak	Descend from a family or been born in ...	N
Spanish in				
Euskadi	51·6	29·3	76·4	(198)
Catalonia	49·0	30·3	88·2	(295)
Galicia	39·3	31·4	77·4	(81)
More Spanish than ... in				
Euskadi	70·8	23·9	65·7	(24)
Catalonia	64·9	32·7	89·2	(70)
Galicia	39·2	35·6	85·4	(23)
As ... as Spanish in				
Euskadi	68·0	32·2	68·6	(194)
Catalonia	60·5	34·5	81·9	(380)
Galicia	40·9	39·6	85·1	(209)
More ... than Spanish				
Euskadi	74·7	38·2	69·1	(84)
Catalonia	64·1	45·5	71·8	(116)
Galicia	35·5	40·5	71·5	(56)
Basque (in Euskadi)	79·8	28·3	41·2	(279)
Catalan (in Catalonia)	51·5	27·0	77·2	(151)
Galician (in Galicia)	52·2	53·6	76·8	(120)
Total in				
Euskadi	69·2	30·4	60·7	(779)
Catalonia	56·5	33·3	82·4	(1012)
Galicia	42·7	41·8	80·3	(489)

Note: The percentages are based on those expressing agreement or disagreement with each item ignoring the "no answer" (n.a.) and "don't know" (d.k.) answers; because multiple answers could be given, the columns add to more than 100 percent; for clarity, the base for the largest number answering on any one item is given.

Source: Survey by Gunther *et al.*, forthcoming.

born in Valencia or descend from a Valencian family." The Spanish Basque country is the one in which, after Valencia, the largest number chose the alternative "to live and work" in the region, 69·2 percent; but fewer, 60·7 percent, selected "to have been born in the Basque country or descend from a Basque family." The contrast with the French Basque country, where only 45 percent opted for "living and working" while 67 percent mentioned descent from a Basque family, is striking when we consider the intensity of Basque nationalism in Spain and its weakness in the French Basque country. The same difference between the two Basque countries appears when it comes to language, with only 30·4 percent mentioning it in (Spanish) *Euskadi sur* and 59 percent in (French) *Euskadi norte*. This difference made us think that the categorization used by a nationalist movement tended to emphasize the territorial definition of membership rather than a primordial one.

This hypothesis is confirmed by the very different pattern of response in Galicia, a region with a distinct culture in which a very large proportion of the population speaks the language and where the number of immigrants from other parts of Spain is small. It has experienced a cultural revival and an affirmation of its linguistic personality, but the nationalist parties have been weak and demands in relation to the center have been limited to autonomy. Galicia would be a prime example of the region where the distinctiveness of the population leads to an affirmation of primordial elements rather than to a territorial definition of membership in the community. Only 42·7 percent opted for the alternative "to live and work," while 80·3 percent considered "to have been born in Galicia or to come from a Galician family" as the defining characteristic. In Catalonia, 56·5 percent chose the phrase coined by the Catalan leader Jordi Pujol (1976) of "living and working" in Catalonia. But also a very large proportion, 82·4 percent, chose "to have been born in Catalonia" or "descending from a Catalan family." It would seem as if Catalonia were occupying an in-between position in the continuum between the primordial and the territorial conceptions. As we shall see, this is the result of contradictory conceptions among different segments of the Catalan population resulting from the presence of a large number of non-Catalan immigrants and their descendants.

If we compare the five regions under consideration, we discover that it is in the one where the ethnic identification is weakest, the French Basque country, that the primordial characteristic of language is chosen most often, followed by Valencia, where one cannot speak of a real nationalist sentiment and movement although aspirations for autonomy and a cultural revival have had considerable support. Most surprisingly, the emphasis on language is not very strong in Catalonia for complex reasons we will discuss later; and it is weakest in the Spanish Basque country with only 30·4 percent mentioning it. This latter part is less surprising in view of the large number of native Basques and descendants of Basque families who do not know or speak Basque. Of these regional comparisons, we should retain as the most striking the relatively weak emphasis on primordial characteristics in the most nationalist of all those regions as well as the surprising emphasis there on territoriality. If we were to interpret our findings in a somewhat simplified way, we could say that the French Basque country represents the purest case of primordial sentiments and the Spanish Basque country a case where modern nationalism has moved away from the primordial emphasis to a territorial conception of membership in the community. The case of Valencia lies somewhat outside of our consideration and could be characterized as one of regional identity in which residence and descent are considered about equally significant. In Galicia the consciousness of distinctiveness based on birth and descent is central but primordial claims overall are weaker as evidenced by the relatively low emphasis on language.

Identity and Primordialism v. Territoriality

In all the regions it was asked: "Nowadays when one speaks so much about nationalities, would you say that you feel Spanish [in France: French], more Spanish than Basque [or, as applicable, Catalan or Galician], as Basque as Spanish, more Basque than Spanish, or Basque." In the case of Valencia a trichotomy was used: "Spanish," "identifying with the Catalan countries," and "identifying with the Valencian countries," to take into account the possibility of identification with greater Catalonia or Valencia as distinct communities. The responses to these questions were analyzed to determine the necessary characteristics of a Basque, Catalan, and so on, as defined by those with regional v. those with national identities.

In some of the regions under consideration the choice of national identity makes relatively little difference in defining who belongs to a particular community. So, for example, in Valencia those who identify as Spanish mention "living and working" in Valencia in 86·5 percent of the cases, and those who identify more as Valencian mention it in 78 percent. Certainly those identifying as Valencians are more likely than those identifying as Spanish to mention descent and birth as well as language; that is, they are more likely to emphasize the primordial characteristics. But since the proportions identified as Spanish and Valencian are relatively similar, the overall picture is one of considerable consensus in the definition of regional identity.

This is not the case in the Basque country, where we find considerable differences of definition based on national identity. In view of all the literature emphasizing the distinctive culture and personality of the Basques, it is surprising that those who define themselves only as Basques, rejecting thereby any Spanish identity, should be the ones who more often choose "living and working," 79·8 percent compared to the regional average of 69·2 percent. This is followed in descending order by those who identify themselves as more Basque than Spanish, 74·7 percent, as Spanish as Basque, 68 percent, and the low of 51·6 percent of those identifying themselves as Spanish. It is the "outsiders" who more often mention birth and descent, 76·4 percent compared to only 41·2 percent of those identifying as Basques. Language is mentioned by a similar proportion irrespective of identity, with the exception of those identifying themselves as "more Basque than Spanish." This is the group where the voters of the Partido Nacionalista Vasco (PNV), the more moderate nationalists, heirs of the traditions of Sabino de Arana, are more numerous than the new *abertzale* extreme left nationalists, who have gained most of their support among those identifying as just Basque. In fact the difference between these last two groups indirectly confirms our hypothesis of displacement of the primordial by the territorial conception of identity in the extreme nationalism of today. If we consider both descent and language together, it is among those who are more Basque than Spanish or those who are as Basque as Spanish where the primordial self-definition is strongest. These points gain support when, reversing our procedure to now, we examine the national identity of the groups that embrace each of the possible definitions of who is a Basque (see Table 10.2).

In Catalonia, once again, those who identify themselves as Spanish are more likely to choose primordial criteria in defining who is Catalan, and particularly descent or birth rather than the purely territorial definition of membership in the Catalan community. It is among those who consider themselves more Catalan than Spanish, the group that tends to vote most for the Catalanist parties, where the territorial definition of "living and working" in Catalonia finds most support, but still appreciably less than in the Basque country and among the most nationalist of the Basques. It is this group that identifies as more Catalan than Spanish, but still as Spanish, and that therefore favors autonomy within the Spanish state, which considers language the central element in defining who is Catalan, 45·5 percent. In Catalonia, therefore, we find those identifying as Spanish most

Table 10.2 *National Identity of Those Considering "Living and Working in the Basque Country" a Necessary Condition for Someone to Consider Himself Basque*

| Identity | To live and work in Euskadi | | Sample total |
	Yes	No	
Spanish	18·7	39·2	25·0
More Spanish than Basque	3·0	2·8	2·9
As Basque as Spanish	23·3	24·6	23·7
More Basque than Spanish	11·6	8·8	10·7
Basque	43·5	24·6	37·3
	(541)	(241)	(782)
Total	69·2	30·8	100

Note: Not classified; 147 cases.
Source: As Table 10.1.

likely to define as Catalan those born in Catalonia or of Catalan descent, a definition which leaves open the opportunity for the children of immigrants to become Catalans but does not imply that immigrants themselves, for the fact of living and working there, should consider themselves Catalans. In fact those identifying as Spanish, or as more Spanish than Catalan, are most likely to be immigrants, living and working in Catalonia. For them, there are two communities within the territory.

The French Basque country, which we have characterized as an area where primordial conceptions of Basque identity predominate, shows relatively little difference between those who consider themselves as "French" or "more French than Basque" or "as French as Basque (see Table 10.3). They all are likely to emphasize descent (around 70 percent) and language (around 60 percent) as defining Basqueness. In *Euskadi norte* too those most nationalist, the small minority identifying as more Basque than French, or just Basque, are more inclined to mention "living and working," although they also mention language and birth in the region in approximately the same proportion as those identifying as French. However, the contrast in the number mentioning "living and working" in the French Basque country, 56 percent, with the 80 percent among Basques in the Spanish Basque country (see again Table 10.1) is quite striking and confirms our basic hypothesis about the shift from primordialism to territoriality.

In Galicia among those who identify only as Galicians (an identification which, as the research by DATA and others shows, does not necessarily imply a nationalistic choice, but to some extent a lack of sophistication that prevents many of the

Table 10.3 *Conditions Necessary for a Person to Consider Himself Basque in the French and Spanish Basque Country, on the Basis of National Self-Identification*

Conditions necessary to consider oneself Basque	French Basque country				Spanish Basque country (Euskadi)					
	Total sample	French or more French than Basque	As French as Basque	More Basque than French or Basque	Total sample	Spanish	More Spanish than Basque	As Spanish as Basque	More Basque than Spanish	Basque
To speak	59	58	60	62	22	21	21	12	20	32
Descent from a Basque family	67	70	69	60	30	39	37	28	26	30
To be born in Basque country	46	47	46	49	39	44	44	40	32	40
Live and work in Basque country	45 (386)	42 (214)	47 (110)	56 (45)	70 (1011)	56 (141)	67 (57)	79 (267)	74 (122)	67 (386)

Note: The study in the French Basque country was carried out by Institut Français de Demoscopie; responses of "don't know" and "no answer" do not appear.

Source: Postautonomy referendum survey, DATA, 1979.

peasants from thinking about themselves as anything but Galicians), language is more often mentioned than among those with a dual identity or a purely Spanish identity. Birth and descent are mentioned by large numbers in all groups, but slightly more among those with a dual Spanish and Galician identity. Here too the relatively small proportion identifying only as Galicians is more likely than the rest of the population to emphasize "living and working." In this case it is not a moving away from the primordial, but a combination of both the primordial and the emerging territorial definition, congruent with the newly won autonomy.

In Valencia where nationalist parties and movements have been even less successful than in Galicia, those identifying as "Valencian" are most likely to mention the primordial elements, 59 percent language and 85 percent birth and descent. They cite "living and working" in the region in 78 percent of the cases, less than among those identifying as Spanish, 86·5 percent. To the extent that in that region there is a sense of distinctiveness it is still exclusively a primordial one.

The more detailed analysis of data for the Basque country will allow us to specify even further the extent to which extreme nationalism and the desire for independence are associated with an emphasis on territoriality rather than primordialism.

Centralism, Autonomy, Federalism, and Independence, and Who Can Be Considered Basque or Catalan?

In a number of surveys following the referendum on autonomy we have asked a complex question that allows us to discover the extent to which the respondents prefer differing relations with the state. Four alternatives were offered: a centralist conception of a Spanish state, a recognition of autonomy, a more advanced stage of autonomy closer to what we could call federalism, or a desire for independence. The cross-tabulation between those preferences and the elements defining the Basque or Catalan identity will allow us to confirm further the patterns we have described. The main results are presented in Table 10.4.

Among those who favor a centralist state, the definition of who is a Basque is fundamentally one of birth and descent, embraced by 80·3 percent, while among those favoring independence for the Basque country the proportion so defining Basques is only 45·5 percent. The territorial definition of "living and working" in the Basque country is chosen by 56·7

Table 10.4 *Attitudes toward Centralism, Autonomy, Federalism, Independence, and Characteristics Defining Who is Basque or Catalan*

Characteristics to be considered Basque/Catalan	Favoring				
	Centralism	Autonomy	Federalism	Independence	Total
Living and working in Euskadi	56·7 (122)	67·4 (355)	67·7 (101)	74·0 (183)	67·3 (761)
Speaking Euskera	36·3 (121)	29·4 (347)	28·1 (94)	30·9 (170)	30·7 (732)
To be born in Euskadi or to descend of a Basque family	80·3 (130)	62·3 (353)	59·1 (104)	45·5 (174)	61·1 (761)
Living and working in Catalonia	64·2 (206)	46·6 (629)	78·4 (115)	65·7 (118)	55·5 (1068)
Speaking Catalan	36·7 (182)	26·3 (572)	45·0 (98)	30·4 (99)	30·7 (951)
To be born in Catalonia or to descend of a Catalan family	86·7 (212)	88·8 (604)	61·0 (104)	71·1 (103)	83·8 (1023)

Note: The number of those responding to each item varies slightly and, therefore, the bases for the percentage differ.

Source: Gunther *et al.*, forthcoming.

percent of the centralists in contrast to 74 percent of those favoring independence. Even language is mentioned by 36·3 percent of the centralists and 30·9 percent of the pro-independence group. The same patterns appear when we compare the autonomists with those preferring independence: 62·3 percent of the former and 45·5 percent of the latter emphasized birth and family origin, and 67·4 percent and 74 percent respectively use the definition "to live and work." This means that the closer one is to extreme nationalism the less emphasis is placed on the primordial, and the more on the territorial, conception. The aspiration for autonomy, therefore, is still anchored to a considerable degree in primordial elements, while the extreme nationalist desire for independence tends to reduce the saliency of the primordial and to emphasize instead the territorial principle.

The patterns we have just described for the Spanish Basque country are not found to the same extent in Catalonia, although there are signs that things might be moving in the same direction. Centralists certainly favor birth and descent more in defining who is Catalan than do those favoring independence, but not more than does the large number of autonomists. There is no difference between centralists and the proindependence group in defining regional identity in terms of living and working in the area. But the federalist alternative already shows signs of desire to incorporate the immigrants into the Catalan community. Federalists are, however, ambivalent, since they are also, together with the centralists, the ones who emphasize most the linguistic distinctiveness of Catalonia, 45 percent and 36·7 percent respectively. If we keep in mind that the desire for independence in Catalonia is the choice of only a very small proportion of the population and that most of the nationalists are more inclined to an advanced stage of federalism, we see that the Catalan response to the problem of identity emphasizes both language and territoriality. This is a conception that involves a community open to those who integrate themselves into it by accepting the language and culture of Catalonia. The rank-and-file autonomists have not yet accepted "living and working" as defining Catalan identity, although the Catalanist leadership, as well as the leftist parties favorable to autonomy, defend just that definition. They do not emphasize language as a categorizing element as much as we might have expected, but like the centralists, they see birth and descent as the main defining characteristics. In a sense we could say that there is much more ambiguity and multidimensionality in defining who is a Catalan in Catalonia than who is Basque in the Basque country.

Nativity, Mixed Parentage, Immigration, and the Definition of Who Is Basque

In view of the presence of a large number of immigrants, a fairly large cohort of offspring from two immigrant parents, and the not negligible group of descendants of mixed parentage, it is interesting to see how these different groups and those of second-generation pure Basque origin define being Basque. The results are summarized in Table 10.5.

The data, which will have to be confirmed by other studies, show fairly complex and certainly less clearly defined patterns than those based on identity and political choices. "To speak Euskera" is chosen slightly more often by those with two Basque-born parents than by those with only one; it is chosen least often by those with two immigrant parents. Curiously it is named fairly frequently by those who are themselves immigrants. The primordial criterion of language is obviously disturbing for those of immigrant background, since very few of them have learned Euskera. Descent from a Basque family

Table 10.5 Native or Immigrant Origin and Defining Characteristics to be Considered Basque

Defining characteristics of a Basque	Origin of respondents				Immigrants	Sample Total
	Both parents born in Basque country	Only father born in Basque country	Only mother born in Basque country	Both parents immigrants into Basque country		
To live and work in Euskadi						
yes	65	68	72	74	74	70
no	33	29	26	25	24	28
To speak Euskera						
yes	26	21	23	10	21	22
no	71	79	74	88	74	74
To descend from a Basque family						
yes	30	32	37	33	29	30
no	66	66	58	65	67	66
To be born in Euskadi						
yes	38	47	44	39	38	39
no	59	53	54	59	57	58
	(446)	(38)	(57)	(97)	(374)	(1012)

Note: Responses of "don't know" and "no answer" are not shown.
Source: Postautonomy referendum survey by DATA, 1979.

is mentioned almost equally by all groups, but perhaps more often by those with a Basque mother. To be born in the region is among the more often mentioned characteristics independent of origins, although those of mixed parentage seem to stress it slightly more.

In view of the opportunities for integration into the emerging Basque community, it should not be surprising that immigrants and children of immigrants should choose more often "to live and work" in the area as a criterion. Those of pure Basque parentage, both father and mother born in the Basque country, are the ones least likely to use the territorial criterion, 65 percent compared to 74 percent of those with two immigrant parents.

However, the most striking finding here is the relative insignificance of the differences by origin and the broad consensus on the definition of who is Basque. By contrast, we find significant differences when we classify the responses by subjective identity or by preferences about the national future of Euskadi. The contrast between the relationship of the more objective and the more subjective characteristics, and the definitions used in determining who is Basque, is further evidence that those definitions are not just a reflection of integration into the primordial community, but largely of political and ideological commitments.

Sex and Age Differences in the Definition of Who is Basque

In any society we might expect women to feel the primordial ties more strongly, and this is quite true in Euskadi. In fact, if we were to take seriously some of the literature on the matriarchial character of traditional Basque society, we would expect it to be even truer. However, it might be worth notice that in mixed marriages between Basques and immigrants the mother transmits the language, while the father seems to transmit a stronger Basque national identity and more nationalist politics to the offspring. From another perspective, however, the greater politicization of men would lead us to expect the more nationalist stance on their part; therefore, if primordialism were the basis of those sentiments, primordial criteria should be stronger among them. However, our data summarized in Table 10.6 show that the territorial conception is stronger among men than among women, while the primordial one (whatever indicator we use) is weaker.

Table 10.6   *Age, Sex, and Necessary Conditions for Someone to Consider Himself Basque*

	Age			Sex	
	18–24	*25–54*	*55+*	*male*	*female*
To live and work in Euskadi					
yes	73	71	66	76	64
no	27	28	31	24	33
To speak Euskera					
yes	21	23	22	20	24
no	74	73	75	76	71
To descend from a Basque family					
yes	22	30	36	26	34
no	74	66	61	70	62
To have been born in Euskadi					
yes	23	39	48	36	43
no	73	57	50	62	54
	(141)	(624)	(242)	(503)	(508)

Note: Responses of "don't know" and "no answer" do not appear.
Source: As Table 10.5.

There is a clear trend with advancing age toward greater emphasis on the primordial criterion of descent or having been born in Euskadi and a reverse trend in the emphasis on living and working, quite congruent with the more nationalistic position of the young, their strong support for Herri Batasuna (HB) and Euskadiko Ezkerra (EE) (the two left *abertzale* parties), and the greater appeal of the PNV for the older generations. In fact students, who generally have less knowledge of the Basque language due to their more urban and middle-class origin, are among the most nationalistic groups in the society, and are also among those emphasizing the territorial criterion most.

The Combinations of Primordialism and Territoriality in Euskadi

For the case of the Basque country, we have cross-tabulated in Table 10.7 the different characteristics chosen to define who is a Basque and have developed a typology of responses based on the relative strength of territorial and primordial criteria. We find that 36·9 percent elected only a territorial definition. Another 31·5 percent combined territorial with primordial criteria, including very often one that only by stretching the

Table 10.7 National Identity and Characteristics used to Define Who is Basque in Euskadi

Identity	(1) Only territorial	(2) Territorial and one primordial	(3) Territorial and two or more primordial	(4) [= (2) + (3)] mixture	(5) Only primordial	(6) n.a.	N
Spanish	26·2	9·9	16·5	26·4	31·9	5·0	(141)
More Spanish than Basque	35·1	8·8	24·6	33·4	21·1	10·5	(57)
As Basque as Spanish	47·6	10·1	19·9	30·0	13·1	6·0	(267)
More Basque than Spanish	45·1	11·5	17·2	28·7	15·6	10·7	(122)
Basque	31·1	13·7	19·7	33·4	20·7	10·1	(386)
Male	42·3	14·5	17·9	32·4	15·5	7·4	(503)
Female	31·7	13·8	16·9	30·7	23·0	9·6	(508)
Total sample	36·9	14·1	17·4	31·5	19·3	8·5	(1011)

Note: Responses of "don't know" do not appear.
Source: As Table 10.5.

222 New Nationalisms of the Developed West

concept can be considered primordial, namely, being born in the Basque country. Finally, only 19·3 percent opted exclusively for one or several primordial criteria. In fact those choosing three primordial criteria and rejecting the criterion of "living and working" were only 2·3 percent. A few, 8·5 percent, were unwilling to answer the question.

The comparison of the criteria chosen by those who identify themselves exclusively as Basque and exclusively as Spanish reveals considerable parallelisms in the definition of who is Basque, but also some very interesting differences. The purely territorial definition of living and working in the region, which in terms of their interests the immigrants (who mostly identify as Spanish) could be expected to emphasize, is actually chosen in only 26·2 percent of the cases, less than the 31·1 percent among those who identify as Basque. Those identified as Spanish give considerably more preference to primordial criteria (although with a slight edge to being born in the Basque country) than do those identifying as Basque, 31·9 and 20·7 percent respectively. Those identifying as Basque, however, are somewhat more likely to combine territorial and primordial criteria, 33·4 v. 26·4 percent among those identifying as Spanish.

The difference we have been discussing heretofore is not an artefact of greater agreement with a large number of characteristics, but is significant and can be confirmed when we compare the purely territorial and the purely primordial choices. The more detailed data in the tables confirm the weak emphasis on language as the only criterion, not surprising given the large number of Basques who do not know Euskera. What is surprising is that descent from a Basque family should be mentioned so infrequently and that, when mentioned, it is often in combination with birth in Euskadi.

These data are certainly difficult to reconcile with the standard interpretation of peripheral nationalism as an assertion of primordialism in a world threatening the values identified with it. It might very well be that the initial upsurge of nationalist sentiment, the initial ideological formulations like those of Sabino de Arana (1865–1903), were an expression of primordial sentiments (Arana Goiri, 1978, chs. 4.2, 4.4 and 4.5). At the level of the mass of the population, however, the distinctiveness of the Basque today is not clearly formulated in primordial terms, except in part by those not belonging to and not identifying with the Basque community. It would be interesting to compare these responses of the population with those of the Basque intellectuals, of the elites of the nationalist movement, and of the active members of Basque parties.

The various responses of those voting for different Basque parties in the 1979 elections give us a hint of an interesting division in the conception of Basqueness between the centrist and traditional nationalist party (the PNV) and the *abertzale* left (HB and EE), and even within the latter camp (see Table 10.8). The PNV supporters give appreciably more weight to primordial criteria and not only in combination with territorial ones: 24·3 percent of the PNV adherents compared to 8·3 percent among the voters of EE, and 17·2 percent of those of HB, chose only primordial characteristics. The supporters of these two radical nationalist parties mentioned much more often as their sole criterion "to live and work" in Euskadi: 47·2 percent of those of EE, and 41·4 percent of those of HB compared to 30 percent of those of the PNV. It is interesting to note that the EE, the party that most explicitly combines Basque nationalism with Marxist ideology, and which is attempting unsuccessfully to hegemonize working-class politics in the Basque country; which has fused with part of the Spanish Communist Party in the Basque country (the PKE–PCE); and which had some success among the immigrant workers in the 1979 elections, should be the one whose followers opt overwhelmingly for a territorial definition, either exclusively or in combination with primordial ones, but practically never for a purely primordial one (8·3 percent compared to 18·2 percent for the electorate as a whole, and 24·3 percent among followers of the PNV). These data, demonstrating the relative emphasis on a territorial v. a primordial conception, confirm the generational ideological shift that has taken place within Basque nationalism.

If we needed any further confirmation, we could find it in the responses of those who hold different images of terrorists, a group which has played such an important role in the political conflict in the Basque country.[5] The most extreme nationalist position is represented by the minority of the population that in 1979 believed that the terrorists were patriots, while the most extreme rejection of nationalism is represented by the minority that defined them as common criminals. Table 10.9 cross-tabulates support of terrorism with the definitions of Basqueness. Those who thought of the terrorists as patriotic freedom fighters were the least likely to define the Basque in pure primordial terms (13·7 percent) and most likely to adopt the criterion of living and working in Euskadi (41·1 percent). Even if we look at the mixed responses, those who see the terrorists

Table 10.8 *Characteristics Used to Define Who Is a Basque, by Voters of Different Basque Parties*

Voters of:	(1) Only territorial	(2) Territorial and one primordial	(3) Territorial and two or more primordial	(4) [= (2) + (3)] mixture	(5) Only primordial	(6) n.a.	N
PNV	30·0	12·2	21·2	33·4	24·3	11·8	(255)
EE	47·2	15·3	15·3	30·6	8·3	9·7	(72)
HB	41·4	12·6	16·1	28·7	17·2	11·5	(87)
All those voting	33·9	12·3	18·7	31·0	18·2	6·2	(764)

Note: (N = 1011); responses of "don't know" do not appear.
Source: As Table 10.5.

Table 10.9 *Characteristics Used to Define Who is Basque, by Those Holding Different Images of the Terrorists*

Respondent's Image of terrorists	(1) Only territorial	(2) Territorial and one primordial	(3) Territorial and two or more primordial	(4) [= (2) + (3)] mixture	(5) Only primordial	(6) n.a.	N
Patriots	41·1	17·3	14·3	25·6	13·7	7·7	(168)
Idealists	37·9	13·6	16·1	29·7	18·2	11·2	(330)
Manipulated	30·8	16·8	18·6	35·4	21·9	7·2	(292)
Madmen	37·7	16·9	18·2	35·1	22·1	3·9	(77)
Criminals	30·0	10·0	18·0	28·0	32·0	4·0	(50)
n.a.	40·4	9·9	18·4	26·9	18·4	9·2	(141)

Note: Responses of "don't know" are not included.
Source: As Table 10.5.

as patriots are the least likely to combine a territorial definition with more than one primordial criterion. In contrast, it is the segment of the population most intensely hostile to the ETA terrorists, those defining them as criminals, who mention most often a purely primordial characterization (32 percent) and least often a purely territorial one (30 percent). These data undoubtedly run counter to the image that the nationalist terrorism is supported by communalist sentiment in the population. Even those who see the terrorists as idealists rather than patriots are more likely to mention a territorial conception than a purely primordial one. Those who define the terrorists as either manipulated and, therefore, in a sense alien to the Basque national community (thereby avoiding the perception of a conflict between Basques and Spaniards) or as (irresponsible) madmen choose most often some combination of territorial and primordial criteria, while tending to give slightly more significance to the primordial than those who see the terrorists as patriots. These data are perhaps the clearest confirmation both of the ideological shift in Basque nationalism that the ETA theorists have achieved and of the complexity of the Basque question. They lead us to suspect that autonomy within the Spanish state and the recognition of the cultural demands based on primordial loyalties are not likely to satisfy the extremists, who see the Basque community as comprising all those living and working in the Basque country and who aim to achieve political independence.

After All, Primordialism

Our discussion has highlighted how in the Basque country a territorial definition of who may consider himself a Basque has gained ground, particularly among nationalist Basques. But is it really true that the Basque self-identity today is based on living and working in the Basque country? Do those living in Euskadi feel Basque independently of their speaking Euskera, descending from Basque parentage, or being born in the Basque country?

The answer is basically no. There is undoubtedly a minority of immigrants who do not speak Basque and yet who fully identify themselves as Basque and nothing else, and a larger number of such persons who identify as both Spanish and Basque; but in spite of all the pressures in the period of our research, 51 percent of non-Euskadi-speaking immigrants identified themselves either as more Spanish than Basque or as just

Spanish. At the other end of the territorial–primordial continuum 77 percent of Euskera speakers born in Euskadi of Basque parents call themselves just Basque and another 13 percent more Basque than Spanish. Only 9 percent of the group feel themselves as much Basque as Spanish, and only 1 percent as partly Spanish, or as more Spanish than Basque. Primordial characteristics certainly do not explain identity completely, but there can be little doubt that a purely Basque identity is found most often among those whom the primordial criteria would identify as Basque. There are those who identify with the Basque community and the Basque nation, using the term somewhat loosely, on the basis of their living and working in Euskadi; but contrary to the hopes of the political nationalists, they are a minority. At most the territorial principle is the basis for a dual identity, a dual solidarity that gives only limited support to political nationalism and to its most extreme expression, secessionism.

In fact our data in Table 10.10 show clearly that each of the primordial characteristics contributes somewhat to the choice of identity. Irrespective of the knowledge of the Basque language, those of full Basque parentage are more likely to define themselves as Basque, or as more Basque than Spanish, than those with one non-Basque parent. In turn having one Basque parent leads to a greater identification with the Basque community than being born in the Basque country of non-Basque parents. Finally, even the tiny minority of immigrants who have made the effort to learn the Basque language is less likely to identify as Basque than is the first generation born in Euskadi with the same knowledge of the language.

Independent of family background, of being born in Euskadi, or even of having immigrated, command of the language contributes much to the identity. To be *Euskaldun* (speaker of Basque) is the strongest determinant of Basque identity; but since only a minority of those of mixed parentage, and even fewer of those of immigrant parents and only a tiny minority of the immigrants are Euskaldunes, language contributes to Basque identity in the population mainly among those of Basque descent. Among those whose father and mother were born in the Basque country, it is the understanding of Euskera that makes the greatest difference, although speaking it reinforces national identity slightly. Among those speaking or understanding Euskera, 77 and 71 percent respectively choose the Basque identity, while among those who do not understand the language at all the proportion is 41 percent. The

Table 10.10 Nativity, Parentage, Knowledge of Euskera, and Identity

Identity	Both parents Basque			One parent Basque			Both parents immigrants			Respondent is immigrant		
	Speak Euskera	Only under-stand it	Do not under-stand it	Speak Euskera	Only under-stand it	Do not under-stand it	Speak Euskera	Only under-stand it	Do not under-stand it	Speak Euskera	Only under-stand it	Do not under-stand it
Spanish or more Spanish than Basque	1	2	10	—	—	7	—	18	16	6	15	51
As Basque as Spanish	9	7	34	6	25	41	—	36	41	50	46	34
More Basque than Spanish	13	20	15	18	19	22	33	18	8	6	15	8
Basque	77	71	41	76	56	29	67	27	32	39	23	8
N	(224)	(55)	(157)	(17)	(16)	(58)	(6)	(11)	(75)	(18)	(26)	(303)

Note: Percentages sometimes do not add to 100 due to rounding errors.
Source: As Table 10.5.

weakness of the Basque identity as an exclusive one is largely due to the fact that 36 percent of those with two Basque ancestors do not know the language. Their speaking Spanish does not lead them to reject a Basque identity—only 10 percent of them think of themselves as Spanish or more Spanish than Basque—but rather to choose a dual identity. The fact of having one parent not born in the Basque country reduces the knowledge and use of the Basque language; but, independent of that, it reinforces the dual identity. Among those children of mixed marriages who do not speak Basque, only a small proportion makes a clear and exclusive choice of either the Basque identity (29 percent) or the Spanish (7 percent).

Those born in the Basque country of immigrant parents, who have probably lived and worked all their lives in Euskadi, are still not likely to have learned the language. Despite speaking only *Ederra* (the Basque word for Spanish), a significant number of them claim to be only Basque (32 percent) and another 8 percent more Basque than Spanish; however, a plurality chooses a dual identity, 41 percent. Only the very small minority that has become Euskaldun approaches the level of Basque identity of those with at least one Basque parent. In their case one might wonder whether the knowledge and use of the language are not the result of the choice of identity. Similarly, Euskaldun immigrants, a tiny minority, opt decisively for a dual or for a purely Basque identity, in contrast to those immigrants who do not understand Euskera. Language is certainly a characteristic that can be acquired, but Euskera is not easy to learn: recall that only 13 percent of the immigrants claim to understand it and only 5 percent to speak it. The 39 percent of the Euskera-speaking immigrants who identify only as Basque, therefore, comprise only 2 percent of an immigrant population that in our sample accounts for over one-third of the population of Euskadi.

Generational Differences

Identity, as we have said, is not simply a reflection of descent, birth, or length of stay in the Basque country. The political and ideological climate to which different generations have been exposed is beyond doubt also strongly related to identity. Those with two Basque parents, those of mixed heritage, those born in the Basque country of immigrant parents, and immigrants themselves born after 1950, that is, adolescents from the late years of the Franco regime and from the period of transition to democracy, are appreciably more likely to identify as Basque than are their elders. Particularly those born between 1931 and 1950, who grew up in a period in which nationalism was persecuted and who, on account of their age, were less likely to become involved in the agitation following the death of Franco, are less likely to identify as Basque even when they come from a Basque family. While 72 percent of those born after 1950 of two Basque parents identify as Basque, only 57 percent of those born of similar parentage between 1931 and 1950 do so. Among those of mixed parentage, the proportions in the two generations are respectively 61 and 33 percent, with 10 and 16 percent identifying as Spanish or more Spanish than Basque. Among immigrants, the proportions are respectively 16 and 9 percent, with 35 and 48 percent identifying as Spanish or more Spanish than Basque.

Independent of family background the youngest generation growing up in the atmosphere of the late Franco period and the turmoil of the transition has moved toward Basqueness. This runs somewhat counter to the idea that those growing up in the period of Franco's anti-Basque cultural policies would react more strongly against them. There is, however, some indication that among the older generations those born before 1930 and particularly before 1920, that is, those who experienced adolescence under the republic (1931–9), felt their Basque identity more strongly. On the other hand, it is true that children of immigrants born before 1931 in the Basque country, in spite of the length of their stay there, retained their Spanish identity. The same is largely true for the older immigrants, although here a significant minority, perhaps as the result of the length of their stay, identified with the new homeland.

Family background is still the dominant factor, if we consider that even in the youngest generation 72 percent of those with two Basque parents and only 41 percent of those with immigrant parents identify as Basque, while 3 and 35 percent respectively identify themselves as Spanish, or as more Spanish than Basque. Even in a period in which, as we have shown elsewhere, the Spanish identity is likely to have been subject to a "spiral of silence" in the climate of nationalist Basque self-consciousness, only the descendants of immigrants, and among them only the younger generation, are ready to forsake their Spanish identity in significant proportion.

Our data, particularly those by generation, show that the *Zeitgeist* of a particular historical period, the pressure of the climate of opinion, and in the last analysis the positive and negative sanctions used by the society's rulers can change identities and reinforce those derived from primordial loyalties. Still, as the repression of Basque national identity and nationalism during the Franco period shows, primordial loyalties are ultimately the strongest basis of national identity.

In view of the data it would seem that the progressive supplanting of a primordial conception of Basque identity by a territorial one is clearly linked to political changes, to efforts at mobilization, and to a generational change. This shift undoubtedly has social and political consequences, but at the same time a comparison with the reality we just described shows that Basque identity is an ideology—or should we say a utopia? It is an ideology in the senses that: (1) it masks the reality of a society in which much of the population feels a dual Spanish and Basque identity; (2) it tries to ignore the fact that two cultural, social, and linguistic communities are living together in Euskadi, each with its own identity; and (3) it attempts to create a sense of community against the Spanish state that would incorporate those not sharing the primordial characteristics. It is a utopia in the sense that it proclaims the ideal of a community that could ignore the complex realities derived from almost a century of immigration, the linguistic losses of Euskera over an even longer period of time, and the differing strength of primordial ties within the Basque community itself. As we know, ideologies and utopias can change the world, but they can also engender bitter conflicts, insoluble problems, and a threat to living and working together irrespective of identity. The recognition of Basque and Spanish primordial identities, the combination of both in the course of generations, might be a better basis for a free Euskadi in a free Spain than the utopia of a territorial Basque community.

Nationalism and Class in Ethnically Heterogeneous Society

Nationalism has been seen by both its supporters and its critics as an integrating ideology, bridging such other conflicts in the society as class struggle and, unless nationality is identified with the religious tradition, the secular–clerical division. It is no accident that fascism should have transferred the class struggle to the conflict between poor and rich countries, that Nazism should have been a "catch-all" party substituting the *Volksgemeinschaft* for the class-divided society of Weimar, and that today the left in the Third World very often tries to create an alliance between the national bourgeoisie and the masses against imperialism and its internal allies. The theory of internal colonialism is another effort, in this case within a leftist perspective, to unite the popular sectors of the society against outside domination, even where that domination is purely economic. Many movements and parties representing national minorities have been interclass parties, and in quite a few cases they have found the Christian Democratic interclassist ideology congenial. Nationalism in many of these forms, therefore, has been seen as an alternative to class conflict, and for a long time the left wanted to hold on to the idea that proletarians had no nation.

Highly industrialized peripheries, with their unavoidable class conflict, pose a difficult problem for the nationalists, who want to channel all energies into the national struggle. The difficulty is compounded when the industrialization has attracted a large number of immigrant workers of different national bakground, or when a particular class has been in the forefront of the national struggle. In such a context, which is the one that prevails in the Spanish Basque country and in Catalonia, ideologists and political leaders inevitably have to debate the relationship between class and nation. The history of the ETA shows how painful and divisive those debates can become.

Early Basque nationalism, as formulated by Sabino de Arana in the context of the industrialization of Vizcaya, could avoid the question of class conflict by describing Basque society as a harmonious community that greedy capitalists threatened to disrupt by attracting immigrant workers from other parts of Spain to their mines and industries. Those capitalists, with their liberal politics, their intra-Spanish and international ties, and their increasing identification with the Spanish monarchy (which generously granted them titles of nobility) could be defined as alien to the *Volk*—religious, communal, middle-class, small business, artisan, peasant, and small-town society. The new working class was alien not only in its origin, but on account of its growing secularization and susceptibility to the appeals of a socialist "godless" labor movement. In that context, whatever solidarity existed between big capitalists and the immigrant workers was something alien and outside the Basque community, whose self-assertion would thus eliminate a double threat.

In the first decades of the century, and particularly in the 1930s, the nationalists of the Partido Nacionalista Vasco (PNV) would increasingly opt for the Christian Democratic interclass ideology, developing like similar parties elsewhere in Europe their own trade union movement, the Solidaridad de Trabajadores Vascos (STV), their farmers' organization, and so on. In this way they created a community separate from the powerful socialist trade union, the Unión General de Trabajadores (UGT), and from the Spanish bourgeois left–socialist alliance in politics on the one side, and from the capitalists of Bilbao identified with the Spanish monarchist right on the other. Within the Basque community only a small segment—Acción Nacionalista Vasca (ANV)—split off, rejecting the Catholic and clerical stand of the PNV that had led it to collaborate with the Spanish right against the laïc republic in the hope that an autonomous Basque region would be able to regulate separately its relationships with the church and the Vatican. Once that dream was shattered, cooperation with the Spanish right became more difficult, and the adroit politics of the Socialist leader Indalecio Prieto brought the PNV closer to the Republicans. The military uprising, and with it the exaltation of Spanish nationalism, forced the Basques into an uneasy alliance with the Republicans and the working-class organizations in a joint but not common struggle against the invading army. The fact that a corps of that army was Navarrese Carlist units made the struggle even more painful for those who considered Navarra part of Euskadi, and the fact that the Catholic Basques should side with the godless Marxists made the Basque nationalists even more abominable to the Spanish right. In exile the Basque nationalists found succor in their identification with the Christian Democratic international and its rejection of both fascism and Marxism.

The accelerated industrialization and immigration, the identification of the Bilbao financial and industrial oligarchy with the Franco regime, and the passivity of their nationalist elders that set in with prosperity, created for the younger generation of nationalists, including a number of priests and seminarians inspired by Vatican II, a new context in which to analyze the relationship between class and nation. Third World ideologies, the Jewish struggle for independence, and the intellectual impact of Marxist thought would in the 1960s lead to endless debates about strategies in the national struggle and the role of the immigrant proletariat, about Marxism and violence. Paradoxically the emerging revolutionary utopia of some of the ETA ideologists comprised, in place of the classless golden age of the primordial communal society, a new classless, communist self-managed society, born out of revolution against the Franco state.

The new nationalist left could struggle in the name of the whole Basque people against the Franco regime, against its representatives regardless of their origin, and against the big business oligarchy allied with Franco. That some of the immigrants, and particularly their daughters and sons, joined in the struggle, was further proof of the unity of the Basque "nation". Although the "oligarchy" was Basque by descent and to some extent in its way of life, it could be excluded from the emerging community by a Basque version of the Third World struggle against capitalists, imperialists, and colonialists. This political version of the theory of internal colonialism had obviously to ignore the fact that the dominant elite in Basque society was Basque. The tension between the financial oligarchy and small and medium business, which sometimes fell into financial difficulties, made it easier to ignore subsequent conflicts between workers and employers.

As the struggle against the Spanish state became more widespread, however, ideology could not ignore the strategic question: should priority be assigned to the class struggle, incorporating the immigrants, or to the national liberation struggle and the emphasis on language and identity? This issue engendered bitter confrontations in the secret assemblies of the ETA movement and inspired successive splits and conflicts too complex even to summarize here; yet the underlying issue is essential to an understanding of the political fragmentation in the Basque country after the death of Franco. The original division of the terrorists into an ETA *militar* and an ETA *político-militar* and the presence today on the ballot of two revolutionary Basque lists, Herri Batasuna and Euskadiko Ezkerra, as well as the split of the Communist Party in the Basque country in 1982 and many of the latent tensions within the PSOE in the transition period, can ultimately be traced back to it.

In an industrial class society class differences and conflicts inevitably either divide a nationalist movement into different parties or inspire an international class solidarity that subordinates nationalism to the defense of class interests. The latter may take the form of working-class parties that attract voters from both communities or of bourgeois alliances—often inspired by early working-class successes—to better resist the workers. In any case united action by the nationalists to achieve either independence or stable consociational relations with the central state becomes difficult, and policies derived from primordial identity are postponed, at least for the time being, in an effort to achieve some political stability within the territorial framework. Energies are transferred in part to politics within the community and, within the framework of autonomy, away from nation-building.

Only minorities connected to a millenarian effort of creating a new social and national community can, to some extent, avoid the dilemmas that class politics inspires within the emerging community. Their voluntarism, the solidarity created by direct action, and the secrecy of the terrorists' brotherhood allow them to combine revolutionary chiliasm with the national liberation ideology and to end up with a definition of nationhood based on the common struggle against a state seen as an agent of the capitalist system. An idea of nation that includes all who hate that domination and who are willing to participate in the struggle against it serves to overcome the objective fragmentation of the population, its different subjective identifications, and the expression of its heterogeneity in the voting of normal democratic politics (Aranzadi, 1981). The immigrant who dies executed by Franco or in a shootout with the police is certainly Basque. Basques are those who persist in the struggle against the existing political and social order, even now that it is a democratic order legitimated by referendums and elections. The "people" now assume a reality beyond any aggregation of individuals with different characteristics, different identities, and different choices. It is a reality beyond any social reality, a reality in the mind of the believer.

To try to capture these voluntaristic definitions we added in a postelection survey in December 1981–January 1982[6] two new items to the list of "conditions to be considered Basque" used earlier: "the will to be Basque" and "the defense of the Basque nation." Fully 82 percent of the population agreed with "the will to be Basque" (92 percent among the voters of the PNV). The "defense of the Basque nation," a more militant option, found less agreement, 70 percent. Among PSOE voters, 80 percent agreed with the "will to be," but only 58 percent said yes to the "defense of the Basque nation" (34 percent said no). This alternative, so congruent with the ETA ideology, is the defining characteristic most often chosen by the voters of HB, 88 percent, slightly more than by those of the PNV, 83 percent, and the EE, 80 percent. The difference between 76 percent of HB supporters considering the "will to be" a condition of Basqueness (compared to 92 percent among those of the PNV) and the

88 percent opting for a definition based on a more militant stance is further evidence of the varieties in conception within the Basque community of who is Basque. The nuance reflected in these two answers reminds us in some respects of the difference that split the Mensheviks and Bolsheviks in their historic debate about the definition of party membership.

In a class-divided society, particularly one in which a significant segment of one of the classes does not share the language, culture, traditions, and so on, of the emerging nation, as is the case with the immigrants in the Basque country and Catalonia, nationalists who reject an interclass nationalist movement, or who try but fail to achieve one, face difficult choices. The problem is more acute in the first case, particularly when the goals of national and social liberation are fused, as in leftist nationalist movements.

The struggle for national freedom, when it is identified with the struggle of the subject classes for their social liberation, can have two rather disturbing consequences. One is the increasing rejection of any solidarity or common political action with the privileged dominant classes, although they might share the ethnic cultural characteristics, concretely the denial of a common national identity with the oligarchy of Bilbao in the Basque case. The second possible consequence is the emergence of a common front, whether for radical or for piecemeal social change, with workers who do not share the ethnic characteristics and, consequently, a readiness for cooperation with the larger working-class movement not only in the regional community, but in the larger state. The result, as was actually the case when the group identified as Oficina Política controlled ETA in 1965–6, is a decreasing emphasis in the appeals, the propaganda, and the ideologies of nationalist themes and an increasing saliency of the terminology of class conflict.[7] The ambiguities that result are well reflected in this text:

> Therefore, if some worker having arrived from abroad wants to make a Spanish revolution, we encourage him and we support him ... but, we remind him that the Spanish revolution will have to be made in Spain and not in Euskadi or in some other place. We consider them and their sons, however, more Basque than those capitalists with long Euskaldun (Basque) names. (Quoted in Jáuregui Bereciartu, 1981, p. 262).

The drift in this direction soon impelled the ethnolinguistic faction into tactical alliance with the Third-World tendency, leading to the expulsion of Oficina Política and to one of the first splits in the ETA.

The bourgeois nationalists, when unable to mobilize the working class for the nationalist cause in an advanced industrial society, and when pushed into a minority position by either regional or statewide working-class parties, face a similar problem of whether to ally across ethnonationalist boundaries in common defense of a social and economic order. However, since the defense of those bourgeois interests is unlikely to have been articulated in our time in ideological terms, the pragmatic compromises are less likely to be as divisive. Still, they certainly constrain the dynamics of the nationalist movement, as the recent history of the bourgeois Catalanism of Convergéncia i Unió and to a lesser extent of the Basque PNV shows.

To the extent that the nationalist movement is fundamentally one of cultural defense, of assertion of primordial values within broader state and even national politics it might be able to retain a broad basis even in a modern and industrial society, cutting across class lines as would be the case with the Swedish minority in Finland. The problem becomes serious when the nationalist movement aspires to govern within a territory, either after the attainment of political autonomy or in an independent state. In a modern society governing—except in small and marginal or rural areas—inevitably involves policy decisions that, under conditions of freedom, are unlikely to be agreed on by all classes. Ultimately, the saliency of class alignments leads to the incorporation into the politics of the emerging community of those who do not share the primordial characteristics and therefore, inevitably, to an emphasis on a territorial rather than a primordial conception of the nation.

Two Communities in Spite of the Ideology of "Territorialism"

One of the paradoxes of the conflict in multinational, multilingual, multicultural societies like the Basque country is that, when asked if there are significant differences between the native population and the immigrants into the area, both natives and immigrants tend to deny it. The same is true of those supporting the most nationalist alternative. These patterns are in a sense congruent with the decreasing emphasis on the primordial differences, and we suspect that in an earlier phase of the nationalist movement, around the turn of the century, the responses would have been very different. Undoubtedly the fusion of populations through mixed marriages,

the great economic and social equality derived from industrialization and the consumption society, and the solidarities
based on social class have tended to reduce the visibility of
differences based on primordial elements. These responses, on
the other hand, make it more difficult to understand the intensity of the nationalist sentiment.

There is a latent contradiction between the decreasing
saliency of the categorization based on primordial elements and
the limited emphasis on differences in the mentality and way of
life of natives and immigrants. At the same time people's
responses to questions about who are their neighbours and,
above all, who are their friends partially contradict those
denials. These responses show that most people are quite aware
of the different identities of the two communities in the region,
particularly when it comes to friendship, where we find a considerable degree of homogeneity. The same pattern emerges in
the relatively low proportion of mixed marriages among immigrants' parents. Unfortunately we have no data on the present
marriage patterns of immigrants. It would seem as if the objective distinctiveness of the communities were increasingly denied
at the ideological level. We obviously cannot know how sincere
the responses to the more "ideological" questions are. But even
if we were to assume that there is a certain reluctance today to
admit to anything that might sound like racism and that the
responses are more a result of the ideological formulation of
some of the leftist parties than the expression of real feelings,
those subjective answers are real in their consequences and are
sociologically relevant.

How many "Basques": the Implication of Alternative Definitions of Who is Basque

The implications of a definition of membership in the Basque
community—whether in terms of primordial characteristics,
territoriality either as place of birth or of "living and working,"
subjective national identity, or finally political national
consciousness—will quickly become apparent when we turn to
the data of our 1979 survey. Although these data are not to be
taken as an exact reflection of actual population distributions,
since they are subject to sampling error, they give us a fairly
good picture of the heterogeneity of the population using those
four complementary and in part competing criteria.

Taking as the least demanding primordial characteristic

descent from parents born in the Basque country, we find 45 percent of our sample with both parents born in the region, 5·7 percent whose mother was Basque but whose father was immigrant, and another 3·8 percent whose father was Basque but whose mother was immigrant; that would add up to 54·5 percent of the population Basque on the basis of descent. Another 9·5 percent are first-generation Basque with both parents born elsewhere (see Table 10.11). It is not clear if by the criterion of descent we should consider them Basque; certainly those nationalists who use primordial criteria of descent would not consider them Basque. They, however, and the remaining 36·1 percent born in other parts, in Spain, could be defined as Basque if the territorial definition of living and working were to be applied.

If we were to add to the criterion of origin the speaking of the Basque language, the 45 percent in the second generation would be reduced to 22·5 percent to which we could add between one-tenth and one-quarter of the children of mixed marriages who say that they speak the language (see Table 10.12). The use of a less stringent criterion of understanding (but not speaking) Euskera would increase the primordial community only slightly. It could be argued that those immigrants and children of immigrants who have learned the language could be considered members of the "primordial" community. Even using the less demanding criterion of understanding the language would add only some 6·5 percent to the Basque community. The combination of the criteria of descent (of at least one Basque-born parent) and understanding the language would leave the Basque community reduced to slightly less than one-third of the population (see Table 10.13).

The criterion of subjective national identity expressed in terms of feeling Spanish, more Spanish than Basque, equally as Basque as Spanish, more Basque than Spanish, or Basque, again shows the population divided with 39·7 percent Basque, 12·5 percent more Basque than Spanish, 27·3 percent equally as Basque as Spanish, and 20·5 percent either Spanish, or more Spanish than Basque. Let us note that in some other surveys taken in a moment of less nationalist Basque exaltation the proportions were slightly less favorable to Basque identity. This subjective identification does not have a one-to-one correspondence with the objective characteristics. So, for example, among those whose parents were Basque-born, 63·7 percent identified as Basque, 14·2 percent as more Basque than Spanish, 17·4 percent as Basque and Spanish and 4·4 percent as more

Table 10.11 *Nativity, Parentage, and National Identity in Euskadi*

	Identity				
	Spanish or more Spanish than Basque	As Basque as Spanish	More Basque than Spanish	Basque	
Both parents born in Euskadi	(20) 4·4* / 10·1 / 2·1	(79) 17·4 / 29·7 / 8·1	(62) 14·2 / 50·8 / 6·4	(277) 63·7 / 71·8 / 28·5	(438) 45·0
One parent born in Euskadi	(5) 5·4 / 2·5 / 0·5	(29) 31·5 / 10·9 / 3·0	(19) 20·7 / 15·6 / 2·0	(39) 42·4 / 10·1 / 4·0	(92) 9·5
Born in Euskadi of immigrant parents	(14) 15·2 / 7·0 / 1·4	(35) 38·0 / 13·2 / 3·6	(12) 13·0 / 9·8 / 1·2	(31) 33·7 / 8·0 / 3·2	(92) 9·5
Immigrant	(160) 45·6 / 80·4 / 16·4	(123) 35·0 / 46·2 / 12·6	(29) 8·3 / 23·8 / 3·0	(39) 11·1 / 10·1 / 4·0	(351) 36·1
Sample total	(199) 20·5	(266) 27·3	(122) 12·5	(386) 39·7	(973)

* In each cell entries appear as follows:

N	row percentage
column percentage	total sample percentage

Note: Thirty-eight respondents giving no answer to the identity question have been excluded, and the percentages that appear here are based on the reduced total.

Source: As Table 10.5.

Table 10.12 *Distribution of the Sample of the Population of Euskadi, by Parentage, Language, and Identity*

Identifies	Basque parents understands	does not	Mixed parentage understands	does not	Immigrant parents understands	does not	Immigrants understands	does not
Basque or more Basque	24·9	8·6	2·8	3·0	1·1	3·0	2·0	4·7
Equally as Basque as Spanish	2·3	5·3	0·5	2·4	0·4	3·1	2·1	10·1
More Spanish or Spanish	0·3	1·6	—	0·4	0·2	1·2	0·5	15·5
	27·5	15·5	3·3	5·8	1·7	7·3	4·6	30·3

Note: There are 3·8 percent of the sample (1011) not answering one of the questions on which the typology is based.
Source: As Table 10.5.

Table 10.13 *Identity by Nativity and Language*

Identity	Both parents Basque-born		One parent Basque-born		Born in Basque country of immigrant parents		Immigrants	
	understands Basque	does not	understands Basque	does not	understands Basque	does not	understands Basque	does not
Basque	76	41	67	29	41	32	33	8
More Basque than Spanish	14	15	18	22	24	8	11	8
As Basque as Spanish	8	34	15	41	24	41	46	34
More Spanish than Basque or Spanish	1	10	—	7	12	16	11	51
N	(279)	(157)	(33)	(58)	(17)	(75)	(46)	(303)

Note: Percentages do not always add to 100 due to rounding errors.
Source: As Table 10.5.

Spanish. Basque origin, therefore, does not exclude a Spanish national identity. In turn, among the immigrants, 35 percent already identify as equally as Basque as Spanish and 19·4 percent as more Basque or Basque. Among the sons and daughters of immigrant parents, those identifying as Basque are 33·7 percent, and 13 percent are more Basque than Spanish, while 38 percent express a dual identity.

The combination of four groups of origin and four basic alternatives of identity shows the heterogeneity of the population that the combination of primordial, territorial, and subjective criteria produces. Those with at least one Basque-born parent identifying as Basque constitute 30·5 percent of the total population, while those who by descent would be Basque but by subjective identity are at least equally Spanish are 13 percent. On the other hand, the subjective criterion adds to the Basque community 7 percent of immigrants and their children who identify as Basque, and another 4·1 percent who feel more Basque than Spanish. Using the subjective criterion combined with origin, we find 17·2 percent either descendants of immigrants or immigrants themselves who feel more Spanish than Basque, compared to 15·7 percent who feel both identities equally. If the national community were to be built on the basis of origin and identity, even loosely defined as more Basque than Spanish, the maximum would be 38·8 percent of the population.

Summarizing these complex data, it is obvious that primordial origin (of at least one parent born in the region, regardless of his or her origin) would define as Basques little over one-half of the population; and subjective identity, the feeling "Basque" or "more Basque than Spanish," would also characterize around one-half of the population. Combining descent and subjective identity, as we have seen, reduces the Basque community to 38·8 percent. In view of these data it is not surprising that many nationalists should reject the primordial criterion of who is a Basque and should favor the territorial criterion that allows a significant minority of immigrants and children of immigrants to identify as Basque, or at least as more Basque than Spanish (11·4 percent of the population). The combination of either descent or, for those of immigrant background, subjective identity, still leaves 17·2 percent of the population classified as fundamentally alien and not very much inclined to integrate into the Basque community.

The Basques can only be a significant majority of the population if they do not reject those of Basque ancestry who identify as "as Spanish as Basque," 10·7 percent, and if they are willing to include in the community those either of immigrant background or immigrants themselves who feel at least "as Basque as Spanish." The exclusion of those Basques who identify as "more Spanish" or "Spanish," and of those of immigrant background not identifying as "more Basque than Spanish" or "Basque," would exclude more than one-third of the population. Therefore, the question of who is Basque, which appears so simple in most of the writings on peripheral nationalism, turns out to be enormously complex. We have left out the French Basque country and the population of Navarra, in which only a small minority identifies as Basque, or to some extent, as Navarrese and Basque. The inclusion of these two areas, which for the nationalists are part of the Basque community, would reduce even further the number of those who by any combination of primordial and subjective criteria would be defined as Basque (Linz, 1982; Linz *et al.*, 1983).

Things would be easy if all those defined by the combination of primordial and subjective criteria as Basque were also committed to a Basque nationalist political opinion, would vote for Basque parties, and would support independence in principle; but unfortunately for the nationalists, things are not that simple either. To give just a few examples: of those with two Basque ancestors, 56·5 percent (which means 73 percent of those actually voting) voted in 1979 for one of the three Basque parties, but only 42 percent of all voters said that their choice was for nationalist rather than social and economic considerations. There are strong indications that when it comes to political choices, subjective identity is more important than descent or language. In addition, we should not forget that a vote for one of the Basque parties is not identical to support for a drive of independence. Even among those of purely Basque parentage, only 17 percent expressed a "very great" desire for independence, 22 percent "fairly great," 16 percent "fairly small," 10 percent "very small," and 19 percent expressed no desire for independence (see Table 10.14). That means that quite a few of second-generation Basque background who vote for Basque nationalist parties do not favor independence.

If we were to combine primordial characteristics, subjective identity, and politically conscious Basque nationalism, those satisfying all three criteria would be a very small minority of the population.

Table 10.14 Nativity, Parentage, Subjective Identity, and Desire for Independence for the Basque Country

Desire for independence	Both parents Basque				Mixed parentage				Immigrant parents				Immigrants			
	Ba	+Ba	=SpBa	Sp	Ba	+Ba	=SpBa	Sp	Ba	+Ba	=SpBa	Sp	Ba	+Ba	=SpBa	Sp
Very great	24	11	3	—	21	16	7	—	26	17	—	—	36	10	5	1
Fairly great	42	31	6	—	44	21	14	30	35	50	20	7	26	24	11	10
Fairly small	12	29	24	5	15	32	21	—	29	—	17	14	13	28	16	9
Very small	8	5	22	10	3	—	24	—	—	17	20	14	3	7	17	15
None	10	16	39	75	10	37	31	50	3	25	37	50	15	21	43	57
n.a.	4	6	8	10	5	—	7	—	6	—	6	14	10	7	7	8
N	(277)	(62)	(79)	(20)	(39)	(19)	(29)	(4)	(31)	(12)	(33)	(14)	(39)	(29)	(123)	(159)

Ba = Basque
+ Ba = more Basque than Spanish
= SpBa = as Basque as Spanish
Sp = Spanish or more Spanish than Basque
Source: As Table 10.5.

Political Implications of the Choice between Primordialism and Territoriality

The different categorizations used in defining who belongs to the ethnic community or nationality have important social, political, and cultural implications which cannot be analyzed here in depth but which deserve further discussion. Undoubtedly the territorial definition of who is Basque, Catalan, and so on, implies an openness on the part of natives accepting that definition to incorporate the aliens to the primordial community, either by the sheer fact of residence or by a combination of residence and willingness to integrate themselves. At first sight, it would seem that this position is the most generous and, ultimately, the least conflictual between communities; but it can also be interpreted as involving serious potential conflict in the future, since it might imply that all those resident in the territory have to feel identified with and loyal to the emerging community and perhaps nation-state. Certainly it provides the basis for a policy of cultural assimilation. The definition of living and working in the region implies that there are not two cultural, linguistic, and social communities with their own distinctiveness, their own rights, and potentially their own political expression: any effort to maintain that distinctiveness by cultural, social, or political action on the part of the "alien" immigrant community will be perceived as undesirable, threatening, and disloyal to the new emerging national community. It is a definition that excludes the patterns usually associated with consociational politics such as proportionality and the assignment to the minority of areas of autonomy; and obviously it excludes any defense of that minority and its right by a central government (in which the minority is majority) as an external interference in the new autonomous community.

It is the model implicit in the policies of the monolingual cantons of Switzerland and increasingly in the linguistic regions of Belgium (with the exception of Brussels), where those with a different linguistic background must accept the monolingualism in public life of the subunit in which they live, while enjoying citizenship rights. It is a model that serves for the construction of a truly multinational, multilingual state. It would seem an adequate model when internal migrations are not important, when the number of immigrants and children of immigrants not culturally assimilated is small, and when the consciousness of a broader national identity linked with the culture of the immigrants is not strong. None of these circumstances holds in the Basque country or in Catalonia, where large numbers of immigrants and significant numbers of sons and daughters of recent immigrants have passed the age of cultural assimilation in school, where links are strong to the larger Spanish nation or culture, which is still the majority culture of the whole country, and where bilingualism is guaranteed by the Constitution. In such a context the assimilationist model implicit in the territorial definition involves the danger of a lack of recognition of the rights of the minority and thereby of serious conflict in the medium run.

On the part of the immigrants the categorization in territorial terms of who is Basque or Catalan implies that they have the option to integrate, to identify with, and to feel as totally equal members of the emerging autonomous community as a society and subpolity. The success of those claims obviously depends on the extent to which the majority native population also accepts such a territorial definition or insists consciously or unconsciously on emphasizing a primordial conception of its ethnic identity. Such a claim by those alien to the primordial community offers opportunity for identification, assimilation and integration. However, it also involves a claim to equality and rights that might conflict with the defense, reaffirmation, and hegemony of the primordial culture and way of life that initially gave rise to the movement for national autonomy or independence. In a sense it makes the alien element more threatening to the revival and hegemony of the primordial culture, since it cannot be considered a distinct community, as Sabino de Arana did when he advocated that immigrants should be denied citizenship and expelled. On the other hand, it encourages the nationalist and separatist tendency of peripheral nationalism, since it tends to loosen the ties with the larger polity, in this case Spain. If the aim were to create a multinational, multilingual state, it could be positive if both natives and immigrants shared the territorial definition, and if the immigrants were ready to identify with the new community, integrate themselves into it, assimilate culturally, and ultimately abandon their own "primordial" identity. Then it could be the basis for stable new model of a multinational state. However, if the nationalist movement aims at independence, the acceptance of a territorial definition by the "aliens" would reinforce that drive and thereby, in the medium run, be one more factor in exacerbating the conflict, since it would make any consociational politics between the autonomous region and the larger state, and between communities within the autonomous region, more difficult. Should the nationalists achieve independence, it would however make difficult any assertion of their "primordial" identity in the new state.

Acceptance by both natives and immigrants of a primordial definition of the ethnic identity is not conflict-free; but if there is an acceptance of the common state, and if within the autonomous region consociational solutions are found to the coexistence in the same territory of two communities with their own distinctive social, cultural, and political organizations, that could lead to complex but stable relations between the state and the autonomous region and between the communities within the region. However, the model will inevitably lead to conflict if the nationalist primordial community seeks full political independence, since in that case the conflict will be not only with the larger state but between two national communities, one majority and one minority defined by primordial characteristics. Independence in that case will require either full assimilation of the minority or more or less deliberate discrimination against them and perhaps a policy that encourages a return to their places of origin.

A situation in which the native population maintains the primordial definition of the ethnic community and where the immigrant population and the descendants of immigrants accept a territorial categorization is also a source of tensions. The immigrants are likely to claim total equality with the natives in the emerging community, either by accepting a voluntaristic self-integration and identity (which might be rejected since they would not share the primordial elements defining membership in it) or by asserting, as in the past, that those primordial criteria should be either secondary or limited to certain spheres. In fact the immigrants in that context might be divided between those who feel frustrated in their attempt to integrate and assimilate, encountering difficulties in the process due to the strong emphasis on primordial elements, and those who feel that the territorial principle defines membership in the community, irrespective of whether one shares the primordial elements.

An "Essential" Definition beyond Primordialism and Subjective Identity

The data we have just presented may explain why the extreme nationalists, in situations like the one described, turn toward metaphysical conceptions of the nation and speak in the name of "the people" but reject the idea that the people should speak or vote before the conscious vanguard changes the objective conditions. Sometimes this means creating a spiral of silence for other options, even terror, that suppress alternatives and expel from the community those rejecting the nationalist solution. No referendum or plebiscite can decide the fate of the nation. Those who share the primordial characteristics but refuse the subjective identity, and even those who assume the identity and reject the political implications that the nationalists derive from it, are defined as traitors and therefore excluded from the national community. The nation becomes a transcendental reality that cannot be questioned and exists independently of the actual beliefs and actions of those supposed to be part of it. Temporary majorities or minorities become irrelevant; the nationalist vanguard must carry on the fight, largely in the hope that its actions will produce a conflict and a forced choice between an outside enemy and the primordial mythical community.

It is no accident that so many nationalisms should have been profoundly a- or antidemocratic and that extreme nationalism should reject consociational democracy, the type of democracy in which even majorities cannot decide matters that are intensely felt by minorities. This is true for the extreme nationalists of the periphery no less than for those of the center. The integrity and essence of the nation, be it Spanish or Basque, then becomes something that cannot be endangered by the decision of the individual members of the community. From this perspective the democratic methods of decision-making and the even more complex methods of consociational democracy are unjustifiable and therefore inadequate, and the problem becomes insoluble.[8] Obviously there is always one solution, but even that one in many cases proves unworkable: decision by violence and force. We should not forget that a number of the most serious and least tractable conflicts of our time have been generated by exclusivist conceptions of national identity. To mention only a few in which democratic institutions were potentially available: Ulster, Cyprus, Israel, Lebanon, and Czechoslovakia before World War II. Only a full acceptance of a nonexclusivist conception of the nation, a commitment to a dual national identity like that of over one-third of the population of the Basque country and a larger proportion of Catalans, together with respect for the cultural identity of the two communities and common citizenship for all those living in the territory, is compatible with the freedom of democracy.

A territorial categorization of membership in an ethnic, cultural, linguistic minority is ultimately ambiguous. On the one hand, it facilitates a new political integration by establishing a basis for loyalty to the new form of political organization, independently of whether one shares the primordial characteristics. It is thus conceived with the purpose of reducing ethnic conflict and creating a broad front in relationship to the center. On the other hand, it is a source of new conflict, since it excludes the possibility of two communities retaining their social and cultural identity and implies ultimately discrimination, assimilation, or expulsion.

Initially the elements of the majority in the minority within the territory might be willing to support a territorially based desire for autonomy, but the implications we have just noted are likely to lead to conflict at a later stage and to make it difficult to find consociational solutions within the new territorial organization of the state. On the other hand, the radical nationalist is likely to find the territorial definition dangerous because it ultimately dilutes the distinctiveness of the ethnic, cultural, linguistic, national community. It is, therefore, no accident that, within the territorial framework, the more radical nationalist would add a further condition for membership: the will to identify with the emerging community. The territorial principle entitles those who do not share the primordial characteristics to join the primordially based community, but it also requires the will to do so, to identify a Basque or Catalan, rather than just the fact of living and working in the Basque country or Catalonia.[9] In that case, nationalism has gone full circle from the demands for recognition of primordial distinctive elements to demands of loyalty to the new emerging political community, irrespective of culture, linguistic, or other characteristics.

The new nationalists ultimately do not conceive a political community any differently from the old nation-states, which have demanded, in the past, that same loyalty and identification from all their citizens irrespective of their primordial self-categorization. Identity, and the loyalty that is linked with it, is the ultimate criterion of membership in the emerging political community. However, nationalism is not likely to abandon fully the primordial elements that initially gave rise to its demands. The new claim is that all those in a particular territory, irrespective of their primordial background, must identify with the community and share its language and culture.

There is no room left for separate communal identity for the minority within the former minority.

Notes: Chapter 10

1 The data used are from the following sample surveys: for the Basque country, unless indicated otherwise, survey by DATA, November 1979, after the referendum on the Autonomy Statute. For the French Basque country, survey by DATA executed by Cofremca, November 1979. For Catalonia, Valencia, and Galicia, survey by Richard Gunther, Giacomo Sani, and Goldie Shabad of 5439 Spaniards over 18, carried out by DATA between mid-April and mid-June 1979, with an oversampling in those regions (NSF grant SOC77–16451): see Shabad and Gunther, forthcoming; Gunther *et al.*, forthcoming. I want to thank the authors for having made their data available to me, for further analysis.

2 On peripheral nationalisms and their political manifestations in Spain, see the following publications of the present author (with extensive bibliographic references): Linz, 1973, 1975, 1980a, 1980b, 1981, 1982; Linz *et al.*, 1981, 1982, 1983. For further recent contributions, see Shabad and Gunther, forthcoming; Gunther *et al.*, forthcoming; García Ferrando, 1982.

3 The literature on internal migrations in Spain is extensive, particularly on the migrants and their place in Catalan society: see Pinilla de las Heras, 1979; Solé, 1981. On nationalism, class, and immigration in Catalonia, see *Quaderns d'Alliberament*, 1977, 1978. Recently more attention has been devoted to the immigrants in Basque society at the turn of the century: Corcuera Atienza, 1979; Fusi, 1965; Olábarri Gortazar, 1978. Beltza (pseud.), 1976, provides an analysis from a Marxist left–radical–nationalist perspective. On the political attitudes of descendants of immigrants and of the migrants themselves, see Linz *et al.*, 1983.

4 The political writings of Basque nationalist ideologists, lately mostly of the left, and the academic literature on the Basques are so extensive that we must refer the reader to the bibliographic references in our other publications (see n.2). In English, see Payne, 1975; Clark, 1979. For a recent review, consult Puhle, 1982. In Spanish, see Arana Goiri, 1978; Elorza, 1979; Corcuera Atienza, 1979.

5 The literature on the ETA movement and its many factions and organizations, its role in the struggle against Franco, and its ideology is too extensive to be cited. On the group's continuing and intensifying terrorist actions after free elections, total amnesty, the granting of autonomy to the Basque country, the election of a Basque regional Parliament, and the constitution of an autonomous government, see Muñoz Alonso, 1982. For the responses of the population, see Linz *et al.*, 1983.

6 Data from the survey planned by R. Gunther, J. Linz, J. Montero, H. Puhle, G. Sani, and G. Shabad, with the support of the Volkswagen Foundation, executed by DATA. Incidentally, the responses to the items repeated from the 1979 survey have demonstrated no changes beyond those that can be attributed to sampling variations.

7 On the internal debates on nationalism and class in the ETA movement, see Jáuregui Bereciartu, 1981.

8 On the rejection by Basque nationalists and their opponents in Navarra of the referendum to decide the integration of Navarra into Euskadi, see Linz *et al.*, 1983.

9 On the different responses of Catalan intellectuals and politicians to the problem of defining the Catalan identity, see Marsal *et al.*, 1979; Mercadé, 1982. For qualitative interviews on the question of identity in Catalonia, see Hernández, 1981.

References: Chapter 10

Arana Goiri, Sabino (1978), *Obras escogidas, Antología política* (San Sebastian: L. Haranburu).

Aranzadi, Juan (1981), *Milenarismo vasco (Edad de oro, etnia y nativismo)* (Madrid: Taurus).

Beltza (pseud. of E. López Adán) (1976), *Nacionalismo vasco y clases sociales* (San Sebastian: Txertoa).

Clark, Robert P. (1979), *The Basques. The Franco Years and Beyond* (Reno, Nev.: University of Nevada Press).

Corcuera Atienza, Javier (1979), *Orígenes, ideología y organización del nacionalismo vasco, 1876–1904* (Madrid: Siglo Veintiuno de España).

Deutsch, Karl W. (1966), *Nationalism and Social Communication* (Cambridge, Mass.: MIT Press).

Elorza, Antonio (1979), *Ideologías del nacionalismo vasco. Industrialismo y conciencia nacional* (San Sebastian: L. Haranburu).

Fusi, Juan Pablo (1965), *Política obrera en el País Vasco, 1880–1923* (Madrid: Turner).

García Ferrando, Manuel (1982), *Regionalismo y autonomía en España, 1976–1979* (Madrid: Centro de Investigaciones Sociológicas).

Geertz, Clifford (1963), "The integrative revolution: primordial sentiments and civil politics in the new states," in C. Geertz (ed.), *Old Societies and New States: The Quest for Modernity in Asia and Africa*, (New York: The Free Press). pp. 105–57.

Gunther, Richard, Sani, Giacomo, and Shabad, Goldie (forthcoming), *The Making of a Competitive Party System. Spain after Franco* (Berkeley, Calif.: University of California Press).

Hernández, Francesc (1981), "El nacionalismo catalán y la socialización nacionalista," *Sistema*, vol. 43–4, pp. 151–69.

Jáuregui Bereciartu, Gurutz (1981), *Ideología y estrategia política de ETA. Análisis de su evolución entre 1959 y 1968* (Madrid: Siglo Veintiuno de España).

Linz, Juan J. (1973), "Early state-building and late peripheral nationalism against the state," in S. N. Eisenstadt and S. Rokkan (eds.), *Building States and Nations: Models, Analyses, and Data across Three Worlds* (Beverly Hills, Calif.: Sage), Vol. II, pp. 32–112.

Linz, Juan J. (1975) "Politics in a multi-lingual society with a dominant world language: the case of Spain," in Jean-Guy Savard and Richard Vigneault (eds.), *Les Etats multilingues. Problèmes et solutions* (Quebec City: Les Presses de l'Université Laval), pp. 367–444.

Linz, Juan J. (1980a), "La política en sociedades multilingües y multinacionales." in Fundación de Estudios Sociológicos (Fundes), *Como articular las autonomías espanõlas* (Madrid: Fundes), pp. 83–107.

Linz, Juan J. (1980b), "The Basques in Spain: nationalism and political conflict in a new democracy," in W. Phillips Davison and Leon Gordenker (eds.), *Resolving Nationality Conflicts: The Role of Public Opinion Research* (New York: Praeger), pp. 11–52.

Linz, Juan J. (1981), "La crisis de un estado unitario, nacionalismos periféricos y regionalismo," in R. Acosta (ed.), *La España de las autonomías (Pasado, presente y futuro)* (Madrid: Espasa Calpe), Vol. II, pp. 651–751.

Linz, Juan J. (1982), "Peripheries within the periphery?," in *Mobilization*

Center–Periphery, Periphery Structure and Nation Building: A Volume in Commemoration of Stein Rokkan (Bergen: Bergen Universitets Forlaget), pp. 335–80.

Linz, Juan J., Gómez Reino, Manuel, Orizo, Francisco A., and Vila, Darío (1981), *Informe sociológico sobre el cambio político en España 1975–1981. Fundación Foessa, IV Informe Foessa* (Madrid: Euramérica), Vol. I, pp. 509–83.

Linz, Juan J., Gómez Reino, Manuel, Orizo, Francisco A., and Vila, Darío (1982), *Atlas electoral de Alava, Guipúzcoa, Vizcaya y Navarra* (Madrid: Centro de Investigaciones Sociológicas).

Linz, Juan J., Gómez Reino, Manuel, Orizo, Francisco A., and Vila, Darío (1984), *Conflicto en Euskadi, Estudio sociológico sobre el cambio político en el País Vasco 1975–1980* (Madrid: Espasa Calpe).

Marsal, Joan F., Mercadé, Francesc, Hernández, Francesc, and Oltra, Benjamín (1979), *La nació com a problema. Tesis sobre el cas català* (Barcelona: Edicions 62).

Mercadé, Francesc (1982), *Cataluña: Intelectuales, políticos y cuestión nacional. Análisis sociológico de las ideologías políticas en la Cataluña democrática* (Barcelona: Ediciones Peninsula).

Muñoz Alonso, Alejandro (1982), *El terrorismo en España* (Barcelona: Planeta-Instituto de Estudios Económicos).

Olábarri Gortazar, Ignacio (1978), *Relaciones laborales en Vizcaya (1890–1936)* (Durango: Leopoldo Zugaza).

Payne, Stanley G. (1975), *Basque Nationalism* (Reno, Nev.: University of Nevada Press).

Pinilla de las Heras, Esteban (1979), *Estudios sobre cambio social y estructura de clases en Cataluña* (Madrid: Centro de Investigaciones Sociológicas).

Puhle, Hans-Jürgen (1982), "Baskischer Nationalismus im spanischen Kontext," in H. A. Winkler (ed.), *Nationalismus in der Welt von heute* (Göttingen: Vandenhoeck & Ruprecht), pp. 51–81.

Pujol, Jordi (1976), *La immigració: problema i esperança de Catalunya* (Barcelona: Nova Terra).

Quaderns d'Alliberament (1977), *Questió nacional i lluita de classes*, No. 1 (Barcelona: La Magrana).

Quaderns d'Alliberament (1978), *La immigració als paísos catalans*, No. 2 (Barcelona: La Magrana).

Shabad, Goldie, and Gunther, Richard (1982), "Language, nationalism and political conflict in Spain," *Comparative Politics*, vol. 14, no. 4, pp. 443–77.

Shabad, Goldie, and Gunther, Richard (forthcoming), "Spanish Regionalism in the 1980s," in S. Payne (ed.), *Europe in the Eighties: A Comprehensive Assessment of Politics, Economics and Culture* (Princeton, N.J.: Karz-Cohl).

Solé, Carlota (1981), *La integración sociocultural de los inmigrantes en Cataluña* (Madrid: Centro de Investigaciones Sociológicas).

11

Catalan Nationalism
some Theoretical and Historical Considerations

ORIOL PI-SUNYER

Introduction

In a recent editorial Foreword the editors of *Comparative Studies in Society and History* (1980, p. 144) note that "Outbursts of violence attract social scientists the way volcanic eruptions draw geologists, as specific events inviting measurement that promise to reveal subterranean forces which may in turn reflect still more basic structures." This observation is equally valid for the phenomenon of nationalism, for such movements have attracted increasing public and professional attention as their militancy has grown.

For the most part social scientists have scored poorly in anticipating the strength of contemporary nationalism, in particular nationalism within Western societies. At the risk of some simplification liberal scholarship has tended to look at nationalism, when it has done so at all, as an antique evil bound to give way to progress. Marxist theories generally treat nationalism as an ideological manifestation of some less-evident infrastructure. Again it is not perceived as a rational political response (the genuine issues are those of class interests), but as a case of false consciousness—what appears to be is not really so at all. It took decades and many hard lessons for Western governments and Western scholars to recognize the strength of nationalism in their colonies. In our postcolonial world the wars of national liberation in the colonies seem inevitable, but the perception was different a generation or more ago. In this respect we should remember the attempts to meet these challenges by force—the roster of "emergencies" and "police actions" is very long—or through the offer of membership in a "community" or "union" dominated by the metropole.

In due course, first the political and later the economic agendas of independence achieved recognition, but the interpretation given to these forces and movements continued to reflect Western preconceptions. For our purposes, what needs to be stressed is that the nationalism of former colonies could, in substantial measure, be attributed to the demonstration effect of doctrines that had lost much of their currency, or much of their power to galvanize opinion, in their countries of origin. It was a comfortable hypothesis.

Furthermore, the internal political problems and cleavages confronting the governments of so many new countries could be interpreted as the growing pains of states that were still in the process of establishing institutions and a sense of shared history. It was also to be expected that as countries with little experience in modern politics, particularisms of various types— the old affinity groups of tribe, caste, religion, family, and region—would continue to make themselves felt for some time to come after independence. However, the assumption was that these archaic challenges to the state were bound to recede as "nation-building" progressed, a process that combined administrative consolidation with various forms of modernization and secularization.

Of course, more often than not, events have taken a very different direction. The perturbations that have shaken many non-Western societies, movements, and ideologies that have variously been termed "nationalistic," "fundamentalist," and "liberational," typically make use of just those ties of social solidarity that were assumed to be on the wane. This is not what was predicted. For example, K. H. Silvert (1963, p. 19) in the introduction to the widely-read *Expectant Peoples: Nationalism and Development*, bluntly states, *"Nationalism is the acceptance of the state as the impersonal and ultimate arbiter of human affairs"* (emphasis in original). According to this definition, the state becomes the entity of highest allegiance, while government functions as an impersonal administrative and redistributive authority.

Such a view of the state as arbiter and manager, and of nationalism as its binding ideology, is more than anything else an idealization of what an advanced state system was *expected* to look like; it bears little relationship to the all-too-common phenomenon of the levers of power falling into the hands of a particular interest group, a "capture" of government that is the antithesis of power exercised in the common interest.

Obviously political models and interpretations that stress the primacy of the state are likely to obscure internal political and cultural heterogeneity as well as underplay the realities of international and transnational interdependence.

The specifics of models may be of concern only to political scientists and other specialists in policy and government, but the general concepts form part of a much more extensive system of belief and values. It is difficult to argue the evidence that the specialists reflect—as well as influence, of course—broad frames of intellectual reference and deeply established concepts in majority popular cultures. This chapter is hardly the vehicle to argue the case in detail, but we might take note of the role of the French state's intellectual patronage and control in the elaboration of a state-supported high culture and the concept of France as a people within "natural" frontiers.

Turning our attention to Spain, we can easily identify an "españolista" position, a perspective that combines an emphasis on strong central control with a distrust of minority nationalisms. What is particularly interesting is that this viewpoint has been, and continues to be, shared by political and intellectual figures all along the political spectrum: socialists, liberals, communists, monarchists, fascists, and republicans. For intellectuals especially, this perspective is validated by a denial of major cultural and institutional differences within the boundaries of the Spanish state.

Thus, while Spain is multiethnic and multilingual (Linz, 1975), it is not seen as such by the outside world. In part this is due to the very important fact that the majority language is not only an Iberian language, but also a major global language. This language can be glossed as "Castilian" or as "Spanish", the latter being the preferred form outside of Spain. Under these circumstances it is especially easy for foreigners to suppose that much as German is the language of Germany, Spanish is the language of Spain. But these factors of perception are not independent of politics and power. Some Spaniards who speak the majority language insist that Castilian *is* Spanish, the common and universal language of all Spaniards, the language of a great literature and a glorious historical past, a link with those many countries originally colonized and settled by Spain.

Catalan nationalism would seem to fit reasonably comfortably into the general category of Western nonstate nationalisms. True, in the early decades of this century, Spain had the appearance of a political anomaly—a sort of displaced "Balkan" country—to many observers from other Western societies. It was poor, and mostly agrarian, a land in which the role of such traditional groups and classes as the military, the clergy, and the landlords was very much in evidence; and of course, it was a state with deep cleavages of class, region, language, and nationality.

Today the economic and social profile of Spanish society shows many similarities with that of other Western countries. At the same time, almost everywhere in the West, the challenges to the state, its authority and legitimacy, have grown enormously. A significant component of this challenge is nationalism in one form or another. Thus in some respects Spain has become more "European" but at the same time many Western societies have discovered that they are not immune to the play of forces that had previously been considered as peculiarly "Spanish".

We can perhaps, first, agree that the process of "development" does not automatically spell the decline of nationalism. This would seem to be the case whether we stress the shift toward a market economy or examine the transformation of traditional political systems in the direction of the liberal nightwatchman state. There is also little to indicate that the consolidation of totalitarian regimes spells the end of nationalist aspirations.[1]

We are not suggesting an absence of linkage between nationalism and political–economic factors. On the contrary, one of the most interesting characteristics of nationalist movements is the manner and degree to which they undergo critically important changes in response to alterations in the economic and political environments within which they are positioned. This plasticity is evident in structural, organizational, and ideological changes over time as well as in the intensity and political penetration of such movements. The very fact that nationalism can mean so many different things to different peoples, as well as to the same reference group at different points of time, is probably one reason why social scientists have often approached nationalism as a manifestation of something supposedly more substantial.

What, then, should we understand by nationalism? As a preliminary definition, I suggest that nationalism entails two components, political and cultural. All nationalisms have in common a political dimension of systematic action and a cultural dimension of group membership uniting the collectivity. Politically nationalism is something more than loyalty to political institutions, and culturally it is more than belonging to a group.

It is no less a manifestation of cultural cohesion, as informants will repeatedly insist. An explanation or definition that takes this cultural dimension into consideration does not require of us that we discount the evidence of our experience and the expressions and sentiments of those we work among.

We are not, needless to say, required to take the specific cultural explanations and validating myths of our informants as other than an "emic" expression, *one* level of reality. The distinction between "emic" and "etic" approaches to social and cultural analysis derives from linguistics, and in particular the work of Kenneth Pike (1954). Much as linguists commonly differentiate between phonetics and phonemics, students of cultural systems are asked to distinguish between phenomena that can be examined independently of informants' cultural judgment (etics) and phenomena that can only be assessed in terms of the patterns of meaning of a particular group (emics). The distinction between the two approaches has been well expressed by Sydel Silverman:

> In etic analysis, the reference point for verification is the community of scientific observers; the usefulness of methods of observation and units of analysis depends upon their applicability to all cultures and observers. In contrast, the adequacy of an emic analysis is judged by the responses of the natives themselves ... more or less the way a linguist would ask native speakers whether or not statements generated from his own model of the grammar constituted grammatic speech. (Silverman, 1977, pp. 9–10)

Advantages are likely to accrue to methods of inquiry that do not discard cultural dynamics. As a case in point, one of the really knotty problems faced by students of nationalism is finding good and sufficient reasons why members of minority nationalities—and often the whole reference group—that are perfectly conversant with the ways of the majority culture, and have all the formal qualifications to participate in it, continue to insist on their distinctiveness. In not a few cases the groups in question are far from marginal and have been part of state society for centuries.

It would seem that purely economic and political arguments do not explain why groups such as the Catalans and Scots continue to maintain a separate identity. Similarly, without recourse to an element of cultural explanation, it is difficult to understand why the modern state, with the enormous advantages it enjoys in propaganda and the control of educational structures, has not managed to convince its minority citizens that nationalism (other than that sanctioned by the state) runs against the inexorable tides of history, or is an archaic and parochial sentiment.

I do not suggest that we should opt for a "black box" theory of nationalism and simply assume that "something" goes on "in there" that can only be intimated by its effects or consequences. We should indeed study nationalism at all levels. However, there is nothing "unscientific" or "unprogressive" in resisting the temptation to reduce nationalism to an epiphenomenon. In *Les Damnés de la terre*, Frantz Fanon (1961, pp. 174–5) after pointing out that "national culture" should not be confused with folklore, populism, or tradition, goes on to state: "National culture is the sum of efforts by which a people describe, justify and celebrate the struggle through which they were raised and preserved." We shall return to the matter of explanation, but Fanon's stress on description, justification, and celebration is a good point to leave the discussion.

Structural Continuities

If, as it has often been claimed, nationalism is a potential inherent in all ethnic and/or linguistic collectivities, it is nevertheless quite evident that of the many possible candidates only a relatively small number have opted for the path of nationalism. There are many reasons why this should be so, but two sets of factors certainly facilitate the emergence or maintenance of nationalism: the presence of *institutions and structures*, developed over time, that strengthen group identity and aid mobilization; the establishment or definition of *goals* to which mobilization may be directed.

This section examines some aspects of Catalan cultural and institutional history of special pertinence to group solidarity and organizational potential. The section to follow will be concerned primarily with nationalist strategies during the nineteenth century.

A distinctly Catalan society first began to take form in the aftermath of the Islamic invasion of the Iberian peninsula (Lewis, 1965; Glick and Pi-Sunyer, 1969, p. 148). The peoples who escaped the initial and powerful thrust of the Moorish conquest became differentiated into five Romance-speaking cultural groups: Catalan, Aragonese, Castilian, Leonese, and Gallego-Portuguese. The Basques comprised a distinct entity antedating Romanization and Germanization.

By the late Middle Ages the kingdoms of Catalonia, Aragon and Valencia were grouped in the federation known as the Crown of Aragon. In the words of Stanley Payne (1970, p. 15), this federation had "developed one of the most advanced—if not the most advanced—constitutional systems in fourteenth-century Europe," an opinion shared by other historians (Elliott, 1964; Schneidman, 1970).

This constitutional system was essentially an alliance between the Crown and the various commercial and industrial interests, urban and rural. The role of the aristocracy was secondary and essentially limited to military responsibilities. Following the Black Death, the Catalan–Aragonese contractual state faced many strains, but the essentials of the political system survived.

The union of the Spanish Crowns in 1478–9, foreshadowed by the marriage in 1469 of Ferdinand, heir to the throne of Aragon, and Isabella, the heiress of Castile, created a royal patrimony, but not a unified nation, or even an administratively centralized state.

Much of the structure of constitutional pluralism survived until the early eighteenth century. Indeed, after a general uprising in 1639–40 against attempts at centralization, the Crown made formal recognition of Catalan political liberties and of the strict limits of royal authority in an agreement of 1653.

One of the consequences of this successful political confrontation was that the traditional directing classes in Catalonia, the upper bourgeoisie, retained their economic and political primacy. In the century of absolutism, and with the model of Louis XIV across the border, Spain continued to be an empire of separate territories, each one having a distinct identity and a separate constitutional relationship to the Crown.

In its heyday the Crown of Aragon can best be considered as a highly successful combination of political stability and mercantile expansion. It is to the economic dimension that we now turn our attention. Vicens Vives graphically describes the dynamic quality of the late mediaeval economy:

A swarm of merchants underwrote the maritime expansion, sending the sailors of Barcelona and Mallorca from the Sea of Azov to the coasts of Senegal. Sicily, Sardinia, and the center of

the Barbary Coast were her fiefs. Nor should it be forgotten that
Catalan merchants competed with Venetian and Genoese
merchants in the traffic in spices ... and in the trade in Mediterranean products between Naples and Bruge. Until 1420 they
occupied second place in Brugge, center of the Nordic commerce, as well as a leading position in Alexandria, key to the
markets of the Far East. (Vicens Vives, 1972, p. 74).

This prosperity, a prosperity that touched not only sailors and
merchants, but also the textile and metal trades, other manufactures, and an increasingly market-oriented peasantry, did not
survive the crises of the late fourteenth and fifteenth centuries.
Catalonia's protocapitalist economy, oriented strongly to trade
and foreign markets, may have been particularly vulnerable to
a Pan-European disequilibration of political and economic
systems. As the center of economic and political gravity shifted
away from the Mediterranean, Catalonia had the choice of
stagnation or carrying out a restructuring of significant
proportions.

Some of the best evidence for such a restructuring comes
from the countryside. Between the mid-fourteenth century and
the end of the fifteenth century the population of Catalonia
declined almost 40 percent, but between 1550 and 1620 there
was a spectacular demographic recovery, in part because of
mass emigration from France. By the beginning of the seventeenth century, some 20 percent of the total male population of
Catalonia was made up of French immigrants (Elliott, 1963, p.
26). While Spain as a whole in the period 1600–1750 belongs to
the category of sick economies, Catalonia enjoyed a "moderate
prosperity ... based on a commercial intermediate role"
(Wallerstein, 1980, p. 188). And De Vries notes that "only in
Catalonia did a permanent agricultural advance occur during
this otherwise deperate era" (De Vries, 1976, p, 51).

Again and again at the end of the seventeenth century
Catalan commentators stress that commerce and industry must
be the salvation not only of Catalonia, but of all of Spain. The
model to be followed, one is told, is the Dutch. Holland, of
course, was an entrepreneurial state *par excellence* (Vilar, 1979,
pp. 351–2).

In the War of Spanish Succession the Catalans sided with the
English, another commercial society. But the move proved to
be a disastrous political mistake, for the English, weary of a
long war, abandoned their allies and signed the treaties of
Utrecht of 1713–14. The Catalans fought on until the city of

Barcelona fell after a long siege on 11 September 1714. The defeat spelled the end of a formal constitutional identity.[2]

The main motive for these actions seems to have been a growing frustration with the economic mismanagement of Spain. The Catalan directorate, supported by broad sectors of the population, backed one of the claimants to the throne in the expectation that success would permit the modernization of Spain and allow Catalans to play an important role in the political and economic revitalization of Spain and its empire.

This frustration is perfectly understandable when we contrast the general decline of the Spanish economy with the vitality of Catalonia after 1650. In short, we have a major asymmetry: "peripheral" development and "central" stagnation.

We can hardly doubt that the substantial economic success of Catalonia, together with political and institutional continuity, helped to reinforce group identity.

Catalonia and the Colonial Market

The eighteenth century began badly for Catalonia; yet by the end of the century military defeat and the loss of political liberties had been transformed into general prosperity and notable economic expansion.

A critically important factor in the changing fortunes of Catalonia was the transformations that were taking place in the Spanish Empire. Between the early decades of the eighteenth century and the Napoleonic invasion of 1807–8—very slowly at first—the new Bourbon dynasty put into operation a series of economic and administrative reforms designed to strengthen the kingdom and its American dependencies. Between 1714 and 1790 Catalonia's population doubled to 1 million inhabitants, a much higher growth rate than that experienced by the Spanish state as a whole. The change was most pronounced in the cities. By the end of the century Barcelona had been transformed into an industrial metropolis of over 100,000 inhabitants, a city that produced an extensive range of commodities: metal goods, dyes, soap, armaments, spirits and much else, but most important of all, textiles. During the 1790s the port of Barcelona shipped some 2·5 million meters of cotton cloth overseas annually, a figure that represented almost one quarter of the Catalan output (Ardit *et al.*, 1980, p. 68). Several other towns also became important as manufacturing and processing centers.

Already by the middle decades of the eighteenth century it is legitimate to speak of some factory production. As the century progresses we find, first, the concentration and the regimentation of a growing proportion of the industrial laborforce, and then around 1780 the introduction of much more advanced textile machinery. Originally from England, these jennies, mules and water-frames required substantial amounts of capital. In part because of costs and also due to problems of delivery, the English prototypes were soon copied and improved upon.

The rural population did not decline; on the contrary, records and descriptions refer to expanding villages and the constant pressure to colonize and exploit marginal lands. As a case in point, there was not only an increase in the amount of land planted in vineyards, and hence more wine available for export, but the development of an important brandy industry shipping to markets as far afield as the Baltic and the Americas.

The countryside, having made a very substantial shift in the direction of intensive cultivation of commercial crops, was very much articulated with the cities and markets previously discussed. The rural equivalent of the Barcelona entrepreneur was the farmer-capitalist with commercial links to market towns and the many small trading ports of the coast.

For this period, there is little evidence of conflict between state and peripheral elites. The peripheral elites, including those of Catalonia, increasingly identified with the state, or at least perceived no contradiction between "nation" and "state". Catalan elites, with links not only to the state but also to the empire and its markets, initiated a diglossic shift which increasingly transformed Castilian into the language of business, science, and serious discourse. Castilian, however, was little used by the gentry and smaller merchants and virtually unknown among the peasantry and urban workers.

It is also very relevant to the whole issue of core–periphery relations to take note of the fact that many of the best statesmen of eighteenth-century Spain came from the provinces and overseas: cultured nobles like the Asturian Jovellanos and the Aragonese Count of Aranda, as well as many administrators of humble birth who owed their position to royal favor. Certainly there were never enough of these men to transform the Spanish bureaucracy, but for some decades the core tapped the talents and energies of an extensive hinterland. A secure and reformist government, optimistic toward the future, felt much less threatened by real or imaginary internal enemies, and it could well be that this was the last opportunity of bringing about the transformation of what was still a powerful state into a modern society.

For a variety of complex reasons, the restructuring of Spanish society did not take place. First, there was the destruction of the Napoleonic Wars, a destruction that was not only economic, but also social and political. Not unrelated to this long episode of invasion and occupation was the loss of the American colonies which achieved independence at a time when the power and prestige of the state were at a particularly low ebb.

If the loss of colonial markets was a painful reality, the abrogation of the liberal Cadiz Constitution of 1812 by the reactionary Ferdinand VII was an equally disturbing political development. While the Constitution was perhaps too liberal to survive, it appealed strongly to most sectors of the Catalan bourgeoisie. When it was rescinded, protests in Catalonia were widespread, and by no means limited to the comfortable classes. The Catalans had fought tenaciously against the French invader—and paid the usual price for resistance. A reversion to bad autocratic government was bound to alienate Catalonia; we can in fact trace the origins of modern nationalism, in the standard nineteenth-century guise of a literary revival coupled to doctrines of the enduring relationship of land, people, and language, to this period of economic crisis and political discontent.[3]

Nineteenth-Century Limits of Growth

By 1820 the one-time colonial markets, if not completely lost, were nevertheless open to all manner of competition, in particular from an economically and politically ascendant Britain.

Under the circumstances it is understandable that the Catalan bourgeoisie and, in particular, the larger manufacturers lobbied for legislation that would bar or impede foreign merchandise from what remained of the metropolitan and colonial markets: Spain, Cuba, Puerto Rico, and the Philippines. A small enough market by the standards of 1800, but all the more precious given the competition elsewhere.

The motivations of the bourgeoisie are in keeping with what we might expect: attempts at market protection phrased in the idiom of the common good. However, the structural position of this class in the state power structure does not fit the accepted models.

To begin with, it was a class that encountered great difficulties in establishing coalitions with other elite and middle sectors such as the long-established mercantile interests of Cadiz and Malaga, the shipbuilders and merchants of Bilbao and San Sebastian, the latifundia owners of Andalusia, and the professional–bureaucratic classes of Madrid and interior Spain. At certain times and under certain circumstances it proved possible to form alliances with some of these groups for profit and politics, but what never occurred was a lasting arrangement leading to class consolidation.

If there were problems of alliance formation in nineteenth-century Spain, part of the reason is that all classes in Catalonia, including the bourgeoisie, never lost their ambivalence toward the state, an attitude that does not rule out calls for state support and protection. It would be simplistic to attribute this reluctance to some kind of liberal–conservative division in state politics, for not only were there conservative elements in Catalonia, but the ideology of liberalism was to be found in important components of Spanish society.

Perhaps these disjunctures are sharper in retrospect than they appeared to be early in the century, for we should note that the Catalan elite did indeed attempt to consolidate its position. Industrialists not only called upon the state to protect the "national" industry (by which they meant the industry of Spain, which was virtually all concentrated in Catalonia) but attempted to rally a base of support. This was not inconsequential, but most of the groups and classes who directly or indirectly depended on the fortunes of Catalan industry lived in Catalonia itself. It thus proved impossible to translate economic power at home and a degree of political influence at the state level (primarily on economic policy) into secure power at the center.

Between 1833 and 1901 one can count a total of 902 ministerial appointments in the various Spanish governments, liberal and conservative, monarchist and republican; of these portfolios, only twenty-four were allotted to Catalans (Balcells, 1977, p.78). Lluis Domenech i Montaner, a leading Catalan political economist, noted accurately in 1914 that Catalonia, "the most advanced, richest [region] and [the one] best related to the other civilized countries, is scarcely represented in the government of the state" (Domenech i Montaner, 1914, p. 57).

How should we assess this phenomenon of a bourgeoisie that does not achieve hegemony? Clearly the issue is not one of *late* development, and hence comparisons with the power structures of the contemporary Third World are unlikely to shed much light on the subject (Pi-Sunyer, 1974, 1975). I also find unconvincing Hansen's (1977, pp. 24–55) thesis which would explain much of Catalan history as the consequence of a "premature" bourgeoisie.

What should be recognized is that events in Catalonia could hardly have followed the evolutionary processes traced out by larger industrial societies and, in particular, politically independent ones. Much of the difficulty is due to the fact that the major models of political–economic transformation take as their point of departure the large core states and their respective histories and institutions.

Broadly speaking, this is as true of models derived from Adam Smith as it is of those inspired by Karl Marx. It is certainly understandable, given the context of the times, that Marx and Engels took the English example as most representative of mature capitalist development, although the industrial primacy of Britain does not explain a bias in favor of "great nations," a perspective traceable to Hegel.

The Catalan case illustrates that capitalism is capable of developing in different ways, even directions; and it should not really surprise us to find a bourgeoisie, such as the Catalan, that is not linked to the construction and consolidation of the state. Since the option of consolidation was hardly feasible, the Catalan directing classes pushed for a confederation structure that would have allowed a high degree of political autonomy coupled with economic integration—a proposal that was coolly received in Madrid.

We find, therefore, that the political and economic process in Catalonia runs counter to many accepted theories on the nature of capitalism, much as it runs counter to the often postulated relationship between underdevelopment and ethnic militancy. It would be difficult to interpret Catalan nationalism and, more broadly, Catalan political frustrations as a simple response to economic subordination, such as has been elaborated by Michael Hechter (1975, p. 39), in whose formulation the superordinate group is "ensconced as the core" and seeks to consolidate its economic and political advantages.[4]

We can compare this model, based on the uneven benefits of the Industrial Revolution in Britain, to the observation of Pierre Vilar that

Within Spain, [capitalism] created the sort of relationship of underdeveloped country to metropolis, between the country as a whole and the industrialized regions with all the resentments that these relations imply.

But in this case, the colonized are the majority. And they have the state! This cannot last. Here is the origin of the schism. (Vilar, 1980, p. 561)

This "schism" would manifest itself in many ways. If there were conflicts of interest dividing the Catalan elite from that of the center, an essentially new group of individuals, the intellectuals, were in the process of reestablishing a linguistic and literary high culture.[5] This movement, the *renaixenca,* was distinct from, but not unrelated to, the political and economic discontents that moved the industrial elite.

As the century progressed, however, the Catalan business elite tended to move further to the right socially and politically. While there were exceptions, this class was becoming increasingly conservative in habits and social attitudes and ever more fearful of civil unrest, especially in the form of worker militancy. These fears tended to overshadow, although never to displace, the distrust of Madrid and the dislike of Spanish administration: in the last analysis it was the repressive powers of the state that secured property and profits.

Such considerations, however, did not influence the thinking of the middle class to anywhere near the same degree. This class was growing in size and developing an awareness of role and position. We must think of it as an entity made up mostly of salaried and professional people, not employers of labor, not capitalists in the strict sense of the word. It was a culturally conscious middle sector which read a good deal and attended all manner of meetings and performances—characteristics which reached right down into the class of artisans and small shopkeepers.[6]

The importance of the middle class in the development of Catalan nationalism was pivotal. Certainly no group "discovered" or "invented" the movement or phenomenon, for the good social and historical reason that it was always there in some form. But the intellectuals gave it a contemporary ideology (or, perhaps more correctly, a set of ideological options) and lasting cultural institutions. While the business elite remained important and influential, it steadily lost ground not simply as a Spanish political force, but, inevitably, also as a Catalan one.

It is not within the scope of this chapter to follow the paths leading to the development of middle-class consciousness in

Catalonia. Nor can we trace out the process that transformed a literary movement of the *Félibrige* type into a cultural movement of broad appeal. As elsewhere in Europe, the success of progressive politics was closely tied to the changes brought about by the Industrial Revolution, not the least being new class alignments, growing urbanization, the spread of literacy, and the emergence of a popular press.

We cannot follow the history of the labor movement in Catalonia in any degree of detail, but we should take note of a phenomenon that has no real parallel outside of Spain: the success of anarchism. Only in Spain did this ideology develop a mass organization with a strong revolutionary drive. Already by 1870 anarchism had developed sufficiently to make possible the first conference of the "Spanish region" in Barcelona. Some ten years later the number of anarchists throughout Spain was of the order of 60,000, with most adherents clustered at the northern and southern peripheries of Iberia: the latifundia lands of Andalusia, the area of most extreme rural misery, and the industrial heartland of Catalonia.

This may seem a curious distribution, but it reflects certain structural similarities. To begin with, there was already a migratory movement from the south to the industrial north, although on nothing close to the scale it would achieve in our century. Also, in both places we are dealing with a proletariat who had no reason to trust a state whose policies were often hostile to its interests. Finally, there was another common strand: a general suspicion, born of long experience, of all hegemonic forces. For anarchists, this category encompassed not only the triad of state, church, and capital, but those ideologies and labor organizations that did not espouse libertarian communism.

Barcelona, the largest city in Iberia and the only one for many decades with a substantial industrial working class, soon became the headquarters of the anarchist movement. By 1917 the CNT, the anarchosyndicalist National Confederation of Labor, could count on a membership of over 700,000 throughout Spain, but concentrated mostly in Catalonia and Andalusia. This was a figure five times that on the rolls of its closest rival, the socialist UGT, the General Union of Workers.

In the early twentieth century three ideologies of the left can be found competing for the allegiance of the working class in Catalonia: the anarchosyndicalist unions and political federations, and the respective socialist and communist bodies. Names and initials change over time, but the main competition faced by the anarchists came from PSOE, the Spanish Socialist Workers Party, and its UGT union. The socialists, and later the communists, tended to be exceedingly cautious, in fact often negative, on the nationalities issue. As parties with a centralized organization and the aspiration of governing the state, they tended to distrust philosophies of self-determination as well as revolutionary scenarios.

The anarchist position was significantly different. As Raymond Carr (1980, p. 59) has noted, they believed that bourgeois capitalist society was doomed "not by some ineluctable historical process, the 'objective conditions' of the Marxist analysis, but by its moral decrepitude." Given this view, they had no desire to take over the levers of what they regarded as a corrupting power. This perspective helps explain why notable figures from the Catalan nationalist left maintained close relations with anarchist bodies and why anarchists did not find it ideologically incompatible to support Catalanist causes.

The interplay of competing ideologies with center–periphery cleavages has been one of the tragedies of left-wing politics in modern Catalonia. It has meant conflict within the proletariat of a type that one does not normally encounter in politically independent societies. The conflict can in part be understood as a reflection of the attempt to deny Catalonia what it surely deserves: a labor movement that is not the satellite of external political establishments. While anarchism as a vital political force did not survive the Civil War, some of its aims and achievements, in particular a deep sense of community and a genuine faith in humanity, continue to influence the left in Catalonia. While it would be a simplification and a distortion to co-opt anarchism as a direct manifestation of nationalism, it is certainly valid to approach it as an ideology highly compatible with any movement leading to greater pluralism and decentralization. Anarchists themselves, it should be remembered, claimed to be essentially apolitical.

Conclusion

What can we learn from the Catalan case respecting the nature of nationalism? Perhaps the most important contribution that emerges from a study of the Catalan data is the absolute necessity for a much more sophisticated, more multidimensional, approach than is commonly offered by those writing on the subject. Besides the semantic and analytical sloppiness typical of so much scholarship, there is the lamentable disregard for history (not simply on issues touching nationalism) so typical of the work of social scientists. I have commented on this limitation with respect to Spain and Catalonia (Pi-Sunyer, 1970, 1974), and in the broader frame of Mediterranean studies John Davis (1977, pp. 239–57) takes anthropologists to task for a superficial and selective use of history.

Turning to theory, we can examine the degree of fit between general explanatory models of nationalism and the Catalan specifics. One body of theoretical analysis links capitalism, the dominant economic mode, to nationalism, the dominant political one. The Catalan evidence does indeed support the case for some degree of relationship, some linkage, between nationalism and the transformations brought about by the Industrial Revolution. But contrary to many models which stress economic dependency and underdevelopment, Catalan nationalism simply cannot be understood as a response to *economic* internal colonialism. Much the same observation has been made by Marianne Heiberg (1975) concerning Basque nationalism, in particular the fact that it cannot be attributed to the frustrations of "blocked mobility" and similar individual impediments.

The frustrations felt by Catalans during the nineteenth century, and at several other times, did not concern matters of social status. There is very little evidence of a colonized mentality, of "provincialization," and of the resulting negative self-images.[7] Catalans, and in particular the Catalan bourgeoisie, did complain about inadequate political representation and the expense of supporting a lumbering and incompetent administration. A society, or segments of it, can feel aggrieved without having to be impoverished or feeling inferior. Indeed, one does not have to look far for examples of nationalism among well-to-do, some would even say privileged, communities and groups: Basques and Catalans in Spain, American colonists, Czechs in the Austro-Hungarian Empire, Armenians and Greeks under Ottoman rule, the United Provinces in the sixteenth century, to cite but some of the most obvious cases. This is quite a varied assortment, but none falls into the category of economically deprived populations, and some represent the advanced segments within their respective polities.

Can one reverse the question of socioeconomic causation and consider nationalism as abetted by wealth rather than generated by poverty? The Catalan case, as argued in this chapter, supports such a hypothesis, but with the proviso that equally important is the use to which wealth is put. Clearly great advantage may accrue to a nationalist movement in a relatively prosperous area. In Catalonia we find not only sufficient wealth to support a variety of political enterprises, including labor movements, but also the institutional and organizational structures to make the best use of such resources.

In this respect Catalonia has always been very modern. From the Middle Ages to the present Catalans have preferred to organize their political and economic activities, and much of their social life, on the basis of corporate groups and similar associations (Pi-Sunyer, 1971, pp. 126–33, and 1974, pp. 118–24). This is very different from structures based on clientelism and dyadic alliances. The former are institutions of long duration with a recognized membership, a set of procedures, and some goal or aim. The latter are social groupings composed of unequal individuals bound together in personalized reciprocal relationships, and are inherently unstable.

For Catalans, their ordered social life is very much a part of their cultural patrimony. Catalans have worked together in groups for centuries and are very conscious of the fact that entities with corporate functions represent something more than the sum of the membership at any given moment of time.

The modernization/nationalism conundrum can be approached, though only partially resolved, by examining the relationship in a very different manner from the one espoused by dependency and core-periphery advocates. Thus Ernest Gellner, far from regarding nationalism as the ideological response to the imposed order of capitalism, makes it an organizational requirement of all modern societies. His argument, in brief, is that industrial and industrializing societies are inevitably politically centralized, occupationally specialized, and individually mobile. Societies of this type, he claims, are not compatible with the existence of "cultural chasms between segments of the population" (Gellner, 1981, p. 775).

The elimination of such "chasms," he insists, demands strong states able to carry the burden of public order and underwrite expensive and complex educational systems:

Education is central, prolonged and universal, or very nearly so. It must be carried on in the same linguistic and cultural medium. This cultural and linguistic medium acquires an enormous importance, greater perhaps than it ever had before. (ibid., p. 761)

Taking the argument one step further, it follows that "Nationalism is essentially the transfer of the focus of man's identity to a culture which is mediated by literacy and an extensive, formal educational system. It is not the mother tongue that matters, but the language of the *école maternelle*" (ibid., p. 757).

How useful is this provocative thesis? Its main value, I would suggest, is that it stresses essentially *political* considerations: conflicts within systems, power dispersal and power concentration, authority, and the hegemonic attributes of the state. This concern with the means of coercion, as distinct from the means of production, is an important corrective. Similarly, it is a point well worth making that nationalism and modern society are not antithetical.

But, however well argued, Gellner's theories only take us part of the distance. One major flaw, well illustrated in Catalonia, is a failure to distinguish between state and non-state nationalisms. What we may term state-sponsored nationalism takes much of its shape from the necessity of demarcating and defending boundaries between the state and like polities, while in the case of nonstate nationalism the entity in question pits itself against the weight and power of the state. To recognize only state nationalism as legitimate (in the sense that it is brought into being by the complex organizational requirements of modern society) is, basically, a functionalist position not unlike that of the developmentalists of two decades ago.

Furthermore, I am not at all convinced that modern society must perforce be culturally homogeneous because of the imperatives of industrialization. The composition of present-day Western Europe with its millions of immigrant "guest-workers" hardly supports such a hypothesis. And if it be argued (which Gellner does not) that these are all people in the process of acculturation, we must still account for the successful industrialization of such multinational states as Switzerland. I do not believe that the answer lies directly with the imperatives of modern economic systems, but rather with the much more subtle needs of identity and security, needs that have surely grown with the pace of industrialization.

Gellner strips down culture to effective communication and puts much stress on language. But if language were only a form of communication, a code, switching from one language to another would be dictated by efficiency. Turning our attention once more to Catalonia, it is clear that this has not happened. What is significant of modern Catalonia is that faced with the choice of two languages, the majority of the population opted to speak Catalan. The relationship between language and its speakers is reciprocal, or as Vilar writes:

> It is without a doubt because they spoke Catalan that the Catalans were able to preserve a group consciousness. But it is above all when they have most keenly felt this group consciousness that they have refused to forget Catalan. (Vilar, 1980, p. 573).

Why should this be the case? At the heart of the matter is that Catalans have not had to change their language or relinquish their culture. There has been plenty of pressure to do so, but even in the grimmest of times they have kept sufficient economic resources under their control and known what to do with them. This has only been possible because, fundamentally, neither language nor culture has proved to be an impediment to change and modernization.

With respect to language, all Catalans are at least bilingual. In fact, for several generations now, educated Catalans have spoken at least three languages: their own, Castilian, and one of the major European languages. In the professional and scientific world there is a growing use of English (displacing not only Castilian, as a language of wider communication, but also French and German).

In conclusion, it does not seem at all unreasonable to me that Catalans are nationalists and that their nationalism is rooted in their culture. Materialist approaches to nationalism tend to reduce it to the economic base and seldom allow any degree of autonomy to ethnicity/nationalism. I find it hard to come to terms with economics independent of culture and society. Even capitalism, an economic structure embedded in Western institutions, shows significant variations over time and space. As Gellner notes, there is—and always has been—the state; the power of coercion, at times integrated with the power of capital, at other times much less so.

The lesson from Catalonia is not that economic and political forces should be disregarded—on the contrary, they should be studied with consummate care—but that these alone will not explain the phenomenon of nationalism. Not because nationalism does not respond to these forces, but because they will be interpreted and altered by specific cultures and societies— which are themselves undergoing change.

Throughout this chapter, I have stressed that while nationalism has many meanings and attends to many issues, it functions as a mechanism for solving problems, problems that at times may be fundamentally economic, at others essentially political, but always social in the sense that it is concerned with issues of group membership. Nationalism is definition and category, and differentiates what is from what is not; as Fanon noted, it describes, justifies, and celebrates the experiences of a people in ways that have meaning for the collectivity. Regardless of the needs that are satisfied by expressions of nationalism—needs that may be shared by other comparable groups—each and every nationalist movement derives its frame of reference and its legitimacy from a specific culture. And each culture is, at the core, a specific way of ordering belief and experience, of giving meaning. The success or failure, even the emergence, of a particular nationalist manifestation must be looked for not simply in terms of the impact of overreaching forces, political or economic, but the response to these according to a distinct cultural frame of reference.

Notes: Chapter 11

1 Marxist–Leninist states, although following policies that should theoretically protect them from the problems of ethnic and nationalist demands, have had their share of difficulties, as events in the Soviet Union, China, Czechoslovakia, Laos, Romania, Vietnam, and most recently Yugoslavia, indicate.

2 With the termination of self-government, the authority to pass laws, levy taxes, mint coinage, maintain consulates abroad, and raise regular troops was abrogated. The distinct Catalan Civil Code, tied to property rights and inheritance, did survive.

3 The urban and rural working classes were to remain solidly Catalan-speaking until the end of the century and the extensive migration from Murcia and Andalusia. That knowledge of written Catalan was fairly widespread early in the century is indicated by the 1832 publication of a Catalan New Testament by the London Bible Society.

4 Hechter in several recent conference papers (including "Internal colonialism revisited," in this volume) has revised his internal colonialism theory to take into account "segmental" as well as "hierarchical" cultural division of labor. This adjustment, while in the right direction, does not seem to sufficiently attend to the problem of conflict of political interests.

5 Intellectuals as a group or entity begin to be identified as such substantially later— around the turn of the century.

6 This petit-bourgeois stratum is the subject of Santiago Rusiñols' modernist novel, *L'Auca del senyor Esteve*, of 1907. That the life history of a typical Barcelona shopkeeper should be the subject of successful literary work tells us a good deal about the society and its values.

7 There have, of course, been time and cirumstances when some sectors of the Catalan population emulated foreign ways: the higher aristocracy, a group of rather limited influence, became substantially Castilianized in the sixteenth century; and we have mentioned the changes during the second half of the eighteenth century; and in much more recent times a very small minority of the bourgeoisie have become Castilian-speaking. There have also been periods of substantial French influence.

References: Chapter 11

Ardit, M., Balcells, A., and Sales, N. (1980), *Historia dels països catalans de 1714 a 1975* (Barcelona: Adhesa).

Balcells, A. (1977), *Catalunya contemporánea I (Siglo XIX)* (Madrid: Siglo XXI).

Braudel, F. (1972), *The Mediterranean and the Mediterranean World in the Age of Philip II* (New York: Harper & Row), Vol. 1.

Carr, R. (1980), *Modern Spain 1875–1980* (Oxford: Oxford University Press).

Editorial foreword, (1980), *Comparative Studies in Society and History*, vol. 22, no. 2, pp. 143–4.

Davis, J. (1977), *People of the Mediterranean: An Essay in Comparative Social Anthropology* (London: Routledge & Kegan Paul).

De Vries, J. (1976), *The Economy of Europe in an Age of Crisis* (Cambridge: Cambridge University Press).

Domenech i Montaner, L. (1914), *Estudis polítics* (Barcelona: Biblioteca Popular de l'Avanc).

Elliott, J. H. (1963), *The Revolt of the Catalans* (Cambridge: Cambridge University Press).

Elliott, J. H. (1964), *Imperial Spain* (New York: St. Martin's Press).

Fanon, F. (1961), *Les Damnés de la terre* (Paris: Maspéro).

Gellner, E. (1981), "Nationalism," *Theory and Society*, vol. 10, no. 6, pp. 753–76.

Glick, T. F., and Pi-Sunyer, O. (1969), "Acculturation as an explanatory concept in Spanish history," *Comparative Studies in Society and History*, vol. 11, no. 2, pp. 136–54.

Hansen, E. C. (1977), *Rural Catalonia under the Franco Regime* (Cambridge: Cambridge University Press).

Hechter, M. (1975), *Internal Colonialism: The Celtic Fringe in British National Development, 1536–1966* (London: Routledge & Kegan Paul; Berkeley and Los Angeles, Calif.: University of California Press).

Heiberg, M. (1975), "Insiders/outsiders: Basque nationalism," *European Journal of Sociology*, vol. 16, no. 2, pp. 169–93.

Lewis, A. R. (1965), *The Development of Southern French and Catalan Society, 718–1050* (Austin, Texas: University of Texas).

Linz, J. J. (1975), "Politics in a multi-lingual society with a dominant world language: the case of Spain," in Jean-Guy Savard and Richard Vigneault (eds.), *Les Etats multilingues. Problèmes et solutions* (Quebec City: Les Pressés de l'Université Laval), pp. 367–444.

Payne, S. (1970), "Catalan and Basque nationalism," *Journal of Contemporary History*, vol. 6, no. 1, pp. 15–51.

Pike, K. (1954), *Language in Relation to a Unified Theory of the Structure of Human Behavior* (Glendale, Calif.: Summer Institute of Linguistics), Vol. 1.

Pi-Sunyer, O. (1970), "The perception of the past: Spanish historiography," *Bucknell Review*, vol. 18, no. 2, pp. 110–20.

Pi-Sunyer, O. (1971), "The maintenance of ethnic identity in Catalonia," in O. Pi-Sunyer (ed.), *The Limits of Integration: Ethnicity and Nationalism in Modern Europe*, Research Report No. 9 (Amherst, Mass.: Department of Anthropology, University of Massachusetts), pp. 111–46.

Pi-Sunyer, O. (1974), "Elites and noncorporate groups in the European Mediterranean: a reconsideration of the Catalan case," *Comparative Studies in Society and History*, vol. 16, no. 1, pp. 117–31.

Pi-Sunyer, O. (1975), "Of corporate groups and vanishing development: a reply to Hansen, Schneider and Schneider," *Comparative Studies in Society and History*, vol. 17, no. 2, pp. 241–4.

Schneidman, J. L. (1970), *The Rise of the Aragonese-Catalan Empire, 1200–1350* (New York: New York University Press).

Silverman, S. (1977), "Patronage as myth," in E. Gellner and J. Waterbury (eds.), *Patrons and Clients* (London: Duckworth), pp. 7–19.

Silvert, K. H. (1963), "Introduction: the strategy of the study of nationalism," in K. H. Silvert (ed.), *Expectant Peoples: Nationalism and Development* (New York: Random House), pp. 3–38.

Vicens Vives, J. J. (1969), *Conyuntura económica y reformismo burgues* (Barcelona: Ariel).

Vicens Vives, J. (1972), *Approaches to the History of Spain*, 2nd ed. (Berkeley, Calif.: University of California Press).

Vilar, P. (1979), *Catalunya dins l'Espanya moderna* (Barcelona: Curial) Vol. 1.

Vilar, P. (1980), "Spain and Catalonia," *Review*, vol. 3, no. 4, pp. 527–77.

Wallerstein, I. (1980), *The Modern World System. Vol. II, Mercantilism and the Consolidation of the European World Economy* (New York: Academic Press).

Young, A. (1787), "A tour in Catalonia," *Annals of Agriculture*, vol. 8, pp. 193–275.

12

Nationalism and the Noncolonial Periphery
a Discussion of Scotland and Catalonia

JACK A. BRAND

Michael Hechter's model of internal colonialism (1975) offers an attractive explanation for the development of nationalism. Although plausible in certain cases, this model is not a general explanation for the development of nationalist movements. One can save the hypothesis but, in doing so, it becomes a truism (Hechter, 1978).

Broadly speaking, Hechter's argument does not work in Scotland or Catalonia, because both were rich, strong economies when modern nationalism was first expressed. In Tom Nairn's (1977) terms these are cases of "overdevelopment." Of the two, Catalonia never has been an internal colony. On the contrary, it is the strongest regional economy in Spain.

At the time when nationalism acquired mass support, it was the only industrial economy in Spain, second only to Britain in its productive capacity and technical superiority in the textile industry. Scotland's case is more complicated. It might be argued that it is a type of internal colony today, but when Scottish regionalism first became important in modern times—in the 1880s—its economy was perceived to be extremely healthy. It did not in any sense fit the model of an internal colony.

This chapter is divided into two main sections. In the first I shall state briefly what I believe to be the main indicators of internal colonialism. In order to show where my two case studies deviate from the model I feel that it should be sketched here. Next I shall indicate where the deviations take place and raise measurement problems. In the second part I suggest another way of explaining the rise of nationalism in these two areas, arguing that a phenomenon such as nationalism is probably not explicable in terms of one law or rule, but rather that different conditions may produce the same result. Combinations of circumstances are required. No single cause is either necessary or sufficient.

(1) The Thesis of Internal Colonialism

The idea of internal colonialism is that, under some circumstances, a state divides into a core and a periphery. In general, peripheries will be less prosperous than cores but certain peripheries will have a relation to the core similar to that experienced by colonies. Peter Mathias describes a colonial relationship in the context of the British Empire:

> Associated with the intention of protecting home industry was another general aim of the regulatory system, the control of colonial economies. In 1750 the making of steel, the refining of iron and manufacture of finished articles from iron were prohibited in the North American colonies. They were to act as protected markets for the export industries of the mother country; hence their own spontaneous economic development and foreign trade had to be checked when it ran counter to these principles. The obverse of this was the encouragement of colonial economies as primary produce suppliers to the metropolitan economy. (Mathias, 1976, pp. 85–6)

In studies of the economic history of Spain there are similar statements in which the details of the control vary but the principle is the same (Vincens Vives, 1969, p. 393). In *Internal Colonialism* Hechter applies such a model of this relationship to what he calls the "Celtic" nations of the United Kingdom: Ireland, Scotland, and Wales, suggesting that these are internal colonies on the periphery of the metropolitan country. In Hechter's terms they qualify for this status because of two characteristics: First, there is the relation described by Mathias; secondly, they have a cultural distinctiveness from the metropolitan country.

Problems of Measurement

One of the problems of Hechter's analysis is that the nature of this cultural distinctiveness remains vague. Let us clear the less important measurement problem out of the way before we go into why Scotland has the level of cultural distinctiveness sufficient for an "identity take off," while the north of England or the west, let us say, do not. To be fair, Hechter is no less clear than other studies of nationalism, but this still leaves the difficulty that one of the major prerequisites for ethnoregional parties, as he puts it, is vague. For Hechter, who gives quantification a major place, this is even more important. The other major prerequisite is in no better a state. Not only must there be a cultural (undefined) division, but also a cultural division of labor. He himself admits that this is not defined and, therefore, cannot be quantified (Hechter, 1975, p. 42). The whole point in Hechter's first discussion of the cultural division of labor is, however, that the economic activity of the periphery will be subordinate to that of the metropolis or core.

Problems of Theory

Michael Hechter agrees that his original description of internal colonialism does not fit several cases, including Scotland (1980, p. 4). The problem has to do with the cultural division of labor. For a colonial situation to exist, the colony must have the lower status and less skilled jobs in a much higher proportion than is true of the economy of the core. Certain key functions must be controlled centrally, for example, the allocation of capital.

Even though these functions are still performed in the "colony," Hechter believes that a cultural division of labor may still lead to nationalism. He has moved to a new position which he calls the segmental cultural division of labor. In this case the division will not be hierarchical, but segmental. In order to explain this Hechter takes the example of the Jewish community in the United States. This is a self-conscious community, he argues, because not only do they share an ethnic background with a similar culture, myth of descent, and language, but also work in a small number of occupations. This brings them together and makes them aware of their common needs and interests (Hechter, 1978, p. 312).

The attraction of Hechter's initial model was that it tried to explain the rise of a social movement in an elegant fashion. It referred to the effects of deprivation and the whole theory was tied into a wider Marxist model of society. His present position bears no relation to that put forward by Lenin (1956). It makes no sense to call this "internal colonialism."

The second problem about this new model is precisely the

measurement difficulty mentioned in relation to the original model. There is no quantifiable indicator which would tell us when the society was sufficiently segmented to support nationalism.

Let us be generous. Let us ask whether impressionistically there seem to exist conditions of segmentation which would make this theory work in Scotland.

In Scotland the occupational breakdown of the population does not seem to have the feature which Hechter identified among American Jews. It might be argued that a larger proportion of Scots than of, let us say, Tynesiders, were engaged in agriculture and that this was true both when modern Scottish political feeling began to be shown in the 1840s and 1880s and even today. On the other hand, it is notorious that, of all occupations, agricultural workers are the most difficult to organize. Much of this has to do with sheer geography. Two hundred men in a factory can be contacted in half an hour. It may take three weeks in the countryside. Hechter makes this point and adds that there must be meeting sites and not just similarity in occupations or other activities. He might further reply that, during the seedtime of modern Scottish nationalism, the center of Scottish life was in the shipyards and heavy engineering where there was a high concentration.

Table 12.1 *Employment in the United Kingdom and Scotland, 1907–24*

Industry	1907		1924	
	UK (%)	Scotland (%)	UK (%)	Scotland (%)
Mines and quarries	13·8	15·3	16·3	17·8
Iron and steel, engineering, and shipbuilding	22·0	26·7	19·7	23·2
Other metals	1·6	0·6	1·6	0·5
Textiles	17·9	16·3	15·9	16·2
Clothing	10·8	8·8	8·6	6·0
Food, drink, tobacco	6·6	8·2	6·5	8·2
Chemicals	1·8	1·1	2·6	1·9
Paper and printing	4·7	5·2	4·6	5·0
Leather, etc.	1·2	0·7	1·5	1·5
Timber	3·4	4·0	2·6	2·9
Clay and stone	10·4	9·3	9·4	7·6
Miscellaneous	0·7	0·5	1·2	0·9
Public utilities	4·9	3·4	9·6	8·2

Source: Historical Record of the Census of Production 1907–70, London, HMSO, 1978.

There is no evidence that support for Home Rule came from this section of society. It is difficult to explore the occupational bases for Gladstonian Home Rule in a systematic fashion. It seems to have spread through all parts of Scottish society (Hanham, 1969). It is significant, for example, that all the Bills introduced into the Commons from 1893 to 1920 were supported by the overwhelming majority of Scottish M.P.s and several attracted petitions signed by the conveners of all the Scottish county councils and the lord provosts of the cities. This covered a very wide range of occupation and social station. It is difficult to see how this could be made the basis of a segmental division of labor such as Hechter describes.

Hechter also attempts to explain the existence of national feeling in Scotland by pointing to the personnel of the institutions protected under the Settlement of 1707: the law, the church, and education. The first problem about this explanation is that the proportion of Scots involved in these institutions is very small. Secondly, even if we allow that their centrality outweighs their small size, there is very little evidence that they were important in the early regionalist or nationalist organizations. On the contrary, it has been a continual problem of nationalism in Scotland that these specifically Scottish "establishments" have not been sympathetic. The lawyers were too conscious of the privileged position they enjoyed. The Church of Scotland only started to support Home Rule after World War II. By this time it was a rapidly declining force in Scottish society. In any case, the support of the church could never be described as full-throated.

From Hechter's point of view, Catalonia is more promising. It might be that it is part of a segmented division of labor. Salvador Giner (1980, pp. 17–18) described Catalonia as having a social system which has been distinct from that of the rest of Spain from the end of the eighteenth century. This is the part which first became a modern European industrial economy. With the exception of the Basque country, this was the only industrial region of Spain until the 1950s.

Even now, it is incomparably more industrialized than other regions. The province of Barcelona has the largest share of the market of all the Spanish provinces in the food industry, textiles (where it is ten times bigger than its nearest rival), timber-based industry, paper products, chemicals, all material used in the building industry and the metal industries apart from basic metal industries (Instituto de Estadística, 1980, pp. 565–7). That is seven out of the eleven types of industries listed. On that basis it is tempting to argue that nationalism grew in Catalonia because of this segmentation. There are problems with this explanation.

The first is that Catalonia's economy and thus its social system have become industrialized. On the other hand, if we take Hechter's point about concentration, we must point out that the industrial workers of Catalonia, especially those of Barcelona, were the most difficult to recruit for the Catalan cause. It was only on particular occasions that they voted for a nationalist party or alliance before 1936 and then only for tactical reasons. The creed of the Catalan working class as for the immigrant workers from other parts of Spain was anarcho-syndicalism (Fraser, 1979). The anarchosyndicalist federation, the CNT, and the smaller anarchist organization, the FAI, despised the nationalist Esquerra as a representative of middle-class interests. They were right. Where the early nationalists, the Lliga Regionalists, had represented the upper bourgeoisie, the Esquerra was firmly grounded in the lower middle class (Poblet, 1976).

The heart of the matter seems to be that, if there are concentrations in particular occupations, or other activities; where there are sites which provide meeting places, it is very likely that the people meeting there will share opinions. A point of view will develop. This does not answer the question as to why a nationalist point of view specifically should grow up.

Hechter's Later Model.

Before I move from this section, I must comment on Hechter's expansion of the model of internal colonialism. Some of this is contained in his contribution to this book. I have already suggested that he moves far from the original idea when he brings in the notion of segmentation. In the complete model there are other elements which are interesting but which do not always help him in the explanation. His general approach is that of Neil Smelser (1964). Hechter refers to Pinard's study (1971) which specifically uses this framework.

The fact that this is now far from Internal Colonialism is not important. On the other hand, we do have to consider the fact that Hechter relies on the "rational actor" model in a way which really does not seem to work. His discussion is divided into an explanation for the increase in party membership and an increase in the votes for ethnoregional parties. He suggests that the first depends most on "the availability of patronage and other selective benefits available through the party" (Levi and Hechter, in this volume, pp. 136–7). In supporting this argument he points to the number of patronage places available through the Secretary of State for Scotland. This is totally irrelevant. These appointments are not in any way available to the Scottish National Party (SNP). If one looks at the growth of party membership between, let us say, 1961 and 1976, there was no point at which this could have been encouraged by the sorts of selective benefits which Hechter describes. Under Conservative secretaries of state appointments went to Conservatives and under the Labour administrations they went to Labour sympathizers. This application of the rational actor model simply does not work, because there were no selective benefits available to prospective SNP members and thus there was no sense in which these benefits increased over this period and, in this way, acted as a growing incentive to new party members.

Hechter explains the increase of the vote, as opposed to party membership, as a response to the availability of nonselective benefits guaranteed by the SNP. The party is seen, in other words, as a credible pressure group. The history of Scotland in the 1960s and early 1970s helps to support this. Scotland was certainly perceived as receiving more government aid because of a fear that more and more votes would sweep over to the Nationalists. Survey data show that the SNP was regarded as good for Scotland in this sense by a large section of Scottish voters: even those who did not vote for the Nationalists (Brand, 1984). There is a problem. In the period when the SNP was building up to being a credible party, putting successful pressure on government, it was, in this sense, not credible by definition. The rational actor model cannot really explain the dynamics of this takeoff phase.

The Importance of Hechter's Model

Hechter's later version does not have the elegance and economy of the earlier one. In Hechter's favor it should be said that he has provided us with an example of what such a theory should look like. He also identifies a process which is very important in the growth of some nationalisms. The Irish case is the one which immediately springs to mind. Because there are other quite different cases, however, our final position must be that Hechter's argument is not at a sufficient level of abstraction to be generally useful.

(2)   An Alternative to Hechter

In what follows I shall not offer a complete theory to explain nationalism. I shall take up various points in Hechter's discussion to see whether anything more satisfactory can be said, starting with the idea of culture.

The Idea of Culture

I understand by "culture" a system of shared norms, values, and symbols on the basis of which a society communicates. It is safe to say that both Scotland and Catalonia had, and have, popular cultures. It is true that a large proportion of the popular culture in both areas contains elements which are British and Spanish respectively. In neither case have these latter elements obscured the "peripheral national" elements. Thus in the historical part of popular culture an ordinary Scot can be aware, however vaguely, of Britain's imperial history and also of the part which he believes that Scottish regiments played in it. In another part of the realm there are specifically "Scotch comics." Harry Lauder was the best known outside of Scotland but there are scores of them, including Billy Connolly. In Catalonia Clave's working-class choirs and a particular type of music-hall is again self-consciously Catalan as opposed to being Spanish. There are also the more specific examples of Scottish or Catalan sentiment such as the national football teams. All of this constitutes a culture which identifies its members for themselves and others. A means of communication is provided and so is a set of symbols.

One factor which is closely associated with nationalism and with culture is language. As a symbol of the people's unity, it is widely used to create a culture and it sets boundaries to the society. On the other hand, there are many nationalist movements in countries which do not have their own language. The American Revolution is a case in point. In Andalusia there is a powerful and widespread movement now, although Andalusians speak Castilian. Finally, in Scotland, the Scottish National Party has never used Gaelic as a vital part of its platform as language is in Catalonia or Wales. Although Gaelic has the status of being the original language of the people, at the present only 5 percent of the population speak it. Scottish nationalism and American nationalism do not need a special language. The popular culture is strong enough to maintain the consciousness of the people without it.

The same point can be made of religion. It is useful to have a distinctive religion such as the Church of Scotland or national religious institutions such as the Catalan Abbey of Montserrat. In both cases they have been important in maintaining national consciousness. They did so as part of the popular culture and by acting as rallying institutions and as providers of a national elite. In other circumstances another type of symbol or rallying institution would have played the same role.

Culture is, then, the defining symbols and values that hold a social system together. In general, the boundary feature important for the growth of nationalism is the existence of symbols that define the boundary. One such symbol is that of the historical existence of a separate state in the region which shares other cultural characteristics. Any area which enjoys that symbol is fertile ground for nationalism. It is important to realize that it is not simply the existence of the symbol which matters, but its exploitation. In the eighteenth century Scots and Catalans were well aware of their country's separate history but it was in the second half of the nineteenth century that both nationalist movements started. It was only then that the symbols were manipulated or became salient.

National sentiment is the most recent form of a primeval emotion of community. There are two implications of this point. First, it is a virtually permanent part of human consciousness. Secondly, nationalism is the form which can only be expressed under certain circumstances.

When we speak about nationalism or national sentiment, we are speaking about a wider community, self-sufficient in the sense of being a sovereign state. It is, then, not possible to have nationalism unless there is a state of this type. If the political unit is simply a collection of territories linked together by the marriage contracts of one particular strong man or his threat or terror, national sentiment is unlikely to develop until he or his descendants are able to hallow these arrangements by tradition. Once this process of hallowing has taken place and especially if it is founded on cultural identity, then the way is clear for the growth of national identity. Nationalism is thus the form of community identity which is expressed by the modern state (Poggi, 1978).

The next obvious question concerns the time at which the modern state begins. I believe that it begins, for our purposes, long before the French Revolution. The condition for national identity was first established for those who lived in areas with communication to the center. It was more a reality for the town-dweller than for the peasant. But there were times when the consciousness of the national would become both more widespread and more salient. An important instance was the Napoleonic invasions, which forced peoples with notoriously particularistic identities to unite; such unity went right down the social scale to those whose economic position and place of birth had given them few previous links with what it was to share nationality. The invasion of Edward's army into Scotland in the thirteenth century had the same effect as did the English invasion of France during the time of the Capets or, much later, the Napoleonic invasion of Spain and Germany. National identity did not have a regular increase, but came and went. It could not exist, however, without a unified state.

The other implication of seeing nationalism as the modern form of a primeval emotion is viewing it as a permanent feature of modern human society, one of the most important possible lines of cleavage and conflict in human society. The histories of Scotland and Catalonia show that cleavage based on national identity has alternated with other cleavages as the basis of politics. In Scotland the country was united against the English as early as the thirteenth century. In the fifteenth and sixteenth centuries much of politics was based on the pro-English or anti-English parties. The time of the Union in 1707 saw vigorous anti-English feeling on the part of the common people (Daiches, 1977). At other times, other cleavages were more salient. The fight between the Catholics and the Reformers made for cross-national alliances. In our own century it has been the class cleavage which has outbid the others as the basis for politics. In Catalonia it was class matters which drove the Catalan *haute bourgeoisie* from the leadership of nationalism in favor of the protection of the Spanish army and the civil guard (Maura, 1975). Earlier, at the end of the eighteenth century and the beginning of the nineteenth century, Catalans who shared the modern values of other Spaniards made common cause with them against the traditionalism of the Carlists. In both countries, however, and in many other countries, national identity as a basis for national politics was a recurrent theme.

I believe that Kedourie and Gellner were both right in their different ways in seeing a change in society as a prerequisite of nationalism (Gellner, 1964). They were wrong in putting the change too late, in the arrival of mass politics or industrialization. Any traumatic change which widens people's consciousness of and identity with the self-governing or potentially self-governing society of which they are a part, creates nationalism. The essential point is that there is nothing new about nationalism. The real question is under which conditions this standing cleavage can be made salient over the others.

The Nineteenth-Century Take-off of Nationalism

I have demonstrated that there is a culture for Scotland and Catalonia. In both cases the culture contains the idea of a nation at one time independent. I must now turn to an explanation of why nationalism in Catalonia became a political movement in the second half of the nineteenth century and why the nationalist political party won the majority of Catalan seats by 1932. In Scotland, by contrast, there was support for some autonomy from the 1880s onwards but it was not till the 1960s that a nationalist party commanded more than 10 percent of the vote. What is the reason for this late development?

My first point in explanation is that the success or failure of the nationalist parties has no direct relation to nationalist feeling. Nationalists may believe that they can work through one or other of the statewide political parties which is more sympathetic to their aims. The Liberal Party was just such an organization in nineteenth- and early-twentieth-century Scotland. Many present-day Catalans believe the same of the Spanish Communist Party. Nationalism may take many forms other than the formation of a specifically nationalist party. It may also not take the form of a claim for outright independence. On that definition the Catalan Convergencia is not nationalist, since it asks only for autonomy within the Spanish state. This is also the program of the Basque National Party.

The lack of a nationalist party (in the wide sense of claiming some self-government rather than total self-government) does not mean that nationalist feeling did not exist in the nineteenth century. Yet why did nationalism take an open, direct form in Catalonia much earlier than it did in Scotland? Why was there mass support for Catalan autonomy so early as compared with Scotland?

Scotland and Catalonia are different sorts of peripheries. Scotland falls into the category which is more familiar: one which is both depressed and economically exploited, because it is not as near to world markets as London. Catalonia has better contacts with European markets than the rest of Spain, because of its position astride some of the main historical trade routes from France. This positioning has led to cultural contacts with Europe which were distinctive too. It is to the eonomic position that we should turn first.

Scotland and Catalonia were among the first parts of Europe to be modernized. The actual details of this modernization cannot be discussed here. I want only to point out that both regions are subject to the international conditions which affect parts of the economically developed world, and hence to the trade cycle. For a very large number of people at certain times, this meant unemployment and misery. The conditions in which they lived meant that this would give rise to working-class organizations. The international spread of working-class parties was to be particularly important for the development of nationalism, although in very different ways (Gellner, 1964).

The economies of both Britain and Spain were also deeply affected by the fact that both were major imperial powers. Thus the early modernization of Scotland and Catalonia depended on the fact that they were part of an economy which enjoyed a large and guaranteed foreign market. In both cases the merchants of these areas were refused access to trade in the empire. Central and Southern America were dependencies of the Crown of Castile and it was only in the eighteenth century that Catalonia, as a part of the Crown of Aragon, was allowed to trade with the North American colonies.

The subsequent histories of the empires are different. In the nineteenth century, the seedtime of modern nationalism, Britain developed its empire. The American colonies detached themselves but India and Africa provided an extremely prosperous second empire. The west of Scotland around the city of Glasgow was one of the major British centers which benefited from this vast market.

Compare the situation in Catalonia. Spain's Latin American empire disappeared by 1824 with the exception of Puerto Rico and Cuba which were to go at the end of the century. They were trifles compared with what Spain had held before 1800. After the victories of Bolivar and San Martin, it was not even possible to keep up an economic empire because the goods produced in Spain were more expensive than British or North American manufactures. Thus, in the nineteenth century, Catalonia was part of a declining (or declined) imperial power which could not provide Barcelona and the other industrial Catalan towns with a guaranteed market. By contrast, Scotland was part of the great imperial money-making crusade. Under these circumstances the very last thing that the Scottish bourgeoisie wanted was to cut themselves off. Their interests were the same as those of industrialists and merchants in Birmingham and London. The Catalan bourgeoisie, controlling virtually the only industry in Spain, had interests different from those of the other Spanish elites. We shall see that the Catalan nationalism of the 1880s to the first decade of this century was built on the desire of the Catalan bourgeoisie for tariffs to keep out foreign goods.* Most of the rest of Spain was, until this century, more interested in cheap goods and food irrespective of their origin.

There is more to be said about the effect of the empires. The Scots, in common with other Britons, were proud of the empire up to its dissolution by the early 1960s. When it went, it was largely part of a (relatively) pacific and gradual process. Compare this with the calamity of South America. The crowning blow, the loss of Cuba in 1898, is one of the most dramatic episodes in Spanish history leading to an atmosphere of national gloom. For the Scots, it was good to be British. This was true even for the early Scottish Nationalists working out the relations of an independent Scotland with England, and "The party, having regard to the large contribution made by Scotland in building up the British Empire, [is] desirous of increasing the interest of the Scottish nation in the affairs of the Empire" (Brand, 1978, p. 201). For Catalans, as for all Spaniards, the empire was a chapter of mismanagement, corruption, and human suffering.

It was not only the empire which was a source of pride to Britain, but the system of politics itself. For the middle classes at least, the British system of parliamentary government was regarded as the best in the world. Many other British institutions enjoyed the same reputation among their consumers: the police, the monarchy, and so forth. It was hard for the average Spaniard to feel a parallel enthusiasm for Spanish political institutions in the nineteenth century. Certain parts of the countryside seemed to be constantly in rebellion sparked off by Carlists or by radicals either from the middle-class or working-class movements. This was also the century of the *pronunciamiento* in which senior and sometimes not so senior soldiers challenged the existing government. Through all this the government, whichever one it was, seemed to be remarkably unable to deal with the situation.

It is also worth looking at the condition of the working-class movement in both countries. In the more industrialized Britain, the Labour Party was more important than was in Spain the Partido Democratico Socialista Obrera, now the PSOE. In any case the organized Spanish working-class movement was largely

*See also the discussion by Pi-Sunyer, in this volume, p. 264.

anarchist or anarchosyndicalist with no parliamentary representation. Although one might argue that the Labour Party cast
upon its shoulders the "Home Rule all round" mantle of the
Gladstonian Liberals, one could also point to the *federalista*
mantle which fell on the PSOE. When the harsh winds of real
politics blew, both mantles were swept off. Both socialist parties
were and are basically centralist but both are happy to support
Home Rule when it is tactically convenient.

One enormous subject which must not be ignored is the effect
of war. In Britain the effect of fighting two world wars was that
the claims of the nationalist parties were overridden. Spain had
a Civil War which resulted in victory for the side which wanted
to suppress all peripheral nationalism in favor of Spanish nationalism. The first effect was as intended. In Catalonia,
however, after the worst days of the repression, it worked in a
different direction. Nationalists and working-class activists
found themselves in the same prisons and subject to the same
persecution. This led to a readiness to understand each other's
position. The effect of this after Franco's death was that the
Catalan socialists and communists supported the nationalist
claim (Benet, 1948). Their fellow party members in Madrid
were not always in complete agreement. In contrast, the Labour
Party in Scotland had to be forced to accept the policy of
devolution by Transport House. The Scottish section of the
party saw devolution as the doctrine of the enemy (Keating and
Bleiman, 1979).

Let us now compare Scotland and Catalonia in terms of the
world circumstances, or the circumstances of the state of which
they are a part. If we look at any period from the beginning of
the nineteenth century up to the middle of this century,
Scotland enjoyed many more benefits from its membership of
the United Kingdom than Catalonia did from being a part of
Spain. I have suggested that this was the case in psychological
terms, and in economic terms, because Scotland's industries
were heavily export-oriented and depended on the international
market commanded by Britain. In these circumstances we
would expect a weak nationalist movement in Scotland and, at
least, the possibility of a strong one in Catalonia. This would
assume, of course, that the circumstances in these areas were
themselves conducive to this development. We know that this
was more or less what happened. By the end of the nineteenth
century nationalism was fully developed in Catalonia. In 1901
the Lliga Regionalista won twelve seats in Catalonia and commanded a place in the Spanish Cabinet. At the elections of 1907

Solidaridad Catalana carried forty-one of the forty-four Catalan seats. By the foundation of the Second Republic demand for autonomy was overwhelming and the government had no option but to grant the statute.

The situation in Scotland is quite different. There was a Home Rule movement in the 1880s but it was not a healthy child. A fully nationalist movement, demanding complete separation, was founded in 1928 but it had no real success until the 1960s. The SNP vote went up almost continuously until the high point of the 1974 (October) election, when it got eleven of the seventy-one Scottish seats and 30 percent of the Scottish vote coming second only to Labour which took 36 percent.

There were important changes in Scotland's external environment which may explain this change. Scotland was no longer part of an empire and even the British parliamentary system, so long revered, was subject to prolonged criticism. Parliament was seen to be lumbering and to hinder the expression of opinion. The monarchy was ridiculed. The British economy was in crisis, and this crisis was to get worse. The fact that other European economies were in the same condition was no comfort and, in any case, was probably not clearly perceived. It was no longer so nice to be British!

The problems of the British economy had a particular effect on Scotland. Since the end of the last century Scottish firms had been taken over by English companies or multinationals. When recession came, it was the Scottish branches which were closed down first. This process, so characteristic of the 1960s and 1970s, is, I believe, more important than the discovery of oil in the North Sea announced in 1971. The nationalist advance had started before this with many skilled men thrown out of work. North Sea oil gave hope to a people who were deeply uneasy about their economic future.

That most of the independent units of the Scottish economy have been taken over by firms with headquarters outside of Scotland has additionally led to an outflow of the best talent from the country to London or abroad. Compare this situation with that in Catalonia. Catalan businessmen do move to Madrid but, until very recently, Barcelona was the commercial capital. In many ways it still is. In any case, there is no strong incentive for a Catalan to move to the political capital. He can be more prosperous by staying where he is. In the same way, there is very low representation of Catalans in the civil service and the armed forces. These are the traditional channels of upward mobility for Spaniards, but neither they nor other methods of upward mobility were as promising and attractive as what already existed in Catalonia. The effect of this was that an elite exists and flourishes in Catalonia. The equivalent is, in Scotland, only a shadow of what it was. Add to this the fact that the Catalans perceived themselves as having an interest quite different from that of Madrid and there is a great likelihood of a movement for autonomy.

It was not only the business elite that left Scotland. I have suggested that Catalans were not represented in the civil service in proportion to their numbers in the population. On the contrary, Scots in all walks of life streamed to the capital. Where the University of Barcelona enjoyed the same prestige as the University of Madrid, Scots universities could not compete with Oxford or Cambridge. The best young men and women, broadly speaking, go there even if they, first of all, spend some years doing a Scottish degree. In general, where Catalan institutions have a status of equality with all Spanish institutions, and where Catalans are happy to spend all their lives in Catalonia because there are rich rewards there of every sort, the same is not true of Scotland. For the bright young man or woman, "the road winds ever on" and it winds south.

The effect of this is that, in every field of Catalan life, there is a native elite ready to provide leadership for a political movement. Scotland has been stripped of its elites. The nationalist movement shows a disastrous inability to lead and the party seems to operate with no strategy.

Conclusion

In this chapter I have looked at two countries with nationalist movements which are significant in politics but are of varying strengths. The other characteristic which they share is that they are both highly developed in an economic sense. Scotland has moved, and is moving, from this position in an economic sense.

The burden of my approach has been that we cannot get a satisfactory explanation of the takeoff of nationalist movements in many countries by any form of the "internal colonial" model. On the contrary, I have pointed to two central features which characterize both Scotland and Catalonia. An independent popular culture, including the symbol of past independence, is very crucial. The other important factor is the world position of the country and the extent to which this allows the society to develop and build a consciousness of its own interests. In this last regard Scotland and Catalonia are strikingly different.

References: Chapter 12

Benet, J. (1948), *Catalunya sota el regim Franquista* (Barcelona: Blume).
Brand, Jack A. (1978), *The National Movement in Scotland* (London: Routledge & Kegan Paul).
Brand, Jack A. (1984), "National consciousness and voting in Scotland," Papers on Government No. 15, University of Strathclyde, Glasgow.
Daiches, David (1977), *Scotland and the Union* (London: John Murray).
Fraser, Ronald, (1979), *Blood of Spain* (London: Allen Lane).
Gellner, Ernest (1964), *Thought and Change* (London: Galloway).
Giner, Salvador (1980), *The Social Structure of Catalonia* (London: Anglo-Catalan Society).
Hanham, H. (1969), *Scottish Nationalism* (London: Faber).
Hechter, Michael (1975), *Internal Colonialism* (London: Routledge & Kegan Paul; Berkeley and Los Angeles, Calif.: University of California Press).
Hechter, Michael (1978), "Group formation and the cultural division of labor," *American Journal of Sociology*, vol. 84, no. 2 (September, pp. 293–318.
Hechter, Michael (1980), "Internal colonialism revisited," paper presented at Conference of Europeanists, Washington, D.C., 23–25 October, mimeo.; revised version, in this volume.
Instituto de Estadística (1980), *Anuario Estadístico de España* (Madrid: Instituto de Estadística).
Keating, Michael, and David Bleiman (1979), *Labour and Scottish Nationalism* (London: Macmillan).
Lenin, V. I. (1956), "The development of capitalism in Russia," in *Collected Works* (Moscow: Foreign Languages Publishing House), Vol. 13.
Levi, Margaret, and Michael Hechter (1980), "The rise and decline of ethno-regional parties," paper presented at Conference of Europeanists, Washington, D.C., 23–25 October, mimeo.; revised version, in this volume.
Mathias, Peter (1976), *The First Industrial Nation* (London: Methuen).
Maura, R. (1975), *La Rosa de Fuego* (Barcelona: Grijalbo).
Nairn, Tom (1977), *The Break-Up of Britain* (London: New Left Books).
Pinard, Maurice (1971), *The Rise of a Third Party* (Englewood Cliffs, N.J.: Prentice-Hall).
Poblet, Josep (1976), *Historia de l'Esquerra* (Barcelona: Dopesa).
Poggi, G. (1978), *The Development of the Modern State* (London: Hutchinson).
Smelser, Neil (1964), *The Theory of Collective Behavior* (New Haven, Conn.: Yale University Press).
Vincens Vives, Jaime (1969), *An Economic History of Spain* (Princeton, N.J.: Princeton University Press).

13

Living in the House of Power
Welsh Nationalism and the Dilemma of Antisystem Politics

PHILLIP RAWKINS

Introduction

All opposition movements within liberal democracies depend in large part on the political opportunities that others, deliberately or unwittingly, create. In the present economic difficulties of Western industrial states political scientists and journalists alike take for granted that opposition parties do not win elections; governments lose them. Minority nationalist parties, particularly in unitary political systems, depend more than other oppositions on the provision by others of political space. The approach adopted by such parties to political action is hence as likely to be opportunistic as to derive from a considered strategy. Indeed, nationalists' perception of the weight of external constraints will largely define their objectives.

In examining specifically the development of nationalist politics in Scotland and Wales what is particularly striking is the extent to which the respective nationalist parties have been shaped in their practices and outlook by the ideological impact of the British political model. A number of factors have been at work here: the relative tolerance of the British political system toward expressions of dissent, if couched in ideologically "reasonable" terms; the centralist bias of the political system; and the numerical weakness of the Scots and Welsh as territorial minorities within an English-dominated state. Cultural factors of importance have included: the integrationalist bias in education and the mass media, and the absence in the post-1945 period of a cultural division of labor, in terms of which the Scots and Welsh would be denied access to valued rewards on the basis of nationality. For such reasons, in their considerations of the range of choices open to them, Scottish and Welsh nationalists have been as much influenced as their centralist opponents by R. A. Butler's concept of politics as "the art of the possible".

The Shadow of Westminster

This study focusses, though not exclusively, on Plaid Cymru, the party that since at least the 1930s has formed the political spearhead of the Welsh nationalist movement.

Since its formation in the 1920s Plaid Cymru has been obliged to confront, however obliquely, a set of fundamental and interrelated problems. First, the mobilization of support: how to reach the mass public of Wales, and how to bring nationalist ideas to their attention? Only in the 1960s and 1970s did Plaid Cymru succeed in reaching significant numbers of voters and in convincing them to view the party as a credible electoral contender. As will become clear, the party's opportunity was not of its own making. But in order to take advantage of the opening that presented itself the party was obliged to modify its *ideology* and to link its basic philosophy to a *coherent program* of action and proposed legislative change.

A coherent program is not enough. In addition, there is what might be termed *issue-salience*: the party's ability to articulate a short list of easily comprehensible issues, relevant to the most immediate concerns of voters and expressed so as to achieve a certain resonance in popular consciousness. While taking the necessary steps to reach the voter and to court media attention, the emergent party must also maintain *a distinct political identity*.

These problems—mobilization, ideology, program, issue-salience, and identity—are barriers any political party must clear in order to expand. In its early years, and up to the late 1950s, it was by no means clear that Plaid Cymru really sought to become a political party or to to win political power. Entrenched in its rural fastnesses, as the focus of a broader cultural movement, the party that was not quite a party found it easy to sustain itself. At the same time the party could make no impression on the larger political system. In the mid-1960s, following five or six years of internal disorder and disputation, the party committed itself unambiguously to electoral politics. In doing so, Plaid Cymru's leaders found it both expedient and necessary to place in abeyance the dilemma, often raised in speeches and pamphlets by nationalist leaders, of whether the party attached a greater priority to "making nationalists" or winning votes (Rawkins, 1979a).

In the mid-1960s, sensing the opportunity to win public support as never before, yet not quite understanding why, the party leadership understandably followed the path of least resistance. With hindsight, it is apparent that in doing so the party was taking some considerable political risks. Since the 1979 British general election the costs of electoral and constitutional politics have seemed to nationalist intellectuals and activists alike to have outweighed the benefits.

Parties are often formed initially around certain individuals and within the context of a relatively small and clearly defined community. Under such circumstances parties easily maintain satisfactory links between leaders and followers and experience little difficulty in ensuring that party ideology fits the political preferences and psychological needs of the members. In liberal democracies political parties are distinguished from social movements and pressure groups principally through their search for power. They seek to win credibility in the eyes of voters; in order to do so they enter the political system as participants committed to electoral competition.

In following such a path a party will naturally lose many of its communitylike qualities. (1) In its initial phase the organization is likely to be characterized by strong personal links among members, along with adherence to a set of common symbols and beliefs that separate the ingroup from its perceived opponents. (2) In seeking to expand its social base the party attempts to mobilize support through the relevance of its activities and goals. At the same time party organization undergoes transformation, and a small community dissolves into a looser association, open to a wider population. (3) In the long term it hopes to convert a broad-based and disparate association into a large community defined by common interest and a degree of commitment to a distinctive ideology and program (Blondel, 1978, pp. 56–67).

For a time, in the late 1960s and until the later 1970s, it appeared that Plaid Cymru had made this three-stage transition successfully. The outcome of the two general elections of 1974 and, more dramatically, of May 1979 provided concrete evidence to the contrary. Outside of parts of the Welsh-speaking counties of Gwynedd and Dyfed it was clear that, neither at a membership nor an electoral level, had the party succeeded in convincing large numbers of disaffected citizens that they should make their political home with Plaid Cymru.

Between October 1974 and May 1979, with a minority Labour government whose survival depended on the support of nationalist and /or Liberal M.P.s in the House of Commons, Plaid Cymru's three M.P.s made the most of their place at the center of things. However, their moment in the spotlight owed more to Labour's difficulties than to Plaid Cymru's success at the polls. In neither of the general elections of 1974 had the party succeeded in matching the peak of its electoral achievement, 12 percent of the Welsh vote, recorded in 1970. In October 1974 the party had polled 11·6 percent of the vote, with its share falling to 8·7 percent in 1979. In all four of the general elections of the 1970s Plaid Cymru had contested all thirty-six Welsh constituencies.

In March 1979 the government's proposals to establish a Welsh Assembly with modest powers were defeated in a referendum by a 4:1 margin. This decisive reversal appeared to many to signify that any prospect of electoral advance for Welsh nationalism might be written off. The party's poor showing in the general election two months later only reinforced this impression. As one of the party's M.P.s remarked ruefully to the author in the summer of 1980, the party, thrown back on the shrinking Welsh language "heartland", had become Plaid Cymraeg ("the party of the Welsh-speaker"). Even this comment exaggerated the strength of the party's social base. Although the ability to speak Welsh remains the chief predictor of a predisposition to vote for Plaid Cymru, the majority of the country's 20 percent Welsh-speaking minority vote for other parties.

If the objective of Plaid Cymru has been to mobilize the Welsh nation as a political force, its twenty-year venture in serious party-building must be termed a failure. Examination of Plaid Cymru's history, along with a perusal of election statistics, would probably lead the observer to conclude that the party of Welsh nationalism had reached the limits of its potential.

For some time now Plaid Cymru has occupied a modest corner of what Max Weber termed "the house of power." To take the metaphor literally, Plaid Cymru's two present M.P.s owe their well-apppointed Westminster office, with its fine view over the Thames, to the public relations efforts of the previous Labour administration, as it sought to secure the protection of a few extra votes in the latter stages of its life as a government.

This is not to suggest that the nationalists were bought off by the government. The point is rather that the party can only hope to win concessions by becoming a pawn in the strategy of a larger party. To put the matter in a different way, at a time of rising unemployment and social discontent, the commitment of the nationalist party to electoral politics may offer a convenient safety-valve to the politically disaffected. Hence, despite itself, the nationalist opposition might find itself serving as a handmaiden to government, assisting it in fulfilling the largely ritual function of legitimation (Finer, 1980, pp. 224–31).

In the first eight months of 1980 Welsh nationalism received more sustained attention from the mass media than in the whole of the previous year: a year which had included the referendum on the Wales Act and a general election. This state of affairs had little to do with Plaid Cymru as an electoral force. It resulted from the arson campaign directed at "second homes" and other targets, and from the intense campaign for a coherent Welsh-language TV service on the newly available "fourth channel."

Since the political awakening of the Welsh-speaking intelligentsia in the mid-1960s broadcasting had been second only to education as a target of demands for greater use of the Welsh language (see Rawkins, 1979b; Morgan, 1981, chs. 12 and 13). Following some years of agitation, sit-ins at TV studios, and the interruption of broadcast transmissions, all political parties in Wales had pronounced their acceptance of the so-called "one-channel" solution to Welsh-language broadcasting. The concept of the "Welsh fourth channel" (Sianel 4 Cymru) had also been endorsed by no less than four government commissions of inquiry. With the government making plans to introduce a fourth channel for TV transmission throughout the United Kingdom the proposal was for all Welsh-language programming to be concentrated on the new channel, allowing additional time for English-language broadcasts on the other channels. As the Association of Welsh-Language Broadcasters pointed out (*Western Mail*, 24 February 1981), the proposal would cater to the aspirations of the Welsh-speaking minority, while providing a wider range of programming to English-speakers.

With the return of Margaret Thatcher and the Conservatives to power, commercial broadcasting interests obviously pressured the government to reverse its position (Madgwick and Rawkins, 1982). In September 1979 the government indicated its intention to reject the concept of the "Welsh channel." This position was formalized in the presentation of the revised Broadcasting Bill to the House of Commons (Parliamentary Debates, 24–25 June 1980): "If all Welsh language programs were to be placed on that channel in Wales, there would be a considerable reduction in the advertising revenue likely to be raised." The announcement of the government's decision in September 1979 galvanized Welsh nationalists to launch a massive campaign of protest. It also provoked a storm of criticism from Welsh elite circles. Significantly those speaking out against the government's position included leaders of the Labour Party, the trade unions, and the Anglican Church, and not merely the "Welsh cultural establishment."

The Welsh Language Society resumed its earlier campaign of limited property damage to TV studios and transmission installations in England and Wales. Plaid Cymru members were encouraged to hold back payment of their TV license fees. Finally, in April 1980 Gwynfor Evans, party president since 1945, announced his decision to begin a hunger strike on 9 October unless the government accepted the one-channel solution.

Throughout the summer months a series of minor concessions was made. By September 1980 the total of those refusing to pay their TV license fees had risen to 2500. The courts had already shown themselves unwilling to send to prison three distinguished academics who had admitted damaging a TV transmitter. Finally, a week after receiving a delegation of Welsh notables, the government backed down in the face of the mounting onslaught. The dramatic breakthrough occurred just three weeks before the date set for Gwynfor Evans's fast (Madgwick and Rawkins, 1982; *New Statesman*, 16 January 1981; *Western Mail*, 8 and 18 September 1980).

This provided a much-needed surge of adrenalin to Plaid Cymru at what would otherwise have been a low point in the party's history. However, the party was immediately confronted with the problem of how to use the victory to political advantage. As on many earlier occasions, the party found itself lacking a sense of direction.

As the party's former vice-president Phil Williams observed, unless the party could follow up its successful campaign for the TV channel with dynamic action for English-speaking Wales, the result might well be to distance English-speakers even further from the nationalist movement (Williams, 1981, pp. 101–2). The TV campaign, combined with the emphasis on the achievements at Westminster of the party's two M.P.s (each a Welsh-speaker from a Welsh-speaking constituency), might simply serve to reinforce the existing public stereotype of Welsh nationalism. Without a coherent strategy, the party might discover that to secure publicity for its "success" would merely create public resentment at the privileged treatment accorded an unrepresentative linguistic minority.

The Devolution Years and the Making of Party Strategy

By the early 1970s Plaid Cymru, like the Scottish National Party, had been dramatically transformed from a tiny, other-worldly movement to a broadly based popular organization. Its membership was now drawn to an approximately equal extent from English-speakers and Welsh-speakers. The party was led by a professionalized and politically sophisticated elite (Rawkins, 1979a, 1978).

The work and influence of this "modernist" elite, in conjunction with the experience gained in fighting a series of parliamentary by-elections in the late 1960s and early 1970s, led the party to rebuild its organization for more effective electoral competition. It cannot be said that the modernists were merely political opportunists. From 1966 to 1974 they developed a wide range of economic and social policies which, in large measure, reflected the group's concerns for social reform. However, once the party tasted power, both through the winning of parliamentary seats and through its new-found success at local government level in the 1970s, the cutting edge of modernism was understandably blunted in the search for enhanced public credibility.

An Antisystem Party?

No party is likely to increase its share of the popular vote by courting controversy and creating divisions at every opportunity. As the rather different histories of the Communist parties of France and Italy have demonstrated, the pursuit of power requires a broadening of the party platform, a dilution of ideology, and a willingness to compete with more centrist parties on their own ground. In other words, the search for public credibility is a vital step toward power. Yet the logic of such parties' basic political role, whatever the conscious strategy pursued by their leadership, places them in opposition to the political system.

Consider the case of Italy, where the Italian Communist Party (PCI) appears to have lost significant fundamentalist support as a result of its cooperation with the Christian Democrats. In other words, as it has sought to extend its popular base of support by ideological moderation, so it has been threatened by a weakening of its link with the deeply imbedded *inciviste* political subculture which provides its core constituency (Allum, 1973, pp. 62–8; Jaggi, 1977; Hobsbawm and Napolitano, 1977; Barkan, 1980). As the antisystem party succeeds in attracting votes from its more moderate opponents so it stands in danger of becoming the victim of the system it challenges. While the PCI gained public credibility from its efficient and human administration of major municipalities, so it became the guardian of a system whose limitations and deficiencies it could not control.

It need hardly be emphasized that the PCI has possessed a far stronger hand in its delicate formal and informal negotiations with the Italian political establishment than has Plaid Cymru in its relations with Westminster. However, the PCI has been obliged to recognize that in supporting the Christian Democrats wherever they have sponsored social reform, it has been reinforcing the position of a party whose political objective has been the destruction of its unwanted ally. By moderating its criticisms while supporting reforms, arguably, it has allowed the Christian Democrats to claim credit for the new measures and to enhance the breadth of their popular appeal. Further, as the policy of the PCI has moved closer to social democratic norms so it has facilitated the journey of a proportion of its voters to the Socialist Party.

Similarly, Plaid Cymru, in a position of unaccustomed political influence, became ensnared by the dominant concern of the Labour Party to maximize its own electoral prospects and to maintain power at Westminster. Devolution, except for a small band of the committed within the Labour Party in Wales and Scotland, was always a means to this end. Further, because Plaid Cymru—unlike the French Communist Party (PCF) or even the Scottish National Party—had little in the way of votes to deliver, it was obliged to play a self-consciously low-key role in the interparty discussions prior to the 1979 referendum campain, as well as in the campaign proper. Thus Gwynfor Evans wrote, a year prior to the campaign:

> We must do our utmost to ensure that the elected assembly becomes a fact. This will require, however invidious we may find

it, that leadership must be taken by the government, the Labour party and the unions. (*Welsh Nation*, January 1978)

In the event, the government failed to support its own devolution policy and a short while later Labour lost the 1979 general election. However, in those constituencies of industrial South Wales where Plaid Cymru has provided the principal opposition, Labour's strategy appeared to have been successful. The nationalists were brushed aside, with the "Welsh dimension" failing to take root as an election factor. Scotland rather than Wales, of course, had provided the initial catalyst to the government's devolution strategy. Here, the only region where Labour gained ground, the Callaghan strategy grasped considerable electoral rewards, with Labour's substantial advance taking place chiefly at the expense of the SNP.

In the runup to the referendum campaign Plaid Cymru took credit for creating "a new political dimension in Wales itself." It was also claimed that "we have taken the Welsh question to the heart of British politics, sometimes to the irritation and even the anger of the then London establishment" (*Welsh Nation*, November 1978). However, the temporary foothold of the "Welsh question" in the Palace of Westminster was in large part an accident of the unfolding of the broader pattern of British politics. The passage of the Wales Bill through Parliament has been treated by government and opposition alike as an irrelevant nuisance. Welsh devolution was, essentially, a ripple of the more substantial problem Scotland represented for Westminster and its managers. For all this, on other matters Plaid Cymru took full advantage of its new visibility to extract a notable series of policy concessions. In many ways the record suggests that within the House of Commons the three Plaid Cymru M.P.s operated more judiciously and successfully than did the larger SNP group. However, on devolution, the party leadership appears to have flattered itself at the extent of its influence. Depending on Labour to "sell" the Welsh dimension to the Welsh people, they failed to take account of the opportunity the referendum campaign and the atmosphere surrounding it might present to the party, particularly in attracting English-speaking voters.

During the 1970s Plaid Cymru had been effective, as a pressure group, in drawing attention to the economic problems of industrial Wales, but it had failed to mobilize the English-speaking vote in support of its *national* platform. As the analysis of opinion poll data for the 1974–9 period demon-

strates most emphatically, the party has remained disproportionately one of Welsh-speaking voters (Balsom, 1979). Its
support among English-speakers remains ephemeral and its
capacity for expansion limited.

By 1974, although the party had formed the spearhead for
the growing self-assertiveness of the Welsh-speaking middle
class, it no longer monopolized the politics of Welsh identity.
The Labour Party, in particular, had adapted to the revitalization of the Welsh dimension. Yet Plaid Cymru's elite, particularly in Welsh-speaking Wales, appeared complacent about
the party's role in presiding over what was seen as the inevitable
resurgence of what Gwynfor Evans called "the national will."
That attitude appeared to stem from an almost sublimal preoc-
cupation with the Welsh-speaking areas, and from an unspoken
assumption that politics were merely a means to the salvation
of language and culture.

Certainly there is considerable evidence to demonstrate that
consciousness of Welsh identity remains strong throughout
Wales, and not merely among Welsh-speakers. Analysis of data
derived from the Welsh Election Survey of 1979 (based on a
representative national sample) indicates that of those inter-
viewed, 57 percent think of themselves as Welsh, 33 percent as
British, and 8 percent as English. Given the presence of a
significant number of citizens of English origin in Wales, these
figures are quite striking, particularly in comparison with
Scottish data deriving from the equivalent survey, conducted
during the same period. In the case of Scotland 52 percent
identify as Scottish, 35 percent as British, and 2 percent as
English (Balsom *et al.*, 1982; Brand, 1981).

Plaid Cymru's performance in by-election campaigns has
demonstrated that "Welshness" may, on occasion, be harn-
essed in support of nationalist politics. However, at general
elections, when British, not Welsh, issues predominate, the
party has remained very much an outsider. For the most part
it appears that, outside of the Welsh-speaking population,
Welsh identity has minimal political salience.

For Welsh nationalists, the problem is how to utilize its
restricted opportunities to stimulate and transform national
consciousness, and thus, to endow the national question with a
new political immediacy. In this regard, for precisely the same
reasons, Phil Williams (former party chairman and vice-
president) argued passionately in favor of taking a hard line on
devolution, while Dafydd Elis Thomas and Emrys Roberts
(party vice-president, 1978–80), each of whom shared many of

Williams's reservations about the party's general direction, supported the moderate, low-profile position favored by party leader Gwynfor Evans. For Thomas, what was critical was to transform the political situation by creating governmental institutions in Wales. Hence despite the limited powers to be granted to the assembly, its establishment could transform Welsh politics by creating a *Welsh* forum and focus for political debate. Plaid Cymru was obliged to depend on Labour and the Welsh Trades Union Council (TUC) to deliver the necessary referendum vote. However, as a result of a "yes" majority, it could find itself occupying a strategic position in a new political force-field. It would no longer face the apparently insurmountable obstacle of creating a Welsh campaign in an election atmosphere saturated by media inputs from Westminster-oriented politicians and commentators. As Gwynfor Evans put it, summarizing the argument for the "devolutionist" strategy: "The reality is that whatever we can achieve at Westminster has to be done through some other party. And there was no way we could have disassociated ourselves from the devolution proposals even if we had wanted to" (*Arcade*, no. 25, 30 October, 1981).

The argument has force, but it also lacks perspective. What was proposed in the Wales Act was devolution of administrative responsibility, not devolution of power. Not only would the assembly have lacked legislative powers, it would also have possessed no means of raising its own revenues, remaining entirely dependent on a block grant from Westminster. As Hunt and Peacock pointed out in their Memorandum of Dissent from the Report of the Kilbrandon Commission on the Constitution, a strong democratic argument could be made for independent revenue-raising powers for the assembly. Only "the possession and exercise of these powers will, we believe, foster among the people both a sense of independence and a sense of extra involvement in their own affairs" (HMSO, 1973, p. 104). Even with an assembly, Plaid Cymru would find itself constrained to considering how best to work for achieving the goal of equipping it with greater powers. Once again, such an analysis might lead to an emphasis on the need for moderation in order to encourage the Labour Party's support for fundamental demands for a stronger assembly.

More generally, as Phil Williams had pointed out, by playing the game strictly according to the rules of those who support the status quo, the party reinforces the trend toward compromise of nationalist demands. It also allows the "real" nationalist position to be defined as outside of the limits of serious political consideration. Once Plaid Cymru accepted devolution, what had been at one time the moderate position became the extreme. It was no accident that Plaid Cymru found itself fighting in the referendum for a simple "yes" vote to proposals it felt fell far short of what was necessary.

The gradualist or moderate strategy, while it may make sense strategically, becomes a habit. The party adjusts to the political culture, while its objective involves transforming it. It is possible, as the party's new president (since October 1981), Dafydd Wigley, M.P. for Caernarfon, has argued, to view the hard-line and moderate approaches merely as alternative strategies, to be employed deliberately by the party at different times for different purposes (*Welsh Nation*, January 1977). However, it is hard to avoid the conclusion that the gradualist approach has become enshrined as an aspect of the party's philosophy.

The work of forging a politically relevant *national* identity remains to be done, The party has been unable to transform the antigovernment, anti-Labour sentiment, which brought it local election victories in the southeast in the 1970s, into support for an alternative politics. As the referendum campaign demonstrated, the same voters who supported Plaid Cymru in its by-election spectaculars of earlier years, and its local election victories of the mid-1970s, were entirely unmoved by the prospect of a Welsh Assembly.

The continuing search for respectability will inevitably push the party further in the direction of "electoralism," and of a willingness to compete for political spoils on the terms set by the dominant parties. To pursue this approach is to over-emphasise the "instrumental" dimension of the movement's activities, and to risk destroying the internal solidarity generated by its past adherence to the symbols and emotional trappings of nationalism, language, and cultural identity.

What faces the party, however, is a complex dilemma. To emphasize the party's philosophy risks reinforcing the old stereotype of Welsh nationalism as essentially a sectionalist movement, defending the cultural heartland. The party's present position is an uneasy compromise, reflected in the persistence of what Phil Williams has termed the "pressure-group mentality."

Viewed as a pressure group, Plaid Cymru has had a considerable effect in rejuvenating the Welsh dimension of British politics over the past twenty years. At the level of "bread and butter" politics, it has also drawn the attention of media and government to social and economic problems in Wales. This has won the party a modicum of public recognition without yielding it the real dividends of political credibility. Available survey data suggest that, while Plaid Cymru is seen to be "good for Wales," it is also associated in the public mind with "extremism" (see Balsom *et al.*, 1982; Balsom, 1981).

One element in the success of the "no"-vote campaign in the referendum had been the assertion that a Welsh Assembly would be dominated by a Welsh-speaking elite. As a result, it was claimed, English-speakers would find themselves at an increasing disadvantage in competing with Welsh-speakers for public sector employment. One factor in Plaid Cymru's decision to play a low-key role in the referendum campaign was the fear of provoking an English-language backlash. Ironically, by associating itself closely with the Labour devolutionists in the Welsh Assembly campaign, the party contributed inadvertently to a situation in the 1979 general election where nationalists found themselves to be distinguishable, from the voter's viewpoint, exclusively in terms of their identification with the Welsh language.

The issues which potentially unite a Welsh majority on nationalist grounds are those which portray all regions of the country as the victims of a system of political and economic decision-making which operates independently of local needs. In the referendum campaign the party found itself associated with the system against those who were successful in mobilizing popular, antigovernment sentiment. As a decentralist, antibureaucratic party, it was ironic for Plaid Cymru to see Labour politicians reaping the benefits of popular support by utilizing the "antisystem" line.

Like the Scottish nationalists, Plaid Cymru has succeeded on occasion in persuading a significant section of the electorate that a vote for nationalism is likely to draw the attention of Westminster. The diversion of substantial public resources to the Carmarthen constituency following Gwynfor Evans's first parliamentary election victory there in 1966 bears eloquent testimony to the wisdom of an electoral shift toward nationalism at a time of government weakness. As Jack Brand has put it, in commenting on the electoral support amassed by the SNP in the early 1970s, nationalist voters saw the party as one which would fight their battles—on such issues as threatened unemployment and industrial decline—at Westminster (Brand, 1981, p. 37; Miller, 1981). The solution to their problems lay in obtaining a better hearing from government. While the solution to Scottish problems is still perceived to be found at Westminster, the typical SNP voter is unlikely to become a committed partisan. Labour, the traditional party of that part of the Scottish population most vulnerable to the effects of economic setbacks, remains the party which is closer to power and the resources of government.

Both the SNP and Plaid Cymru found themselves trapped by the devolution issue. As Gwynfor Evans has suggested, by the late 1970s the logic of the situation was that neither party could have avoided being identified in the public eye with the proposals contained in the Scotland and Wales Acts. Although the final result in Scotland was extremely close, it appears that the government devolution strategy effectively "cooled out" the issues of nationalism, creating an impasse such that in the 1979 general election neither nationalist party found itself able to mount a campaign perceived to be relevant to voter priorities.

For the "antisystem" party, it is sound strategy to take advantage of opportunities within the conventional political game. However, if the strategy is to bring about sustained advance, the party must be prepared to switch to a higher-risk game, where it will attempt to create its own issues and carve out its own opportunities. Whatever the potential for creating a national sentiment in favor of self-government in Wales, Plaid Cymru will only test the limit of its possibilities by obliging the state to act where it would prefer not to do so. As Richard Rose has pointed out, "to secure Westminster's attention, groups must voice demands in such ways that Westminster's calm is disturbed" (Rose, 1979, p. 22).

The dilemma for Plaid Cymru is that where it has succeeded in mobilizing public sentiment against state action—as in its campaign against the flooding of the Tryweryn Valley in the ealry 1960s (Fishlock, 1972, pp. 102–8), and more recently in the fourth-channel campaign—it has also reinforced its image as the party of the Welsh-speaker. As had been predicted, the party's success in the TV campaign has only served to allow those seeking to arouse the English-language backlash to describe the Welsh-language TV service as a symbol of separatism. At the same time, the opponents of bilingualism have been able to depict "Sianel 4 Cymru" as an unjustified subsidy (the estimated cost to the Treasury of the new service is between £30 and £40 million per year) to an already privileged minority (*Western Mail*, 19 February 1981).

In considering further the limits to Plaid Cymru's potential, and the possibilities for a transformation in the party's fortunes, it may be instructive to turn to consideration of a comparison between nationalism and its supports in Wales and Quebec.

Nationalism in Wales and Quebec: Parallels and Contrasts

Nationalism has a lengthy history in both Wales and Quebec; but as in Brittany, the Basque country, or Corsica, it was only in the 1960s that nationalism emerged as a radical force, with its influence percolating through a wide range of social, cultural, and economic institutions. In both cases it was the political and intellectual mood and situation of the 1960s which provided fertile ground for modern, reformist movements to emerge.

In both Canada and the United Kingdom, as in the United States, the 1960s saw the emergence of an atmosphere of greatly increased tolerance to reform. The Pearson and Trudeau administrations in Ottawa, and the Lesage government in Quebec, all sponsored reform in a wide variety of spheres of social activity. Similarly, in the United Kingdom the Labour government of 1964–70, and to a lesser extent its Conservative predecessor, was responsible for major liberalizing reforms. There are a variety of explanations for the emergence of the new climate of tolerance. Its principal foundations would seem to derive in part from the growing expectations of citizens, fueled by the growth of state intervention in economy and society, and the escalation of promises made by successive governments from 1945 on. At the same time, the openness to pressure for reform in the decade in question was also the consequence of the vulnerability of government and the decline in political authority in the face of the emerging crisis of the Western economies (Perrow, 1979, pp. 192–211).

Neither the reformed Plaid Cymru nor the Parti Québécois emerged in a vacuum; each drew on the work of predecessors. In the case of Plaid Cymru the apparent continuity indicated by retention of the party name disguises a quite radical transformation in political orientation and organizational form very similar to that which occurred in Quebec. Each party was able to draw on elites trained in other movements and parties. As the parties began to grow they dislodged resources from other groups and organizations operating within the same territory (Freeman, 1979, p. 176).

In the case of Plaid Cymru the party was able to draw on the experience of activists in various cultural organizations and youth movements, in the Labour Party in some cases, in the Campaign for Nuclear Disarmament (CND), and student politics. This ensured that in the late 1960s the party came to be equipped with a leadership core possessing the necessary organizational experience and political self-confidence to enable it to compete with its more established electoral opponents. The new recruits in turn were able to utilize their existing social networks to emphasize the new credibility of the revitalized movement. In this way, other recruits were attracted, and the social base of the party was broadened quite considerably.

In the case of Quebec the intensity of the experience of modernization, the rapid transition from a rural to an urban society, and the transformation of Montreal from an Anglophone-dominated to a Francophone city, all took place in or at least continued into the post-1945 period. In Wales the situation was very different. The impact of modernity and the transition to an urban society had been felt much earlier, and in a different political era. Further, unlike Quebec, Wales did not possess a focal metropolis to constitute a center for political mobilization and for the dissemination of nationalist ideology.

In Quebec social reform and nationalism reinforced each other. In association with the "Quiet Revolution," nationalism ceased to be a defensive ideology of rural and small-town Quebec. It now became a modern, outward-looking ideology, seeking to embrace change rather than reject it. Leadership now had passed into the hands of a new urban middle class: the technocratic intelligentsia, associated with the expansion of public sector employment, and particularly those engaged in education and administration (Guindon, 1978, pp. 212–46).

In Wales too it was this group, in both urban and rural areas, which provided the reformist elite. However, by contrast with the situation of Quebec, nationalism was not destined to become a crucial component in the world-view of this class as a whole. Nationalists, as in other social classes, were to remain a minority.

In any case there did not exist in Wales a set of territorially based institutions around which nationalists might seek to concentrate their demands for change, and whose activities they might seek to control. In contemporary Wales, as in Quebec, the public sector is of disproportionate importance as a source of employment. However, by contrast with the Quebec situation, in Wales public sector employment is concentrated in regional branches of statewide bureaucracies.

Hence in Wales the nationalist program is focussed, by necessity, on the creation of Welsh-based political, economic, and cultural institutions. At the same time, its campaigns must be aimed at a public oriented to London rather than Cardiff for redress of its grievances. In Quebec it was precisely the existence of a set of distinctive institutions, whose scope was expanded considerably during the "Quiet Revolution", which provided a necessary basis for the emergence of a large, self-confident urban middle class for whom nationalism was to become (though not exclusively) a matter of the pursuit of their economic interest.

Further, the persistence into the 1970s of a cultural division of labour at elite levels in private industry and commerce between Anglophone and Francophone, along with the limited success of the provincial Liberals in ensuring that French became the language of work in the private sector, provided a fundamental issue around which to mobilize mass support. As the center of a movement, the Parti Québécois (PQ) appealed to voters as the vehicle for the logical extension of the politics of the "Quiet Revolution" and for undertaking further actions to ensure the full equality of Francophones within their own province (Fournier, 1976; Rioux, 1971; McRoberts and Posgate, 1980; Arnopoulos and Clift, 1980).

In Wales, by contrast, language continued to divide the nation rather than to bind it together. In a rather limited sense Plaid Cymru's success in winning and retaining two parliamentary seats in rural Wales, in Gwynedd, has been due to its position as a party protecting the interest of the Welsh-speaker. In other words, where the language remains relatively strong, though threatened by the forces of change, the party wins electoral support on a basis somewhat like that which brought the PQ to power (Williams, 1980; Rawkins, 1979b). But here the parallel ends.

Plaid Cymru: Retrospect and Prospect

Plaid Cymru's most significant organizational achievement has been to construct and maintain a coalition of groupings divided by ideological preferences, class composition, geographical origins, social experience, and linguistic status. To many of its members in rural, Welsh-speaking Wales the party has functioned principally as a cultural association. In the eyes of its modernist elite, and to those who have come into contact with it in formal political circles, the party has exhibited instead what Dafydd Wigley summed up a few years ago as a "coherent set of policies in the social democrat slot" (personal interview, July 1975).

The party has maintained its internal coherence through its ability to offer either concrete or symbolic rewards to all its elements (Rawkins, 1979a). The coalition was built largely by the modernist elite, which first emerged to play a significant role in the mid-1960s. It has held together until now, and appears likely to continue, despite the ideological splits now so apparent within the leadership, and expressed in the contest between the party's two M.P.s for the party presidency in 1981.

At an elite and activist level the PQ is divided by ideology between two groups often described as the "participationists" (or the left) and the "technocrats" (see Murray and Murray, 1979; Nevitte, 1981). The present division within Plaid Cymru is similar. As in the PQ, the "left" has emphasized internal party democracy. Through the mobilization of activist support they have scored notable victories in policy debates at annual conferences and in national council meetings. Yet the less militant "technocrats" retain control of actual decision-making, as well as the direction of overall strategy.

Neither party is likely to resolve its divisions, but both have devised sophisticated informal systems of containing conflict. In each case it appears that ultimate authority resides in the hands of those able to deliver the greatest measure of power. However, unlike the PQ, Plaid Cymru has sustained a set of withering political reverses in the past few years. It is precisely because the elite has been unable to deliver the goods during the past two years that the left opposition has succeeded in mobilizing a significant challenge, and in drawing attention to an alternative version of nationalism.

Since 1966 the party has moved where opportunities have enabled it to go. Its journey through the electoral maze came to an abrupt end in 1979. Yet the path that was followed from 1965 to 1980 was not entirely accidental. The party's leadership, activists, and members were for the most part comfortable with the direction taken, and capable of performing the tasks entailed. In any case the party's achievements were probably limited more by its status as a territorially based, minority party in a unitary political system than by any organizational failure or inadequacy of effort or initiative.

Like the PQ, Plaid Cymru is, in essence, a populist party. As such, it seeks to mobilize the population of Wales around a

broad concept of nationalism. Since it acts in the name of
Wales, it must seek to expand yet further the breadth and depth
of the coalition it has built at an elite level. It must continue to
work to accommodate, however uneasily, a broad set of
economic and social interests. The PQ has accomplished this.
It lives and will continue to live with the contradictions such
strategy implies (McRoberts and Posgate, 1980, p. 207). Plaid
Cymru must learn to do the same. Within the nationalist
spectrum specific issue groups and more sectionalist language-
or class-based organizations will from time to time draw
resources and media attention away from Plaid. On other
occasions the party will be able to co-opt the resources of these
groups in advancing its own campaigning.

In the short term the political situation is one which appears
to offer little promise to nationalists. The Social Democratic
Party (SDP), like the Liberals in October 1979, appears capable
of further reducing nationalist support. However, there appears
to be little prospect that any of the British parties will succeed
in confronting the now well-entrenched structural decline of the
economy of Wales.

It is on the very uncertainties of the direction of social change
and social conflict in the 1980s that Welsh nationalism's hopes
must depend. Most of our conventional wisdom on political life
in Britain and other advanced industrial societies is derived
from a rather narrow base: the experience of the postwar
period. Drawing on this experience, the rise of the SDP might
stand out as a more significant indicator of the shape of politics
in the 1980s than the riots in Brixton or on Merseyside. As we
move further into the 1980s it is quite probable that the "rule
book" will prove to be a distinctly less helpful guide to the
directions and limits of political change. Whether Welsh nationalists will be able to count themselves among the innovators
or the casualties of the period remains to be seen.

Note: Chapter 13

This chapter is based on continuing research work conducted in Wales by the author
from 1972 to 1980. The research was supported, at various times, by the Canada
Council, the SSHRC (Canada), and the SSRC (UK). I am grateful to Dean Terry Grier
and the Arts Division of Ryerson Polytechnical Institute and to Professor Richard Rose
of Strathclyde University for their encouragement over the years. The continuing
courtesy and helpful attitude shown to me by the members and leaders of Plaid Cymru
made the task of this researcher far easier than he had any right to expect.

An earlier draft of this chapter was presented at a seminar held at the University
College of North Wales, Bangor, in November 1981. Discussions with Denis Balsom,

Charlotte Aull Davies, and Ken McRoberts after the presentation assisted me in clarifying my thinking on a number of points.

References: Chapter 13

Allum, P. (1973), *Italy: Republic without Government* (New York: Norton).

Arnopoulos, S., and Clift, D. (1980), *The English Fact in Quebec* (Montreal: McGill-Queen's University Press).

Balsom, D. (1979), *The Nature and Distribution of Support for Plaid Cymru*, Studies in Public Policy No. 36 (Glasgow: University of Strathclyde Press).

Balsom, D. (1981), "Looking north to south", (review of W. Miller's *The End of British Politics*), *Arcade*, no. 24 (16 October).

Balsom, D., P. Madgwick, and D. Van Mechelen (1982), *The Political Consequences of Welsh Identity*, Studies in Public Policy No. 97 (Glasgow: University of Strathclyde Press).

Barkan, J. (1980), "Italian communism at the crossroads," in C. Boggs and D. Plotke (eds.), *The Politics of Eurocommunism* (Boston, Mass.: South End Press), pp. 49–76.

Blondel, J. (1978), *Political Parties: A Genuine Case for Discontent* (London and Boston: Routledge & Kegan Paul).

Brand, J. (1981), "National consciousness and voting in Scotland," ms. (University of Strathclyde, Glasgow).

Finer, S. E. (1980), *The Changing British Party System, 1945–1979* (Washington, D.C.: American Enterprise Institute for Policy Research).

Fishlock, T. (1972), *Wales and the Welsh* (London: Cassell).

Fournier, P. (1976), *The Quebec Establishment* (Montreal: Black Rose Books).

Freeman, J. (1979), "Resource mobilization strategy: a model for analyzing social movement organization actions," in M. Zald and J. McCarthy (eds.), *The Dynamics of Social Movements* (Cambridge, Mass.: Winthrop), pp. 167–89.

Guindon, H. (1978), "The modernization of Quebec and the legitimacy of the Canadian state," in D. Glenday, H. Guindon and A. Turowetz, *Modernization and the Canadian State* (Toronto: Macmillan of Canada), pp. 212–46.

HMSO (1973), *Royal Commission on the Constitution 1969–1973, Volume II, Memorandum of Dissent by Lord Crowther-Hunt and Professor Allen Peacock* (London: HMSO).

Hobsbawm, E., and Napolitano, G. (1977), *The Italian Road to Socialism* (Westport, Conn.: Lawrence Hill).

Jaggi, M. (1977), *Red Bologna* (London: Writers & Readers Publishing).

Jones B., and Wilford, R. (1979), *The Welsh Veto: The Politics of the Devolution Campaign in Wales*, Studies in Public Policy No. 39 (Glasgow: University of Strathclyde Press).

McRoberts, K., and Posgate, D. (1980), *Quebec: Social Change and the Political Crisis*, 2nd ed. (Toronto: McClelland & Stewart).

Madgwick, P., and Rawkins, P. (1982), "The Welsh language in the policy process," in R. Rose and P. Madgwick (eds.), *The Territorial Dimension in UK Politics* (London: Macmillan), pp. 67–99.

Miller, W. (1981), *The End of British Politics? Scots and English Political Behaviour in the Seventies* (Oxford: Clarendon Press).

Morgan, K. (1981), *Rebirth of a Nation: Wales 1880–1980* (Oxford: Oxford University Press).

Murray, V., and Murray, D. (1979), "The Parti Québécois: from opposition to power," in H. Thorburn (ed.), *Party Politics in Canada*, 4th ed. (Scarborough: Prentice-Hall of Canada), pp. 243–54.

Nevitte, N. (1981), "The Parti Québécois: leaders, members, and supporters," paper presented at the Annual Meeting of the American Political Scciene Association, New York, September.

Osmond, J. (1981), "Gwynfor's legacy," *Arcade*, no. 25 (30 October).

Perrow, C. (1979), "The sixties observed," in M. Zald and J. McCarthy (eds.), *The Dynamics of Social Movements* (Cambridge, Mass.: Winthrop), pp. 192–211.

Rawkins, P. (1978), "Outsiders as insiders: the implications of minority nationalism in Scotland and Wales," *Comparative Politics*, vol. 10, no. 4, pp. 519–34.

Rawkins, P. (1979a), "An approach to the political sociology of the Welsh nationalist movement," *Political Studies*, vol. 27, no. 3 (September), pp. 440–57.

Rawkins, P. (1979b), *The Implementation of Language Policy in the Schools of Wales*, Studies in Public Policy No. 40 (Glasgow: University of Strathclyde Press).

Rioux, M. (1971), *Quebec in Question* (Toronto: Lewis & Small).

Rose, R. (1979), *From Steady State to Fluid State: The Unity of the Kingdom Today*, Studies in Public Policy No. 26 (Glasgow: University of Strathclyde Press).

Williams, E., and Thomas, D. E. (1981), "Commissioning national liberation," *Bulletin of Scottish Politics*, vol. 1, no. 2, pp. 139–60.

Williams, G. (1980), "Industrialization, inequality and deprivation in rural Wales," in G. Rees and T. Rees (eds.), *Poverty and Social Inequality in Wales* (London: Croom Helm), pp. 168–84.

Williams, P. (1981), "Minority report," in *Report of the Commission of Inquiry* (Cardiff: Plaid Cymru), pp. 94–115.

14

The Political Economy of Contemporary Nationalism in Wales

GLYN WILLIAMS

One of the striking features of the emergence of minority nationalism concerns its relationship with the involvement of the state in economic activity. In the nineteenth century it was argued that, within a "free" market economy, no producer could ignore competition from other producers; consequently the only role of the state was to create the judicial bases for economic competition. In reality, of course, the state has played a central role in the emergence of the very competition of capital which has served to suppress liberalism. Rather than organizing competition, the state stimulated it to the extent that monopolistic tendencies emerged. Such monopolism is unable to operate in a vacuum and depends upon the support of the state. Thus two simultaneous processes operated: first, the inevitable tendency toward the politics of centralization, legitimized by an ideology of egalitarianism; and secondly, the increasing trend toward the predominance of state capitalism, creating a situation where the state is seen to permeate most aspects of the lives of its citizens.

There is little doubt that state intervention has intensified during the past thirty years. The state has been predominantly responsible for the reorganization of capitalist space within both Britain and Wales and, as a consequence, for the reorganization of the social structure. I contend in this chapter that ethnicity is not to be seen as an abstract self-definition, but as a quality which is imposed in the sense that it represents the only form of expression for certain actors as a consequence of such economic and sociostructural changes. I shall try to develop this theme by considering the specific nature of spatial economic organization and its relationships to class and ethnic configurations. I will argue that nationalism has to be understood in terms of the antagonisms which result from this process of state intervention.

Much of the analysis focusses upon social reproduction, and it might be useful to discuss the manner in which social class is conceptualized before proceeding to the empirical discussion. While the analysis is located in the Marxist problematic, there are two issues of orthodox Marxism that require attention. First, orthodox Marxism tends to treat classes as homogeneous, unified entities acting in their own interests, either in their own right or in relationship to one another. Yet nothing prevents us from distinguishing fractions of one and the same class. Such fractions are more than simple strata, since they coincide with important economic differentiations and, as such, can even take on an important role as social forces, a role relatively distinct from that of the other reactions of their class. Secondly, while Marxism defines classes principally by their members' place in the productive process, political and ideological places also have an important role. Thus within the following discussion both class fragmentation and the ensemble of social practices which pertain to social class will be central.

Economic Structural Change in Wales

The Welsh economy at the beginning of the century clearly emphasized primary production: almost half of the male labor-force was employed in mining, quarrying and agriculture. From the onset of the Industrial Revolution external capital had mainly influenced the large-scale developments in the Welsh economy, although with the expansion of the coal industry toward the end of the nineteenth century a native Welsh bourgeoisie appeared. However, the coalmines had become limited companies after 1875 and became oligopolistic at the turn of the century. The economy in Wales at this time was labor-intensive and there was little sign of an integrated Welsh economy.

In the rural areas the gentry families, which had consolidated their positions as early as the fifteenth century, began to sell off parts of their estates, much of this land being purchased by tenants who farmed relatively small units. As a consequence, the percentage of Welsh agricultural holdings farmed by the owner increased from 10.6 percent in 1909 to 63.7 percent in

1970. With the size of the holdings averaging less than fifty acres, this development constituted the emergence of a native petite bourgeoisie rather than a bourgeoisie. This tendency was consolidated by the substitution of capital for labor which not only proletarianized many of the smaller farmers, but also eliminated much of the agricultural proletariat. The number employed in agriculture declined by 27 percent between 1911 and 1951. At the same time, the quarrying industry which was dispersed throughout the rural areas virtually collapsed.

The crisis, reflected at this time by the displacement of the proletariat in rural Wales, was also evident in the industrial south. With two-thirds of the laborforce in South Wales engaged in the production or transportation of coal, steel, and tinplate in 1923, the contraction in world trade during the 1920s and 1930s was a severe blow. Output in South Wales coal declined by 38 percent, the number of miners employed by 42 percent. With the owners of the private mines seeking to guarantee their profits by reducing wages, this was a period of considerable labor militancy in the South Wales coalfields. The steel and tinplate industries also experienced considerable difficulties. Several steelmills were relocated at coastal locations, and the inland valleys experienced severe depopulation. Throughout South Wales the unemployment rate exceeded 30 percent for years on end.

During the 1930s it was explicitly acknowledged that the state had a direct role to play in restructuring the economy to resolve the crisis. Such restructuring can be seen as an alternative to a different form of state involvement, in that during the depression as much as one-half of the capital expenditure of many settlements in South Wales derived from the Exchequer, while public assistance accounted for one-half of the total ratable value. Such a change of policy also fitted into a more general adjustment from the export orientation of capital goods to consumer production for the home market. That led to a regional diversity based upon light industry, the growth points for which were quite different from those of the earlier industries which had been located at or near the coalfields. As a consequence, the older areas, including those of industrial Wales, tended to suffer.

Recently Cooke (1981) has argued that the militancy of the South Wales laborforce, or at least the perceived militancy, was an important factor in the place that was allocated to Wales in the process of economic restructuring within Britain. He claims that the new industrial developments, as well as some of the residual enterprises, sought to maximize their surplus value by seeking a nonorganized laborforce which was not able to force up the price of labor. Associated was a tendency to "deskill" the production process, so that the laborforce was expanded rather than being contracted by specialization. He argues that such a development was detrimental for the redevelopment of much of industrial Wales which was held to have a militant and highly organized laborforce. Indeed, he goes so far as to claim that Welsh labor was deemed undesirable even when it consisted of those who had migrated to England as a consequence of the depression.

Whatever the merits of this argument, the advent of World War II made Wales a highly desirable location for industry. Although as many as 130,000 people were employed in the war industries in Wales in 1943, the combination of migration and conscription led to a loss of 100,000 people between the end of the 1930s and the end of war, a number which corresponds to the number unemployed before the war (Humphreys, 1972, p. 39). The choice of locations such as South Wales over more favored ones in southeast England was held to involve the abandonment of "economic considerations for the location of industry." Shadow industries were established, and the laborforce consisted primarily of specially trained females. The coal industry also found advantage in the war conditions, and the war years were ones of considerable prosperity for South Wales. Whatever prejudices existed against either the location or the laborforce disappeared. The "new" industries appeared unhindered by the locational prejudices that were evident during periods of normalcy.

This was the springboard for what are conventionally referred to as "regional development programs." They involve lowering the price of labor and capital by state-sponsored taxation and subsidies in order to "induce" firms to relocate in the periphery. Public funds are employed as an inducement to private "enterprises." It is implicitly assumed that such locations are somehow the opposite of the "natural preferences" of industrial companies. Such a policy is justified as a form of welfarism, where a benevolent state acts to rescue a powerless laborforce from unemployment. Consequently, the structure of social relations is not questioned and the state is seen as acting in the interest of the peripheral population rather than of the private sector. Only when the contradiction is observed—of a state which simultaneously seeks to relocate certain forms of labor while claiming to create work for others of the local laborforce—is the logic of this argument brought into question.

Two kinds of recent changes have affected the economy in Wales: on the one hand, the changes in the capitalist world-system (Wallerstein, 1974); and on the other, the restructuring of the regional division of labor within Britain. Obviously both of these are to a degree facets of the same phenomenon, as is evident in the unseen capitalist development. It is claimed by Rawkins (1978) that the British economic history of the past thirty-five years has involved a decline from a core status, with many international ties, to a semi-peripheral status, in which many of the international activities persist but Britain is also the locus of substantial external investment. He claims that some of the recent industrial developments in Wales are a consequence of this change. The regional division of labor, on the other hand, involves the spatial distribution of growing and lagging sectors and of the associated skill capacities within these sectors. Cooke describes the latter stages of the development of this structure in the following terms:

> Ultimately a form of the use of regional space designated the "branch circuit" is formed. In this, for a given sector or "branch" of industry, capital takes advantage of and reinforces the uneven inter-regional division of labour which has emanated from the process of earlier rounds of capitalist expansion. This takes the form of an intense concentration of high-skill tertiary activity in one region, and the polarization of lower order production activity to cheap labour regions. (Cooke, 1980.)

The regional typology which emerges from this process involves *headquarter regions* with high-value labor power of executive, research, and other high-skill activities; *skill regions* such as the component enclaves with average labor power of lower-order technical and professional labor; and *labor reserve regions* with low skills and value of labor deriving from the disintegration of archaic capitalist forms of production but also including the industrial platform function. Depite the high level of generalization associated with such a typology, it is none the less useful. Within a dynamic context it serves to demonstrate how regions which at one moment are characterized by high-skill, high-remuneration employment may subsequently be transformed into regions of considerable deskilling and reduction of labor power.

Within Wales we can identify subregional aggregations of economic activity. The old areas of primary production are, as we have seen, subject to significant denudation but are supplemented by a certain amount of subsidiary industrial platform development. The industrial platforms also constitute the major developments in the smaller towns and the rural growth poles. Within this concentration the manufacturing enterprises tend to be small in scale and pay relatively low wages to a largely female laborforce. In contrast, the only semblance of a headquarter region is Cardiff, the national capital, where many devolved headquarters of British enterprises are located. This concentration links up with the industrial enclave, along the coastal belt of South and northeastern Wales. Here we witness the large, capital-intensive units of the multinational and the component industries which often resort to international subcontracting in order to take advantage of the low cost of employing an unskilled laborforce for relatively high wages in regional terms. They depend neither on local resources nor on local markets, thus retaining external control.

Superimposed upon these private sector manufacturing developments is the laborforce associated with the tertiary or service sector. Most of this is concentrated in the enclave and the headquarter center. Much of this employment involves professional and scientific employment and what might be termed "miscellaneous services" involving hotel workers, shop assistants, and so on. Northeast Wales and the northern coast also contain significant service sector employment. As might be expected, the various subregional administrative centers contain significant proportions of public service employment. It is also here, as a consequence of the strong emphasis on tourism, that the miscellaneous service employment is also high.

The impact of these economic changes is evident in the data on employment in Wales. Tables 14.1 and 14.2 illustrate the broad changes in the occupational structure between 1951 and 1979. They emphasize the huge decline in primary production and the corresponding increase in manufacturing activity and in occupations in the service sector. While these tables are in themselves of value in demonstrating the scale of the economic and occupational changes, they mask the subregional variations described above. These are presented with reference to manufacturing and services, the two main growth areas in Tables 14.3 and 14.4.

Table 14.3 indicates the huge increase in the number of manufacturing jobs in the South Wales coalfield and the proportional growth in manufacturing in much of rural Wales. It seems that the South Wales industrial axis lost manufacturing

Table 14.1 *Employment Changes in Wales by Broad Sector,*
1951–76 (Change in 000s)

Industrial sector	1951–63	1963–71	1971–6
Agriculture	−12·2	−10·5	−2
Mining	−36·1	−55·0	−9
Manufacturing	41·3	40·8	−8
Metals/shipbuilding	2·4	−8·1	−13
Construction	14·2	−4·7	0
Transport	−18·2	−11·3	−4
Other services	78·1	12·8	71
Total change	67·5	−34·0	35

Source: Williams, 1982.

Table 14.2 *Employment Changes in Broad Sector, 1974–9*
(Estimated Employment in 000s)

Sector	September 1974	September 1979	Change (in 000s)
Agriculture	26	22	−4
Mining	43	38	−5
Manufacturing	254	236	−18
Metal manufacturing	84	69	−15
Construction	67	69	2
Transport	61	57	−4
Other services	470	521	51
Total	1005	1012	7

Source: As Table 14.1.

Table 14.3 *Manufacturing Employment Change, 1959–75, by*
Subregion

Subregion	1959	1975	Change (%)
Central and eastern valleys	77,300	111,600	44
West South Wales	70,800	81,200	15
South Wales coast	80,700	76,200	−6
Northeast Wales	30,800	33,400	8
North Wales coast	3,200	5,900	84
Northwest	7,800	11,900	53
Central Wales	1,500	6,200	313
Southwest Wales	2,600	6,000	131

Source: Fothergill and Gudgin, 1979.

Table 14.4   *Service Employment Change, 1959–76, by Subregion*

Subregion	*(1)* *1959*	*1971*	*(2) Percentage change*	*(4)* *1971*	*1976*	*(5) Percentage change*
Central and eastern valleys	61,300	62,000	1	71,450	96,560	35
West South Wales	67,200	67,800	1	77,880	88,120	14
South Wales coast	132,000	148,700	13	172,110	180,730	5
Northeast Wales	22,600	25,100	11	28,880	36,740	28
North Wales coast	23,500	23,700	1	26,480	30,500	15
Northwest Wales	33,000	35,800	9	41,470	43,560	5
Central Wales	14,600	14,000	−4	15,890	16,250	2
Southwest Wales	34,100	31,700	−7	36,740	45,380	22

Note: Owing to the use of different data bases by the two sources, two 1971 subregional estimates have been included; the figures in columns 4 and 5 are crude estimates.

Sources: Columns 1 and 2: Fothergill and Gudgin, 1979; columns 4 and 5: *Welsh Economic Trends*, 1979.

jobs during this period. This is a manifestation of the inward movements of non-Welsh-owned branch plants which extended into all parts of nonmetropolitan Wales. This involves a skill distribution factor with the higher-skilled jobs being located in the larger towns and cities of the South Wales enclave and lower-order assembly work in the declining coalfield and rural Wales. We should also note that many of the enclave branch plants are foreign-owned (Lovering, 1983a), while those outside of the enclave tend to be British-owned.

The decline registered for South Wales in Table 14.3 does not indicate decline in overall employment, as is evident from a scrutiny of Table 14.4. Changes in manufacturing employment are often contradicted by changes in service sector employment. While service sector employment stagnated during the 1960s, it grew rapidly during the 1970s. Substantial increases were registered in Northeast Wales, the metropolitan center of the South Wales enclave, and the rural adminstrative centers. Between 1974 and 1979 the two categories "financial, professional and miscellaneous services" and "public administration and defense" showed an increase of 14·3 percent in the number employed, compared with an increase of 8·8 percent for the overall British figures.

These figures obscure one important feature of the economic reorganization. Between 1951 and 1971 the male activity rate declined from 86·2 to 78·4 percent, while the female activity rate rose correspondingly from 24·95 to 35·56 percent. This

Table 14.5 *Male and Female Employment, Welsh counties, 1981*

County	Percentage female activity rate	Percentage women at work	Percentage men at work	Percentage married women at work (age 16–59)	Increase in percentage married women at work (1971–81)
South Glamorgan	59·3	54·8	74·6	55·9	10·4
Mid-Glamorgan	55·4	48·8	71·6	52·9	11·8
West Glamorgan	56·8	50·7	72·6	53·8	13·8
Gwent	56·2	50·3	73·3	53·3	11·1
Powys	53·8	49·8	81·8	50·4	8·5
Gwynedd	51·8	46·5	75·4	46·0	11·4

Source: 1981 Census returns.

process has continued during the 1970s, as Table 14.5 indicates. The considerable decline in the traditionally male-dominated primary and manufacturing employment has corresponded with an increase in the number of women employed in the growth areas of service and new manufacturing activities. This feminization of the laborforce is even more striking when we consider the overall employment structure in Wales (Table 14.6).

Women constitute a relatively unorganized laborforce which works for low wages. Furthermore, as much as one-quarter of the employed females are part-time workers. During the 1960s there was an increase of 45,000 in the number of jobs in Wales but a decline of 49,000 in the number of males employed. While the female employment rate was increasing at an annual rate of 1·5 percent, the male rate was declining at a rate of 0·8 percent annually. This trend has accelerated during the 1970s.

While capital formation in Wales has been well above the British average—£260 million a year between 1958 and 1964—this investment does not appear to have increased employment, although it has served to restructure the economy. This is partly because much of the money that was invested was destined for capital-intensive projects which did not integrate with any Welsh process of manufacturing. Humphreys (1972, p. 42) has suggested that the United Kingdom has gained more from this investment of capital than Wales itself. What is evident is that there has been a distinctive rundown of the traditional industries and a growth in manufacturing activity involving the establishment of branch plants of already

Table 14.6   *Welsh Employment Structure, 1977*

Employment category	Number employed (in 000s)	Percentage of work force	Percentage female
Professional/scientific services	167·3	16·7	71·0
Engineering and allied	109·0	11·0	26·4
Distributive trades	102·3	10·3	58·0
Miscellaneous services	101·3	10·2	61·0
Public administration	83·6	8·4	39·0
Metals	80·0	8·0	7·0
Construction	64·4	6·5	6·0
Transport and communications	57·6	5·8	15·0
Manufacturing, general	50·2	5·0	32·0
Mining and quarrying	41·0	4·1	3·7
Textiles and clothing	29·2	3·0	60·0
Insurance, banking, etc.	26·6	2·7	53·0
Agriculture, forestry, fishing	23·9	2·4	21·0
Chemicals and coal-petroleum	23·3	2·3	21·0
Gas, electricity, water	19·3	1·9	17·0
Food, drink, tobacco	18·5	1·9	42·0

Source: *Welsh Social Trends/Tueddiadau Cymdeithasol*, No. 5, 1982, p. 18.

established British and overseas enterprises. Indeed, it is highly likely that foreign firms now account for as much as 20 percent of manufacturing employment in Wales (cf. Davies and Thomas, 1976). The service sector has also grown substantially. In both of these developments there is an evident feminization of the laborforce.

Marginalization

I have sought to suggest that the changes in the structure of the economy in Wales as a consequence of state intervention have not been spatially uniform. Developments in the metropolitan center and the industrial enclave are quite distinct from those in the other areas of development. I shall return to the precise nature of these differences. For the moment I would like to consider how the concept of "development" tends to imply that changes in the economic structure are unidirectional, thereby ignoring the tendency for such changes to lead to the elimination of other economic features.

Much of the manufacturing and retail developments tend toward monopoly. The foreign companies of the enclave depend upon neither local resources nor local markets, while giving the host country a minimum of control over their activities. Their impact upon local companies is minimal. Perhaps the marginalization effect is most evident in the retail sector. It is here that we witness the purchase and amalgamation of competing enterprises within the locality, or alternatively the simple process of an economy of scale, enabling the branch enterprises to undercut the prices of any local competition. Such a process of marginalization is among the more evident features of "regional development."

A study of the multiplier-effect of such development in Anglesey (Sadler *et al.*, 1973) suggests other, less evident, features of the same process. The work introduced there demanded only low skill, with women earning only 40 percent of male wages. Much of the labor was part time. In contrast, the management and supervisory staff were well paid. By and large the firms were seeking secondary labor; as a consequence, they tended to use few local firms and marketed most of the production outside of Wales. Furthermore, these enterprises were vulnerable to trade conditions, being dependent on those consumer markets where competition was strongest. Perhaps the most interesting finding was that the increase in the income of the major beneficiaries of these developments, namely, the lower professional and managerial groups, could actually cause a reduction in the activity of the rest of the county (Lovering, 1983b).

In other locations marginalization derives from the inability of most of the population to participate in the new developments while also being made even more remote from the scarce infrastructural resources. This is not a matter of choice, as conservative discourse would imply, but is imposed by the planning of development. Often policy dictates that most of the benefits will cluster around growth poles, with a subsequent deprivation of benefits from other locations. Even rudimentary benefits become scarce and their absence is a manifestation of the progressive marginalization. Ownership of private transport becomes an essential job qualification, subsistence costs are higher than in the growth poles, and services taken for granted elsewhere are conspicuously absent. Local residents lucky enough to obtain employment at the growth poles tend to spend much of their earnings in the cheaper retail outlets at such centers. The resultant falloff in trade frequently results in the closure of local retail outfits, thereby complicating further the lives of the old and the unemployed.

A multivariate analysis of deprivation (Grant, n.d.) indicates some interesting patterns. Not only do some geographical areas show an unusually high incidence of indicators of deprivation, but more interestingly the deprived areas reveal a high incidence of Welsh-speakers and a low incidence of recent immigrants. These types of relationship are the very ones which have been ignored in the simplistic accounts of nationalism which derive from the correlation between voting behavior and language (Madgwick *et al.*, 1973; Balsom, 1982). Where the relationship has been noted, a form of culturalist explanation for deprivation is offered with the inevitable stigma of a Welsh "culture" (Grant, n.d.).

Within the marginalized sector the surviving enterprises are obliged to reduce production costs in order to remain competitive. Lovering (1983a) suggests that the marginalized sector can be divided into two components, the "competitive capitalist" component and the "marginalized laborforce" component. The former exists between the integrated monopolistic sector and the activities and services that are only part of the capitalistic orientation. It employs cheap labor to provide for the domestic market and to service the higher-income groups of the integrated sector; it thereby transfers value upward to those groups. The link between the two components constitutes the evident feature of the split labor market (Bonacich, 1972). The limits of job opportunities oblige the worker to accept lower-paying employment or to seek some form of employment, even if it be self-employment, outside of regular, integrated markets. Despite the plight of the marginalized proletariat, it is the "black labor" of this kind which is the source of substantial criticism from the Conservative and Liberal lobby. It is here that cheap labor is most evident, much of it being family or self-employed labor which works long hours for extremely limited returns.

A recent survey has indicated the extent and nature of the marginalized sector (Wenger, 1981). Within the survey area the manufacturing activities were limited and tended to employ part-time female labor at very low wages. Perhaps the most significant feature of the male laborforce was the high incidence of self-employment and multiple job holding. One-quarter of the active male population was self-employed, while a further 12 percent of all household heads were occupied in more than one capacity. Also significant was a very high incidence of mobility in both directions between the "skilled worker" (proletarian) and "self-employed" (petit-bourgeois) categories, with as many as 18 percent of the male laborforce being mobile from the former to the latter category and a further 16 percent in the opposite direction. This is yet another indication of the insecurity of self-employment within the marginalized sector. Yet there is a small bourgeoisie in such areas which earns extremely high wages and this further highlights the plight of the proletarian population.

It is this marginalized sector which has been particularly hard hit during the present recession. While the sheer scale of the multinational enterprises will usually guarantee their survival, as also is true of many of the British monopolistic enterprises, the scarcity of capital undermines small local enterprises during recession. This, of course, merely hastens monopolization. The few manufacturing establishments tend to be satellites of firms with their headquarters in England, and these branches are the first to close. This reluctant private sector, combined with the shrinking public sector, wreaks havoc in many areas. Much of the marginalized space has depended heavily upon the injection of state funds and its multiplier-effect. It has been estimated that this redistribution of income added 12 percent to the average income in Wales (Lovering, 1983a), and the slowing down of state aid to Wales has intensified the crisis created by the repercussions of state intervention in the private sector.

Changes in Class Configuration

Sociologists have tended to conceive of class in statewide dimensions, without any consideration of regional or subregional configuration and variations. Yet if there is an uneven feature to the development of capitalism, the local variation in class structure should be central to any class analysis.

A second problem which has plagued a Marxist analysis of class in contemporary capitalism is what to do with the public sector and also with those large areas of the private sector where "ownership" is at best a nebulous feature. The works of Wright (1980) and Poulentzas (1973) have helped resolve this dilemma. They both emphasize the role of political and ideological relations in resolving the seemingly contradictory class locations, class not being determined simply by reference to economic criteria. This allows them to distinguish between mental and manual labor on the one hand, and to emphasize the importance of supervisory and decision-making functions on the other.

The most evident feature of the new developments in Wales involves the bourgeoisie of the private sector. Tomkins and Lovering (1973) indicated that at the end of the 1960s, before the advent of the multinational companies and before the recent entry of many of the branch plants, only 39 percent of the industries employing more than twenty-four workers were Welsh-owned. There is every reason to believe that this situation has declined still further during the past decade. It is also true of many of the retail establishments which are branches of firms with their head office in England or overseas. Not only is the ownership external, but so also are most of the managerial personnel. The latter usually consist of "spiralists," that is, those whose careers consist of a combination of social and geographical mobility and whose period of residence in Wales is often limited. Such personnel are usually recruited outside of Wales. The skilled fraction of the proletariat is often introduced from the outside, since the main attraction of Wales for many of these firms is the existence of an unskilled, unorganized laborforce. It is also claimed that the English managerial group tends to give priority to English applicants for the more lucrative of the lower administrative and higher manual sections of their laborforce. The bulk of the proletariat consists of low-paid local employees, many of them being women who work part time.

Within the enclave there is less of a tendency for the administrative bourgeoisie to be non-Welsh, partly because of the dominance of the overseas establishments in this sector and the resultant tendency for local recruitment rather than already established career hierarchies. This local recruitment also applies to the lower part of the laborforce. Thus much of the laborforce is local and is paid higher wages than in the branch enterprises.

The bourgeoisie of the headquarter establishments located around the national capital of Cardiff also tends not to be Welsh, and the same pattern of career structure and external recruitment as holds for the branch factories applies to this sector of the economy. The same is true of the branch retail establishments, which are scattered throughout the industrial area and the towns of the nonindustrial areas. Once again much of the lower-level labor consists of local females.

Within the rural areas most of the agricultural establishments are too small to permit the employment of labor. The petits bourgeois who own and run these establishments tend to be the descendants of those who purchased their farms when the large estates broke up at the turn of the century (Williams, 1980). Two other developments stand out in such areas, tourism and the construction of power plants. In the former the larger enterprises tend to be owned by non-Welsh personnel, although this is not exclusively the case, while the smaller enterprises tend to be locally owned. Most of the labor in tourism tends to be seasonal and poorly paid, consisting of both local and transient labor. The construction projects tend to be of limited duration and draw upon labor mainly from outside of Wales, although again there are exceptions that derive from local pressure. After the completion of the construction, the supervisory personnel in the power plants are invariably drawn from outside of Wales.

Within the marginalized sector the undermining of the residual private sector establishments results in the process of proletarianization of the petite bourgeoisie. One suspects that a significant intergenerational mobility between this declining petite bourgeoisie and the public sector arrests this process, which none the less should not be ignored.

In the public sector, as should be evident from what has been said about the growth of the service sector in general, there is a much greater involvement of local labor at all levels. Here there is a need to distinguish between local and state-administered services, albeit local services are subject to state supervision in one form or another. A number of state agencies have been decentralized, most of them to the headquarters and enclave regions, although other areas are also influenced. While many of the personnel in this sector are non-Welsh, a large proportion at all levels tends to be local employees and a number of conspicuous occupations carry Welsh-language qualifications. This can serve to generate a restricted form of limited spiralism within a career structure which is specifically Welsh. The new bourgeoisie which has been created by such developments is particularly significant. This is particularly true of the mass media, which tend to be concentrated in the headquarter region, and of the higher education sector, which has a somewhat wider geographical distribution. Most of the personnel in lower-level employment within this sector tend to be local.

The "professionals" within the local administration do tend to show a diffused recruitment pattern, but again a significant number of jobs carry a Welsh-language qualification, especially in the fields of educational and social services, most notably in the marginalized locations. Again the lower-order employment tends to be recruited locally.

Nationalism

Unfortunately the limited studies of nationalist voting in Wales have related it either to spatial or to occupational class categories. As a consequence, their value for a Marxist interpretation is limited. However, it might be useful to consider this evidence briefly. The most obvious feature of the geographical distribution is the concentration of nationalist voting in what we have referred to as the marginalized areas—the rural areas away from the growth poles and the industrial enclaves, and the declining industrial areas. With few exceptions, support for nationalist candidates in the enclave and the headquarter region has been limited (see, for example, Balsom, 1979).

Since the data that would allow us to discuss voting behavior in Marxist class categories and the public/private sector distinction are not available, it might be more useful to try to analyze social conflicts over other issues that pertain to nationalism. The most important such issue involves the implicit conflict over the role of the state in economic policies. It is this, rather than more radical features of socialism, which distinguishes the two major British parliamentary parties in theory, although things may be quite different in practice. From our point of view the most important features of this conflict are the extent to which it fragments the class structure and how this fissure is related to factors of ethnicity.

The heterogeneity of the low-income groups in the marginalized sector, together with the false sense of economic opportunity associated with self-employment opportunity, generates a cohesion which cuts across class and militates against the development of a proletarian consciousness. It also serves to cloud the issue of what, or who, is responsible for their marginal status and relative deprivation. The relationships between the dominant classes and the marginalized groups are increasingly precarious, unstable, and fragmentary. For the marginals, the state despite the limitations of its service, remains the major source of survival. Still, many of them remain outside of the state's compensatory mechanisms, and many see also that the state, in its collusion with capitalism, is responsible for their marginal position. At the same time, they are stigmatized for seeking benefits. Their marginality is produced by the necessity for capitalist accumulation in the dominant economic sector; marginality provides an effective means of reducing demands on scarce capital while contributing to its accumulation.

The disarticulation of the economic positions and the social relations that are attached to them makes class action difficult. There is a contradiction between opposition to the capitalist class and the idea of progress and industrialization. The types of economic arrangement characteristic of marginalized economies tend to individualize the problem of making a living. This obscures the exploitation of the proletariat while emphasizing the limited economic opportunity for the enterprising individual.

The proletariat in the marginalized sector differs markedly from its counterpart in the enclave. The relation of each to the system of domination is quite distinct, and the opportunity for meaningful coping with deprivation also differs. This makes it clear that an understanding of deprivation cannot be divorced from an understanding of power in society. Much of the marginalized population remains outside of the trade unions. The unemployed are not integrated, neither is much of the labor in the rural areas, hence the advantage to the "new" industries. Among unionized workers, there are marked differences of advantage, awareness, and integration. Within the larger enterprises of the enclave, that is, those enterprises which operate for the British or international market, there appears a high level of class consciousness characterized by a high level of integration. Such enterprises often dominate the local source of proletarian labor, giving a coherence to the internal structure of the proletariat and its organization (Massey, 1980). The highly mechanized production process formalizes it and removes the producer from the direction and conception of production. Such enterprises are often able to undermine government attempts to control the cost of labor, thereby making the state appear either to be impotent or in a subversive collusion with capitalism. The instrumentalist orientation of the workers in the enclave sector results in their viewing the unions not so much as a unified representative of the collective proletariat, but rather as a means of putting pressure on the government and their employers to respond to the demands of their own small sector. The publishing of a wages "league" involving the various proletarian workgroups severely undermines the creation of a unified proletarian struggle.

Thus the trade union movement is fragmented into various

unions which correspond to broad occupational categories and which thereby find themselves in competition with one another rather than with the bourgeoisie. This form of competition serves the interest of those members of the proletariat who exist within the enclave but works against those in the lower-paid sectors, the unemployed, and the nonunionized. This fragmentation can extend to a geographical dimension, thereby further cleaving the proletariat. It can extend to a cooperation between the stronger trade unions and the government in power, so that while the members of such unions may benefit other members of the proletariat may suffer.

This politicization of the trade union movement involves a willingness to use political parties as a means of intervening in the state—proletariat struggle with the apparent intention of gaining benefits for the proletariat. However, parties such as the Labour Party which claim to represent the interests of the proletariat often find themselves tied to policies which are often forced upon them by their integration into the international capitalist system and which severely curtail their ability to operate on behalf of proletarian interests.

Thus the labor movement embodies a dualism, on the one hand claiming to defend the community, and on the other hand merely seeking advantage for that part of the proletariat which is materially already better off. Some of the demands which the stronger unions push on behalf of the more highly paid workers can suffice to liquidate some of the smaller firms of the marginalized sector, and thereby jeopardize the poorest workers' ability to earn a living. There is an inability to recognize that the community and the state are in mutual opposition. The workers are divided along lines which Touraine (n.d.) has referred to as "defensive" and "offensive."

The situation is complicated by the fact that the Labour Party, the very party which claims to represent the interests of the workers, fails to implement socialist policies, but rather encourages "foreign" capitalism to exploit local labor while simultaneously marginalizing a major part of the residual proletariat. For many, the Labour Party has long ceased to be a radical party in Wales, a party which represents the interests of the underdog. It has gained the image of a party which serves the interests of external capitalism and an unrepresentative trade unionism.

Under such conditions the adversary can only be defined as the capitalist system imported and directed by "foreigners," but the class which does this remains in the marginalized sector.

Thus it is difficult to make a class struggle involve the idea of "progress," since it opposes the means that claim to achieve such "progress." It leads to a fragmentation of classes with fractions opposing one another because of their different relationships to the system of domination. This is strengthened by the disparities between the workers in different industries, in different regions: disparities which derive from the different relationships with the sector that is linked to the flow of capital, and usually the support of the state. In such situations there will be a tendency to align along ethnic divisions in opposition to both the master and the "foreigner," who are usually one and the same, the emphasis being upon community defined by exploitation, or by an exclusion which demands collective action.

Here we are discussing the manner in which the status group consists of the community—a collectivity drawn together across class lines—which does not define itself simply by exploitation, but also by exclusion. Within the resultant discourse the community consists potentially of all those threatened with being left out of the integrated sector, those whose economic survival is threatened by the encroachment of the "new" developments. It also includes those faced with inadequate housing and without resources, because they are enclosed within a dependent society which is not in control of its own means of production and mode of development, and whose resources flow either toward the "foreigners" or toward those sectors which are dominated by them. This opposition is to a certain extent defined by a sense of exploitation on the part of the collectivity and by submission to a power which is in some way "foreign." Thus the conflict cannot simply be a class conflict within what they define as a national economy, but is equally the defense of the community against the external forces which serve to undermine it.

Given the disarticulation of class relationships, the classes constitute themselves as social agents only through their relationship to the state. If the state is actively associated with reinforcing the fragmentation of the proletariat, which is the inevitable consequence of the collusion between the state and capitalism in the regional development policies, a political opposition arises which naturally comes to struggle against the state in the name of the people rather than in the name of the proletariat. The state may well seek to disguise its intentions by operating through devolved bodies such as the Welsh Development Agency or the Development Board for Rural Wales, and may even allocate funds to counter the social consequences of its economic actions, but when the actual agents of "development" are evidently "foreign", the ploy is revealed.

This process is particularly evident when the dominant indigenous stratum is threatened by the externally based bourgeoisie of the enclave. Local identity is employed to create a local solidarity against the outside. The "spiralists" drawn from the English core define themselves and their actions not in terms of Wales, but of Britain, which for most is coterminous with England. They reject the idea of integration on any terms which might be regarded as "Welsh" and expect to be accepted on their own "British" terms. In this respect they are often supported by those members of the local bourgeoisie who are integrated into the "new" developments and who stand to benefit from them. The "alien" bourgeoisie expect to be integrated into the local political system on the basis of their status, but their inability and unwillingness to integrate culturally prevent them from mobilizing popular support. Consequently, they resort to the formation of various local pressure groups, whose issues and activities become a battleground between, on the one hand, the indigenous bourgeoisie and petite bourgeoisie who emphasize the concept of community and, on the other, the "alien" bourgeoisie who emphasize their opposition to the concept of local community (Williams and Roberts, 1982). This conflict develops into one of ideology between the nationalism of Wales and the British nationalism which the capitalist class, in collusion with the state, employs to mask and justify continued disparities in the geographic division of labor. It is based upon an awareness that ethnic groups are stratified within the general division of labor.

Inevitably this conflict comes to focus upon the very elements which sustain the local community. Where the institutions of the community serve to minimize risk, the idea of community serves as a basis for mobilization. Community and state are seen as mutually opposed, and a struggle ensues in which the state seeks to integrate risk minimization into the state's welfarism and into the associated official discourse of benevolence. It is within these same networks and institutions that the local petite bourgeoisie achieves leadership, a function which cuts across the local communities to the wider ethnic community, thereby generating a regional or national leadership. Integration into such community power discourses allows members of the proletariat to draw upon the patronage of the local or regional petite bourgeoisie and bourgeoisie as a basis for risk minimization and even social mobility.

The "new" nationalism is not in any way new, but is merely the reexpression of a continuing state of dependency. Rather than seeking a culturalist explanation involving primordial attachments, I have sought to identify economic processes that generate group formations with contradictory positions. In so doing I believe I have answered those criticisms of the internal colonialism thesis (Hechter, 1975) which point to an absence of internal diversity and an overly conspiratorial view of economy by stressing the manner in which class fragments are generated. Within this perspective culture becomes a symptom of the emerging opposition rather than its cause. The process is well expressed by Touraine:

> there is a reaction against dependence. Here it is not a class but a territorial collectivity, whether regional or national that is defending itself against an external domination. This dimension may separate itself off from others in order to give birth to a vague, very easily manipulated nationalism or populism, but it is necessarily present in a dependent social movement. It is fairly directly linked to the existence of "marginality" which is to say, the powerlessness of dependent society to bring a large section of the population into participation in economic growth. (Touraine, 1977, pp 427–8)

While I would object to the implication of nationalism as "false consciousness" in this statement, I concur with the claim that certain types of economic change generate a form of consciousness which associates with the emergence of minority group formations out of inchoate ethnic enclaves wherein a variety of factors change the pattern of integration between the minority and the larger society.

References: Chapter 14

Balsom, D. (1979), *The Nature and Distribution of Support for Plaid Cymru*, Studies in Public Policy No. 36 (Glasgow: University of Strathclyde Press).

Balsom, D. (1982), "The political consequences of the Welsh identity," in A. H. Richmond (ed.), *After the Referenda: The Future of Ethnic Nationalism in Britain and Canada* (Downsview: Institute of Behavioural Research, pp. 111–50.

Bonacich, E. (1972), "A theory of ethnic antagonism: the split labor market," *American Sociological Review*, vol. 37, no. 5, pp. 547–59.

Cooke, P. (1980), "Dependency development in UK regions with particular reference to Wales," *Progress in Planning*, vol. 15, no. 1, pp. 1–62.

Cooke, P. (1981), "Local class structure in Wales," *Papers in Planning Research*, no. 31.

Davies, G., and Thomas, I. (1976), *Overseas Investment in Wales: The Welcome Invasion* (Swansea: Christopher Davies).

Fothergill, S., and Gudgin, G. (1979), "Regional employment change: a sub-regional explanation," *Progress in Planning*, vol. 12, no. 3, pp. 155–219.

Grant, G. (n.d.), "A social atlas of Gwynedd," ms. Gwynedd County Council, Caernarfon.

Hechter, M. (1975), *Internal Colonialism: The Celtic Fringe in British National Development, 1536–1966* (London: Routledge & Kegan Paul; Berkeley and Los Angeles, Calif.: University of California Press).

Humphreys, G. (1972), *South Wales* (Newton Abbot: David & Charles).

Lovering, J. (1983a), "Uneven development in Wales: the changing role of the British state," in Glyn Williams (ed.), *Crisis of Economy and Ideology: Essays on Welsh Society, 1840–1980* (Bangor: BSA Sociology of Wales Study Group), pp. 48–72.

Lovering, J. (1983b), *Gwynedd: A County in Crisis*, Occasional Paper No. 2 (Harlech: Coleg Harlech).

Madgwick, P., Griffiths, N., and Walker, V. (1973), *The Politics of Rural Wales* (London: Hutchinson).

Massey, D. (1980), "Industrial restructuring as class restructuring: some examples of the implications of industrial change for class structure," Centre for Environmental Studies Working Note No. 604.

Poulentzas, N. (1973), "On social classes," *New Left Review*, no. 78, pp. 27–54.

Rawkins, P. (1978), "The global corporation, ethno-nationalism and the changing face of the European state," *World Affairs*, November.

Sadler, P., Archer, B., and Owen, C. (1973), *Regional Income Multipliers* (Cardiff: University of Wales Press).

Tomkins, C., and Lovering, J. (1973), *Location, Size, Ownership and Control Tables for Welsh Industry* (Cardiff: Cyngor Cymru).

Touraine, A. (1977), *The Self Production of Society* (Chicago: University of Chicago Press).

Touraine, A. (n.d.), "An Introduction to the Study of Social Classes in a Dependent Society," ms.

Wallerstein, I. (1974), *The Modern World-System. Vol. I, Capitalist Agriculture and the Origin of the European World-Economy in the Six-teenth Century* (New York: Academic Press).

Welsh Office (1979), *Welsh Economic Trends*, No. 6 (Cardiff: HMSO).

Wenger, G. C. (1981), *Rural Industrialization: Development and Deprivation* (Cardiff: University of Wales Press).

Williams, G. (1980), "Industrialization, inequality and deprivation in rural Wales," in G. Rees and T. Rees (eds.), *Poverty and Social Inequality in Wales* (London: Croom Helm), pp. 168–85.

Williams, G., and Roberts, C. (1982), "Language, education and reproduction in Wales," in B. Bain (ed.), *Sociogenesis of Language and Human Conduct* (New York: Plenum Press).

Williams, G. A. (1982), "Women workers in Wales," *Comment*, vol. 20, no. 6 (20 March), p. 10

Wright, E. O. (1980), "Class and occupation," *Theory and Society*, vol. 9, no. 2, pp. 177–214.

15

The Religious Factor in Contemporary Nationalist Movements
an Analysis of Quebec, Wales and Scotland

NEIL NEVITTE

Religion is rarely included in the cluster of variables significant for explaining nationalism, particularly nationalist movements in industrially advanced societies. This is an oversight. This chapter contends that "the religious factor," to borrow Gerhard Lenski's phrase, while certainly not the most important variable, has contributed to nationalism particularly during the early phases in the life-cycle of these movements. Furthermore, it will be suggested that religion continues to interact with contemporary nationalism in less direct but none the less significant ways. In an attempt to clarify some of the theoretical issues the first part of the chapter will consider some of the traditional ways in which the relationship between religion and nationalism is posed. The remainder will focus mainly on the relationship between religion and nationalism in the case of Quebec; the cases of Wales and Scotland will be considered briefly for comparative purposes.

The significance of the religious factor has been discounted partly because of the way in which the theoretical relationship between religion and nationalism has been posed. Carlton Hayes, an influential historian of nationalism and a representative exponent of the traditional view, contends that nationalism competes with and successfully displaces religion as a vital force in modern societies. Nationalism competes with religion, according to Hayes, because it is itself a religion (Hayes, 1960, chs. 12 and 13; see also Baron, 1947). The thesis is appealing because of its symmetry, economy, and seemingly benign conclusion, a conclusion hardly challenged at all. One reason why the conclusion is difficult to contend with is the fact that it represents the culmination of different kinds of argument. First, it is argued that nationalism is a religion because it has the same structure; for example, there are parallel systems of rituals. Nationalism, Hayes points out, has "liturgical forms of saluting the flag," "solemn feasts and fasts," and the national anthem "is the Te Deum of the new dispensation; nationalism has its processions, pilgrimages, holy days and temples" (ibid. pp. 155–66). The inherent limitation of this structural view is that there are no guidelines for discriminating *between* those phenomena that meet the structural minima of a set of events. In effect, no distinction is made between religion, a political ideology, or any cause to which groups may be committed.

A second thread of the traditional perspective offers a historical interpretation which links nationalism with the evolution and consolidation of modern, especially West European, states. The Reformation and the French Revolution are regarded as critical historical junctures because they mark the state's advance in eclipsing the church as the mainspring of political authority; the state progressively displaced the church by placing an overriding claim on the allegiance of its citizens. Of course, the Reformation and the French Revolution were critical junctures for the emergence of the modern state. But this interpretation gives a limited perspective. It confines the relationship between religion and nationalism to the institutional struggle between church and state and encourages a state-centric interpretation of nationalism, where nationalism is viewed merely as the ideology of the state.[1]

A third argument in support of the traditional view stresses the functional equivalence of nationalism and religion. Nationalism, so the argument goes, has been able to displace and become a substitute for religion, because "it serves men's religious sense." Hayes writes: "As the masses grow cold about the historic Christian faith and practice, they have tended, rather, to accept other and more attractive substitutes" (ibid. p. 15). The Industrial Revolution is regarded as instrumental to such a transformation by encouraging "indifference to Christianity." The result?—"A kind of religious void," and Hayes explains, "any such void is unnatural and an urge arises to fill the void with a new faith" (ibid. p. 15). That faith is nationalism. The assertion that nationalism is anathema to religion seems to be underwritten by the questionable assumption that man's "religious sense" is a sort of fixed quantum. But the broader and more important proposition, to the effect that secularization is the engine of nationalism, requires a more careful consideration.

Discussions about secularization and the place of religion in modern society, particularly the effects of modernization on religious change, inevitably call up serious conceptual issues which continue to be thrashed out in the sociological literature (Douglas, 1982). It has been argued, for example, that the term secularization is loaded with so many meanings that it should be dropped altogether (Martin, 1965; Shiner, 1970). This is not the place to rehearse that complex debate except to make the observation that, by the mid-1960s, the dominant secular paradigm of the 1950s, which held that modernization undermined religion in several ways, was being called into question. The disagreement was not over whether modernization and the differentiation of institutional authority had disengaged religious institutions from the public sphere. Traditional church religion kept its religious functions but it was pushed to the periphery of modern life. What was problematic was the place of religious *values* in modern society. Evidence of the resurgence of religious values, even while religious institutions languished, suggested (contrary to the predictions of the secular paradigm) that religion was not disappearing—rather it was relocating and reappearing in diffuse forms (Marty, 1982).

The secular paradigm was influential with other social scientists who looked to factors other than religion, notably class, to explain political phenomena, such as participation in advanced industrial societies. But this focus has been adjusted too. Rose and Urwin, for example, in their analysis of survey data for seventeen Western countries, concluded that "religious divisions, not class, are the main social bases of parties in the Western world today" (Rose and Urwin, 1969, p. 12). In short, there is considerable evidence indicating that the religious factor, albeit in a more attenuated form, is present in advanced industrial societies and that it continues to be relevant in explaining contemporary political phenomena. Precisely how it relates to contemporary nationalism remains to be explored.

One objection to the traditional way of formulating the relationship between religion and nationalism was that it reduced the problem to a matter of church–state conflict and encouraged thereby a state-centric view of nationalism. As pointed out elsewhere (for example, Nielsson, in this volume), the boundaries of the nation and the state do not necessarily coincide, notwithstanding the expectation that the forces of modernization would erode national differences within states, and nationalist politics has proven to be remarkably resilient even with the most technologically sophisticated states.

Comparative Historical Considerations

The primary interest here is in those cases where nations reside within states. Cases where religion has influenced nationalism but where the nations have their own states, for example, Ireland or some East European countries, will not be considered. A brief survey of the historical background of Quebec, Wales, and Scotland is instructive because it suggests, contrary to the traditional interpretation, that religion has been instrumental in ensuring the continuity of the national cultures from which contemporary nationalist movements draw.

For the purposes of discussion it is useful to trace the relationship between religion and nationalism in Quebec in three stages: the first deals with the role of the Roman Catholic Church during the period of settlement until the end of the French regime, until 1759; the second encompasses the period of British conquest, until 1867; and the third continues until the "Quiet Revolution" of the 1960s (for a general history, see Wade, 1968, chs. 1–3).

It is a well-documented fact that the Roman Catholic Church was a crucial actor in the settlement of New France. It preceded and acted on behalf of the state and commercial interests in the colonization process. In fact the terms of settlement of New France explicitly gave the church monopoly over migration with the result that the colony developed into a community which was religiously and linguistically more homogeneous than France itself. During the consolidation of the French regime the church became increasingly entrenched as the vital social, political, and economic, as well as spiritual agency. It ran the schools, hospitals, provided welfare functions, and performed quasi-legal services. In short, the church was the central agent of social and political organization with the parish acting as basic community focus. In so far as the church had an extensive and coherent administrative structure, one frequently used by the formal agents of the state, there is good reason to view the church as the major integrating force behind French-Canadian society.

The impact of the British conquest was to consolidate and

augment rather than challenge the place of the Roman Catholic Church. There were several reasons for this. First of all, military defeat meant that the French colonial apparatus was dismantled and many of the major commercial interests discontinued their operations. In other words, the withdrawal of the governmental and economic leaders left the church as the only remaining organization linking French-Canadians. Given its historic role in settlement, the scale of involvement, and the departure of competing elites, it is not surprising that the church emerged as the undisputed leader and spokesman for the interests of the nation. The interests of the church and the interests of the nation were, in effect, fused and were consolidated by the church's ability to project the whole nation's missionary purpose in North America, a continent hostile to Catholicism (Brunet, 1973).

The style of British colonial administration was a second factor augmenting the position of the church within Quebec. Britain was interested in an efficient administrative system which would not place excessively heavy demands on British administrative personnel. Colonial experience elsewhere taught that it was more effective to co-opt and utilize indigenous authority structures rather than trying to dismantle and impose alien systems of authority on colonized people. This policy was followed notwithstanding the fact that Britain had yet to give Roman Catholicism any official status. Since in practical terms the church provided the only set of indigenous elites, British toleration toward Roman Catholicism in Quebec was almost certainly due to overriding pragmatic concerns (Moir, 1967). Because the church was the elite structure capable of effectively governing French-Canadians, it was in a strong position to bargain for and extract extensive guarantees which in turn enhanced its own position. The church's bargaining power was further enhanced by the strategic significance of French-Canadian neutrality to Britain's ability to defend its North American interests. The position of the church changed from time to time. Essentially it can be traced in the evolving set of agreements between French and English Canada. Starting with the Articles of Capitulation of 1759, it continued through the Treaty of Paris, 1763, the Quebec Act, 1774, the Constitutional Act, 1791, the Act of Union, 1840, and culminated in the British North America Act, 1867. The important point is that in negotiating with the British colonial elite the church successfully entrenched its interests through the guaranteed protection of religious rights. Given the role of the church in French-

Canadian society, and given the fact that the church had established itself as the spokesman for the French-Canadian nation, the guaranteed religious rights operated as surrogates for national rights.

As long as the church's position remained unchallenged, arguably until the 1960s, the institutional church continued as the leader of the national cause. One of the ironies in the evolution of the church's position was that the Durham Report, which informed the Act of Union, 1840, simultaneously proposed the assimilation of French-Canadians, "for their own good" as Durham put it, as well as the need to maintain the place of the church in French Canada. That the church, from the British point of view, was important for "resisting the arts of the disaffected," and that it was also instrumental for maintaining French-Canadian identity (Craig, 1963, pp. 141–71), helps to explain why traditional Quebec nationalism tended not to be inclined toward separatism or independentism. The extent to which traditional nationalism has disappeared in contemporary Quebec is open to conjecture, but most scholars agree that traditional nationalism held sway at least until the 1960s.

The positive contribution of religion to nationalism is not unique to Quebec. A very brief survey of some other examples is sufficient to make the point and to provide material to suggest, in broad outline, some of the comparative implications.

Religion in Wales, though organized in a much less hierarchical fashion than in Quebec, has played an important role in maintaining the Welsh national culture. The continuity of the Welsh language, for example, has been explained partly as a result of the fact that the Bible was translated into Welsh in the sixteenth century (Jones, 1973). The Acts of Union of 1536 and 1542 threatened Welsh culture not only by imposing English law and administration, but also by prohibiting the use of Welsh in legal and official matters. The Methodist break with the Established Church in the early nineteenth century led to the development of uniquely Welsh forms of Nonconformism. To a certain extent the major religious division corresponded to a significant class division. Historically the Anglican Church in Wales is linked with the landowning interests, the anglicized middle classes and support for the Conservative Party, whereas the Nonconformist denominations are made up of the Welsh lower-middle classes in rural and industrial Wales (for a class/colonial perspective, see Nairn, 1977).

With the attacks on Welsh religion and education in the

famous Blue Books episode of 1847, church leaders and other Nonconformists became spokesmen for the forces which wanted to counteract anglicization. It was this same group that, in the late nineteenth and early twentieth centuries, advanced nationalist claims principally for separate legislative consideration. They championed the establishment of national institutions such as the University of Wales; supported the Welsh-language press; were leading figures in the Welsh literary renaissance; and consistently pushed for the use of Welsh in schools. Religious issues such as denominational education, the payment of tithes to the Established Church, and the temperance and church endowments took on the mantle of national issues. It is not surprising then, that disestablishment eventually realized in 1920, became a national cause (Morgan, 1970; Jenkins, 1975; Butt-Philip, 1975).

Disestablishment did not signal the end of the link between religion and nationalism in Wales. In fact Nonconformist church leaders were instrumental in the reorientation of the movement in the interwar period. They were active in the formation of the Welsh nationalist party in 1925, the first president of which was a minister. One study of 540 churches in the Swansea area reports that approximately 40 percent of the chapel leaders were involved in Plaid Cymru. The party platform at the time expressed concern with the future of Christianity, the Welsh language, and identity (Butt-Philip, 1975, p. 15). Of course, not all Nonconformists were equally enthusiastic in their support for the movement, but the Independents, Baptists, and Congregationalists all regarded their involvement as an extension of the idea of religious and civil liberty. Some saw the future of the churches as inextricably linked with the future of Welsh civilization as a whole (loc. cit.)

It is true that chapels are no longer the meeting place of society and that nonreligious elites play a larger role in a Welsh nationalism that has taken on less of a traditional character. But from the language crisis precipitated by union to disestablishment—to the formation of Plaid Cymru—to its support for cultural pressure groups such as the League of Youth and the Welsh Language Society, as well as high levels of activism in the Plaid today, the record attests to the continuity of the religious factor in Welsh nationalism.

The case of Scotland provides more evidence suggesting a close connection between religion and national identity. As Jack Brand points out, the Church of Scotland "has certainly been one institution if not *the* primary institution which has expressed the Scottishness of Scottish society" (Brand, 1978, p. 130). The link between religion and nationalism in Scotland can be traced at least as far back as the seventeenth century. The Reformation in Scotland produced a Scottish nationalism which, as in Quebec, advanced in the belief that Scotland was uniquely a covenanted nation (Reid, 1973, p. 22). The Church of Scotland has a history of speaking for the nation; the General Assembly regards itself as an authentic voice for Scottish interests. In fact in the seventeenth century the assembly of the church did perform parliamentary functions when the Scottish Parliament did not meet. The Union of Scotland and England, in 1707, in one sense enhanced the position of the church in that the rights of the church were entrenched. As Christopher Hill argues, the Act not only had the immediate economic effect of expanding the free trade area, it also gave Presbyterians access to Parliament and guaranteed the existence of Presbyterian universities.[2]

As in the cases of Quebec and Wales, the church has a record of resisting the forces of anglicization. The kirk, like the parish and the chapel, provided the cornerstone of community life and was the chief conduit for projecting national and religious values. The church provided leadership in and active support for a myriad of national cultural institutions ranging from national universities and literary societies to rights organizations (Hanham, 1969, ch. 2). It continues to take an active interest in the political, economic, and social life of the nation as is evident in the proceedings of the Church and Nation Committee. And since World War II that committee, along with the General Assembly of the church, has continued to lobby for increased legislative independence for Scotland.[3]

The historical summary of the relationship between religion and nationalism in Quebec, Wales and Scotland is intended as illustrative rather than exhaustive. The findings, in my view, challenge the traditional way of formulating the relationship. These and other cases (including, for example, the Basques, Catalans, and Irish) suggest that religion can and does contribute to nationalism. Obviously Quebec, Wales, and Scotland are very different in important respects and so any comparative judgments must be guarded. Nevertheless, it is possible to speculate about the general conditions under which the religious factor is likely to contribute to nationalism, namely:

(1)   where the national minority is distinguished by religion from the dominant culture of the state;

(2)   where the national church (one or more institutions) has the institutional capacity to speak for the nation;
(3)   where religious values are a significant part of the national culture in question.

It is hardly surprising to find church involvement in nationalism when the roots are traced as far back as the sixteenth and seventeenth centuries. After all, religion and politics are hardly distinguishable in traditional societies and infrastructure of the state was hardly developed, remote, and unpopular. Under these circumstances national churches were one of the few institutions with the capacity and the reach to speak for the nation. Similarly, the circumstances were favorable for the clergy to emerge as national elites not only because of their relatively high literacy rate, but also because the national churches offered the opportunity to achieve upward mobility within the nation. In other words, participation in the dominant culture of the state was not a prerequisite for upward mobility as was the case in other sectors.

The fact that national churches took it upon themselves to act as agents of the nation in agreements with the state could have, plausibly, at least two consequences. First, it may make the nation, as a unit to the bargain, more politically self-conscious; and secondly, it may cement the church's identification with the national cause. However, in the case of Quebec in particular, and possibly also in the Scottish instance, it is clear that church leaders did not adopt an independentist orientation. In the case of Quebec the church's strategic position at the nexus of the arrangements linking the dominant culture of the state to the national minority was turned to its own advantage. In fact the state (represented by the British colonial administrators) and the church developed an interdependent relationship. The church hierarchy persuaded the British not only to entrench religious rights, but also to extend tithing and other privileges, privileges which were resented by the flock. The position of the church *within* the national society was dependent on the *external* link with the state as much as its *internal* support from the national community. On the other hand, colonial administration could only be effective and serve colonial interests if the indigenous national elites were capable of "delivering" the French-Canadian population.

In the final analysis the ability of churches to act as national institutions depends on their ability to mobilize the national community. There is little question that the churches of

Quebec, Wales, and Scotland have become progressively disengaged from the public sphere and correspondingly their role as national leaders has diminished. However, notwithstanding the unrevised secularization paradigm, and contrary to the expectations of Hayes and others, there is scattered evidence pointing to the fact that religious institutions and values are still a relevant part of contemporary nationalism. In Wales, for example, where church attendance rates are significantly higher than in England, the Nonconformist churches continue to speak out on national issues such as bilingual education, Welsh broadcasting, Home Rule, and the use of Welsh as an official language. Butt-Philips's analysis of Plaid Cymru activists, although ten years old, shows that support for the national party is much higher among non-Anglican denominations. Moreover 7 percent of the financial contributions to the party come from ministers, although they account for less than one-tenth of 1 percent of the population (Butt-Philip, 1975, appendix B). In Scotland it is reported that church attendance rates are three times greater than those in England, indicating the comparative significance of religious values to Scottish political culture. There too the Church of Scotland continues to identify itself with a range of national issues (Harvie, 1977). More systematic data are available in the case of Quebec and this allows for a more detailed exploration of the relationships between religious values, national identity, and Quebec nationalism.

Nationalism and Religion in Contemporary Quebec

Nationalism is one of the constants of Quebec political life. Differences between the Quebecois and their political parties arise over *how* the interests of the national community can best be protected in what appears to be a culturally hostile environment. The traditional answer was that the Quebecois should work for greater political autonomy within the Canadian federal system; it was an approach encouraged by the Roman Catholic Church.

Most scholars point to the early 1960s as a dramatic turning-point in Quebec. The transformation was peaceful but fundamental, none the less. The "Quiet Revolution" was signaled by the surprise defeat of the Union Nationale, a defeat which gave the reformist Liberal Party its opportunity to initiate a far-reaching set of institutional changes. The state took over and expanded important activities, in the areas of education, health, and social welfare, which had historically belonged to the church. The Quiet Revolution was widely regarded as Quebec's transition from an old order to a new one. In effect, new aclerical elites argued that the grip of the church was responsible for Quebec's social, economic, political, and cultural retardation (Trudeau, 1958, p. 300). Thus for the transition to be effective enough to allow Quebec to take its place in the modern world, the church's hold on public life would have to be challenged and dismantled.

There is little question that the institutional changes were sweeping. The role of the state expanded as dramatically as the church's contracted. The educational reforms deconfessionalized postsecondary education for the first time in Quebec history; educational opportunities broadened and educational curricula were tuned to the demands of a technologically sophisticated society. At the same time, the church became increasingly disconnected from interest groups in society, interest in the priesthood declined, as did attendance rates for mass. It is not surprising, then, that most observers interpreted the institutional changes as the reflection of a more basic shift in the values of the Quebec population (Dion, 1967; Rioux, 1969; Dumont, 1971). Religious values, it appeared, had been replaced by secular values. The emergence of the Parti Québécois in the late 1960s and its electoral victory of 1976 seemed to confirm the passing of traditional values and with them the traditional solution for the problem of protecting Quebec's cultural, economic, and social position. It was assumed that there would be a new solution—independentism, but that has yet to be realized.

In a sense, the lineage of the Quiet Revolution hypothesis can be traced to the secularization paradigm of the 1950s. In fact the hypothesis has been so widely embraced that attention has been deflected from serious consideration of the religious factor in contemporary Quebec politics. The following discussion is based on survey data designed to explore the religious factor in Quebec; they were collected through mail questionnaires in November 1976.[4]

Space does not permit detailed analysis of the findings of the 1976 study. Instead the focus will be on answering three questions which follow from the theoretical and historical discussion above:

(1) To what extent is Quebec a religious culture?

(2)   Is there a relationship between religion and national identity?

(3)   What is the nature of the relationship between religion and nationalism in Quebec?

Francophone Quebecois are almost exclusively Roman Catholic for historical reasons, and so any analysis of the religious factor has to aim at distinguishing between Quebecois along other dimensions. Table 15.1 presents two dimensions of religion: what might be called personal religiosity—private religious beliefs; and cultural religiosity—the extent to which religious values are a part of the French-Canadian communal identity. Quebecois who are personally religious may or may not subscribe to the view that religion should take on anything but private dimension. Implicit in the definition of a secular society is the idea that religious values are privately held. The critical issue, then, is to what extent do Quebecois link religious values to the collectivity.

Table 15.1 indicates that even though there is a high association between both measures of religion ($\gamma = 0 \cdot 7$), 19 percent of those who are personally very religious attach little or no importance to religion for the French-Canadian culture, and 45 percent of those for whom religion is personally important attach little or no importance to religion for the collective culture. Only 57 percent of those who are personally most religious are also culturally most religious. A more significant finding is shown in the marginal distributions of the table. Only 29 percent of the respondents view religion as unimportant to French-Canadian culture, whereas nearly one-half of the sample report that religion is very important or important to the culture.

On the basis of these data it is difficult to argue that Quebec is a secular culture. A more detailed analysis of these data reveals that younger Quebecois, those under 35 years of age, are both personally and culturally more secular than other cohorts. Furthermore, the data indicate a strong relationship between education and a secular view of French-Canadian culture. Probing these data suggests the conclusion that the educational reforms of the 1960s were instrumental in producing a distinctly defined cohort which holds Quiet Revolution values; these secular orientations are not evident in the most highly educated strata of other cohorts. Although longitudinal data are necessary to confirm this view, the data indicate a more limited application of the Quiet Revolution hypothesis.

Table 15.1 *Options of the Quebecois on the Personal and Cultural*
Importance of Religion

Personal importance of religion	Importance of religion to French-Canadian culture (%)				
	Very important	Important	Less important	Not important	Totals
Very important	57·3	23·9	9·8	9·0	100% = 255 (32·0)
Important	16·8	38·1	29·7	15·5	100% = 155 (19·4)
A little important	8·5	25·8	42·3	23·5	100% = 213 (26·7)
Not important	0·6	5·7	17·2	76·4	100% = 174 (21·8)
Totals	24·0	23·2	24·0	28·9	100% = 797 (100·0)

Note: Personal religiosity is measured with the question: "Quelle importance attachez-vous à vos croyances religieuses?" Cultural religiosity is measured with the question: "Certaines personnes pensent qu'il est important que la religion occupe une place importante dans la culture canadienne-française. Partagez-vous cette opinion?"
Source: Survey conducted by Nevitte and Gingras, November 1976.

Table 15.2 presents the relationship between nation-state identification and cultural religiosity. The data show that the least culturally religious Quebecois are more likely to regard themselves as Quebecois only, or Quebecois first, while the most culturally religious tend to give equal or more attachment to their Canadian identity. However, it is noteworthy that most of the culturally religious do not identify primarily with the state; slightly more than one-half of this group identify themselves equally as Quebecois and Canadian. Simultaneous identification with the Canadian state and the Quebec nation is a characteristic of traditional nationalism. It is the culturally secular who tend to identify exclusively with the Quebec nation.

Given the tendency of culturally religious Quebecois to identify with the state as well as the nation, it would be unlikely that religious national identifiers would express their national claims as independentists. This expectation finds support in Table 15.3 which indicates more than one-half of those who have an entirely secular orientation toward French-Canadian culture, those of the Quiet Revolution cohort, prefer the modern political solution: independentism. Fully 70·3 percent of the culturally religious are anti-independentists. While the culturally secular Quebecois dominate the ranks of the independentists, only 16·2 percent of Quebec national identifiers opposed

Table 15.2   (*a*) *Opinions of the Quebecois on the Cultural Import-ance of Religion, Grouped by their State-Nation Identification* (*b*) *State–Nation Identification of the Quebecois according to their Cultural Religiosity*

State nation identification	Importance of Religion to French–Canadian culture				
	Very important	Important	Less important	Not important	Totals
(*a*)					
Quebecois only	10·4	10·4	23·9	55·2	100% = 134
Quebecois first	16·6	28·3	27·5	27·5	100% = 247
Equally Quebecois and Canadian	33·9	24·7	20·8	20·5	100% = 283
Canadian first*	29·5	25·0	23·5	22·0	100% = 132
Totals	23·9	23·5	23·9	28·8	100% = 796
(*b*)					
Quebecois only	7·4	7·5	16·8	32·3	16·8
Quebecois first	21·6	37·4	35·8	29·7	31·0
Equally Quebecois and Canadian	50·5	37·4	31·1	25·3	35·6
Canadian first*	20·5	17·4	16·3	12·7	16·6
Totals	190	187	190	229	796

* Includes also Canadian only.

Note: State-nation identification was measured with the following question: "Vous considérez-vous comme étant: Québécois seulement; Québécois d'abord, Canadian ensuite, également Québécois et Canadien; Canadien d'abord, Québécois ensuite; Canadien seulement?"

Source: As Table 15.1.

Table 15.3   *Attitudes of the Quebecois toward Separation According to Their Cultural Religiosity*

Attitude toward separation	Very important	Important	Less important	Not important	Totals
Independentist	20·8	31·7	38·2	50·2	36·0
Undecided	8·9	7·5	15·2	16·6	12·3
Antiindependentist	70·3	60·8	46·6	33·2	51·8
Totals: 100% =	192	186	190	229	798

Source: As Table 15.1

to separation are culturally secular. Cultural religiosity, according to these data, interacts with nationalism to depress the inclination that nationalists will favor the independentist option.

These findings indicate the coexistence of both traditional and modern orientations to Quebec nationalism. They suggest that the values linked with the Quiet Revolution have not percolated throughout Quebec society, and that despite the retreat of religious institutions in Quebec, religious values continue to impinge on contemporary Quebec nationalism in significant ways. The broader implication is that the traditional way of evaluating the relationship between religion and nationalism should be reevaluated and that the religious factor should be considered in the analysis of contemporary nationalist movements.

Notes: Chapter 15

1 The limitation of this perspective is discussed more fully in the Tiryakian and Nevitte essay in this volume (Chapter 3).
2 The move in some nationalist quarters however, was regarded as a sellout of national interests: see Hill, 1961, p. 293.
3 As Brand points out, the record of the church on the matter of complete independence for Scotland is somewhat equivocal; nevertheless, it was critical of the Kilbrandon Report for not suggesting greater devolution: see Brand, 1978, pp. 132–7.
4 The data are derived from a 106-item questionnaire mailed to a regionally stratified sample of 2900 Quebecois. The return rate, a little under 30 percent, yielded about 900 usable cases. The sample analyzed here is slightly smaller, because non-Roman Catholics and non-Francophone respondents have been omitted from the analysis. Further details of the methodology may be obtained from the author.

References: Chapter 15

Baron, S. W. (1947), *Modern Nationalism and Religion* (New York: Harper).
Brand, Jack (1978), *The National Movement in Scotland* (London: Routledge & Kegan Paul).
Brunet, M. (1973), "Historical background on Quebec's challenge to Canadian unity," in D. Thomson (ed.), *Quebec Society and Politics* (Toronto: McClelland & Stewart).
Butt-Philip, A. (1975), *The Welsh Question: Nationalism and Politics 1945–1970* (Cardiff: University of Wales Press).
Craig, G. (ed.) (1963), *Lord Durham's Report* (Toronto: McClelland & Stewart).
Dion, L. (1967), *Le Bill 60 et la société québécoise* (Montreal: HMH).
Douglas, Mary (1982), "The effects of modernization on religious change," *Daedalus*, vol. 111, no. 1 (Winter) pp. 1–19.
Dumont, F. (1971), *The Vigil of Quebec* (Toronto: University of Toronto Press).

Hanham, H. J., (1969), *Scottish Nationalism* (Cambridge, Mass.: Harvard University Press).

Harvie, C. (1977), *Scotland and Nationalism* (London: Allen & Unwin).

Hayes, C. J. (1960), *Nationalism: A Religion* (New York: The Macmillan Co.).

Hill, C. (1961), *The Century of Revolution, 1603–1714* (New York: Norton).

Jenkins, D. (1975), *The British: Their Identity and Their Religion* (London: SCM).

Jones, R. T. (1973), "The Welsh language and religion," in Meic Stephens (ed.), *The Welsh Language Today* (Llandysul: Gomer Press), pp. 64–91.

Martin, D. (1965), "Towards eliminating the concept of secularization," in J. Gould (ed.), *Penguin Survey of the Social Sciences* (Harmondsworth, and Baltimore, Md.: Penguin Books), pp. 169–82.

Marty, M. (1982), "Religion in America," *Daedalus*, vol. 111, no. 1 (Winter), pp. 149–63.

Meisel, J. (1973), *Working Papers in Canadian Politics* (Montreal: McGill-Queen's University Press).

Moir, J. S. (1967), *Church and State in Canada 1627–1876* (Toronto: McClelland & Stewart).

Morgan, K. O. (1970), *Wales in British Politics, 1868–1922*, 2nd ed. (Cardiff: University of Wales Press).

Nairn, T. (1977), *The Break-Up of Britain* (Thetford: New Left Books).

Reid, W. S. (1973), "The nationalism of the Scottish Reformation," *Scottish Tradition*, vol. 3, no. 1, pp. 22–31.

Rioux, M. (1969), *La Question du Québec* (Paris: Seghes).

Rose, R., and Urwin, D. (1969) "Social cohesion, political parties and strains in regimes," *Comparative Political Studies*, vol. 2, no. 1, pp. 7–68.

Shiner, L. (1970), "Meanings of secularization," in J. Childress and D. B. Harned (eds.), *Secularization and the Protestant Prospect* (Philadelphia, Pa.: Westminster Press).

Smith, A. D. (1971), *Theories of Nationalism* (New York: Harper & Row).

Trudeau, P. E. (1958), "Some obstacles to democracy in Quebec," *Canadian Journal of Economic and Political Science*, vol. 24 (August), pp. 297–311.

Wade, M. (1968), *The French Canadians 1760–1867* (Toronto: Macmillan of Canada).

16

Ethnic Cleavages, Labor Aristocracy and Nationalism in Quebec

JACQUES DOFNY

To live in Quebec also means submitting to national oppression that the Canadian "grande bourgeoisie," through the federal State, exercises over the people of Quebec. By imposing its language, its culture and its policies of development, the Canadian bourgeoisie exercises a range of discrimination that affects the Québécois on an economic level as much as on a cultural and political level. Unemployment, poverty, inequality, are some of the many forms of national oppression that afflict the working and popular classes in their daily lives. ("Manifeste du mouvement pour un Québec socialiste, indépendant, démocratique et pour l'égalité entre les hommes et les femmes", 1982, p. 117)

The Black Rock memorial stone in the traditionally Anglo working-class district of Pointe Saint-Charles in Montreal, honoring 6,000 immigrants who died of typhoid fever in 1847.
And they fought the landlords, the bosses, the politicians, the rich millionaires, gangsters posing as gentry on the mountain and then too, the French *habitants* [starved off] their land and moved into Anglo Montreal neighborhoods, taking away Anglo jobs, lowering the wages and level of misery, forcing the Anglo workers into a fatal, unspoken agreement with the Westmount ruling class that in exchange for acting as sort of unofficial garrison troops, the Anglo would receive preferential treatment in the British-owned companies, just like the Protestant Orangemen in Northern Ireland. ("Black Rock Manifesto", Quebec, 1982, p. 139.)

Since the early efforts to build unions or a left political movement in Quebec debate has revolved around three positions: those who claim that there is a single working class in Canada, including Quebec; those who consider a Quebec working class different from the working class of the other Canadian provinces; and those who place the Anglo-Canadian workers living in Quebec in one or the other working class. This is not purely a theoretical debate, as it commands political orientation and options. It is also a question of individual and collective identity. Anglo-Canadians have a greater facility to define themselves as Canadians, while French-Canadians have several options: French in America or French-Canadians or Quebecois. Native French-Canadians are at least Quebecois to most Canadians. They don't travel very often in other provinces; they prefer "the States" on the other side of their southern border. Their professional and social mobility takes place within the Quebec territory, while the Anglo-Canadians of Quebec are not always born in Quebec and easily move themselves professionally and socially throughout the entire Canadian labor market.

If national feelings are therefore different, is class consciousness the same, or different? Is there, or has there always been, a single working class in the past, or two different working classes by ethnic origin, by culture, and by tradition? Was there rather a single working class stratified by ethnic origin and by national affiliation? Finally, was it the same for the natives and the immigrants, or was there rather what Marx and Engels called an "aristocracy of labor"?

In answer to these questions this chapter will, first, examine the influence of the colonial situation of Quebec during the early phase of industrialization upon the structure, the leadership, and the orientations of labour. Secondly, it will discuss the thesis of the aristocracy of labor in the light of a situation where class and ethnicity are mixed.

The Ethnic Structure of the Quebec Working Class

Ethnic Composition of the Population

Compared to the American melting-pot with a single dominant group, Canadian society was built upon two founding nations, one of them imposing its political rule on the other. After the conquest of 1760, Quebec became a colony and was reunited with the actual province of Ontario in 1840 to form a single colony of the British Empire, and finally, melted into the Canadian Confederation in 1867, under the sovereignty of the Queen of England. Since the conquest Quebec society has taken the form of a double social structure: the French-Canadian society and the English society. The two do not mix very often as they are separated by two strong boundaries: religion and language. The two groups played different roles in the process of industrialization. The French-Canadian society, under the leadership, guidance, and social and cultural domination of the Catholic hierarchy and its obedient preindustrial bourgeoisie, in its large majority, stood aside from this process, but gradually provided its laborforce in both agriculture and industry. The English-speaking population controlling the political power, welcomed British investments and immigration. A majority of the entrepreneurs came from England and Scotland as specialized workers and farmers, while from Ireland came a poor and rural population (Connaughts); unemployed Irish workers came also from the United States, and joined their brothers in public works (Corkonians). These two Irish groups entered spectacular conflicts (1847) such as in the canalization of the St. Lawrence River at Lachine and Beauharnois. At this point Irish (mostly Catholic), Scotch and English (mostly Protestant), and Catholic, French-Canadian workers established the basis of the Quebec working class (Table 16.1).

This laborforce was composed of four ethnic origins, and comprised two or three languages; and two religions formed the Quebec proletariat of the early phase of industrialization, that is, waterways and railroad workers, lumberjacks, and longshoremen in the Quebec and Montreal harbors. In Montreal from 1825 to 1844 the immigrants of British origin comprised the majority of the English-speaking group (Table 16.2).

During the second half of the nineteenth century Montreal was the center of the industrial development not only of Quebec, but of Canada as well. In the first half of that second

Table 16.1 *Population of Quebec by Ethnic Origin in 1871*

French	British	Others
929,817 (78·0%)	243,041 (20·4%)	18,658 (1·6%)

Note: The "British" population itself was divided in 1871 into different groups (as percentage of the total population); English, 5·9; Scotch, 4·2; and Irish, 10·4.
Source: Linteau *et al.*, 1979; *Annuaire du Québec.*

Table 16.2 Population Distribution in Montreal (Percentages)

		1844	1901
French-Canadians		42·9	56·3
British		54·9	37·3
English-Canadians	20·0		
Immigrants	34·9		
English	(7·1)		(13·8)
Irish	(21·7)		(15·8)
Scotch	(6·1)		(7·7)
Americans		1·6	
Others		0·5	

Source: Linteau, 1982.

part of the nineteenth century the majority of the working class according to Linteau *et al.*(1979) were English-speaking. In the second half the slowing down of immigration and the acceleration of the internal migration to Montreal of the rural French-Canadians gave a numerical majority to the French-speaking workers (loc. cit.). At the same time, the industry spread in the eastern townships (Sherbrooke), Trois-Rivières, and Quebec, and was distributed among various sectors (Table 16.3).

The Quebec working class is, therefore, made up of two main groups of origin: the French and the British Canadians.

Table 16.3 *Value (in $) of the Manufactured Production, Quebec (1901)*

Food	33,099,000
Tobacco	8,231,000
Rubber	39,000
Leather	20,325,000
Textile	12,352,000
Clothing	16,542,000
Wood	16,340,000
Pulp and paper	6,461,000
Iron and steel	12,842,000
Printing, editing	3,510,000
Transportation equipment	8,058,000
Nonferrous metal	1,497,000
Electrical apparatus	1,815,000
Iron metal minerals	1,630,000
Oil and coal	245,000
Chemical products	4,138,000
Various	1,342,000
	153,574,000

Source: Hamelin and Roby, 1971.

Although this second group is itself divided between English, Welsh, Scotch, and Irish, this subdivision, according to the history or geography, is insufficient in itself. Indeed, if the "French" are homogenized by their religious ideology, practice, and socialization, the same cannot be said for the "English." They are separated between Scotch or Irish Catholics and English and Scotch Protestants. Moreover, English and Scotch can be separated by their national affiliation. This working class is, therefore, fragmented by historic and geographic origin, religion, language, and culture. It is still more fragmented by class relationships. The industrial bourgeoisie is mainly British; that is, English or Scotch. It occupies the sector of large manufacturers, mills, and the technologically advanced sectors, steel particularly, the indispensable basis of the leading industry of the second half of the nineteenth century: railway construction and equipment.

In their competition on the labor market these different groups of workers will play with all of these social characteristics. So the Irish coming from Ireland will fight the Irish coming from the United States (1843—Lachine Canal) or the Irish will fight the French-Canadians (1879 dockers' strike in Montreal). These battles are fights taking place at the bottom of the internal hierarchy of the working class. But there is also the process of upward mobility where the same national affiliation, culture, and language play a role. If the boss is English, Protestant, and speaks the English language, there is a chance that he promotes as foreman, or as a leader of a group of workers, someone who belongs to the same ethnic group, has a similar religious belief, and speaks the same language. This process of upward mobility has given rise in the United States, for a long period, to the major difference between white and black workers. Contemporary sociological researchers have pointed out the fact that foremen and union delegates often present the same psychological and ideological traits. We could add one hypothesis: this situation could help certain French-Canadian workers to become active union members more easily than foremen. If this is valid, we should also find a greater proportion of Irish workers among active unionists. Conditions of social mobility differ between different ethnic groups.

Unfortunately we do not dispose of valid statistics on occupations and professions according to ethnic affiliation. Until more general, available statistics can be constructed, it is only by rare monographic documents or by inference that we can approach this phenomenon. Still, certain elements of the global structure are firm enough to permit a first discussion of the problem. We will concentrate on Montreal, the industrial center of Quebec.

Blue-Collar Workers in Montreal

The blue-collar workers in Montreal worked in three main sectors: the manufacturers, employing many artisans; the new industries linked to steel production (here we find larger proportions of English-speaking workers); and the large mechanized factories: the shoe and cotton industries mainly, with mixed ethnicities.

In order to look at the ethnic composition of the working class we refer, first, to the social inquiry made by an industrialist at the turn of the century (Ames, 1972). H. B. Ames, himself owner of one of the largest shoe factories, investigated west-end Montreal, an area of 38,000 inhabitants mainly composed of craftsmen, factory workers, clerks in a great variety of production: wholesale establishments, a shoe factory, a shirt factory, a cigar factory, a candy factory, a wallpaper factory, a machineshop, a foundry, electrical works, a box factory, a tobacco factory, flour mills, metalworking, ironworks, asphalt, sugar refinery, rolling mills, silk mills, light and power, woollen mills, lumber, sewing machines, and so on.

In this survey we find the only systematic ethnic distribution of a fraction of the working class in Montreal: 7670 families among which 42 percent are French-Canadian, 34 percent are Irish, 21 percent are British, and 3 percent others. These families according to their religious affiliation are: Catholic, 75 percent; Protestant, 23 percent. The three main groups are distributed on the territory: first, in an area where the French-Canadians are in a majority, another where the Irish are in a majority, and a third with a mixed population of the three ethnic groups. In the mixed area we find 26 percent well-to-do, but 12 percent only where the French-Canadians are in a majority, and 9 percent only in the Irish area.

If we consider the formation of the Montreal population, we could put forward the following hypothesis. French-Canadians are the oldest occupants of the city, and at the beginning of the nineteenth century they provided a large majority of the craftsmen, but by mid-century 57 percent of these craftsmen were English-speaking (Ouellet, 1972). The Irish came as a proletariat with no links either with the French population along with its large kinship network, and its petite bourgeoisie, nor with the dominant group of English industrialists. If the sample that constituted the survey by Ames was representative of the whole working class of Montreal, the Irish would have been for this period at the bottom of the class and ethnic stratification.

But the working class of Montreal was not limited to this area, the oldest industrial area of the city. According to Terry Copp (1974), the section surveyed by Ames had a population density of 35–47 persons per acre (according to the city's figures). The wards to the east were much more densely populated; the greatest part of the French-Canadian working class lived there. Typical of this was Sainte-Marie, with a population of 43,000 in 1900. It had the worst sanitary conditions and the highest infant mortality. Montreal was the most dangerous city to be born in, according to Copp; between 1899 and 1901, 26·76 percent of all newborn children died before they were 1 year old (double the figure of that for New York City). In the eastern part of Montreal the large shoe and cotton fabrics plants employed a low-skilled manpower. In contrast, the steel works and railway works in the western part, and later in the extreme east of the city, employed more skilled workers who were, in a very large majority, English-speaking. One dimension can be added to this sketch. In the best description of the Montreal working class of this period De Bonville (1975) gives an estimate of the importation of 1500 immigrant workers per year from 1881 to 1891. The immigration statistics show that those immigrants were mostly of British origin. Considering the British origin of most of the manufacturers and the inexperience of the French-Canadians in the new industries, there is little doubt that many of these immigrants were specialized workers.

This image of a population of workers of British and of French-Canadian origin (coming from the farms of the province) is also found in Linteau's (1982) article on cosmopolitan Montreal. At the time when trade unions reached their momentum, at the end of the century, there was an important British working class. Of the total Montreal population, those of "British origin" represented 37·3 percent, of which 13·8 percent were "English", 7·7 percent were Scotch, and 15·8 percent were Irish. They were distributed unevenly in the different wards of the city. Sainte-Anne, the oldest industrial ward, was British at 70 percent, of which nearly one-half were Irish. Saint-Antoine in its southern part presents the same characteristics, when the English-speaking bourgeoisie (English, Scotch, Irish, and Welsh) built its "terrace houses" in the upper part of the area. But the image is the opposite when one goes to the three eastern wards: Saint-Louis, Saint-Jacques, Sainte-Marie. Here we find the largest concentration of the French-Canadian working class, but we also find "British" workers in the same three areas: $22 \cdot 1$, $9 \cdot 6$, and $17 \cdot 5$ percent respectively; among them, English and Irish are in equal strength. The British are still a majority in the St. Lawrence section, where we find a larger group of "other immigrants": poor Jewish immigrants from Russia, and Germans, Poles, and Italians. In all, however, these 12,844 "others" do not represent more than $6 \cdot 1$ percent of the city population. It is worth mentioning here that the "British" population was constantly declining from 1875 (45 percent) to 1901 ($33 \cdot 7$ percent) to 1971 (17 percent), while the "others" increased and the "French-Canadians" remained constant. This does not mean that different groups in the same area mixed socially with one another. We know for certain that the English bourgeoisie would not have lived in Sainte-Marie, nor probably would the English petite bourgeoisie, but certain numbers of the French petite bourgeoisie may have. Or if Saint-Louis was inhabited by 22 percent British, these British might have been bourgeoisie or petite bourgeoisie mixed with the French petite bourgeoisie. Still, the moves in the urban succession might have changed considerably in the course of half a century. Moreover, two sides of a street might have little contact if they did not belong to the same ethnic or religious group. This is most likely due to the fact that the Montreal elite and the Catholic Church, in particular, have chosen a tight institutional partition following ethnic and religious barriers: parishes, schools, colleges, welfare agencies, and cultural and national associations. As another indication of cleavage, until recently, French and British children had street fights in mixed areas.

There was at the basis of these particular partitions a dominant fact: the property of the means of production. If one reads the list of the manufacturers, one sees British names in a very large majority. This is not to say that there are no French names, but rather that there are very few. Harvey's important book (1978), an analysis based on the documents of a Royal Commission on Labour in 1889, concludes the section on Quebec as a global society with this analysis: "The upper bourgeoisie is mainly anglophone. It controls the economic power. The petite bourgeoisie, dominated by the francophones, exercises the political and judiciary power." But Montreal itself during the second half of the nineteenth century was ruled by a group of elite Anglophone businessmen and Francophone professionals (Rutherford, 1972).

The same economic structure had effects on the distribution of the workers in the plant hierarchy. Following the information given by the same Royal Commission on Labour, Harvey still concludes:

> The difference between nationalities constitutes also a discrimination at the employment level. We have previously stated that management positions were mostly occupied by the English or Scotch. Cheap labor was recruited among French Canadian and Irish. In the employment process specifically, this silent discrimination operates through preference given to the anglophones in the attribution of the best paid jobs when the French Canadians are looked at for their docility and their modest wage requirements. Among all the railway workers the Commission heard, none was of French origin. We may consider this industrial sector as a fief for the "British" and the English "Canadians". (Harvey, 1978, p.206).

It could be added to this that this "non-melting-pot" structure of the Canadian and Quebec economy was perpetuated by the immigrants, as the example of the ladies' garment industry showed thirty years later, in this recollection of a union organizer: "I remember there in '37 when we started organizing in January, the girls (I was especially working with the girls) because they had no defense, and at that time most of them were French-speaking, who were the operators, and the Jewish girls, some of them were operators, but most of them were finishers, drapers and examiners" (Roback, 1978).

We now advance the hypothesis of a union leadership assumed by English-speaking workers, and keeping the working class in its majority out of the French nationalist stream. Further, if a British "aristocracy of labor" had existed, it certainly was between 1880 and 1914. The salient feature of the labor aristocracies, according to Marx and Lenin, is: (1) their highly skilled training, and (2) the building of craft unions and their rejection of the nonskilled workers. The question, therefore, is: was there a labor aristocracy and was it British, French, or both?

Skilled and Unskilled Workers

First, we must recall that the working-class population in Montreal according to Blanchard and to De Bonville (1975), *grosso modo*, was 30,000 in 1880, 50,000 in 1900, and 80,000 in 1914. The proportion of "British" in the total population of Montreal in 1901 was 37·3 percent as against 56·3 percent of "French" and 6·1 percent "others." We can estimate the British workers between 15,000 and 20,000. We, then, follow the summary of the successive occupational role as described by Reynolds:

(1) The initial development of machine industry in Montreal coincided with a heavy immigration of Irish peasants to the city. The result was a concentration of this group in factory and dock labor lasting at least until 1880.

(2) After 1880 the position of the Britishers in the unskilled labor field was severely challenged, first, by the French-Canadians, and later by the continental European immigrants. The British immigrant of this period, if he had even a smattering of technical skill, could be readily absorbed into the growing "heavy industries," which stood in great need of skilled workmen. A significant segregation of British in skilled occupations developed accordingly, and was at its height in the decade preceding World War I.

(3) The tendency in the postwar period (1918) was for the British immigrant to be almost entirely displaced from general labor and partially displaced from skilled labor. At the same time, the great expansion of white-collar and service occupations afforded a new field of employment for the displaced Britisher or, to speak with strict accuracy, for his children. It would appear that this was to be the most prominent field of segregation for persons of British origin during the next decade or two. Not only were those British skilled workers, but according to Reynolds, "The management, moreover, was usually on their side and smoothed the path for them as much as possible; concentration of British immigrants in the skilled trades became an accepted feature of Montreal's industrial life" (Reynolds, 1935, p. 94).

In charge of these skilled workers were the foremen:

> The proportion of British superintendents and foremen in these establishments (the large steel and mechanical electric, chemical plants as well as insurance companies) is considerably above the average and most of the remaining foremen are English Canadian. (ibid., p. 95)

If it happened that a French Canadian foreman was placed in charge, British workers would quit. (ibid. p. 97)

The relative position of the different ethnic groups in the hierarchy of the working class is shown by well-known social indicators. If we look at six wards (already quoted as typical of the ethnic groups), we find a striking difference (Table 16.4).

In the same manner, if we consider the infant mortality rate (under 5 years) for the period 1876–97, the rate (1/1000) is as follows: French-Canadian, 60·4; Irish, 39·4; and British, 40·9.

Table 16.4 *Population per Acre, 1896*

British majority		French majority	
Sainte-Anne:	71·7	Saint-Louis:	177·7
Saint-Antoine:	87·1	Saint-Jacques:	234·9
Saint-Laurent:	72·9	Sainte-Marie:	229·4

Source: Bernier, 1973.

The Building of Unions

This partition among the workers persisted at the union level. When Knights of Labor came from the United States, via Ontario, they promoted the unionization and the politicization of the working class. Their major obstacle, however, was their condemnation by Rome in 1884, instigated by the Archbishop of Quebec, Cardinal Taschereau. None the less, the Knights of Labor by 1885 had 750 members in Montreal; by July of 1887 they had 2252 members. In the meantime (March 1887) Rome lifted the condemnation in response to an appeal introduced by the American Archbishop of Baltimore. But if the religious obstacle was lifted, the ethnic one still held. In order to coordinate the assemblies established in the Montreal area a special local assembly was constituted, namely, District 114. French-Canadians asked for a separate local assembly. Their demand was at first rejected, they had to be content with a translation in French of the Constitution and the documents of the Order. It was only in 1889 that the French-Canadians obtained their own local assembly: there was, instead of District 114, Local Assembly No.1 (Anglophone) and No. 2 (Francophone).

This example shows, first, how important the position of the church was for those Catholic workers; secondly, how the British workers were the initiators of the movement; and thirdly, how the French working-class majority had difficulty in working with the British workers, as they needed their own union local assembly to feel at home. (Needless to say, this type of relationship between the two groups has been going on up to the present time. The novel *Two Solitudes* describes the relationship between the French and English in Montreal, where each occupies a different level in the social structure.)

We have little information at the present time concerning the proportion of workers of both origins in the unions. But we know that unions of the new industry in most instances came from the United States or Ontario. British workers accompanied British technology and American workers came when the American capitalists replaced their British counterpart. French-Canadians, for a long time, were present mainly in the old industries, that is, textiles, lumber, mining and small branches of the manufacturing sectors. Reviewing the 1930 period, Reynolds points out a common membership in the separate "locals." When the membership of the local was common, English tended to become the language of discussion, if the English-speaking members constituted anything approaching one-half of the total. He writes: "Britishers appear to form a larger proportion of the union officials and executives than they do of the general membership, partly because of their background of union experience in Britain" (Reynolds, 1935, p. 106). It is important to note that there was practically no influence from the unions of France. There is one trace of a French worker's delegation sent by the French government (1904). According to a witness, Alfred Charpentier (1973), later president of the Catholic union, their anticlericalism and their class-strength outlook were not well accepted. Most of the time it was American or British unionists who visited Canadian unions. This was particularly the case when the elimination of the Knights of Labor by the American Federation of Labor (AFL) took place. The Knights of Labor was more of a class

Table 16.5 *Unions in Quebec, 1901–21*

	International (i.e. AFL)	Independent national	Catholics
1901	74	62	—
1905	155	81	—
1916	236	70	23
1921	334	38	120

Source: Rouillard, 1981.

movement, whereas the AFL was typically a movement led by and restricted to skilled workers. This type of unionism, therefore, accelerated the ascendancy of the British workers and their predominance over the French workers even if, by force of number, French-Canadian workers were present and in the majority in many instances (particularly in the Montreal and Quebec Council of Trades). These British workers were also the Quebec delegates to the national (Canadian) federations for the most part. Between 1901 and 1921 the progression of the AFL was striking (Table 16.5).

The Catholic Church Influence

The Catholic Church of Quebec resented the presence of the international unions as non-Catholic and foreign. Since its fight against the Knights of Labor, it had supported the creation of local independent unions. The Confédération des Travailleurs Catholiques du Canada was founded in 1921 with 26,000 members. The ideology of this new confederation was deeply impregnated with the social teaching of Rome. The originality of this type of unionism was its capacity to control the rural population, as the parishes of the Catholic Church were everywhere. It was the Catholic union, therefore, which unionized the province, while the AFL had its fortresses in the Montreal area.

The branches and locals of the AFL followed capitalist development, while the Catholic unions took hold in the country. Given that the French-Canadian Catholics were present throughout the province, it was obvious that the national feelings be present in its rank-and-file. But it took a long time before they supported a claim for independence. Indeed, the Catholic Church in Quebec considered itself as the main depository of the papal authority in Canada. It attributed to the Catholic unions a Canadian mission with the dream of becoming the majority in Canada one day. The church, therefore, and its unions, kept away from an excessive French-Canadian nationalist claim. In fact the Catholic unions never succeeded in extending their influence outside of Quebec and it was only after the laïcization of their unions (in 1960 they changed their name and became La Confédération des Syndicats Nationaux, CSN) that the nationalist trend began its move into this confederation. Indeed, it was only after the birth of the independentist Parti Québécois, and particularly at the referendum on independence, that the CSN declared itself in favor of this option (1979).

For what is discussed here, let us remind ourselves that it will take decades for the Catholic unions to fall numerically in the same range as their competitors from the American and Canadian unions.

The Aristocracy of Labor: Theory and Ethnic Partitions

In a social structure subdivided into classes and ethnic groups class characteristics are combined with the ethnic characteristics, introducing class relationships into ethnic relationships and vice versa, either at the level of the whole structure or in each of the substructures. This proposition places the theory of labor aristocracy in a perspective different from the ones of Marx or Lenin.

The Theory of Labor Aristrocracy

In 1890 Engels wrote: "In England, the unions have been in existence for half a century and the large majority of the workers are not in the unions which constitute an aristocratic minority" (Engels, 1972). In *The Condition of the Working Class in England* (1845) he had stated the same situation already, but it appears that in the early years of the First International (1864) Engels and Marx thought that this situation was evolving and they firmly believed that the English working class was to be the leader of the international socialist revolution. Then came the period when they lost this confidence in the English workers and the argument of the labor aristocracy reappears as quoted above.

Lenin was going to strengthen the argument in his polemics with social democrats. He wrote in 1912:

> The principal historical cause of the specific supremacy and of the strength (provisional) of the bourgeois working class politic in England and in the United States, is its fairly old political liberty and the conditions, extraordinarily favorable in comparison with other countries, of the development of capitalism in length and width. For these reasons, an aristocracy broke off from the working class to come close to the bourgeoisie betraying its class. (Lenin, 1970)

This argument arises repeatedly in Lenin's articles, comments, and debates, but it has been diffused mostly in his book *Imperialism: The Final Stage of Capitalism* (1916–17). Here he indicates that in England economic and political imperialism divides the workers. Quoting a letter of Engels to Marx (1858), he speaks of a "bourgeoisie proletariat":

> The European proletarian party finds itself in a position where it is not their labor, but the labor of the practically enslaved natives in the colonies that maintains the whole of society. The British bourgeoisie, for example, derives more profit from the many millions of the population of India and other colonies than from the British workers. In certain countries, this provides the material and economic basis for infecting the proletariat with colonial chauvinism. (Nicolaus, 1970, p.93)

From this analysis of the consequences of imperialism, he assaults the British trade unions and the Labour Party, as he will attack most of the unions in Europe, not to speak of the American AFL, "bread and butter" politics and their *de facto* alliance with the bourgeois regime.

The difficulty with the concept of "labor aristocracy" is its polemical aspects. To combine the working-class concept with aristocracy and their different historical references is paradoxical. But the fact of a minority of skilled workers trying to control the labor market is a well-known historical phenomenon, with various degrees of importance, reality, and success. (Needless to add, the Leninist concept of "vanguard of the proletariat" appeals to a very proximate type of stratum in the working class).

But the question of the so-called "labor aristocracy" was, and still is, reinforced by the presence of foreign manpower (de Maupeou-Abboud, 1978). This factor has been enhanced recently by the presence in most West European countries of southern Italian, Turkish, Portuguese, Yugoslav, and North African workers. A referendum has taken place in Switzerland on the limitation of stay for foreign workers. The violence in France and Britain, and the right to participate in municipal elections in Sweden, are all events which underline the presence of a proletariat on a second or third level, with the less-paid positions, the most routinized jobs, the highest rate of unemployment, and the least union protection. (This factor appears to differentiate sociology in Europe and the United States. While the former analyzes the social structure of a society in terms of classes, the latter, for a long time at least, has used the ethnic origin groupings to differentiate the active population so much so that the "class" analysis tended to conceal the ethnic differentiation in Europe, while ethnic emphasis tended to conceal or even to deny class differentiation in the United States).

However, this was not a new phenomenon. To return to Marx, while it is obvious that the "national question" was not the core of his theory—quite the contrary—he was aware of some problem of this kind, namely, the "Irish question". Certainly Engels who lived in Manchester when the Irish population was numerous among the working people—and also lived for a while with an Irish working woman and her sister—introduced the national question to early Marxism.

In a document from the Council of the First International Marx and Engels, talking about the domination of Ireland, say: "It is a preliminary condition to the emancipation of the English working class, to the actual forced union (i.e., the serfdom of Ireland) in a free and equal confederation, if possible, in a separation, if necessary."

In the minutes of the General Council of the International (14 May 1872) an intervention by Engels is related. He raised the problem of the affiliation of the Irish sections in England with the British federal council. This decision of the British council, Engels claimed, would never be accepted by the Irish section: "[This decision] would reinforce the widely spread opinion among the English workers, according to which, they are superior beings, in comparison with the Irish, and represent a kind of aristocracy, as the white people in the American Slave States compare themselves with the Blacks" (Marx and Engels, 1972, p.78).

It took a long time before the "national question" was raised at the theoretical level among the Marxists. Indeed, the successors of Marx and Engels who raised the question were mostly the Austro-Marxists: Bauer, Adler, Renner, and Strasser. They could not avoid the claims of so many ethnic groups belonging to the Austrian Empire. Lenin took the same position when commenting on the separation of Norway from Sweden and the support in this matter of the Swedish working class for the Norwegian working class.

Ethnicity and Nationalism

In view of what we have said about the formation of the Quebec working class we can reconsider the theory of labor aristocracy, and the link between this theory and the national question.

(1) First, the labor aristocracy theory. It should be remembered that this theory has two facets. First, it says, and this is the first Marx–Engels approach, that the craftsmen control the unions and keep the unskilled away. Secondly, and this was the later position of Marx–Engels and the strongly polemical position of Lenin, that at the imperialist stage the working class of the imperialist country has a *de facto* alliance with the capitalists exploiting the colonized populations and particularly their working class. Boukharine (1971) softened the argument and talked of a relative, temporary alliance.

From what we know of the Quebec working class it is fairly obvious that Britishers constituted the skilled and most prosperous workers in a large sector of the industry. It is also obvious that they were the dominant group in the unions, not only in the industrial metropolis but also in the Confederation of the Canadian Unions. This was typical of the period 1880–1921.

Although further research by historians of labor will bring more precise information concerning the domination by British workers in the "aristocracy" layer of the working class, there is already little room for doubt regarding this hypothesis.

(2) The presence of the American Union is not a Quebec phenomenon. In 1968, among the unions affiliated with the Canadian Labor Congress, ninety-four were branches of American Unions, and twenty-two were national (that is, Canadian) unions. In Quebec the sections of these federations have a liaison bureau: the Fédération des Travailleurs du Québec (FTQ). The comparison with the nineteenth-century Irish–English relationship is still valid. The section of these "international" unions grouped in Quebec in a bureau are in constant tension with the Canadian Congress and they steadily claim more autonomy, often in the sense of a "special status". It took time before French was admitted as a second language in the Congress.

It is as if in Quebec the two lines of the Marx–Engels analyses, the aristocracy of labor and the Irish union section in England, rejoined, first, at the economic level, and secondly, at the organizational level. But in reality the two theories were already joined in the British working class of the nineteenth century. If it is true that the Irish workers were under the direction of an English aristocracy of labor, they were part of it at a secondary degree or level because they too benefited from the exploitation of the working classes of the British colonies. The same could be said of the Quebec working class, their partially belonging to the American Federation of Labor and their participation in American capitalism.

In the case of the Quebec working class another distinction should be made. After the condemnation of the Knights of Labor by the Catholic Church, the church in 1921 established its own unions (Maheu, 1969; Rouillard, 1981), the Catholic Union of Canada, that might have been more properly called the Catholic Unions of Quebec as their extension in the rest of Canada was always nonexistent. It was viewed by the church as part of its mission to convert the separated Protestants to Catholicism. It was also part of the competition with the Irish hierarchy—and later with the Italians—of the Catholic Church in the rest of Canada. The Catholic hierarchy of Quebec wanted the supremacy in the Canadian hierarchy, as well as the delegation to Vatican Councils. The Confederation of Catholic Unions changed its name to Confédération des Syndicats Nationaux in 1959. This was part of the general laïcization and modernization movement of the 1960s.

Conclusion

The quotations of the two manifestos introducing this chapter express the claim of two groups. The first one speaks in the name of a Quebec working class, in which the overwhelming majority is French-Canadian. The second speaks in the name of the "Anglo working class" which has been, since the early industrialization period, the leading group representing up to 40 percent of the Quebec working class and representing today only a tiny minority without real power in the union organizations.

This is one explanation for the fact that the French-Canadian working class did not launch a political action of its own at an earlier period. During the industrial era no political action of any working class without the backing of its unions ever succeeded. If the Quebec unions had been led by the "Anglo" workers, this would in all likelihood not have led to a working-class type of union, but rather to the AFL type of segregation between skilled and unskilled workers on the labor market.

As the economic growth needed and attracted more and more French-Canadian workers they in turn became the leaders of unions. Why did they not go into political action until the late 1970s? The answer involves numerous variables.

First, the influence of the Catholic doctrine on the vast majority of this working class. According to these teachings, the church had to exercise control over the unions. Catholic unions were consequently set up, where priests had a veto right (up to 1943), and where the doctrine was one of cooperation between workers and owners. The church also opposed any political party of the working class, as it denied any structural class differentiation in the society. At the same time, it was the constant position of these Catholic unions to be opposed to French-Canadian political nationalism. It is only recently that they came to favor political action and a more independent Quebec.

The second factor has to do with the international unions. If, in the early decades of this century, the latter favored the building of a working-class party, they soon became apolitical, in the "Gomperian" tradition. There were repeated efforts to build such a party in certain sections of the unions, but in general it was not their purpose. As for the national question, these unions tended to consider that it was a claim of the French-Canadian bourgeoisie, or part of it. They played a minor part in the American union structure and in the first Canadian unions. For them too, it took a long time to create a liaison among the various "locals" in order to have a public voice in the economic and political affairs of Quebec. But they succeeded, finally, up to the point of giving their support to the first party in power claiming the independence of Quebec.

As for the teachers, their enormous increase in a public system of education permitted them to shift from a corporation to a union. They were the first to become sensitive to the nationalist claim, since a major aspect of this claim was the protection of the French language and culture.

Today, for the first time, the three unions are very close to political action and have taken the solution of the national question as one of their main objectives. To reach this point it was necessary for them to raise the level of both types of consciousness: ethnic and social.

This illustrates how a working-class movement in a

semicolonial situation may be obstructed by a conjunction of otherwise opposite interests.

Long ago Werner Sombart (1976) asked: "Why doesn't socialism exist in America?" We might ask: why isn't there any working-class party in Quebec? Why is it that such a proletarian population did not succeed when, in the rest of Canada, the unions have backed a party and placed it successfully in the political arena?

The answer could lie in the tacit alliance between two groups. On the one hand, an ideological hegemony in the dominated group: the social teaching of the Catholic Church and the attainment of its religious goal in the whole of Canada; on the other hand, dominating politically and economically, the British ruling class.

In a parallel manner it was in the interest of the skilled British workers in Quebec to have a tacit alliance with the same dominant group, at the political level. Their control of the unions prevented the upsurge of a French-Canadian working-class party.

The industrialization of Quebec, the slow but constant numerical decline of the British population, the urbanization, and the laïcization and modernization initiated the changing pattern. In the meantime the expansion of the French middle class modified the role and political function of the traditional working class. The middle class supported increasing state interventions in social and economic affairs, concomitant with the supremacy of the multinational corporations. The middle-class intervention and the multinational corporations' strategy, both at the economic and labor relations levels, push the unions toward claiming control over the state and, therefore, the political field to safeguard their corporatist interests as well as to bring about another society.

References: Chapter 16

Ames, H. B. (1972), *The City below the Hill* (Toronto: University of Toronto Press); first published, 1897.

Bernier, J. (1973), Statistics from "Rapports annuels du Bureau d'Hygiène de la Ville de Montréal," in J. Hamelin (ed.), *Les Travailleurs québécois 1851–1896* (Montreal: Les Presses de l'Université du Québec), ch. 1.

"Black Rock Manifesto" (1982), *Canadian Journal of Political and Social Theory* (Quebec), vol. 6, no. 1–2, pp. 109–38.

Blanchard, Raoul (1960), *Le Canada Français* (Paris: Arthème Fayard).

Boily, R. (1980), *Les Irlandais et le Canal de Lachine*, Annuaire du Québec (Montreal: Editions Leméac).

Boukharine, N. (1971), *L'Economie mondiale et l'impérialisme* (Paris: Anthropos); first published in Moscow, 1917.

Charpentier, A. (1973), "Le mouvement politique ouvrier de Montréal 1839–1929", in F. Harvey (ed.), *Aspects historiques du mouvement ouvrier au Québec* (Montreal: Boréal Express).

Copp, T. (1974), *The Anatomy of Poverty: The Condition of the Working Class in Montreal 1897–1929* (Toronto: McClelland & Stewart).

De Bonville, J. (1975), *Jean Baptiste Gagne Petit, les travailleurs Montréalais à la fin du XIXè siècle* (Montreal: L'Aurore).

DeLottinville, P. (1981–2), "Joe Beef, of Montreal: working class culture and the taverns", *Le Travailleur* (Memorial University of Newfoundland), vol. 8–9, pp. 9–40.

Engels, F. (1972), *Arbeiter Zeitung* (May 1890), in *K. Marx and F. Engels: Le Syndicalisme* (Paris: Maspéro), Vol. 1, p. 195.

Hamelin, J., and Roby, Y. (1971), *Histoire économique du Québec, 1851–1896* (Montreal: Fides).

Harvey, F. (1978), *Révolution industrielle et travailleurs* (Montreal: Boréal Express), p. 206; translation mine.

Lenin, V. (1970), *Textes sur les syndicats* (Moscow: Progress Publishers), p. 213.

Linteau, P. A. (1982), "La Montée du cosmopolitisme Montréalais," in *Migrations et communautés culturelles* (Montréal: Editions Leméac).

Linteau, P. A., Durocher, R., and Robert, J. C. (1979), *Histoire du Québec contemporain* (Montreal: Boréal Express).

Maheu, L. (1969), "Problème social et naissance du syndicalisme catholique," *Sociologie et Sociétés* (University of Montreal), vol. 1, no. 1, pp. 69–88.

"Manifeste du mouvement Socialiste" (1982), *Canadian Journal of Political and Social Theory,* vol. 6, no. 1–2, pp. 109–38.

Marx, K., and Engels, F. (1972), *K. Marx and F. Engels: Le Syndicalisme* (Paris: Maspéro), Vol. 1 p. 78.

de Maupeou-Abboud, N. (1978), *Aristocraties ouvrières d'hier et d'aujord'hui dans différents secteurs de pointe,* communication at the World Congress of Sociology, Uppsala, 14–19 August.

Nicolaus, M. (1970), "The theory of labor aristocracy," *Monthly Review,* vol. 21, no. 11, pp. 91–110.

Ouellet, F. (1972), *Eléments d'histoire sociale du Bas Canada* (Montreal: HMH).

Reynolds, L. C. G. (1935), *The New British Immigrant* (Toronto: Oxford University Press).

Roback, L. (1978), "Organizing the cockroach shops in Montreal," in I. Abella and D. Millar (eds.), *The Canadian Worker in the 20th Century* (Toronto: Oxford University Press).

Rouillard, J. (1981), *Histoire de la CSN, 1921–1981* (Montreal: Boréal Express).

Rutherford, P. F. W. (1972), "Introduction" to H. B. Ames, *The City below the Hill* (Toronto: Toronto University Press).

Sombart, W. (1976), *Why Is There No Socialism in the United States?* (New York: M. E. Sharpe); first published, 1906.

Conclusion

RONALD REGOWSKI

Since most of the essays in this volume were written, over two years and much new research and theorizing have transpired. Questions that then remained open have been answered; and some theories that then held promise have faded, while others, including some then unknown, have gained luster and allure. I, therefore, believe that I do myself and my coauthors no injustice if I attempt here not to summarize or even to draw together our various contributions, but to update some of our work and to indicate, in light of what we now know, the most promising avenues of future research.

What Has Been Established?

(1) The Variety of Nationalisms

Many of the early efforts to explain the new nationalisms, while differing radically in their substance, agreed in seeing all of the movements as alike, pursuing the same goals and aroused by the same causes. Thus for Walker Connor (1972) and for Milton Esman (1977), to take only two examples, all of the new nationalisms were revivals of ancient ethnicity, while for Michael Hechter (1975), all were reactions to internal colonialism.

Evidence quickly compelled revision of these monocolored views. Rawkins, as early as 1974, proposed a fourfold typology of modes of Welsh (and, presumbly, of other) nationalist activism (see Rawkins, 1979, and sources there cited). Hechter himself, confronted with such recalcitrant cases as lowland Scotland and Catalonia, came to see two distinct kinds of ethnic or national mobilization, based respectively on the hierarchy and the segmentation of the cultural division of labor (Hechter, 1978, and this volume; Hechter and Levi, 1979); Mughan (1979) proposed that "cultural" nationalisms be distinguished from "economic" ones, with the Flemish and the Walloon movements in Belgium serving as respective examples. Wood (1981, pp. 110–11; cf. Gourevitch, 1979, p. 305) contended that not all nationalisms had been ethnically based; a further category of nonethnic nationalisms, including at a minimum the cases of the American South and of Western Australia (and, one could perhaps now add, western Canada), was required. Even more recently Meadwell (1983), borrowing Tilly's categories of collective action, has advocated a distinction among "proactive," "reactive," and "competitive" nationalisms; and, in the present volume, both Linz's chapter and mine have explored the implications of more complex categorizations of nationalisms based on various definitions of group membership and of goals.

Perhaps the most significant taxonomic and etiological advance, however, has been that of Horowitz (1981), who has proposed a two-by-two typology based on the relative backwardness or development, first, of the group, and secondly, of the region. Educationally and culturally backward groups in economically backward regions, Horowitz contends, are the likeliest to seek separation, or in some cases a continuation of colonial rule, out of fear of being overwhelmed by more advanced groups. Conversely, advanced groups in backward regions—the Ibo in Biafra are a recent example, the Scots in eighteenth-century Britain (I would add) an older one—have the least incentive to pursue secession, precisely because the larger unit offers outlets for their skills. They will try to break away only under really insufferable persecution, and usually only after being driven back already into their home region. In between lie both backward and advanced groups in economically advanced regions, with the latter marginally likelier to secede, particularly when the existing state offers no especially advantageous markets for the advanced group's products. The goals in the various situations, Horowitz predicts, will also differ: backward groups are most concerned to impose proportionality in hiring (just as advanced groups seek always to avoid such quotas), and advanced regions almost always complain of being "milked" to subsidize their less favored fellows.

While we cannot yet be sure which, if any, of these taxonomies will prove most useful, and while we continue to seek a general theory that can explain all of the kinds of nationalism, we must plainly now admit that there *are* different kinds, which often enough have come into direct and even violent conflict— Union Nationale v. Parti Québécois in Quebec, Nationalists v.

Sinn Fein in Ireland—and that a proper appreciation of these differences is one of the most urgent tasks of current research (Bogdanor, 1982, p. 290).

(2)   The Class Basis of Nationalism

Nothing is by now so clearly established as the white-collar and tertiary-sector basis of nearly all of the new nationalisms, regardless of their goals or economic circumstances: compelling evidence from mass or elite surveys, or from both, now exists for Quebec (Hamilton and Pinard, 1976), Scotland (Drucker, 1980, pp. 115–16), Wales (Khleif, 1978; Ragin, 1979; Rawkins, 1979), Catalonia (Solí, 1981), Belgium (Nielsen, 1980), and even the various movements in France (Beer, 1977, and 1980, ch. 4). A. D. Smith (1981; cf. Weinstein, 1979) has proposed a general model of nationalist evolution that suggests why this should be so, at least in the early and middle phases of any movement. On the other hand, some of the older movements, especially of conservative or defensive nationalism, appear to have drawn their main support from peasants and traditional elites (Nevitte, 1978, and this volume; Ragin, 1979, on the Welsh Liberals; Meadwell, 1983). What seems to be lacking, or to emerge only very late, is any substantial support among the industrial working class, or indeed any correlation between industrialization and nationalism.

(3)   "Competitive" v. "Reactive" or "Developmental" Nationalism

Closely related to nationalism's class basis is the question of whether "reaction," "development," or "competition" principally inspires ethnic and national mobilization (Ragin, 1979). The first view, consonant with older theories of "mass society" (Kornhauser, 1959) and strongly evident in the latter work of Karl Deutsch (for example, 1969, p. 73) on nationalism, connects the rise of nationalism to the impact of modernization on settled ethnic groups: the groups *react*, negatively, to modernization and mobilize to preserve their traditional identities. The "developmental" persepective instead locates ethnic loyalties among the most backward and unassimilated elements of any group. They mobilize precisely because they are *not* "developed." The third perspective, usually attributed to

Fredrik Barth (1969) and, in political science, to the pathbreaking work of Melson and Wolpe (1970), attributes mobilization instead to a national or ethnic group's rise to a position of *competition* with other groups. The empirical implications of these three theories are quite different, and hence they can easily be tested against each other. If the "reactive" hypothesis is right, nationalism ought to be correlated with rapid modernization among previously backward groups and areas; if "development" is the key, the least modern groups and areas should be the most nationalist; and if "competition" is the best explanation, mobilization should be strongest among the most advanced elements of any national or ethnic group, that is, the most highly educated, the most mobile, and the already most urbanized.

Here again the evidence by now seems clear: while for earlier and most traditional nationalisms the reactive or developmental models may hold good (Ragin, 1979; Nielson, 1980; Meadwell, 1983), for almost all of the new nationalisms that have been investigated the competitive model fits the data far better (Nielsen, 1980; Fenwick, 1981; cf. Weinstein, 1979, pp. 350–1; Ra'anan, 1980, introduction; Drucker, 1980, pp. 115–17). This finding lends support to the already persuasive general perspective of Barth and his associates, including their hypothesis of ethnic transference and self-selection (Barth, 1969; see also p. 598) and, at least in the view of some (for instance, Nielson, 1980), impugns not only Deutsch's claims but, somewhat paradoxically, those of Hechter *and* of the theorists of primordial ethnicity.

(4) The Self-Selection of Ethnicity and Nationality

Where many earlier students saw ethnicity as a given, around which individuals might or might not mobilize, Barth and his associates claimed that it was often self-selected, indeed sometimes invented, and that transference from one identity to another, usually for straightforward reasons of social or economic advantage, was entirely possible. On this last point Gunnar Haaland's study (1969) of transference between the agricultural Fur and the nomadic Baggara in the Sudan was especially persuasive. Subsequent research has amply borne out these claims. Nelson Kasfir's (1979) brilliant reflection on the case of the invented Nubian identity in Uganda seems conclusive, but one should see also Weinstein (1979), Green (1982), and Juan Linz's contribution to this volume.

What Theories Now Seem Most Promising?

Some well-developed theories have been impugned by the work already discussed: as Orridge (1981) has argued, virtually the whole set of theories of "uneven development" now seems ripe for abandonment; and so, as I have just tried to show, do the theories of primordial ethnicity and of reactive nationalism. At the same time, recent research and reflection have brought to the fore other possibly crucial factors, some barely noticed a few years ago. Three seem particularly worth closer investigation.

(1)   The Context of Political Institutions and Party Systems

In various ways Brand, Levi and Hechter, Rawkins, and Steiner have all argued in the present volume that pre-existing political institutions, patterns of decision-making, and partisan alignments shape and condition the emergence of nationalist movements. Against the once almost universally accepted claim that decentralized and "consociational" systems blunt and deflect potential separatisms (with Switzerland usually serving as the principal exhibit), both Brand and Levi and Hechter follow Birch (1978) in contending that such institutions do not bar, and may actually encourage, the rise of autonomist movements. Others have pursued similar points. Where Hermens (1938) and Downs (1957) held that plurality, two-party systems were least susceptible to single-issue movements of all kinds, including regionalist ones, both Miller (1980) and I (Rogowski, 1981) have tried to show that such systems may actually be more open to nationalist—and perhaps to other—"passionate" movements. These particular controversies are by no means yet resolved; but there is reason to think that political and party structures may emerge as important and previously neglected explanatory variables.

(2)   The Economic and Class Character of the Existing Political System

Whether the existing state pursues policies of equal opportunity or of discrimination, of regionally equitable or discriminatory taxation and expenditure; whether it embraces capitalist or precapitalist values; and even whether it is free-trading or protectionist—all these have gradually come to be seen as affecting powerfully the incentives to separatism or unity that face groups within the state.

Breton (1964) contended that white-collar, professional, and intellectual strata of minority groups were so often at the forefront of nationalist movements because they contested the rule of merit: they really sought, regardless of ability, to gain a monopoly of these prestigious positions (for example, by restricting access in Quebec to Francophones) and to force others in the society to pay the higher price of their own less competent performance. Breton, however, ignored the possibility, since emphasized by Horowitz (1981) among others, that the existing state might discriminate (or at least permit private sector discrimination) against able members of the minority. In that case, which appears actually to have long obtained in Canada (for example, Innis, 1973, pp. 82–5), a less discriminatory separatist regime might well provide greater efficiency and thus improve the welfare not only of the professional and technical elites, but of the whole group or region. Similarly, central-state policies with respect to taxation, expenditure, investment, and even transportation gradients may, if discriminatory enough, so burden efficiency as to make separation economically attractive.

Nairn (1977), however, has broadened this perspective to ask, from a Marxist viewpoint, whether the existing state is "bourgeois"—roughly, wholeheartedly liberal—or something less. If it is not, separatism finds more and stronger incentives. English hegemony in Britain, for example, reflects not only ethnic snobbery, but far more important, the continued dominance of a precapitalist elite whose values are essentially aristocratic and rural. Thus the British state as now constituted is doomed to both economic backwardness and political stagnation. Somewhat like the old Austro-Hungarian and Turkish empires, it can be modernized—can become fully capitalist, and then ultimately socialist—only be being broken up.

While such a view meshes well with what is known about the class basis of nationalism (see p. 372), some cases seem to speak at once against it: Belgium in the twentieth century and the United States in the nineteenth were classically bourgeois and capitalist states, yet both faced serious threats of dismemberment; nor was the Sweden from which Norway separated at the turn of the century exactly the least capitalist of contemporary European states. None the less, the overall correlation between reluctant capitalism and separatism is strong, as is suggested by such cases as Spain, Canada, the

United Kingdom, and the colonial empires that collapsed after World War II.

In partial contradiction to Nairn but along similar lines, Gourevitch (1979), Horowitz (1981), and in the present volume Pi-Sunyer and Polèse have suggested that protectionist states, by offering large and secure markets to all their regions, make separation less attractive. By this reasoning free trade makes disintegration likelier; and the temporal correlation between the rise of a liberal international order after World War II and the emergence of the new nationalisms can thus be explained.

The logic of the thesis is attractive, and such diverse free-trading cases as nineteenth-century Spain and twentieth-century Belgium, both with powerful separatisms, lend it additional support. On the other hand, an adherent of Nairn might point out, such historically protectionist states as Austria-Hungary and late nineteenth-century Russia also had powerful minority nationalisms; and suggestively enough, these "exceptions" were dominated by precapitalist elites. Worse, some movements have specifically opposed protection and have sought separation at least partially in pursuit of less restrictive trade: the American South, of course, but also Bismarck's "little" Germany (in its aspect as avoidance of a more protectionist *grossdeutsche Lösung*), present-day Singapore, and even western Canada and Quebec. The question for further research must, therefore, be: why is a hypothesis that seems so logically compelling so often contradicted by the evidence?

(3)   The Role of Trade, Product Cycles, and the International Environment

If one asks, as Orridge (1981) has done, why nationalisms seem to ebb and flow together in long cycles and why the nation-state—large up to the end of the nineteenth century, since then often smaller—has been the principal aim of ethnic movements, two kinds of answers now begin to emerge. First, *product cycles* and their concomitant "natural" *scales of production* have an evident importance. As Katzenstein (1982) has observed, the leading products of the nineteenth- and early twentieth-century industrial expansion, above all iron and steel, depended on economies of scale and large markets to a degree that deprived small and decentralized states of all real hope of comparative advantage. Only the uniform property rights and markets of the large nation-state would do. Increasingly in the twentieth century, however, major sectors of production—machine-tools, consumer durables, and electronics—have rewarded precision and quality rather than bigness, so that small states, especially ones with firmly established mechanisms of social cooperation, may actually hold the advantage. According to this argument, then, the nineteenth-century technological environment rewarded the creation of large states, while the twentieth-century one increasingly encourages smaller units.

Similarly, it has frequently been argued, the necessities of *armed defense*, which favored the large state in the nineteenth and early twentieth centuries, now permit smaller units to survive and indeed—by granting them the possibility of lower defense expenditures—give them an additional competitive advantage. On the one hand, the overwhelming dominance of the two superpowers render units like Britain or France less important: surely the "NATO umbrella" would shelter an independent Scotland no less than it does the United Kingdom (Esman, 1977, p. 376; Hechter and Levi, 1979, p. 271; Beer, 1980, p. 34). On the other hand, as Robert Gilpin (1981) has contended, nuclear weapons tend to divorce power from size, by giving even quite small states (for example, Israel) enormous destructive potential. Both factors make small states more viable.

The logic again seems conclusive; but are the premises true? The small states of the Low and Scandinavian regions not only survived in the late nineteenth and early to middle twentieth century, despite some devastating invasions in the two world wars; their economies grew as rapidly as those of the German and American giants, and often enough were principally based (notably in Sweden and Belgium) on heavy industry. Nor has bigness more recently imposed any consistent disadvantage: per capita GNP has grown since 1960 more rapidly in such relative giants as Canada, France, West Germany, and Italy than it has on average in the smaller European countries. Of the larger states, only the United States and the United Kingdom consistently lagged behind their smaller fellows, and since 1973 even America has pulled even (OECD, 1982, p. 40). Militarily, confrontations between nominal allies, or between neutrals and members of one of the two great blocs, have seemed to prove that bigness still matters: Britain v. Spain, Sweden v. the Soviet Union, the United States v. Nicaragua, Britain v. Argentina.

Perhaps, however, the economic variable has simply been misspecified. Smallness, whether of population or of territory, may matter less than a narrow resource base that, by compelling a state to trade, compels it also to seek maximum efficiency

(Rogowski, 1983). In today's world economy a relatively small but largely self-sufficient society may, by pursuing autarky and encouraging uncompetitiveness—as, for example, Spain did during most of the early Franco regime—fare worse than a large but poorly endowed state that accepts its need to trade and remains competitive.

Paths of Future Research

Etiology is not methodology; promising theories do not automatically prescribe promising paths of research. We must go on to specify the techniques that seem best suited to test the hypotheses just discussed.

(1) Further Survey Research

If sophisticatedly designed and properly focussed, this can illuminate the incentives to nationalism, the processes of national identification in the self and among others, and—perhaps most important—the effects of regime character and policies. Among the promising recent attempts are the essays by Linz in the present volume and by Mughan and McAllister (1981) in *Ethnic and Racial Studies*. Where Linz attends principally to questions of identification, Mughan and McAllister take up the issue of motivation, showing among other things that Scottish nationalists, while perceiving Scotland as no more disadvantaged than do Labourites or Conservatives, distinctively imagine both their own and Scotland's opportunities as vastly greater under independence: among SNP supporters, 76 percent believe that Scotland would be better off independent, and 53 percent that they as individuals would fare better; among Labour supporters, the comparable figures were respectively 15 and 9 percent; and among Conservatives, even lower (Mughan and McAllister, 1981, p. 197). At the same time, the authors observe that, on most objective indicators of well-being (education, infant mortality, average weekly earnings, and so on), Scotland is by now the equal or superior of England. What, then, so profoundly convinced the nationalists that independence would improve their lot? Is it only the oil, as most close observers deny (for example, Esman, 1977, p. 275), or has something like Nairn's view come to prevail? Further survey work, perhaps including open-ended items and focus groups, would surely be justified, here and in such similar cases as Quebec and Catalonia.

(2) Diachronic Same-Case Comparison

In instances of major regime or party-system change this would help to establish the importance of the institutional variables now so frequently stressed. Spain, to take probably the richest example, shifted after the late 1950s from an autarkical and relatively feudal regime to a far less protectionist and more pro-capitalist one; and, with the death of Franco, it rapidly democratized and decentralized (the Statutes of Regional Autonomy). France after 1958 changed from a parliamentary to a presidential regime and from a multiparty to an essentially two-party configuration; if the present regime keeps its promises, the country will presently decentralize and resume the use of proportional representation. Canada, largely under pressure from Quebec, has devolved important powers to the provinces over the past two decades. And the United Kingdom and the United States have, at least in the judgment of some analysts (for example, Crewe *et al.*, 1977; Crewe, 1980), undergone a major partisan dealignment since the late 1960s. Changes like these should, according to the various contextual hypotheses, have significantly altered the incentives to nationalist mobilization; but have they done so in fact, and in the predicted direction? Given the strong presumption that, in such same-case comparisons, only the institutional variables will have changed, they seem to provide ideal tests; yet so far as I am aware, no systematic analysis of them has been undertaken.

(3) Comparison with Third World and Older European Nationalisms

While risky, this can help identify the various kinds of nationalism, will permit even more conclusive tests of the "reactive" as against the "competitive" theories of nationalism, and may be crucial in answering what I have identified here as the three major questions still open, namely, the effects of institutions, of the class character of the regime, and of trade and product cycles. The danger of this method is, of course, that the new nationalisms may differ fundamentally from the old (although in that case theorists would have the task of explaining why); not undertaking broad comparison however seems even riskier, for even if one takes into consideration only a few of the leading hypotheses, the number of variables quickly outruns the number of recent European and North American cases.

Examples of such historical and cross-cultural comparison are still rare—for partial exceptions, see Smith, 1972, 1981;

Mughan, 1977; Coakley, 1980)—partly because the breadth of expertise required is also rare. Indeed, specialists in different areas may need to collaborate if any rapid advance is to be achieved.

(4) The Theory of Political Cleavage

Finally, our theorizing and testing will profit most from eventual dissolution into a general, parsimonious, elegant, and well-supported *theory of political cleavage*. This we now significantly lack; or rather all attempts at it, including prominently those of Lipset and Rokkan, have ended in failure wherever they moved beyond description.

To contend that a complicated topic can best be addressed by investigating instead a larger and still more complex subject may sound, but is not, foolish. The fundamental problems of modern chemistry were solved only by treating them as part of the seemingly even more complex world of theoretical physics. Such a strategy may work for at least two reasons: first, the old saw indeed often holds, that we see the forest only by backing away from the trees, or even from the grove; and secondly, we gain by this route, as by the historical and cross-cultural research I have just advocated, a far larger universe of cases for study.

In advocating this strategy I am, of course, implicitly rejecting the perspective that inspired and informed this book: that there was something self-evidently distinctive not only about nationalism as a species of political cleavage, but about the new nationalisms of the developed West. Distinctive they may be, but they are far from self-evidently so; and the basis and the causes of any distinction need still to be stated and theoretically defended.

Was this symposium, therefore, a mistake? No. Indeed, given what was then known, it was in many respects a major advance. But it is now time to move on.

References: Conclusion

Barth, Fredrik (ed.) (1969), *Ethnic Groups and Boundaries: The Social Organization of Cultural Difference* (Bergen and Oslo: Universitetsforlaget; London: Allen & Unwin).

Beer, William R. (1977), "The social class of ethnic activists in contemporary France," in M. J. Esman (ed.), *Ethnic Conflict in the Western World* (Ithaca, N. Y., and London: Cornell University Press), ch. 6.

Beer, William R. (1980), *The Unexpected Rebellion: Ethnic Activism in Contemporary France* (New York and London: New York University Press).

Birch, Anthony H. (1978), "Minority nationalist movements and theories of political integration," *World Politics,* vol. 30, no. 3, pp. 325–44.

Bogdanor, Vernon (1982), Ethnic nationalism in Western Europe *Political Studies,* vol. 30, no. 2, pp. 284–91.

Brand, Jack (1978), *The National Movement in Scotland* (London: Routledge & Kegan Paul).

Breton, Albert (1964), "Economics of nationalism," *Journal of Political Economy,* vol. 72, no. 4, pp. 376–86.

Coakley, John (1980), "Independence movements and national minorities: some parallels in the European experience," *European Journal of Political Research,* vol. 8, no. 2, pp. 215–48.

Connor, Walker (1972), "Nation-building or nation-destroying?" *World Politics,* vol. 24, no. 3 (April), pp. 319–55.

Crewe, Ivor (1980), "Prospects for party realignment: an Anglo-American comparison," *Comparative Politics,* vol. 12, no. 4, pp. 379–400.

Crewe, Ivor, Särlvik, Bo, and Alt, James (1977), "Partisan dealignment in Britain, 1964–74," *British Journal of Political Science,* vol. 7, pt. 2, pp. 129–90.

Deutsch, Karl (1969), *Nationalism and its Alternatives* (New York: Knopf).

Downs, Anthony (1957), *An Economic Theory of Democracy* (New York: Harper & Row).

Drucker, Henry M. (1980), "Scottish nationalism and devolution (stage one, up to 1978): regionalism and the political party system," in U. Ra'anan (ed.) *Ethnic Resurgence in Modern Democratic States* (New York: Pergamon), ch. 4.

Esman, Milton J. (ed.) (1977), *Ethnic Conflict in the Western World* (Ithaca, N. Y., and London: Cornell University Press).

Fenwick, Rudy (1981), "Social change and ethnic nationalism: an historical analysis of the separatist movement in Quebec," *Comparative Studies in Society and History,* vol. 23, no. 2, pp. 196–216.

Gilpin, Robert (1981), *War and Change in International Politics* (Cambridge: Cambridge University Press).

Gourevitch, Peter Alexis (1979), "The re-emergence of 'peripheral nationalisms': some comparative speculations on the spatial distribution of political leadership and economic growth," *Comparative Studies in Society and History,* vol. 21, no. 3, pp. 303–22.

Green, Leslie (1982), "Rational nationalists," *Political Studies,* vol. 30, no. 2, pp. 236–46.

Haaland, Gunnar (1969), "Economic determinants in ethnic processes", in F. Barth (ed.), *Ethnic Groups and Boundaries* (Bergen and Oslo: Universitetsforlaget; London: Allen & Unwin), pp. 53–73.

Hamilton, Richard, and Pinard, Maurice (1976), "The bases of *Parti Québécois* support in recent Quebec elections," *Canadian Journal of Political Science,* vol. 9, no. 1, pp. 3–26.

Hechter, Michael (1975), *Internal Colonialism: The Celtic Fringe in British National Development, 1536–1966* (London: Routledge & Kegan Paul; Berkeley and Los Angeles, Calif.: University of California Press).

Hechter, Michael (1978), "Group formation and the cultural division of labor," *American Journal of Sociology,* vol. 84, no. 2 (September), pp. 296–301.

Hechter, Michael, and Levi, Margaret (1979), "The comparative analysis of ethnoregional movements," *Ethnic and Racial Studies,* vol. 2, no. 3 (July), pp. 260–74.

Hermens, Ferdinand A. (1938), *Democracy or Anarchy?* (Notre Dame, Ind.: The Review of Politics).

Horowitz, Donald L. (1981), "Patterns of ethnic separatism," *Comparative Studies in Society and History,* vol. 23, no. 2, pp. 165–95.

Innis, Hugh R. (1973), *Bilingualism and Biculturalism: An Abridged Version of the Royal Commission Report* (Ottawa: McClelland & Stewart, in cooperation with the Secretary of State Department and Information Canada).

Kasfir, Nelson (1979), "Explaining ethnic political participation," *World Politics,* vol. 31, no. 3, pp. 365–88.

Katzenstein, Peter (1982), "The virtues of necessity: small states in the international economy," ms., privately circulated.

Khleif, Bud (1978), "Ethnic awakening in the first world: the case of Wales," in Glyn Williams (ed.), *Social and Cultural Change in Contemporary Wales* (London: Routledge & Kegan Paul), pp. 102–19.

Kornhauser, William (1959), *The Politics of Mass Society* (Glencoe, Ill.: The Free Press).

Leifer, Erie M. (1981), "Competing models of political mobilization: the role of ethnic ties," *American Journal of Sociology,* vol. 87, no. 1, pp. 23–47.

Meadwell, Hudson (1983), "Forms of cultural mobilization in Quebec and Brittany, 1870–1914," *Comparative Politics,* vol. 15, no. 4, pp. 401–17.

Melson, Robert, and Wolpe, Howard (1970), "Modernization and the politics of communalism: a theoretical perspective," *American Political Science Review,* vol. 64, no. 4, pp. 1112–30.

Miller, W. L. (1980), "What was the profit in following the crowd? The effectiveness of party stategies on immigration and devolution," *British Journal of Political Science,* vol. 10, pt. 1, pp. 15–38.

Mughan, Anthony (1977), "Modernisation, deprivation and the distribution of power resources: towards a theory of ethnic conflict," *New Community,* vol. 5, no. 4, pp. 360–70.

Mughan, Anthony (1979), "Modernization and ethnic conflict in Belgium," *Political Studies,* vol. 27, no. 1, pp. 21–37.

Mughan, Anthony, and McAllister, Ian (1981), " The mobilization of the ethnic vote: a thesis with some Scottish and Welsh evidence," *Ethnic and Racial Studies,* vol. 4, no. 2, pp. 189–204.

Nairn, Tom (1977), *The Break-Up of Britain: Crisis and Neo-Nationalism* (New York: Schocken Books).

Nevitte, Neil H. (1978), "Religion and the 'new nationalisms': the case of Quebec," Ph.D. dissertation, Duke University.

Nielsen, François (1980), "The Flemish movement in Belgium after World War II: a dynamic analysis," *American Sociological Review,* vol. 45, no. 1, pp. 76–94.

Organization for Economic Co-operation and Development (OECD)(1982), *Historical Statistics, 1960–1980* (Paris: OECD).

Orridge, A. W. (1981), "Uneven development and nationalism," *Political Studies,* vol. 29, nos. 1 and 2, pp. 1–15, 181–90.

Ra'anan, Uri (ed.) (1980), *Ethnic Resurgence in Modern Democratic States: A Multidisciplinary Approach to Human Resources and Conflict* (New York: Pergamon).

Ragin, Charles C. (1979), "Ethnic political mobilization: the Welsh case," *American Sociological Review,* vol. 44, no. 4, pp. 619–35.

Rawkins, Phillip M. (1978), "Outsiders as insiders: the implications of minority nationalism in Scotland and Wales," *Comparative Politics*, vol. 10, no. 4, pp. 519–34.

Rawkins, Phillip M. (1979), "An approach to the political sociology of the Welsh nationalist movement," *Political Studies,* vol. 27, no. 3, pp. 440–57.

Rogowski, Ronald (1981), "Nationalisms as single-issue movements: the question of regime accessibility," paper presented at the Annual Meeting of the American Political Science Association, New York City, 2–6 September.

Rogowski, Ronald (1983), "Structure, growth, and power: three rationalist accounts," *International Organization,* vol. 37, no. 4, pp. 713–38.

Sharpe, L. J. (ed.) (1979), *Decentralist Trends in Western Democracies* (Beverly Hills, Calif.: Sage).

Smith, Anthony D. (1972), *Theories of Nationalism* (London: Duckworth).

Smith, Anthony D. (1978), "The diffusion of nationalism: some historical and sociological perspectives," *British Journal of Political Science,* vol. 29, pt. 3, pp. 234–48.

Smith, Anthony D. (1979), *Nationalism in the Twentieth Century* (New York: New York University Press).

Smith, Anthony D. (1981), *The Ethnic Revival* (Cambridge: Cambridge University Press).

Solí, Carlota (1981), "Integración versus catalanización de los immigrantes," *Sistema: Revista de Ciencias Sociales,* no. 43–4, pp. 171–97.

Weinstein, Brian (1979), "Language strategists: redefining political frontiers on the basis of linguistic choices," *World Politics,* vol. 31, no. 3, pp. 345–64.

Wood, John R. (1981), "Secession: a comparative analytical framework," *Canadian Journal of Political Science,* vol. 14, no. 1, pp. 107–34.

Index